T0356050

WHOM FORTUNE FAVOURS

Whom Fortune Favours

THE BANK OF MONTREAL AND THE RISE OF NORTH AMERICAN FINANCE

Volume Two: Territories of Transformation, 1946–2017

LAURENCE B. MUSSIO

Foreword by Niall Ferguson

McGill-Queen's University Press
Montreal & Kingston | London | Chicago

ISBN 978-0-2280-0068-6 (cloth)
ISBN 978-0-2280-0069-3 (ePDF)

Legal deposit first quarter 2020
Bibliothèque nationale du Québec

Printed in Canada on acid-free paper

We acknowledge the support of the Canada Council for the Arts.
Nous remercions le Conseil des arts du Canada de son soutien.

Library and Archives Canada Cataloguing in Publication

Title: Whom fortune favours : the Bank of Montreal and the rise of North American
  finance / Laurence B. Mussio ; foreword by Niall Ferguson.
Names: Mussio, Laurence B., author.
Description: Includes bibliographical references and index. | Contents: Volume II.
  Territories of transformation, 1946–2017.
Identifiers: Canadiana (print) 2019013304X | Canadiana (ebook) 20190133376
  | ISBN 9780228000686 (set ; cloth) | ISBN 9780228000693 (set ; ePDF)
Subjects: LCSH: Bank of Montreal—History. | LCSH: Banks and
  banking—Canada—History.
Classification: LCC HG2710.M63 B328 2020 | DDC 332.1/20971—dc23

Set in 11/14 Sina Nova by Sayre Street Books
Book design by Garet Markvoort, zijn digital

The author dedicates this book to the four living leaders
of the Bank of Montreal, past and present:

W. Darryl White
William A. Downe
F. Anthony Comper
Matthew W. Barrett

Each in their time,
assumed the burden and privilege
of inheriting a remarkable past,
responding to the grand challenges and opportunities of the present,
and renewing their institution for the future that awaits

CONTENTS

VOLUME TWO: TERRITORIES OF TRANSFORMATION, 1946–2017

TABLES AND FIGURES

Tables

Figures

PREFACE

*True observers of nature, although they may think differently, will
still agree that everything that is, everything that is observable as a
phenomenon, can only exhibit itself in one of two ways. It is either
a primal polarity that is able to unify, or it is a primal unity that is
able to divide. The operation of nature consists of splitting the united
or uniting the divided; this is the eternal movement of systole and
diastole of the heartbeat, the inhalation and exhalation of the world
in which we live, act, and exist.*
– Johann Wolfgang von Goethe, *Zur Farbenlehre*[1]

In Volume One: A Dominion of Capital, we analyzed the long-run experience of the Bank of Montreal from its establishment as Canada's first bank in 1817, through the long nineteenth century, and to the end of the Great War. We went on to examine the Bank's experience in the context of some of the momentous changes in Canadian financial and economic life, and transformations in Canada's political economy in depression and wartime. For the Bank of Montreal, the entire period can be seen as one in which the institution acted as a key protagonist in the development of North American finance and the transformation of British North America to nationhood. For many reasons, therefore, the end of the Second World War is an appropriate place for us both to end, and to begin.

Volume Two: Territories of Transformation opens onto a vastly changed landscape for the Bank and for the country. Banking in Canada and in the North Atlantic world was on the threshold of transformation – of markets, technology, regulation, and the customer. The heroic era of finance and nation building was very much in the rear-view mirror. A new and more complex set of challenges emerged in this period.

The Bank of Montreal entered the new era armed with an enviable record of performance, even though in the latter years of the previous era, competitors, circumstance, and context complicated the picture. In retrospect, the post-1945 period can be understood as a struggle – a polarity – between dynamism and form. Of course, the concept oversimplifies to make the point. But it is a relevant point for both the Bank of Montreal and Canadian banking in general. The overriding challenge in the entire period seems to have been one of balancing the need to honour structure and form against the need for change, dynamism, and innovation. Too much attention or emphasis on form at the expense of the dynamic leads organizations to bureaucratic rigidity, an excessive dependence on rules and regulations, and, inevitably, to decline. Worship of dynamism at the expense of institutional stability leads management teams to "live a little," take unreasonable risks, and jeopardize the work of decades and centuries. Goethe saw this phenomenon in nature as the "primal polarity that is able to unify," and in some ways, this applies neatly to the position of the Bank not only as an organization in time but also as an organization in *that* time. As the Bank's long-run experience unfolds after 1945, we see this struggle played out in how its leadership came to terms with multiple transformations and then chose to respond. By so doing, the Bank of Montreal crosses into the multiple territories of transformation that characterized its journey in the decades after the Second World War.

PART FIVE

A Magnificent Facade, 1946–1974

The Bank's business is conducted in an environment of continuous change and innovation. More than ever before, the Bank's success will depend on the results obtained by its capable people.
Foreword to McKinsey's Special Development Programme
for the Bank of Montreal, 1970

When Fortune flatters, she does it to betray.
Publilius Syrus, Maxim 277

Everything we see hides another thing: we always want to see what is hidden by what we see.
René Magritte (Belgian surrealist
painter, 1898–1967)

The Bank of Montreal stepped into the post-war period as a premier Canadian financial institution whose leaders had faced some of the most consequential policy transformations in the history of Canadian finance. As Canadians endured the Great Depression, within its territory, the Bank was thrust into what could be a highly contested political economy. Its leaders were called upon to respond to a remarkable set of events on every conceivable front, from the high politics of sovereign debt to the extension of credit to business and enterprise needing a lifeline to get through an unprecedented economic contraction. As a principal guardian of the integrity of the Canadian banking system, the Bank of Montreal worked hard to ensure the continued stability and financial networks of the Dominion. Its leaders and people distinguished themselves in significant and meaningful ways in Canada's war effort both at home and abroad. Across the country, in both Depression and wartime emergency, regional headquarters and branches delivered the kind of banking services that had characterized the Bank of Montreal as Canada's first bank.

The post-war period would change everything for the Bank of Montreal. The challenges confronting the leadership were multiple: redefining the Bank's role and its mission in Canadian and international banking, a changed competitive environment, newly assertive public policy actors, internal organizational renewal, and technological change. The Bank faced these challenges with over a century-and-a-quarter of demonstrated capacity to respond to the demands of every era.

Canada's long-wave burst of economic growth in the decades following the end of the Second World War offered – really for the first time since the late 1920s – a widely felt hope that long-term prosperity could be sustained. A couple of tables (below) suffice in showing the extent to which those hopes materialized for the country in the post-war period. Gross national product (GNP), from a slow start after 1945, posted strong yearly gains and never looked back. Between 1945 and 1965, GNP increased from $11.8 billion to $55.3 billion; a decade later, it was $165.3 billion (see table VI.1). National income mirrored these gains: between 1945 and 1950, it increased from $9.5 billion to $14.5 billion; by 1965, Canada's national income was $41.2 billion; in 1975, the figure had tripled to $129.7 billion (see table VI.2).

The chartered banks were full participants in the post-war economic surge. Here again, two tables show the health of the chartered banks: assets grew slowly in the immediate post-war period, but then posted significant gains, especially after 1955. By 1975, the combined assets of Canadian chartered banks stood at $77.1 billion (see table VI.3). Loans were also a strong indicator of both bank strength and economic resurgence (see table VI.4). As the saying goes, a rising tide lifts all boats.

Table VI.1 | Gross national product, Canada,
at market prices, 1945–75

Year	$(000,000)
1945	11,863
1950	18,491
1955	28,528
1960	38,359
1965	55,364
1970	85,685
1975	165,343

Source: Derived from Statistics Canada, *Historical Statistics of Canada*
(Ottawa: Queen's Printer), Robert B. Crozier, Section F: Gross National
Product, The Capital Stock and Productivity, Series F56-75, Gross Domestic
Product at Factor Cost, By Industry, 1926 to 1976.

Table VI.2 | National income: net national income
at factor cost, 1945–75

Year	$(000,000)
1945	9,506
1950	14,553
1955	21,908
1960	28,837
1965	41,219
1970	64,235
1975	129,789

Source: Derived from Statistics Canada, *Historical Statistics of Canada*
(Ottawa: Queen's Printer), Robert B. Crozier, Section F: Gross National
Product, The Capital Stock and Productivity, Series F1-13, National Income
and Gross National Product, By Components, 1926 to 1976.

By all key banking measurements – assets, loans, branches, etc. – the Bank
of Montreal was, without question, both a participant and a protagonist in
Canada's rise in economic status. Yet, the apparent prosperity of the Bank's
statistical performance was in some ways a camouflage. What seemed like
one thing actually hid another thing. The Bank's fabled reputation and prestige masked deeper, and more structural, issues in organization, strategy, and
performance. Partly as a result of this, the Bank of Montreal was knocked off
its perch as the largest bank when other chartered banks seized opportunities

Table VI.3 | Total Canadian assets,
Canadian chartered banks, 1945–75

Year	$(000,000)
1945	6,517
1950	8,636
1955	11,575
1960	14,192
1965	21,196
1970	33,616
1975	77,169

Source: Statistics Canada, *Historical Statistics of Canada* (Ottawa: Queen's
Printer) Cat 11-516-X Table J75-106a Chartered Bank Assets.

Table VI.4 | Total loans,
Canadian chartered banks, 1945–75

Year	$(000,000)
1945	1,546
1950	2,941
1955	4,891
1960	6,535
1965	11,549
1970	18,550
1975	45,350

Source: Statistics Canada, *Historical Statistics of Canada* (Ottawa: Queen's
Printer) Cat 11-516-X Table J75-106a Chartered Bank Assets.

and merged with smaller banks. As the following three chapters reveal, the
Bank was growing and getting smaller at the same time.

In other words, in the immediate post-war, the Bank of Montreal was in
some ways a magnificent facade: Its status was undiminished; its financial
influence substantial. Its board of directors comprised some of the most
prestigious men in the country – and, later, one reluctant woman, Pauline
Vanier. But there was no hiding the fact that the values that played a key role
in the Bank's success – conservatism, careful management, an emphasis on

stability – had to be refreshed and overhauled for post-war Canada, and a more competitive environment.

Perhaps the Bank's loss of its role as government banker and, to an extent, coordinator-in-chief of the Canadian banking system played a part in what appeared to be a closing of the managerial mind. Successive administrations did not seem to give serious consideration to the possibilities of a dynamic renewal of strategy and performance. But even this could be characterized less as a "burning platform" – because nothing was actually burning – than as a slow loss of strategic focus.

Of course, the situation was not monolithic. There were areas of intense activity and strategic dynamism from certain corners of the Bank. For example, the branch network was expanding and popping. Yet, by the 1960s, the overall situation had become so noticeable that the Bank of Montreal senior executives began to express concern about just how sclerotic the organization was becoming in terms of personnel, methods that had served their purpose but were approaching their expiration date, technological renewal, and strategic focus. But beyond that, they began taking action to address the situation, as the thematic chapters of Part Five demonstrate.

Chapter 14 focuses on the general history of the Bank in this period and is followed by chapters of singular focus. Chapter 15 examines a key inflection point in the story of the Bank in the 1960s: its reorganization. Finally, Chapter 16 examines the Bank's technological turn throughout the 1960s.

CHAPTER FOURTEEN

Les Trente Glorieuses?
1946–1973

The prosperity of the industrialized world in the three decades following the Second World War was among the strongest and most durable the modern world had ever seen. The remarkable growth of that period would eventually compel economists and observers to reach for superlatives to describe the phenomenon. Some chose a depiction not attributable to human power (economic miracles); others preferred portrayal as a loud, resonating sound (economic boom); more literary types opted for designation as an era deserving of brilliant renown (the "glorious thirty"). Some even called it the golden age of capitalism – an era of growing productivity, per capita incomes, and gross domestic product (GDP), and full employment that could not have been a starker contrast to the era of depression the world had left behind.[1] In the United States and Canada, as well as Europe, more jobs, more money per capita, and more babies being born fuelled a mass-market consumer revolution.

In Canada, the post-war economic boom was powered by several factors. Firstly, Canada benefitted tremendously from the Marshall Plan. Europe, which been destroyed by six years of warfare, was desperate for goods and materials that Canada could supply. Funded by American money through the Marshall Plan, the Canadian resource industry – especially mining, oil, and gas – boomed under the stimulus of European purchases.[2] Secondly, the Canada's population – and therefore both its number of workers and consumers – grew dramatically in this period. Due to unprecedented birth rates and high levels of immigration, Canada's population rose from 12.1 million in 1945 to 22.7 million in 1975.[3]

Of course, down the decades the North Atlantic economy experienced cyclical highs and lows – most notably the recession of 1957–61 – but the overall trend between 1945 and 1973 was unmistakably up. As Robert Bothwell, Ian Drummond, and John English point out in their post-war history of Canada, in the first thirty years after the war, Canadian living standards rose steadily, buoyed by an average productivity growth of 2.5 per cent per year.[4] This increase in productivity was in part thanks to unprecedented levels of new investment. Between 1944 and 1957, investment in new equipment for Canadian industry grew by a stunning 249 per cent.[5] Likewise, output grew every year between 1946 and 1973, except for except for two, 1946 and 1954.[6] Between 1946 and 1956, output grew by 5.3 per cent and consumption by 5.1 per cent. These dropped slightly, to 2.9 and 3.4 per cent, respectively, between 1957 and 1961. Even in downturns, Canada appeared to do remarkably well.[7]

In the North Atlantic world, a set of supranational agreements and institutions focused on establishing post-war order over military security, trade, and financial flows. Those international arrangements complemented the emergence, in some countries, of expanding government institutions more explicitly focused on coordinating monetary and fiscal policy, or providing greater social and income security for its people, and taking a more positive role in economic matters. In Canada, as elsewhere, the collective experience of a Great Depression and a second Great War had changed everything: conditions, expectations, and social relations. What people expected of governments, businesses, and institutions began to change significantly.

This, in brief, was the post-war environment in which the Bank of Montreal's experience would unfold. The Bank arrived at the threshold of this age with powerful capabilities, high trust, and an established, unparalleled record in banking in the North Atlantic world. From the beginning of the twentieth century (and in some ways from the Bank's beginnings early in the nineteenth century) until at least the early 1940s, its bankers were at the centre of the key decisions in banking and public finance. Its executives and directors were drawn from the elites of the Montreal and Canadian establishment. In the new, expansionist era of financial services, the quality of management, the professionalism of bankers, the reputation of the institution, and long-run experience would matter – they always do. But new conditions would demand something more than keeping the structures that had endured: they would demand adapting to change. The roads taken and not taken in the years following the Second World War would determine whether the Bank of Montreal would be able to maintain its prominence and performance as it confronted an economy and society in transformation.

This chapter provides an overview of the life and times of the Bank of Montreal in the three remarkable post-war decades of the twentieth century up to 1974. In many ways, the rhythms of the Bank's long-run experience in this period appear to mirror Canada's broader post-war economic trajectory. While the two are certainly related, the inflection points in the Bank's story are also set by internal dynamics – corporate strategy, the need for renewal, technological change, organizational shifts, and leadership. In addition, this chapter examines the culture and cultural identities of BMO banking during these years.

In the history of any organizations over time, every era and generation has its unique challenges and specific significance. With the Bank of Montreal, the challenges confronted over two centuries – establishing a new venture, creating and maintaining reputation in a trust business, competition, regulation, the establishment of networks, strategy, and performance – would have engaged the energy, will, and insight of its leaders. In this era, the challenges came mainly from within. They focused on the ability of the mid-twentieth-century Bank to respond to a transformed environment by transforming itself. How the leadership and people of the Bank responded to those challenges is the subject of this chapter. We begin with an account of the leadership of the Bank in this post-war period.

The Post-war Nine

The senior leadership of the Bank in the post-war period was guided by a small number of experienced hands in the banking business. George W. Spinney was president of the Bank from 1942 to his untimely death in 1948. His second-in-command, Bertie Charles Gardner, served as general manager from 1942 to 1947, then assumed the presidency from 1948 to 1952. Gordon R. Ball was Gardner's general manager, succeeding to the presidency from 1952 to his death in office in 1959. Arthur C. Jensen served as general manager from 1952 to 1957, when Arnold Hart assumed those responsibilities. Upon Ball's death, Hart was made president – a position he held until 1967, after which he became chief executive officer and chairman (a new post created that year) until 1974. Hart's general managers (in 1967 retitled executive vice-president and general manager, and later chief financial officer) included R.D. Mulholland (1959–67), J. Leonard Walker (1967–69), R.L. Sheard (1969–70), and Fred McNeil (1970–73). It was McNeil who would succeed Hart as chief executive officer in 1974.

These nine Bank of Montreal senior executives were supported by a number of prominent board directors who were styled as vice-presidents: Louis L. Lang, John A. Macaulay, R.G. Ivey, Roger Létourneau, and Hartland Molson, to name a few. These men were joined by H.R. Drummond, Ross H. McMaster, L.J. Belnap, and the Hon. Charles A. Dunning, who made up the executive committee of the board immediately after the war.[8] The board of directors consisted of thirty shareholder-approved positions, although only twenty-eight were filled. Still, to contemporary sensibilities, that was an unusually large number.[9] The larger board of the Bank could have been mistaken for a directory of Montreal and Canadian financial elites of the day. Appointment to the Bank of Montreal board of directors was an incontrovertible sign of social and economic prominence in Canada.

From Spinney to Hart, the nine executives who ruled were, without exception, career Bank of Montreal bankers with a great deal of experience. These men were forged in the bank's culture and its early twentieth-century experience. By and large, these were also bankers at the top of their profession, infused with a classic banker's conservatism and aversion to risk that so marked the Bank of Montreal's culture and approach.

Bertie Charles Gardner, general manager (1942–47) and president (1948–52) was a lifelong banker. He began his banking career in England before entering the Bank of British North America in 1906. Gardner was a tall, athletic man and active sportsman – a rugby player, a rower, and, later, an avid golfer. One observer called him friendly and "approachable as a river wharf."[10] Gardner was described as a "keen advocate of modern principles in banking and a shrewd judge of human nature."[11]

His Canadian banking career began in British Columbia branches, as a teller in some of the most rugged conditions banking had to offer in that time. Gardner then continued in Newfoundland, and eventually in the Montreal head office where he held progressively senior postings, including superintendent of foreign branches. He fought in the First World War, attaining the rank of major and becoming second-in-command of the 43rd Battalion (Cameron Highlanders of Canada). He was severely wounded twice in combat. Gardner was awarded the Military Cross for conspicuous bravery in action at Avion. In the late 1930s and early 1940s, he became part of the Bank's inner cabinet, helping to direct the banker's war effort. Gardner's experience of banking was very much from the ground up and from the perspective of the inspector. His experience in New York City in the 1930s was also formative – at a time when "the Canadian banks never stood higher" as many Americans sought to transfer funds to the Bank of Montreal in the wake of the collapse of so many American banks.[12] Gardner was quintessentially a Bank of Montreal banker: "Although there are bound to be differences of opinions and judgements," Gardner recalled in retirement, "the loyalty of the staff towards each other and to their seniors have never been called in question in my experience. In this respect, I doubt if any industry can make a similar claim."[13]

Gardner's successor, Gordon R. Ball, also worked his way up the ranks and through the branches, with experiences that often mirrored Gardner's (veteran of the Canadian Expeditionary Force in the Great War, and in New York in the 1930s, for example). An intensely hard-working executive and remembered as warm, unpretentious, and humorous, Ball was both respected and admired in national and international banking circles. While heading the Securities Department in New York in the early 1940s, he was in charge of the British Treasury's liquidation of American securities owned by British interests to finance the imperial war effort against the Axis powers.[14] His experience in New York City prepared him well for his senior postings at the Bank after 1947.

George Arnold Reeve Hart joined the Bank of Montreal in September 1931. Like Ball and Gardner, Hart served in the Canadian Army between 1941 and 1946, after which he held postings in Montreal, Edmonton, and New York City. His time in New York was particularly formative, training him to "deal in millions and tens of millions."[15] At the dawn of intercontinental air travel, Hart travelled to the Asia Pacific (in 1953), eventually clocking over 35,000 miles by air during his years with the Bank. He was later proud to claim that those trips were the first of their kind by a Canadian banking executive.

Frederick Harold McNeil was a bit of an exception among the bankers featured here. He came to the Bank of Montreal after careers as a journalist and senior manager, including five formative years at Ford Motor Company of Canada (1960–65). McNeil was born in Saskatoon, Saskatchewan, in 1916 and attended the universities of Manitoba and Saskatchewan. He also served in the Second World War as squadron leader for a Royal Canadian Air Force aircrew, earning the Air Force Cross for his service. This self-described "frustrated cowboy"[16] acquired a reputation as a corporate reorganizer in his work for Braun & Co., MacMillan Bloedel, Powell River Company, and Ford Motor Company. His expertise in organization, personnel, and planning played a critical role in the 1960s as the Bank embarked on a major overhaul of its organization.[17]

Arthur Christian Jensen was born in 1896 in Harbour Breton, Newfoundland. "Erect and tall, fair-headed and blue-eyed like his Scandinavian ancestors [and with an] engaging smile," Jensen joined the Merchants Bank of Canada in 1914, before its merger with the Bank of Montreal in 1922.[18] He served in London, Montreal, and New York in various capacities before moving to the head office in 1931. Jensen served as secretary to G.W. Spinney in Ottawa during the latter's time in the government wartime service overseeing Victory Bonds campaigns (see chapter 14). He became general manager in 1952, vice-president and director in 1954, executive vice-president in 1957, and chairman of the board and Executive Committee from 1959 to 1964.[19] Jensen was also intimately involved with the Bank of London and Montreal (or BOLAM) in the late 1950s. BOLAM was a joint venture between the Bank of

Montreal, the Bank of London and South America, and, after 1961, Barclays DCO. Jensen was also known for his charitable side, especially his commitment to Montreal charities such as the Red Feather campaigns of the 1950s.[20]

Robert David Mulholland (no relation to William D. Mulholland, who would become president of the Bank in the 1980s) was very much in the cut of Bank of Montreal leaders of the day. He joined the Bank in 1923, working for the Peterborough branch. He subsequently served in various positions during the 1930s that took him across Canada and around the world. He joined the Canadian Army during the Second World War, serving for four years. After the war, Mulholland returned to Montreal, where he held progressively more senior positions, including manager of Montreal Branch and assistant general manager. In 1959, he succeeded G.A.R. Hart as general manager, before being promoted to executive vice-president in 1966. A year later, he became the Bank's twenty-second president.[21]

John Leonard "Len" Walker was almost the archetypal banker's banker. He worked his way up from the position of a raw junior at a small branch in Ontario to eventually succeeding R.D. Mulholland as president in 1968. Said to have a "bouncing, stocky and bubbling personality," Walker frequently travelled the length and breadth of the organization to get the pulse of the Bank in an era of change. As one of the principal architects of the Bank's reorganization in 1965, Walker was an active promoter of reform during his tenure as general manager in 1964, senior general manager and chief operating officer in 1966, and senior executive vice-president and general manager in 1967. He assumed the presidency in 1968, adding CEO to the title in 1971. His banking career was cut short when he died suddenly in February 1973 of health-related problems.[22]

Of course, these nine leaders sat atop an increasingly elaborate pyramid of executives, managers, and teams who shaped the execution of strategy as it unfolded in these post-war decades. Yet, as we are reminded every day by the contemporary mantra, leadership matters. In the case of the Bank of Montreal, the greatest challenge facing the "Post-war Nine" was to grasp the need for change, and then establish the direction and speed of change that would move the Bank forward.

After the War

Immediately post-war, the Bank's leadership looked to reassert its long-standing position atop the field of Canadian banking. As President Spinney explained at the 1945 annual meeting: "Long traditions of soundness, sane and experienced management, fair and confidential dealing, plus the competitive spur to progressive outlook and efficiency, have all combined to build this system that is serving the public well. I am confident your Bank is well equipped to do its important part toward meeting the problems and opportunities of the postwar years in a continued spirit of enterprise and helpfulness to the whole community."[23]

Spinney further suggested that people would come to realize that, "in its own way, peace will make its demands no less than war."[24] This commonly expressed sentiment proved prophetic for both the Canadian economy and the Bank.

The economic "reconversion" of the Canadian economy was not to be underestimated. The contracts placed by the Department of Munitions and Supply for the war effort had exceeded $12.75 billion, producing 16,200 aircraft, 28,000 heavy field and naval guns, 1.5 million rifles and machine guns and hundreds of millions of rounds of ammunition, and 2 million tonnes of explosives.[25] By late 1945, the post-war industrial reconversion had begun both domestically and internationally. The measures designed to facilitate international trade included the Dominion Provincial Conference on Reconstruction in Canada and the Bretton Woods Agreement internationally.

The immediate post-war Canadian economy also had to adjust to the relaxation of controls and administrative orders across productive sectors.[26] However, the Dominion government was prepared for an orderly decontrol: $3.6 billion was earmarked for demobilization efforts, including $800 million for the extension of credits to allied countries "to aid in financing their needs and promoting Canada's export trade."[27]

Canadian economic prospects gained momentum by 1946–47. As the Bank's summary reported, "an enlarging flow of income, a diminished rate of saving and increased borrowing have combined to produce record domestic expenditures for Canadian products abroad, financed in part by credit, has resulted in new peacetime marks for export trade." Industry was operating close to full capacity and unemployment was "as near the irreducible minimum as is practically possible."[28] The challenge, however, was inflationary pressures: the rise in prices and living costs. In the United States, business activity was "at the highest level ever attained, except during the peak of wartime production."[29]

By the close of the decade, Canada's GNP was about 80 per cent higher than it had been in 1939; exports were up by 40 per cent and imports by 75 per cent.[30] High employment, well-distributed income, and stable economic conditions allowed the Canadian consumer market to broaden and stabilize.[31] In the banking sector, notice deposits were increasing substantially, as were current loans to the Canadian public.[32]

All the same, the transition to a peacetime economy was not an easy one, since more-experienced hands in the Bank and elsewhere predicted a period of economic dislocation (like the one that followed the Great War).[33] "The cheerful side is that gloomy predictions of postwar decline have so far not been correct," Spinney commented in 1946, and that "business activity has been active in response to insistent world-wide consumer demand and that reconversion has made great progress. The darker aspects of the picture, however, should get very close attention now so that policy may be directed to curing what functional disorders are curable, avoiding whatever disaster is avoidable and advancing whatever real progress can be made."[34]

The Bank's leadership looked to resume some of the plans that were shelved at the onset of the war. One of the top priorities was putting the Bank's real estate into proper order. The estimated post-war expenditure on "Premises," including completion of the new head office in Toronto, which had been started in 1939 and then delayed by the war, as well as other new buildings, extensions, and renovations throughout the country, was estimated to require between $5.8 million and $7.8 million. The latter included the decaying head office in Montreal, which, as the executive committee minutes recorded in 1945, "now extends into three buildings producing an inefficient layout which dilutes the time of senior and junior officers and generally slows down inter-office communications."[35]

As part of its transformation, the Bank also took on a new marketing approach. The informality of the name "B of M" nicely contrasted with the more formal ways of Canadian banking up to the 1930s. In 1946, the Bank of Montreal became "My Bank," the new slogan with which it would forever become associated. An elite institution like Canada's first bank had to move with the times, had to capture the zeitgeist emerging in post-war Canada. As banking strove to appeal to larger and larger publics, such a transformation was a necessity. "The Bank does not deal in money alone," one 1946 advertisement reminded Canadians, quietly emphasizing the Bank's personal touch.

The new slogan came with a new logo, further underscoring the public relations strategy of broadening the Bank's appeal to Canadians. The new slogan and logo were supposed to underscore "the many human relationships arising out of the financial problems of our customers, both of large and small means, but particularly the latter, who seek assistance from a reliable and trustworthy source."[36] In many ways, the new logo captured that new departure in post-war consumer outreach at the Bank of Montreal. The strategy attracted the public relations community's top award of the day: the "Socrates High Award of the Year," for the best bank public relations. "It appears," the award committee concluded, "that the Bank of Montreal has achieved a lasting scheme of forceful advertising … The Bank of Montreal has pointed the way. Its accomplishments deserve, at the very least, the careful study and consideration of similar institutions." Its focus on demobilized veterans, for example, was seen not as a "gesture of heartiness which meant nothing to either bank or veteran. It was, on the contrary, a definite bid for the friendship of the generation who will be the leaders of Canadian thought and accomplishment in the near future."[37]

Other signs also pointed to a more expansive spirit at the Bank. As early as 1945, General Manager B.C. Gardner suggested that it might be time to revisit the Bank's presence in Mexico and Central America, a market from which it had withdrawn during the recession of a decade prior.[38]

The Gardner Bank

In 1948, the sudden death of President G.W. Spinney put Bertie C. Gardner into the presidency. Gardner was a banker of the old school – which was nowhere more evident than in his inaugural address to the annual meeting where he emphasized getting inflation under control and for Canadians to save more. "Capital," he said, "is the product of thrift."[39] Again in 1950, Gardner stressed caution and conservatism in the approach to Canada's economic outlook and to the business of banking: "We live today in an eerie twilight, not between peace and war but between cold war and an all-out struggle. Even while we long for peace and work for peace we must meet the exigencies of the present moment and, as best we may, prepare for what the future may bring."[40] In this "hope for the best, prepare for the worst" message, he reaffirmed the value he placed on saving as a sound foundation for the Canadian economy. In what became a pattern, in 1951 Gardner stated that Canadians apply "a great re-emphasis on the place and value of saving as a force of the side of stability."[41]

At the time, Gardner's cautious approach was understandable. While we now know that Canadians stood at the precipice of a great period of prosperity, in the moment, things did not look so sure. The Canadian economy hit some turbulent waters in 1950, with "ominous signs of recession visible." Matters were made worse by the Korean War, which broke out in late June of that year. Nevertheless, demand for Canadian products in the United States was "phenomenal," and the fundamentals of the Canadian economy were generally strong.[42] Indeed, the most durable trend in the early 1950s was the rise in consumption expenditures by Canadians – as distinct from capital purposes. In 1952, for example, consumer expenditure amounted to $14.3 billion, or 62 per cent of the value of production, with 1953 exceeding those numbers.[43] In other words, Canadians were buying Chryslers, Chevrolets, and television sets in abundance.[44]

Canada's remarkable resurgence in the 1950s was at least partially powered by trade and export demand, especially for agricultural and natural resource commodities.[45] A short-lived recession in 1953–54 slowed the country's progress somewhat, but rebound was quick. By 1957–58, all the usual measures

– consumer demand, and agricultural and mineral production, for example –
were once again indicating that things were cooling off.[46]

The Elite Bank

Despite the initial signs, logos, and slogans, the Bank's strategic position was
unclear and appeared to be tied to deploying an old playbook for a new game.
While B.C. Gardner's conservative agenda in a period of unrivalled growth was
evidence of this, distant early signs could be discerned by 1947. By 1950, based
on a report authored by its economic adviser W.J. Hackett, the Bank was examining its relative position with respect to earning power.[47] The declining profit
position was evidently the spur. In 1948, four banks – the Royal, the Commerce,
BCN, and the Provinciale – reported an increase over 1947, and five – Bank of
Montreal, Nova Scotia, Dominion, Toronto, and Imperial – reported a decline.
Hackett reported that even so, the Bank of Montreal's dividends were in a strong
position with respect to the other Canadian banks – in fact, almost equal to the
Royal Bank's (see table 14.1). Of particular concern was the Bank's investment
in Dominion of Canada government bonds, which on aggregate was higher
than that of other banks (and involved also the length of the deposits). Hackett
concluded that the "processes of wartime finance siphoned money out of savings deposits via Victory Bonds into the government's treasury and from there
out again into industry, to the armed forces and into the hands of many people
who for various reasons were not users of savings deposit facilities to the same
relative extent as those who held surplus cash pre-war."[48] The problem for BMO
was a deterioration of its position as a result of this trend. However, after 1943,
the situation would inch back to its pre-war pattern.

Unlike the other banks, the Bank of Montreal's pre-war clientele and
savings depositors were more the "Tiffany" type. As that pre-war pattern
reasserted itself, those depositors created a predicament for the Bank that
had a bearing on the cost structure, particularly on the issue of interest costs
(which in 1949 were $13.62 million). "With 65% of our deposits in notice
form," Hackett concluded, "the additional annual interest cost would have
been about $716,000, figuring the effective interest rate at 1.2%. With 65%
of our deposits in notice form the additional annual interest cost would approximately be $1.367 million."[49]

Another issue was the Bank's low level of loans. The Bank's immediate post-
war share of Canadian deposits hovered around 25.3 per cent, with the share
of loans averaging about 20.5 per cent (and share of major risk assets at about
22 per cent). What the figures partially obscured was that the Bank was falling
behind the other banks in its share of business lending related to industrial
activity.[50] The Bank was particularly under-represented in the categories of

Table 14.1 | Reported net available for dividends after all expenses and taxes, financial years ending in calendar years

	1947 $(000)	1948 $(000)	1949 $(000)	% Change, 1948 over 1947	% Change, 1949 over 1948
Bank of Montreal	5,423	5,460	5,817	.7	6.5
Royal Bank	4,982	5,559	5,828	11.6	4.8
Bank of Commerce	3,201	3,528	3,616	10.2	2.5
Bank of Nova Scotia	1,992	2,007	2,299	.8	14.5
Dominion Bank	972	1,122	1,001	15.4	−10.8
Bank of Toronto	1,188	1,191	1,156	.3	−2.9
Imperial Bank	841	969	1,115	15.2	15.1
Banque de Credit Nationale	529	590	618	11.5	4.7
Provinciale	322	324	390	.6	20.4
Total	19,450	20,750	21,840	6.7	5.2
B. of M.'s Share of Total	27.9%	26.3%	26.6%		

Source: BMOA, "Confidential Memorandum for Mr Gardner – A Survey of the Bank's Earning Power," 16 March 1950.

brewers/distillers, furniture, rubber, textiles, petroleum and products, mining and finishing, and construction. It was noticeably well represented in financial institutions, and in the builders' supplies and tobacco sectors.

A Liquidity Bias

Hackett got to the heart of the matter. The Bank of Montreal had long-established relationships with large, well-financed concerns. Typically, those enterprises did not need to borrow lots of capital. "Such accounts undoubtedly have prestige and liquidity value and may be directly productive of importance service charge revenue," Hackett argued, "but a preponderance of big accounts, borrowing little, does tend to have an adverse effect on interest earnings in relation to our total operation." However, that was only half the story: "the figures as above analysed do at least put on enquiry as to whether we are getting our fair share of the new desirable lending business arising out of Canada's great industrial expansion in recent years."[51] The $501.3 million of all loans outstanding at the Bank of Montreal (of the $2.093 billion of all bank loans in Canada) was in some ways a misleading figure: the distribution was important; so was the trend line – and neither told a positive story.[52]

The Bank's conservative investment strategy traditionally favoured keeping a higher proportion of assets in cash and government securities than the other major banks, and also a lower proportion in current loans and major risk assets. The Bank's "liquidity bias" had long-term implications for its earning power and rate of return. "The gap between our rate of earnings and that of the other banks is noticeably wide, and widened slightly in 1949," Hackett pointed out. The Bank's 1949 portfolio, for example, held 30 per cent of its net earnings from all Dominion of Canada securities, and 37.3 per cent from interest and discount on loans.[53]

Other actions also pointed out a direction that reinforced the traditional playbook of Bank of Montreal banking. The issue of liquidity was a persistent one in the early 1950s. As one board memorandum suggested, "a bank in a stronger liquid position than other banks will have a higher proportion of its deposits held in cash and short-term government securities and a lower proportion of its deposits invested in loans. In comparison with other and less liquid banks, therefore, it will show a lower rate of average earning power on assets employed. Our own figures display just such a situation in comparison with those of the other banks, as determined from 'Schedule Q.'"[54]

Further evidence of the Bank's conservative strategy came in 1954, when the Bank increased its Rest Fund from $60,000,000 to $72,000,000 by way of transfer from the Contingency Reserves. "Such a transfer would leave the Rest Fund at twice the amount of paid-up capital and would increase the price at which new stock could be issued under the terms of the revised Bank Act." The Rest Fund would grow in the subsequent three years: in 1955, to $92 million;[55] in 1956, to $98.5 million;[56] and in 1957, to $100 million.[57] The executive committee also agreed that "we should place before the shareholders at the next annual meeting a recommendation that our authorized capital be increased from $50,000,000 to $75,000,000. Such an increase would, under the terms of the Bank Act, require the approval of the Treasury Board."[58]

The fact was that the Bank's earning power was not strong, even if there was a silver lining: at least its managers, could claim that they were not expensive operators. "The point is rather that as long as our deposits continue to expand," Hackett wrote, "and as long as the public's demand for ancillary banking services continue to expand, there may be rather narrow limits to what we can do to protect or enhance our profit margin by any really significant reductions in operating costs."[59]

The Excessive Conservatives

In the early 1950s, the question that occupied some of the forward thinkers in the Bank was whether it had fallen into a mentality of excessive conservatism – whether "our managers, over the years, [have] been mentally conditioned to be overly cautious? In the past decade the Canadian economy has been undergoing a tremendous expansion. Have we had our share of the desirable new business arising out of that expansion? Are we in a position to get our share in future? Is there anything further we might properly do to give our managers a lead in this respect?"[60] As Hackett had concluded in his report in 1950: "If we want average or better than average earning power, we cannot afford higher than average liquidity. We can accomplish either result, but not both."[61]

Hackett's analysis of the Bank's situation was not a particular shock to Gardner, but the comparison to other banks was "the striking feature." As he remarked, "the figures are truly astonishing." What could be done? "As to remedies of course the first is more loans – this cannot be achieved overnight," Gardner wrote in response to the memorandum. The entire matter, however, was brought before the board in early 1950, and generated considerable concern.[62] The second was greater earning power from the Bank's portfolio. But the concern President Gardner had was that in order to effect the change in strategy, the Bank would have to draw on its General Loans Reserve, and that would be difficult to justify. "As to a more adventurous lending policy," Gardner mused, "I believe we have been quite reasonable in that respect in the last few years, although our losses are less than the general loss experience."[63] In retrospect, that decision could be called into question as a strategic expression of the Bank of Montreal of a previous generation – made from behind the ramparts of the Bank's conservative intellectual citadel.

The Bank's diffident strategy had other repercussions. Emphasis on its Canadian operations led to withdrawal from Chicago in 1952 – a city in which the Bank had been operating for over ninety years. "In recent years," Gordon R. Ball explained, "there have been changes in the banking laws of the State of Illinois affecting adversely our status as a banking institution in the state. While it is possible that our business in Chicago might have been brought under a different form of corporate organization, its operation there would, in the opinion of the directors, have been unduly restricted."[64] Ball "did not feel that there was any likelihood of our expanding our business in Chicago in the event of incorporation, with the result that we would almost certainly be faced with losses as far as one could see into the future."[65]

The Bank entered into discussions with the First National Bank of Chicago, whose representatives confirmed that "it would be a simple matter" for the Chicago bank to take over the Bank of Montreal's business in the city. Revealingly, the First National Bank's advice was not to retreat, and that "it would be a mistake for the Bank of Montreal to pull out of Chicago because we never interfered with other people's business." The advice was received in Montreal as evidence that the Bank of Montreal could not "expect business to expand if we incorporated a national bank."[66] The withdrawal from Chicago was, again, indicative of a pattern – one of prudence, perhaps excessive prudence. It could have been justified as the right decision of the time, even in retrospect, but it equally appears a hidebound and unadventurous choice – rooted in the more ossified parts of the Bank's culture.

By 1954, however, the Bank began to realize the imperative of action. That year, the company embarked on an aggressive branch-opening policy, which was essentially an attempt to play catch-up with its major competitors. Between 1954 and 1958, the Bank opened 129 branches, which significantly increased deposits – to $134 million in 1958.[67]

A Culture of Bank of Montreal Banking

As with all institutions of a certain size and pedigree, the Bank of Montreal developed a strong, tight-knit set of cultures and subcultures that flourished in the head office and regional headquarters, and across the branch system. Those cultures were defined in a few distinct ways. First, there was the institution itself: the Bank of Montreal, Canada's first bank, with its singular history and leadership in the Canadian banking system. Second, the city of Montreal itself was an important influence in marking that culture as well – specifically, the English-speaking Montreal capitalists and bankers who founded the Bank and managed it generation after generation. Third, over time, cultures of specialization based on function within the Bank – internal audit, securities, marketing, human resources, and personal and commercial banking, for example – also flourished. Finally, subcultures also thrived within the head office and especially in the local and community branches across the country. Each of the hundreds of branches had its own cultural ecosystem – tied, of course, to the larger Bank of Montreal institution through an elaborate system of rules and reporting relationships, vision, and mission, but at the same time separated in geography and practice from the head office.

It is important to understand and analyze the cultures of corporate enterprises in Canada for several reasons. One of the most compelling is simply that those cultures shed light on the values and behaviour of individual institutions, their approach to their business, and the assumptions they make about their place in the world.

Another compelling reason is that, in the contemporary world, people spend a good part of their working lives in those corporate-culture environments. The associations they make, the relationships they form, and the activities they engage in are all filtered through the institutional experience. In the three decades we are examining in this chapter, the Bank of Montreal constituted one of the most consequential corporate cultures of its kind in corporate Canada and particularly in Canadian banking. Of course, you could argue that the Canadian chartered banks are overwhelmingly similar, at least to the casual observer. The differences are subtler, but discernible – in the origins, in "the way things are done," and in the values and approach of organizations in time. In terms of employee culture, a high degree of similarity between institutions within a sector is to be expected. Moreover, the relationships between, say, a Bank of Montreal culture and the broader regional and national cultures and identities that make up the Canadian cultural mosaic are reflected in those corporate cultures.

Being Bank of Montreal

What did it mean to be a Bank of Montreal banker in the post-war period? For the bank's "officer class," it meant belonging to one of the most prestigious banking institutions in the North Atlantic world. It meant being part of an organization whose importance to Canadian economic and financial life was second to none. As well, being a Bank of Montreal banker meant serving an institution that in many ways defined professional banking in Canada. Its presence in cities and towns across the Dominion also made it an important local institution, a trait that persists to this day.

Furthermore, for the bulk of Bank of Montreal bankers in this period, the branches were of overwhelming importance. Consider the remarks of a bank manager reflecting on the 1950s:

> When I first worked in the bank, you know, the bank was the branches or the branches were the bank. There wasn't much else. There was a small head office, you had some regional offices, you had some head office activities like, you know, a small securities department or a small foreign exchange trading department and obviously the offices of the president and so on. There would have been the credit department for the biggest credits and so on but it was basically a branch banking system. The manager of the branch was an important figure in town. And just about all business that was done in banking went through branches. Just about all of it. Whereas, today you have corporate departments and your large trading departments and the folks that get into derivatives and all those kinds of fancy things. You have all of your computer processing activities that didn't exist then because everything was posted at the branch.[68]

Moreover, the relationship between the branches and the head office was highly structured and defined by thousands of regulations and procedures. To give you an idea of the administrative machinery engaged in extending credit, consider the recounting of a senior credit official of the Bank in the 1960s:

The individual branch credit limits were very low. In fact, in smaller branches it could be as low as $3,000, which would enable them to make personal loans but almost no business loans. The way it worked from there, if there was somebody who wanted, say, $50,000, they would have to write up a credit application – breakdown with the balance sheet and so on – and send it to the Ontario division, for example. There you'd have a whole pile of people like me who'd be writing up a reply, but we couldn't approve it. It would then go to a superintendent or assistant superintendent, it was the title in those days, who would look at it and they would – if they thought it was fine, which was extremely rare – they'd sign it. Usually they would send it back and would say "You haven't spoken about so-and-so." Then you'd rewrite it. And then you'd rewrite it. And then you'd rewrite it, and sometimes it would take, it could take weeks before a reply would come back.[69]

Being a Bank of Montreal banker was also marked in other ways. Partly because of the nature of Canadian chartered banking, its hierarchical structure, its size (Bank of Montreal employees numbered less than 10,000 in the late 1940s, growing to about 25,000 in the early 1970s), and the necessity for a regulations-based order, the Bank tended toward a conservative approach and outlook in the functioning of its organization as much as in the conduct of its affairs. The Bank also often resembled a military organization in its approach to people and resources. This included, until the late 1950s, obtaining the Bank's permission to marry. Transfers were also made "wherever they wanted you to go but only [for] the men."[70]

Despite the connotations evoked by Montreal itself as a French and English city, the Bank of Montreal was among the most British and English-Canadian institutions of its kind. Its links with the city of London, its prominence in representing Canadian interests in the London capital market, and its long and close relationships with governments in the North Atlantic world cemented these ties of business and affinity. Many of the Bank's senior executives down the decades were a prominent part of the Canadian ennobled elite, from Lord Strathcona and Baron Mount Stephen to the half dozen or so baronetcies conferred on presidents and general managers of the Bank. It drew the majority of its executives and directors from English Protestant Montreal, giving a deep imprimatur to the Bank's culture that extended from its earliest beginnings to more recent times. One prominent banker recalled some confessional advice offered to him in the mid-1960s: "I remember I was bunking, you know, sharing a flat, a little flat, with a banker and he said, 'You'll never get on in the bank because you don't go to this particular Anglican Church.' So, BMO was an Anglican bank and a notion that a Catholic, although I wasn't a practicing Catholic, but (inaudible) I was, the notion that, you know, an Irish Catholic would ever succeed because if you – and he used this quite earnestly: 'Because I'll tell you if you don't show up in that Anglican Church and they can see you on a Sunday, you'll never get by.'"[71]

Of course, cultures shift over time, and by the 1960s and 1970s the Bank's cultural complexion began to change as the institution and its people responded to the needs and demands of a new era.

To the Banker Born

Throughout these three decades, the leadership and people of the Bank of Montreal were deeply engaged in creating a culture on the inside while also participating in the local, regional, and national dimensions of Canadian life. This wasn't new to the post-war period: participation in the war effort between 1940 and 1945, both at home and abroad, involved thousands of Bank employees. Groups such as the Red Triangle Club of the YMCA, which offered hospitality and a warm meal to servicemen stationed in Montreal or on their way overseas, was one small example.[72] The women of the Bank in Montreal worked hard on hospitality, or meeting troop trains to show solidarity with enlisted men headed for the European theatre.[73] The *Staff Magazine* frequently published letters from members of the staff who were fighting overseas and wanting to keep the "Bank family" abreast of their activities. "I hope to be back with 'the old firm' before another Christmas comes," wrote Major E.A. Royce of Vancouver Branch, "but meanwhile a letter must speak for me."[74] The magazine kept meticulous track of service awards, published obituaries, and provided what news it could in the closing months of the war. After the war ended, the magazine frequently published the first-hand accounts of Bank of Montreal staff in the harrowing circumstances of conflict, prisoner-of-war camps, or on corvette duty in the frigid North Atlantic.[75]

The magazine was an excellent source of personal news such as births, deaths, retirements, staff transfers, promotions, and such. There was also significant space for sports news, keeping the "Bank family" apprised of events, milestones, Christmas parties, and the like. There were all kinds of local, city-based, and regional leagues for cricket, curling, softball (men's and women's), hockey, and bowling. The Montreal Staff Bowling League alone had twenty teams participating in the 1947 season.[76] The number of bankers down the years who played in women's and men's sports leagues across the country is truly impressive – from tennis and fastball to hockey and golf tournaments. Bank employees also took part in plays, floor shows, and small theatre productions. At the beginning of each of these magazine sections, a pithy quote about friendship would invariably appear: "Friendship is the gift of the Gods, and the most precious boon to man. – Earl of Beaconsfield."[77] When the Bank adopted its "My Bank" slogan for the post-war period, it came to fully reflect the participation of its employees in the Bank's culture, on the clock and in the off hours.

Of course, Bank culture did not exist independently from the Bank's main business, and occasionally a supplement would be slipped into the magazine to talk about specific banking issues. One such issue was "Bank's Loss Problems and Remedies," in which bank holdups, misplacement or mysterious disappearances, employee dishonesty, forgeries, and forged cheques were discussed.[78] The magazine also kept readers abreast of developments in the Canadian economy, such as oil and gas development and the expansion of Western Canada.[79] It covered the coronation of Queen Elizabeth II in great detail in the summer of 1953.[80]

On the lighter side, the magazine recounted relationships between branches, such as the Hamilton and Calgary main branches that bet their respective cities would win the Allan Cup football trophy in 1946 (Tigers [sic] versus Stampeders) with each branch upping the ante: "Will take up to $85 on Series at even money. Where is your civic pride?" Hamilton telegraphed Calgary. The reply: "We have plenty of pride and money. We bet $100 even money and if necessary another $50. Please confirm."[81] In the event, Hamilton lost and sent a debit slip to Calgary branch with a mourning band around the slip! News of branch activities and contributors from around the country revealed an active and vibrant local culture. Columns such as "Strictly Feminine"[82] dealt with fashion tips, suggestions from Canadian designers, and social notes in a lighthearted manner. The progress of Bank of Montreal women in advancement, promotion, and retirement was also tracked.

Frequently, the stories appearing in the magazine reflected the service and outreach performed by the Bank. For example, in June 1947, the ss *Waterman* arrived at Quebec with over a thousand immigrants from the Netherlands on board. They came to a new life in Canada carrying liquid assets in the form of travellers' cheques and drafts but no Canadian money. Without Canadian money, they were unable to buy rail tickets to their destination. Without a ticket, they could not leave the ship: regulations prohibited it. The Bank's Quebec branch accountant D.M. Hay secured permission to board the ship with a large team of staffers, a large sum of money, and two loaded revolvers. Thus was born the floating branch of the Bank of Montreal, transacting business for the Dutch immigrants while sailing the St Lawrence. By the time the team ran out of cash, the ship had reached Montreal, where fresh supplies were acquired and "Operation Waterman" continued to its successful conclusion twenty-four hours later.[83]

The broad popular culture of the Bank of Montreal in the post-war period was a remarkably tight-knit entity, organized around the business of banking and cognizant of its role, its prestige, and its responsibilities as a founding Canadian institution – responsibilities to city, province, and country. The culture of its leadership was similar, of course, but had a few unique features, as we have seen. For all its strengths, the danger of that Bank of Montreal culture was in being tied too much to the old ways, relying too frequently on traditional means and faded glories, and not realizing that renewal was a constant imperative if the long-term success of Canada's first bank was to be assured.

Life and Times in the 1950s

The Bank's activities in the 1950s travelled along mainly traditional lines. The volume of applications for credit, short- and long-term notes, and, increasingly, the funding of more ambitious projects reflected the impressive expansion of the Canadian economy. The Bank's loan portfolio touched traditional enterprise such as pulp and paper and steamship lines and new ones such as airplanes. In the case of the latter, the Bank of Montreal, along with the Royal and the Commerce, supported the development of Canadair Limited's construction of fifty Canadair Model DC-4M-4 aircraft for sale to the British Overseas Airways Corporation (BOAC, the precursor to British Airways) in the United Kingdom.[84]

The revisions to the 1954 Bank Act allowed entry of the chartered banks into the mortgage business. By December of that year, the banks' mortgage lending reached $100 million. As B.C. Gardner told the Canadian Club, "Although banks had no previous experience in this field, the setting up of new departments and training of new staffs for the purpose has gone ahead quietly and efficiently." He also noted that the power to lend on real estate "was never sought by the banks, and aroused considerable controversy when the Government suggested it," but the banks were co-operating with government policy on the matter. His view was that the banks should not have been in the business of mortgage lending, but rather should have formed new entities to undertake the mortgage business, "with capital stock subscribed partly by the banks and partly by other lending institutions."[85] Gardner's reluctance and his almost dutiful response to what ought to have been a golden opportunity for Canadian banking is another measure of the times.

The Bank was also intimately involved in national economic security matters. Throughout the 1950s, Gordon Ball was personally active in assisting the leadership of Sun Life Assurance Company with share purchases to forestall a possible hostile American takeover of the Montreal-based institution. In May

1956, the Bank purchased 15,000 shares of Sun Life stock at a cost of US$345 per share "to prevent the shares from falling into the hands of other American interests." The president advised the board executive that the only other large US holding of 17,631 shares was now being offered, "the exact offering price of which is still to be determined." Ball reported that these actions were being coordinated with the Minister of Finance, "who was anxious that the shares be held in Canadian hands and who has undertaken to do his best to see that legislation will be brought before the Dominion Parliament as soon as possible to enable the Sun Life Assurance Company to acquire their own shares." The executive suggested that Ball have a free hand in the negotiations to buy Sun Life shares, "but not exceeding, say, $325, on the understanding that Sun Life will agree to carry compensating balances with the Bank to offset the cost of the shares and will also agree to relieve the Bank of this stock, without loss, within a reasonable time."[86]

The Sun Life struggle against American takeover is one of the most remarkable post-war episodes in the annals of Canadian finance. The threats led to the mutualization of the great Canadian companies. Gordon Ball and the Bank of Montreal were in many ways the heroes, acting in concert with the Dominion government and Sun Life president George Bourke to forestall a possible hostile acquisition from the United States. The episode also shows the very close networks that existed between Canadian corporate elites, especially Montreal elites, and their willingness to offer assistance when one of their own was in trouble.

After a long hiatus, the mid-to-late 1950s saw other Canadian banks beginning to contemplate a new round of mergers and consolidations to gain market share in the sector. The merger of the Bank of Toronto and the Dominion Bank in 1955 restarted the movement. The newly formed Toronto-Dominion Bank then looked for new partners later in the decade. In late 1959, it entered negotiations with the Bank of Nova Scotia about a possible amalgamation.[87] The proposal was kept from the public, but it did occupy the serious attention of the Diefenbaker government and the Liberal opposition. L.B. Pearson discussed the matter with Senator Salter Hayden, who reported to Pearson that the Treasury Board was delaying approval, arguably on the grounds that "the amalgamation might be attacked by the Liberals for political reasons; that it might be associated with the present tight money policy of the government." Pearson himself was in favour of the amalgamation since it did not "contravene a well-established Liberal principle of opposition to combination and monopolies in restraint of trade." Indeed, he argued that "it would in fact, increase competition in the Canadian banking world by putting the amalgamated banks in a stronger position to compete against the powerful banks that remained, i.e. Montreal, Royal, Commerce."[88] In the event, the merger was abandoned after the Treasury Board declined to approve the move.

Two years later, the Canadian Bank of Commerce and the Imperial Bank of Canada amalgamation was approved by the Treasury Board, creating the Canadian Imperial Bank of Commerce (CIBC). "The merger brought together Canada's third largest and sixth largest banks, making the new entity second in size only to the Royal Bank."[89] From the Bank of Montreal's perspective, this merger was more problematic from the standpoint of reputation: it edged the Bank out of second position in the rankings of Canadian chartered banks. The fact that the CIBC would have "a paid-up capital and rest account respectively equal to those of the Bank of Montreal," prompted the executive committee of the board to discuss "desirability of our making a transfer from tax-paid reserves to rest account to make the latter in excess of $120,000,000" to keep the Bank's number two position. No action was ultimately taken, but it was an indication of the concern the Bank's leaders had with the ranking of the institution – short of acting, of course.[90]

The mergers of other banks to gain size and strength in the Canadian market was an important strategic move – and, frankly, perhaps one of the few available – to increase market share and momentum. Here again, the Bank of Montreal elected to stay on the sidelines.

Salaries and Employees

On the inside, one of the most important issues facing the leadership in the 1950s was employee retention. The salaries of Bank employees in the post-war were hardly keeping up with inflationary pressures. "Studies by our Economist's Department," recounted minutes of one board meeting, "indicate that real and disposable income per capital after allowance[s] ... rose on an average of 50% from 1939 to 1947 while earnings of this Bank's employees, similarly adjusted, had in the same period advanced only 14% for officers, 5% for women, and 25% for messengers."[91] The Bank's rates in comparison to those of, say, Bell Telephone Company of Canada were lagging behind. Moreover, comparison with other banks showed that the Bank of Montreal was falling seriously behind its competitors. Not surprisingly, the remedy was to increase wages and salaries and boost bonuses. In November 1948, a series of bonuses were distributed amounting to 16 per cent for non-executives and increases and greater allowances for executives. By 1949, the remuneration to employees in the Bank was, on average, $2,292, while the average for all other banks was $2,078.[92] However, the resource issue was a chronic one. In 1950, the board heard that "too low a commencing salary" was preventing the Bank from attracting a "good caliber of woman entrant and many male applicants, too, have

Table 14.2 | Number of male branch staff (including temporary) and average annual salary at Canadian banks, February 1948

	Age up to 25		Age 26–30		Age 31–40		Age 41–50		Age over 50		
	No.	Average Salary	No.	Average Salary	No.	Average Salary	No.	Average Salary	No.	Average Salary	Total No.
Bank of Montreal	446	$1,379	174	$2,194	878	$2,672	635	$3,169	549	$3,993	2,682
Bank of Nova Scotia	782	$1,091	147	$2,508	466	$2,805	267	$3,557	152	$4,501	1,814
Royal Bank of Canada	655	$1,339	413	$2,263	778	$2,839	471	$3,382	360	$3,786	2,677
Bank of Commerce	817	$1,433	322	$2,181	592	$2,906	517	$3,358	527	$3,859	2,775

Source: BMOA, Minutes of the Executive Committee of the Board, 15 September 1948, "Memorandum for the General Manager."

turned down an offer of employment for this reason. Heavy workloads and excessive hours were also a problem because of the labour shortage. "Not infrequently good women employees are offered positions by other industries at higher salaries." The report cited an example of an "excellent teller at Sun Life Branch, 22 years of age, entered January 1946, receiving $1,682 per annum" who resigned to go with Colonial Air Lines at the considerably higher salary of $2,600 per annum.[93] The Bank was not attracting the better type of applicant, and "the staffing of our branches is becoming an acute problem."[94]

Table 14.2 offers a glimpse into the demographic and income makeup of the Bank's male workforce.

The later 1950s witnessed the beginning of a long process of establishing women on a more equal footing in the Bank. In 1959–60, the Bank established the Bank of Montreal Pension Fund for Women Employees, at the behest of the late president Sir Vincent Meredith and with his bequest of $100,000. A second bequest of equal amount was used to establish a Sick Benefit Fund.[95] Up until then, the Bank had no pension fund for women employees. These first steps in the pension field were a sign of things to come.

The Dangerous Sequel: The 1960s

For several reasons, the decade of the 1960s would prove much more consequential, and turbulent, than the preceding one. Internally, the Bank leadership realized an increasingly serious need to overhaul the company's organization and its technology. Under the leadership of Hart, McNeil, and their teams, the Bank began to respond in a comprehensive way to its competitive situation. Accounts of those reforms are the subject of chapters 17 and 18.

As those reforms took hold, the Bank adapted, at times quite quickly, to a changing social and economic landscape. The infusion of young blood in managerial positions was especially noticeable, particularly the stream of recruits from the United Kingdom. As one such banker recalled: "It was very noticeable, right off the bat, that people were in senior jobs, senior from my perspective, branch accountant or assistant accountant or head of the foreign exchange department or whatever, and they were very young. But of course, in the United Kingdom that would never have happened, and particularly in the Bank of Montreal in the UK because they were going to be in forever so there was no rotation, there was no opportunity. So suddenly, when I inquired about that, they said, 'Oh, there's lots of opportunity in the bank.' So I saw that, my God, people can get promoted here, it's a meritocracy. My accent doesn't matter."[96]

That banker went on to describe the world of Bank of Montreal banking in London, England, which made for both a contrast and a fascinating glimpse into the way banking was perceived and conducted. The Bank's west-end branch was, in fact, a boutique, "private banking before they ever named it." The staff there not only looked after the business of banking but also looked after theatre tickets and the children of wealthy clients. As the same banker recalled:

> We'd get letters of introduction that would come from Canada that "Joe Blow was coming over, he's a very important client. He's got a kid at school over there. Take care of him." So we'd send flowers to the hotel and I'd go and meet them sometimes and I'd take their kids on little tours of London. So it was all that kind of high-touch personal service ... There were no indigenous – we had no clients at all that were purely UK clients. It was all Canadians; there was a Canadian connection and a Bank of Montreal connection. And we were also the bank to a lot of Canadians that were working in the Embassy and working in the Commissioner's Office etc. Because we were well located for that being in Piccadilly.[97]

The Canadian economic and financial landscape changed in the late 1950s. In 1959, the banks came in for a fair bit of criticism over a "tight money situation" that occurred in the country as a result of Bank of Canada expansion of the money supply. The effect was a substantial increase in loans in Canada – by $300 million, or 25 per cent. As a consequence of carrying more loans, the Bank would have to be willing and able to dispose of other assets in an equivalent amount – chiefly in government securities. With the money supply being held constant, by the summer of 1959, the banking system was compelled to slow additions to its loan portfolio to stem the losses incurred, and to shore up their holdings of government securities – which were an important element in the investment mix of the Bank of Montreal and the other major chartered banks.[98] "No banker likes to say 'no' to a credit-worthy applicant, but with broad limiting forces at work over which the banks have no control, such an answer may on occasion be the only answer that can be given."[99]

With the dawn of the 1960s, the Canadian economic outlook became more complex and more ambiguous due to indifferent economic performance and disagreements about economic and monetary policy. "Thus far," Arnold Hart suggested at the 1960 annual meeting, "the 'soaring sixties' have shown little inclination to soar."[100] The problem for the banks continued to be, as Hart put it, "how far we may go in responding to ... lending situations that may properly involve a considerable amount of financing, but under conditions wherein the banks have no indication of the extent to which the loanable resources of the banking system will be permitted to increase."[101] Throughout the 1960s, however, the continuous rise in export-led growth, investment activity, and business capital formation was the major driving force – with outlays for housing, non-residential construction, and machinery and equipment, to cite a few examples, leading the way.[102] These were years of GNP growth touching 10 per cent per annum.[103]

By the late 1960s, the intense growth in the Canadian economy gave way to concerns about inflationary pressures. Hart expressed that concern at the 1967 annual meeting, suggesting that, at 5 per cent, Canada's inflation trajectory was the strongest and most alarming compared to our main export customers – the United States, the United Kingdom, and the European Common Market.[104] Hart placed the blame on runaway government spending and "ever-increasing expenditures," which added fuel to the fire. Inflation was the primary threat to the continued growth of the Canadian economy.

The signs of a changing external environment for Canadian banking were getting more insistent by the early 1960s. Most of the big changes would take place in the parliamentary, legislative, and regulatory arenas. It would begin with Prime Minister Diefenbaker's 1961 empanelling of a Royal Commission on Banking and Finance and continue with the landmark 1967 revisions to the Bank Act. The Canadian banking game would change significantly once those measures were in place.

The Royal Commission on Banking and Finance (Porter Commission)[105] was established on 18 October 1961 on the orders of the Minister of Finance. The Commission was mandated to inquire into and report on: "(a) the structure and methods of operation of the Canadian financial system, including the banking and monetary system and the institutions and processes involved in the flow of funds through the capital market; and (b) to make recommendations (i) for improving the structure and operations of the financial system and, (ii) concerning the Bank Act, the Bank of Canada Act, the Quebec Savings Banks Act, and other relevant federal legislation." The Commission was headed by Justice Dana Harris Porter. The appointment of the Royal Commission resulted mainly from a dispute between the Governor of the Bank of Canada, James E. Coyne, and the Diefenbaker government over the economic policies of the Government of Canada. The dispute reached a climax in June 1961 when the government demanded Coyne's resignation. After the Senate refused to approve a government bill providing for his dismissal, Coyne resigned in July 1961.

In its dealings with Coyne, the government claimed that it did not have control over the Bank of Canada's monetary policy, which was counter to government policy; that Coyne was making controversial public speeches; and that the board of directors increased the governor's pension without informing the Minister of Finance. Consequently, the government directed that a royal commission take a close look at the Bank of Canada's relationship with the Minister of Finance in the field of monetary policy. In his budget speech of 20 June 1961, Minister of Finance Donald Fleming disclosed that it was the government's intention to appoint a royal commission. Fleming told the House of Commons that: "Such broad topics as the pattern and behaviour of interest rates, consumer credit and instalment financing, and the management of the public debt, will be included in the terms of reference. The commission will be asked to study existing financial institutions, such as the chartered banks, the Bank of Canada, and other institutions that perform banking and credit functions, and the various acts of parliament which govern their activities. The commission will also be asked to consider ways and means of encouraging the development of savings institutions."[106]

The Royal Commission of 1961 undertook the first comprehensive review of Canada's banking and financial system since 1933, when the Royal Commission on Banking and Currency, which led to the establishment of the Bank of Canada, was appointed. After 1933, parliamentary committees on the decennial revisions of the Bank Acts, on dominion-provincial financial conferences, and on the Royal Commission on Canada's Economic Prospects undertook further reviews of Canada's financial institutions.

It was expected that the Royal Commission of 1961 would submit its report in time for Parliament's decennial review of the charters of the banks under the Bank Act and the Quebec Savings Bank Act, which expired on 30 June 1964. However, the Commission did not complete its work until 1966, and Parliament had to postpone its review of bank legislation until that time.[107] Hearings were held in Charlottetown, Halifax, Fredericton, Montreal, Ottawa, Toronto, Winnipeg, Regina, Edmonton, Vancouver, and Victoria from 12 March 1962 to 22 January 1963, and ninety-five submissions were received.[108]

The Commission noted the great emphasis placed on the liquidity of and safety of deposits in the Canadian banks – as well as the development of the branch system. This was a major element of attraction to the banks themselves. The result was a high density of banks in Canada – perhaps to excess, it was noted.[109] The Commission noted the banks' general loss of position because of restrictions on what they could offer, and their reluctance to take on additional cost to provide convenience to customers. In the post-war period, the Canadian banks were loaning significantly more to individuals and businesses and away from government securities and liquid assets. By way of example, the share of loans and non-government investments rose from 30.5 per cent in 1945 to 64.6 per cent in 1956.[110]

Response to the Porter Commission Report was mixed. "Chartered Bank presidents are a little startled at what their economists have wrought," reported the *Globe and Mail* when the findings were released.[111] After a long period of study, Arnold Hart suggested that some of the recommendations might lead to more banks and less confidence in the system. Credit systems required judgment and professional discernment, he said, adding that "banks have a function beyond being status symbols."[112]

The 1967 Bank Act

The 1967 Bank Act delivered a major impetus to change in the Canadian banking system. Some economists saw the legislation as official sanctioning of competition within the banking community and between banks and other financial institutions – following the direction set by the Porter Commission.[113] Competition and the application of a "limited range of indirect, general instruments in the hands of the governmental monetary authorities" was the preferred method of proceeding.[114] The act changed the operating basis of the banks across a number of categories. The most significant changes were in lending operations – which ultimately removed the ceiling on interest rates on loans (which were set at 6 per cent).[115] The banks could also now engage in conventional and CMHC-insured mortgage lending (expanding the 1954 Bank Act provisions). The banks were accorded the privilege of selling their own debentures. Cash reserve ratios were set at a 4 per cent minimum for all deposit and certificate obligations except chequing accounts, and the raising of the minimum case reserve ratio to 12 per cent (following on the Porter Commission recommendations).[116] A host of other changes were also put into practice. Banks were now permitted to own leasing subsidiaries so they could plausibly compete with "near banks and foreign competitors."[117] The Porter Commission and the Bank Act that followed based its recommendations were a turning point for the Canadian banking system.

The liberalization of banking restrictions and the promotion of competition were the "means to a safe, efficient, equitable, adaptable, socially responsible banking and financial structure."[118]

The upshot was that the banks were given greater latitude to engage in intermediation functions on better terms.[119] Measures were also taken to ensure that the Canadian banking system remained in Canadian hands by limiting foreign ownership to 25 per cent by foreign residents and to 10 per cent by any single shareholder, foreign or domestic. This was part of a broader effort to limit foreign influence in Canada. Foreign banks were effectively prohibited entry into the Canadian market, though the Mercantile Bank was an exception and restrictions were placed on its future expansion.[120]

Increased competition had been one of the main recommendations of the Porter Commission.[121] John Diefenbaker, by this time in Opposition, considered the Porter Commission's recommendations to open up even greater competition as an important element of reform. He was worried that the Pearson government was not doing enough to live up to the Porter Commission's recommendations. "The opportunity is being lost," he wrote in 1966, "to bring into being, as suggested by the Royal Commission on Banking and Finance, a more open and competitive banking system – carefully and equitably regulated under uniform legislation, but not bound by restrictions which impede response to new situations, enforce a particular pattern of narrow specialization or shelter some enterprises from competitive forces."[122]

Diefenbaker's analysis was characteristically blunt: "A royal commission spent years and thousands of dollars to study the matter in its infinite detail ... The law has been long delayed – too long delayed. This long-drawn indecision has been unnecessary and ridiculous – a product more of political timidity than anything else. The basic, far-reaching change urged by the royal commission did not take place." Where the Commission suggested sweeping competition and transparency across the financial services sector, the legislation was much more either timid or measured, depending upon your perspective. The Commission "would have given Canada more banks, plus a variety of specialized banks (some not over-burdened with expensive networks of branches, as chartered banks now are), plus more protection for members of the public dealing with the companies now called near-banks."[123]

Prime Minister Pearson, however, had reservations about fully implementing the Commission's recommendations, especially in the wake of the collapse of the Atlantic Acceptance Corporation in June of that year, and the difficulties of the British Mortgage and Trust Company, "which have focused public attention on certain weaknesses in the supervision and inspection of financial institutions which are not now adequately supervised."

He concluded that "there seems to be a fairly general feeling that the federal government should go farther in assisting to ensure adequate supervision and the protection of depositors."[124]

Speaking for the Bank of Montreal, President Arnold Hart, too, believed that the Bank Act did not go far enough, citing its timidity and the fact that Walter Gordon, the finance minister, had abandoned most of the Porter Commission's recommendations. The legislation failed "to take into account the realities of the world today and the vast changes that have occurred in the structure of the Canadian financial system and the environment in which it operates."[125] The *Toronto Star* agreed about the necessity for changes, stating: "The big banks are the New York Mets of the financial league – they're born losers everywhere except at the box office."[126]

Foreign Influence and the Mercantile Bank

The 1967 Bank Act also included provisions to limit foreign ownership of Canadian banks. This was part of a long-standing concern about foreign (US) influence. The issue of foreign ownership was initially not on the agenda for the revision of the Bank Act. The issue was forced, however, when in 1965 the Mercantile Bank of Canada was taken over by the US-owned First Citibank of New York. That affair revealed some interesting attitudes toward the changes in Canadian banking, and the competitive position of the Canadian banks in public policy, and so is examined in greater detail in this section.

The Mercantile Bank of Canada was a small Dutch-owned regional bank (thirteen branches, mostly confined to the Montreal area) first chartered in 1950. After the Imperial Bank of Canada takeover of Barclays Bank in 1956, the Mercantile Bank held the distinction of being the only foreign-owned bank in Canada. In 1965 – right in the middle of the Bank Act revisions – the Dutch sold Mercantile Bank to US-owned First National City Bank of New York, which hoped to use the small bank as a launch point to expand further into Canada.[127]

The move came in the midst of an increasing anxiety over foreign investment in Canada and the potential loss of control posed by that investment, especially in relation to the United States. "In our case," one Cabinet document on the question suggested, "allowing foreign agencies to operation freely could in the opinion of the Bank of Canada, lead to serious loss of monetary control."[128] For its part, the Bank of Montreal sided with the Mercantile Bank in the contretemps, in the spirit of maintaining an expanding competitive environment.

In early 1966, despite pressure from Washington, First National City Bank of New York, and the Bank of Montreal, the federal government added new draft provisions to the Bank Act that sought to limit foreign ownership of Canadian banks.[129] The new measures, which held that "no shareholder could own more than 10 per cent of a bank nor could the aggregate of foreign shareholdings exceed 25 per cent," were met with scorn by the US ambassador to Canada, who called it retroactive and discriminatory.[130] Economic nationalists responded in kind: Eric Kierans, former Quebec revenue minister, strongly defended Canada's proposed action. He said the Rockefeller interests had received advance warning before buying the Bank from Dutch interests that Canada might act to limit foreign ownership of Banks.[131]

Reaction did not end there, and pulled back the veil on attitudes about Canadian banks as much as the actual issue of foreign investment. Western-Canadian businessman George MacNamara claimed that special interests and banking elites were limiting foreign ownership in order to preserve their power and influence. The Bank Act's proposed restrictions did nothing to counteract this.[132] A group in Canada, he asserted, commands effective "control, through bank directorships and other means, over 80% of the Canadian money supply."[133] This group would "stop at nothing" to protect "its dominant position in the Canadian economy."[134] The "mother bank" of that group was the Royal, he asserted.[135] The Bank of Montreal did not escape his excoriation, declaring that it was "in deadly fear of its rivals" and that this motive explained why it was the only Canadian chartered bank that came out strongly in favour of permitting the Mercantile Bank to continue operations in Canada on an unrestricted scale. It would be an ally large enough to stave off the others.[136]

McNamara's western populist prescriptions were not widely shared in detail, but the *Financial Times* agreed that the legislation was "like a large abstract painting – you see more and understand less the more you look at it."[137]

Hart's views on the Mercantile Bank and foreign ownership were grounded in an understanding of the competitive environment of Canadian banking, and an idea that liberalization of restrictions was an important principle to advocate for. "Restrictive legislation of this type is surely unworthy of Canada and would be another blow to free enterprise," he told legislators, and the fact that the legislation was aimed at one bank, and obviously so, made it "discriminatory in the fullest sense."[138] Hart was responding to the changes in the competitive landscape with a new vigour, as the Bank began to shake off its lethargic approach and began to deal with the challenges of the era, both internally and externally.

Hart's concern with bank policy expanded to interventions in the late 1960s and early 1970s on matters of overall economic policy. "In reviewing the events of the most economic significance during the past year," he declared in 1971, "it is difficult to escape the conclusion that first place should be given to the breakdown of the international trade policy and payments system signaled by President Nixon's announcement of August 15th … there can be no doubt that resolute account was needed to put the United States economy on a sustainable, non-inflationary growth path and to introduce changes in the international arena such that the United States would be able to continue to make its full contribution to the healthy growth of the world economy." The effectiveness of Canada's response would be "determined essentially by the extent to which the business community remains free to take the initiative in the conduct of its own affairs without forever being on the defensive in the face of what has often seemed to be, and has even been called, 'harassment' at the hands of government."[139]

"Harassment is a very strong term," he conceded, but nonetheless asserted that "business feels harassed and the effects on confidence, initiative and efficiency are the same."[140] These statements came in the wake of a series of reports and legislation that bore the distinct markings of a greater and more complex state involvement in Canadian enterprise. From the Competition Act to the Gray Report (on foreign ownership) to the establishment of a "Competitive Practices Tribunal" – all "betray[ed] a strong tendency to subject the workings of the economy to a regimen of social control through administrative agencies and which in my sincere opinion are fraught with dangers for the continued existence of the free enterprise system which has served this country … so well."[141]

Bank of Montreal president Leonard Walker concurred, adding his voice to Hart's and emphasizing the danger of a volatile interest rate environment. "In 1970, in fact," Walker declared, "we witnessed an all-time peak in interest rates at the beginning of the year, followed by the sharpest decline in Canadian history."[142] The clouded Canadian environment was one reason for the Bank to push into the international arena, where operations had seen the most rapid expansion and assets had grown over 25 per cent per year from 1967 to 1970; by 1970, they represented a quarter of the Bank's assets. The Bank's interventions were a good signal that it was realizing that its position as a premier bank was threatened if it did not assert itself in both strategy and organization as well as in the public square.

Signs of the Times

By the mid-1960s, the atmosphere of change at the Bank began to percolate throughout its operations. A few examples will suffice: while some were of longer duration or greater impact than others, all were significant in their own right.

The Bank expanded in some key areas of finance supporting Canadian enterprise.

The Bank's experience with international trade and exchange was one of its many powerful capabilities. Between 1950 and 1966, Canada's commodity exports more than tripled in dollar terms, equalling $10 billion and equivalent to one-third of the national output of goods.[143] The movement of capital, interest, and dividend payments, in addition to personal and business dealings in the post-war period, was a strong sign of both Canadian prosperity and the fact that the country was tied so closely to the terms of trade.

The Canadian chartered banks were the greatest facilitators of this massive movement, and the Bank of Montreal could rightly assert leadership in this space. The Bank's offices in New York, San Francisco, Los Angeles, and London (two offices) and its representative offices in Chicago, Houston, Paris, Düsseldorf, Milan, Tokyo, and Mexico City provided the necessary networks to mount such an operation. By the 1960s, the Bank's involvement in the Caribbean through the Bank of London and Montreal (BOLAM) was a further indication of the Bank's reach.

The Bank established a Foreign Exchange Department (FED) in 1920 to centralize its growing foreign exchange business – and to defend against and exploit the fluctuations of both the Canadian dollar and the pound sterling.[144] The two currencies were not formally tied, but they moved in tandem, as the proceeds in sterling of Canada's favourable trade balance with the United Kingdom counterbalanced the country's trade deficit with the United States.[145] The fluctuations happened as late as 1949: when the pound was devalued by 30.5 per cent, the Canadian dollar was devalued by 10 per cent.

By the 1960s, the FED had a staff of sixty-two, including two officers in Toronto and a chief trader in Montreal. The FED alone was responsible for massive routine operations in multiple foreign currency accounts through the medium of banking correspondents abroad – and turned over a business of $13 billion per year.

The Bank's involvement in the financing of the Canadian export trade was also important. The Bank of Montreal financed production of goods, development of export trade (including the production of banker's credit reports for the firms they are trading with), dealings with foreign exchange control regulations, and methods of payment.[146]

In 1963, the Bank opened a representative office in Houston, with the idea that Canadian oil and gas companies doing business in the United States – particularly those centred in Calgary – would eventually require banking facilities. The Bank of Montreal was emerging as a clear leader in this area, particularly in the area of financing oil and gas production. Its presence in the market as a big lender facilitated important and co-operative relationships with some of the US banks in the field, particularly in Chicago and Houston. Here, the Bank's reputation for straight dealing earned it a reputation and a status to be envied. "And particularly in the oil and gas business," commented one oil and gas banking veteran, "[straight dealing] is a characteristic that pays off."[147] The Houston experience was indicative of what was possible when an entrepreneurial spirit was combined with the traditional strengths of the Bank – its high trust value, its reputation, and its way of dealing with relationships.

Le Salon: No Men Allowed

In September 1966, the Bank of Montreal inaugurated "Le Salon," Canada's first women-only branch on Sherbrooke Street West in Montreal. The unusual new concept was launched by Hart and Mulholland at a "morning coffee party" in the branch. As the *Globe and Mail* reported, "the branch, looking more like a fashion house than a bank, will serve any woman who has enough cash to maintain the minimum $2,000 account balance required for customers. Men who try to gate crash will be directed to the nearest exit."[148]

Arnold Hart quipped that, "if this branch is successful, we will open others like it in Toronto and several more Canadian cities," adding that "I personally take responsibility for the idea of a bank exclusively for women – and if it fails, I will be fired."[149] As the annual report for that year described, "the décor and appointments of the branch are designed throughout to appeal to feminine tastes."[150] Several US banks tried the same initiative, but this was a first in Canadian banking circles.[151]

In a changing world, these were the initial, perhaps halting, steps toward recognizing the value and importance of women as customers, employees, and, ultimately, equals. In the event, however, the pilot failed to catch on, and no more locations were opened.

Marketing and Public Relations

Marketing came slowly to Canadian banking. By gentleman's agreement, the institutions had refrained from using either radio or television advertising (perhaps considering banking too serious a subject for such a popular medium). By the late 1950s, attitudes were changing somewhat as the natural attraction and power of the medium began to tempt even the most taciturn bankers. In 1957, "the President informed the Executive Committee that notwithstanding the agreement between banks to refrain from advertising on radio or television, we have looked into the matter [as] a competitor might decide to use either, or both, media. The cost of a nation-wide television programme in both French and English under joint sponsorship for 26 weeks of each year would be approximately $500,000 per annum and it was felt that owing to the high cost and the type of service we have to sell, the matter should be left in abeyance."[152] The Canadian banking industry was slowly catching up to the new possibilities of reaching people.

One of the great and lasting symbols of the new era was the 1967 introduction of the new logo, the M-Bar. Designed by Hans Kleefeld, who was also responsible for iconic logos for Canadian giants like Air Canada, Molson, and the Toronto-Dominion Bank, the new logo was hailed by Arnold Hart at the launch as "another major development being taken by the 'new' Bank of Montreal to advance our image of vitality and service."[153] Introduced alongside the logo was "First Bank Blue," the now-famous official colour associated with the Bank of Montreal. The unveiling of the new logo and colour, and as Hart alluded to in his opening remarks, was part of a renewal of the Bank, which is discussed in greater detail in the next chapter.

Introduced to coincide with the Bank's 150th anniversary, the logo was to reflect the Bank's new, contemporary, and more aggressive posture for a new era.[154] "Within the Bank, as well as to the public eye," internal Bank documents reveal, "here is the symbol of an organization in which originality is welcome, staffed by people eager to provide the best and broadest service to individuals and to all enterprises regardless of size and degree."[155] The logo checks all the boxes for an iconic design. As designer Clair Stewart stated, for a corporate logo to have longevity, "it has to be designed well, and the company must be absolutely convinced that the design that's being presented is the right one for them."[156] In this instance, the M-Bar can rightfully take its place among the most iconic corporate logos in Canadian enterprise.

Conclusion

The progress of the Bank of Montreal in the post-war period is shown in tables 14.3 to 14.7. As table 14.3 summarizes, after a slow start, assets began to pick up momentum, particularly in the 1960s and early 1970s. The customer base shown in table 14.4 shows that the number of Bank of Montreal customers grew substantially, especially in the early 1950s, as more and more Canadians required banking facilities. Table 14.5, on personnel,

Table 14.3 | Bank of Montreal assets,
selected years 1945–74

Year	Assets	% Change
1945	$1,715,932,320	
1950	$2,190,529,368	27.7
1955	$2,796,174,000	27.6
1960	$3,485,471,000	24.7
1965	$4,997,145,000	43.4
1970	$8,730,051,000	74.7
1974	$17,650,974,000	102.2

Source: BMOA, Corporate Secretary's Department, Historical Reference
Sources, 1817 Updated to 2004, n.d.

Table 14.4 | Number of customers, Bank of Montreal,
selected years 1946–68

Year	Number	% Change
1946	1,500,000	
1950	1,750,000	16.7
1955	2,130,000	21.7
1960	2,816,000	32.2
1965	3,368,223	19.6
1968	3,925,644	16.5

Source: BMOA, various Annual Reports. Customers were also called
depositors or accounts, and the numbers were not always reported annually.

mirrors a similar story of strong incremental increases and expansion.
Finally, share capital and share price in tables 14.6 and 14.7 tell an important story of powerful profit growth; the possible exception is the early
1960s, a time of slower and more difficult growth.

The statistical portrait of the Bank shows an institution that was growing,
that was profitable, and that was being run competently and professionally.
In the world of Canadian chartered banks, the performance was respectable
over time. But the numbers only begin to tell the story. The relative success
of the Bank in the late 1940s and the 1950s masked some deeper structural
and strategic challenges that only intensified with time. The administrations
headed by Gardner and Ball seemed to have applied a traditional playbook
when it came to growth, expansion, and organizational renewal – in other

Table 14.5 | Number of personnel, Bank of Montreal,
selected years 1952–74

Year	Number	% Change
1952	10,000	
1955	11,500	15.0
1960	14,700	27.8
1965	15,300	4.1
1970	18,253	19.3
1974	24,231	32.8

Source: BMOA, Corporate Secretary's Department, Historical Reference
Sources, 1817 Updated to 2004, n.d.

Table 14.6 | Share capital and retained earnings,
selected years 1946–74

Year	Amount	% Change
1946	$42,000,000	
1951	$51,000,000	21.4
1955	$90,000,000	76.5
1960	$141,850,000	57.6
1965	$163,000,000	14.9
1970	$234,500,000	43.9
1974	$334,000,000	42.4

Source: BMOA, Corporate Secretary's Department, Historical Reference
Sources, 1817 Updated to 2004, n.d.

Table 14.7 | Bank of Montreal per share prices,
selected years 1946–74

Year	High	Low
1946	$22.50	$16.25
1950	$31.25	$27.00
1955	$54.50	$41.63
1960	$60.00	$47.25
1965	$70.50	$59.00
1967	5-for-1 stock split, 23 June	
1970	$17.00	$13.38
1974	$21.00	$11.00

Source: BMOA, Corporate Secretary's Department, Historical Reference
Sources, 1817 Updated to 2004, n.d.

words, they were careful. Very careful – perhaps almost to a fault. Their towering strengths were in the traditional business of banking and in the bank-industry relationships that were required to flourish in Montreal, Toronto, New York, and London. The Bank's transition to a new era marked by broader markets, mass consumerism, and technological transformation would begin, at first haltingly then with greater urgency, under the Hart–R.D. Mulholland (1959–67) and Hart–McNeil (1967–74) administrations. The demographic, regulatory, and technological transformations of this period gathered momentum in the 1950s and really hit a dynamic pace in the 1960s and early 1970s. The challenge of adapting to these transformations was multi-faceted, but principally rooted in the culture of the Bank itself. Its processes, organizational structure, and strategic outlook in the immediate post-war was looking more and more staid and tradition-bound. The leadership in the 1950s and into the 1960s perfectly illustrated the strengths and weaknesses of this approach. On the one hand, they ran the Bank with a great sense of reserve, responsibility, and professionalism. The Bank of Montreal had withstood and could still withstand almost any conditions that the economic cycle could throw at it – and had done so for well over a century and a quarter. At the same time, its bureaucracy was beginning to look increasingly inflexible, its managers and too many of its senior leadership comfortable with The Way Things Are, custodians of a great and important Canadian financial institution, but less and less protagonists.

The Bank of Montreal's overall post-war experience must be set against the wider context of Canadian banking. In the twentieth century, other financial institutions – investment houses, life insurance companies, trust companies, and mutual funds firms, for example – grew substantially in absolute and relative size. This trend began in the early twentieth century and continued unabated up until the Second World War.[157] Private non-bank intermediaries such as trusteed pension funds, mutual funds, finance companies, *caisses populaires*, and credit unions appeared on the scene. In the public sphere, a more activist state became an increasingly central player in finance with control over federal annuity, insurance, and pension accounts; the Central Mortgage and Housing Corporation; and the Canada Pension and Quebec Pension plans.[158]

Between 1950 and 1968, the assets of financial intermediaries grew by 387 per cent. Bank assets grew by 235 per cent in this period, compared to private non-bank intermediaries at 525 per cent. Significantly, public assets became a major player, growing by 380 per cent federally and 1,458 per cent provincially (see table 14.8).

These statistics show clearly that the position of the Canadian chartered banks was strong, but faced increasingly stiff competition from other financial

Table 14.8 | Canadian financial intermediary assets,
selected statistics comparing 1950 and 1968

	% Increase 1950–1968	Assets 1968 $(000,000)
Private: Charted Banks Canadian Assets	+235	28,939
Private: Non-bank Financial intermediaries – total	+525	47,852
Public: Federal – total	+380	19,282
Public: Provincial – total	+1458	4,237

Source: E.P. Neufeld, *The Financial System of Canada: Its Growth and Development* (Toronto:
MacMillan of Canada, 1972), 68.

Table 14.9 | Relative size of individual banks, by market share,
1940 and 1970

	1940 (%)	1970 (%)
Bank of Montreal	26.4	19.5
Royal Bank of Canada	25.3	25.1
Canadian Bank of Commerce (CIBC after 1961)	19.4	
Imperial Bank of Canada (CIBC after 1961)	5.0	22.7
Bank of Nova Scotia	8.8	13.6
Bank of Toronto (TD after 1955)	4.5	12.0
Dominion Bank (TD after 1955)	4.1	
Banque Provinciale du Canada	1.5	2.2
Banque Canadienne Nationale	4.3	4.3
Two largest (%)	51.7*	47.8
Five largest (%)	83.4	92.9

* Neufeld's table states the number as 50.7. This is likely a math error, as
BMO (26.4) + RBC (25.3) = 51.7.

Source: E.P. Neufeld, *The Financial System of Canada. Its Growth and
Development* (Toronto: MacMillan of Canada, 1972), 99.

intermediaries. Indeed, banks in Canada continued to decline in relative size,
and as economist E.P. Neufeld observed, "grew no faster than gross national
product."[159] In the post-war period, particularly after 1950, chartered banks as
a whole continued their slow growth rate relative to mutual funds companies,

consumer loan firms, and other intermediaries. Taking the long-run experience of the chartered banks over a century, there is a decline in relative size of all financial intermediaries of 44 per cent (between 1870 and 1968). By the 1960s, the ratio of chartered bank assets to gross national product levelled off at around 39 per cent – about 7 percentage points lower than in the early part of the twentieth century.[160] One of the reasons frequently cited for this decline is the inherent conservatism of Canadian chartered banks, particularly their preference for high cash ratios and liquidity. In this conservatism, as has been a recurring theme throughout this book, the Bank of Montreal was the de facto leader.

As table 14.9 shows, during this period, the Bank of Montreal's relative size declined from 26.4 per cent in 1940 to 19.5 per cent in 1970. In other words, over the three decades tracked, the Bank lost 6.9 per cent relative position vis-à-vis the other banks. Looking at the Bank's chief rivals, the Royal Bank of Canada managed to hold its own at around 25 per cent (25.3 per cent in 1940 and 25.1 per cent in 1970); the Commerce clocked in at second place at the end of the period, with 19.7 per cent in 1940 and 22.7 per cent in 1970 (with a 6.0 per cent boost from its acquisition of the Imperial Bank in 1961).

A few features of the Canadian chartered banks' approach to the business of banking should be noted. First of all, Canadian banks throughout the twentieth century expressed an increasing preference for liquidity. That liquidity can be defined as how much banks held in Canadian and foreign cash items, plus Government of Canada securities as a proportion of total chartered bank note and deposit liabilities.[161] In 1900, that ratio was 14 per cent; in 1970, it was 36 per cent. Furthermore, as E.P. Neufeld notes, "the banks for years introduced no significantly useful innovation into their debt instruments after they made the crucially important decision just after Confederation to enter the savings deposit business and make banking available to the little man, and not just to the industrial, commercial and agricultural enterprises of the nation."[162] It was only in the 1960s that the banks began to introduce innovations in liability instruments – term notes, debentures, savings plans among them – to spur growth.

The Magnificent Facades

In August 1945, the Bank's former general manager, Sir Frederick Williams-Taylor, died. The Williams-Taylors had made their home in England before moving to the Bahamas. In the obituary notice, the Williams-Taylors were said to be "among [the] closest friends of the Duke and Duchess of Windsor."[163] The death of Williams-Taylor, who had long been remote from the business of the Bank, nevertheless signified a symbolic close to a generation in the life of the Bank of Montreal, one marked by a clearly defined style and an ease of movement among the upper echelons of the social and financial elites of the North Atlantic world. However, the ambiguous legacy of that era would continue to assert itself as the Bank faced a new day and a new world after the Second World War.

In the two decades after the end of the Second World War, the Bank of Montreal's image, its reputation, and its public face reflected its historic and contemporary importance to the financial life of the country. You could say that its image is nicely captured by the "magnificent facades" – the fronts of the historic branches – that defined the architectural presence and heritage of the Bank across the vast geography of Canada, from Halifax to Montreal and Toronto to Winnipeg and Vancouver, and in dozens of second cities across the country.

In a metaphorical sense, that magnificent facade also represented the legacy, the reputation, and the heritage of the Bank conferred on the generation of 1945 from posterity. The Bank's singular record as a nation-builder and key financial point of reference in the emergence of Canada, as the nation took its place in the North Atlantic world, created an image, reputation, and position that, in some sense, gave rise to the magnificent facade of the managerial mind. Facades can be gorgeous, inspiring, and memorable. But facades can also be deceptive and concealing: legacies can hide rigidities; big bureaucracies can mask vast, subterranean deposits of inertia.

In the post-war Bank of Montreal, those magnificent facades of past achievement increasingly masked a loss of vigour. Those grand classical storefronts of the imagination obscured a strategy, organization, and culture content to stand on the shoulders of past generations, of ancient triumphs. The Bank's progress and expansion two decades after the Second World War were also, in some sense, deceptive. The growing numbers in key performance measures were important indicators of the Bank's overall health, but hid deeper issues that were, paradoxically, attacking the inheritance and position of the bank, threatening its claim to greatness. Both its structure and culture combined to hold the organization back from fully adapting to changing times after the Second World War. In essence, the generation of 1945 did not respond either adequately or in good time to the changes transforming Canadian banking.

The simple conclusion is that leadership matters deeply, but that conclusion is as obvious as it is anodyne. What is less obvious (and less anodyne) is that some Bank of Montreal leaders in this era succumbed to the commonplace misapprehension that their generation of leadership was facing unparalleled challenges over which they could exert little or no control. As one military historian reminds us, "so often we forget the power of individuals in the anonymous age of high technology and massive bureaucracies."[164] The post-war Bank of Montreal was in serious need of leaders who could lift their gaze beyond the deceptively reassuring measures of growth and expansion, and perceive that that growth was relative. The problem was not related to the youth or agedness of the leadership, but rather to their strategic perspective and sense of urgency. The times demanded, uniquely in the annals of the Bank of Montreal, a restoration artist – an engineer who could fix a cracked edifice before it came tumbling down.[165] What was needed most was a re-examination and reappraisal of the conventional thinking that caused Canada's First Bank to fall from first, to second, to third in the rankings by the end of the period. The man who came close to this description was Fred H. McNeil, who, significantly, was not a banker by training, but seemed to have the independence of mind and the outsider's perspective to propose the changes that were needed.

McNeil's often-stated self-description as a "frustrated cowboy" takes on a new, unexpected light in this context. The archetype of the Hollywood cowboy is the loner whose "singular fighting qualities alone can save the town when called upon by its beleaguered community." The willingness of outsiders to save the town and then ride off does not quite fit McNeil, but it sure comes close.[166] If McNeil was a cowboy, he was one of the best educated and best prepared that ever existed. Yet overall, at least until the 1960s, there did not exist an overarching purpose, a grand strategy, that energized and electrified the ranks of the Bank of Montreal. At his best, Arnold Hart could deliver and at times link to a greater purpose. But the full extent of these elements would have to await a later generation. To be fair, as the competitive environment got more complicated, as the organization expanded, as it dealt with new conditions and new demographics, a new kind of banker was needed – one who not only knew banking but also was familiar with psychology and sociology in order to respond to the signals of change.

There is another element that emerges from considering the leadership of the period. Their relationship to the Bank's past and experience could be described as unwitting captives rather than purposefully curious students of that remarkable history. They were faithful to the traditions and the culture of the Bank without appearing to understand the patterns that made it strong or caused it to falter. That long-run experience could have acted as a guide to present challenges. In the case of the Bank of Montreal, the men of history featured in this chapter failed to learn from the experience of their own institution and from Canadian banking. In markets, as in ancient and contemporary wars, standout executives and commanders make a difference. They do so partly by understanding what worked in the past and what needs to change. It is why the most successful generals study past battles. Most of the nine leaders would have understood that connection since a majority of them held commissions in one of the world wars.

Changing the corporate and leadership culture from the top on down was perhaps the greatest challenge confronting the post-war Bank. The culture was, quite simply, allowed to rigidify. In strategic terms, the natural-born conservatism of Bank of Montreal banking was transformed from a virtue sensibly exercised to an obstacle preventing fresh thinking. In organizational terms, the Bank's managerial caste increasingly needed rejuvenation. In cultural terms, the Bank's conservatism, which one could claim was infused with a certain agility, ambition, and assertiveness, was largely stripped of its former dynamism. The reliance on, and adherence to, the old forms and behaviours was a prevalent theme in this era.

The position in which the Bank of Montreal found itself, and the mindset it had acquired over time, naturally influenced its strategy and conditioned its leadership. The challenge of maintaining the balance between dynamism and form is especially vital in Canadian banking. The reason is simple: the gravitational pull has typically been toward risk aversion and conservatism for reasons amply demonstrated in the long-run experience of Canadian chartered banks. This tension was, arguably, most acutely felt by the Bank of Montreal. Its history and importance and its quasi-governmental status as the guarantor of Canadian public finance was both a blessing and a burden. The blessing was that it allowed the Bank of Montreal's leaders and people to develop financial networks and relationships in the North Atlantic world that were *sans pareil*. Moreover, the blessings had a return: the Bank capitalized on the consequent irreproducible competitive advantages it acquired that were unique in the annals of Canadian banking.

Paradoxically, these privileges and advantages also came with a price, paid by the Bank's leadership and people: we can call it the burden of history. The cultural inheritance of the past was neither renewed nor pulled forward in a meaningful way in the fifteen to twenty years after the Second World War. Those lost years would cost the bank dearly. It would also compel the later generation of bankers to play catch-up to make up for lost ground. One senior leader of the Bank in the generation following was much more blunt about the legacy of the post-war period, saying that the Bank of Montreal was "the most powerful institution in Canada [in 1930s]. It lost its way after the war. You can trace the decline of the Bank of Montreal from 1945 right down into, and through, the Mulholland era. The bank had been dying and, again, it was outflanked by [institutions] like the Royal and the Commerce doing multiple acquisitions after the war, and bolting on bigger and bigger operations. And the bank lost its pre-eminent position because it was complacent, arrogant and full of hubris that we were the king of the castle, Bank of Montreal. It was the elite bank. Not the mass bank; it was the elite bank."[167]

The judgment is, perhaps, a bit harsh, and could come only from a Bank of Montreal leader whose main challenges were focused on transforming an entrenched historical culture and mindset of the institution. To his generation fell the challenge of injecting a sense of renewal and change without jeopardizing the values and legacy of the Bank. In other words, get rid of the parts that do not work, keep the parts that do, and add the parts you need for the future.

The power of this ambiguous legacy is all the more remarkable when you consider the overall quality of the Bank of Montreal's bankers in this era. The professional quality of the leadership in this era was second to none. Their instinct and skill in many areas of banking could be compared to the best in the business. Indeed, the Bank managed to do a number of interesting things in both domestic and international banking that would bear fruit in later years. Most importantly, this managerial class was eventually able, by the mid-1960s, to begin to understand, and act upon, increasingly serious challenges related to organization, structure, and culture confronting the Bank. By the 1960s, Bank of Montreal leaders began to act.

When they did act, the Bank's magnificent facade began to show signs of stress and eventually began to crumble. The relentless march of time and technological transformation led a growing number of executives to the inescapable conclusion that the Bank was reaching an inflection point. The Hart–McNeil administration had to act, and act decisively, to reverse course. As the facade fell, it revealed a bank whose self-image did not match its desired reality, and whose embrace of a deteriorating status quo delayed a marvellous institution from taking the steps it needed to secure the future. The generation of post-war Bank of Montreal leaders were great professional bankers with noteworthy records of achievement. But they were also products and champions of a system that served both them and the Bank well in the past. They were, in effect, deploying proven methods of conventional warfare in new battlefield situations.

For anything to change, institutions need to acknowledge the problem, analyze it, formulate a plan, and act. That process finally began at the Bank of Montreal in the mid-1960s, and gained momentum into the decade of the 1970s. The transformation of the Bank – its culture, structure, and organization – would become the singular priority in the years to come.

CHAPTER FIFTEEN

Remaking the Bank of Montreal in an Era of Transformation, 1965–1974

A snapshot of the Bank of Montreal in the first half of the 1960s would show a tale of two banks. One was the bank of professional managers with an internationally recognized competence in banking – the bank that had been the cornerstone of the Canadian banking system. The other was the bank that was falling behind in almost all areas of business and desperately required an overhaul.

By the mid-1960s, the Bank of Montreal's relative position within the Canadian banking marketplace was deteriorating. The Bank was falling behind its competitors on a wide range of measures: branch presence, market share, service offerings, and international exchange. Its personnel policies were also not keeping up, and employee retention became a major issue. Its most senior executives knew all this. By 1964–65, they were determined to act.

The organization had become, to a remarkable degree, a rule-bound, bureaucratic institution with unclear chains of command and a lack of communication between departments. These were inherent dangers in any large, mature organization such as the Bank of Montreal. In this instance, however, they threatened to overtake the organization's capacity for adapting and growing. Clearly, a large-scale intervention was required.

The subject of this and the next chapter is how the Bank responded to the challenges it faced and transformed itself over the course of the 1960s. This is the era in which the contemporary bank – the Bank some readers may start to recognize – comes into view. The turning point revolved around two axes: personnel and technology. This chapter focuses on the first element – personnel – and Bank management's attempt to modernize a workforce and talent pool for the challenges ahead.

Management under Arnold Hart's tenure commissioned McKinsey & Company to study the problems of vertical integration, marketing, branch efficiency and branch presence, and market share. McKinsey was, and remains, a management consulting firm of some repute that made a name for itself in providing strategic advice in several fields of specialization that included personnel management and labour relations.[1]

Under the leadership of McKinsey principal Donald K. "Obie" Clifford Jr, a Harvard MBA (1956),[2] the firm conducted extensive research and developed solutions to improve the Bank of Montreal's market position and efficiency. Two McKinsey studies will illustrate. In 1965, McKinsey developed a special program designed to train managers and meet the rising need for qualified bank personnel. In 1967, McKinsey delivered a program designed to maintain the profitability of the Montreal Branch (BMO's most profitable branch office) – and, by extension, other major branches in the system.

Acting partly on advice from McKinsey, the Bank of Montreal embarked on more wholesale reorganization efforts in the early 1970s, this time focusing on four critical areas: branch extension; personnel and personnel training; mechanization; and international banking. McKinsey was a key player in this reorganization after 1970 as well. Their initiatives included, for example, the reorganization of the marketing function. McKinsey investigated the role of the Bank's Marketing Department, both at head office and in divisional offices, and concluded that a marketing reorganization could usefully assist the Bank of Montreal in obtaining its long-term goals.

Already in 1965, the management had begun to recognize the value of overhauling marketing and other functions. One way it attempted to accomplish this was by importing talent from Ford Canada. Gardner Thomas "Gard" Robertson was one such import, recruited to transform the human resources function through PRIDE – performance, review, inventory, development, and education.[3] He was brought in as part of Fred McNeil's team to help transform the organization and culture of the Bank.

Winds of Change

By the mid-1960s, the most senior leadership became increasingly aware and concerned about the Bank's relative position in the Canadian and international marketplace compared to its competitors. The magnitude of the task was not lost on the Bank's president, G. Arnold Hart. When Hart became general manager in 1957, he began to question the way some things were done around the Bank, especially how people were deployed. For example, for decades, the Bank simply did not transfer personnel from province to province – everybody stayed in their own region. By the late 1950s, Hart perceived the need to move around to acquire a better perspective on "what's going on in the country and what their job is," as well as the training required for those positions.[4] Improving the quality of bank managers was the objective: moving them around into different positions across the country was an excellent – and novel – way to do that.

Hart's management team were primed for transformation. It included a young British Columbia banker named Stan Davison, who became the Bank's assistant general manager in the late 1950s. Some years later, in January 1966, the Bank hired Saskatoon-born F.H. "Fred" McNeil as general manager of personnel planning (later, organization and personnel). McNeil's background included service as a squadron leader in the Royal Canadian Air Force and a journalism career in post-war British Columbia. His management consulting career in the 1950s included various stops, most significantly, five years at Ford Motor Company of Canada. Ford was reputed to have understood and absorbed the key lessons of contemporary personnel management – something that would become of central importance to the reform of the Bank of Montreal in the 1960s. McNeil would be named a vice-president in 1967 and then executive vice-president and general manager in 1968.

Hart, Davison, McNeil, as well as President J. Leonard Walker were increasingly occupied with change. As one of the protagonists of that era later recalled, the Hart group was interested in changing things – something that was not easy to accomplish in those days "because the bank was so set in its ways ... because it had been the first bank in Canada and they were kind of living off that."[5] The challenges were made more complicated by the fact that, paradoxically, the Bank was expanding. That sent mixed signals about the urgency of change.

Doing Something about the Bank

By the mid-1960s, the piecemeal approach to reform was effective, but only to a point. One of Hart's key point men on the reorganization issue was J. Leonard Walker, who had been called back from Vancouver to become general manager (head office), and then eventually senior executive vice-president and general manager (1967) before ascending to the position of president of the Bank in 1968.[6]

As one executive of the day recalled, Walker and Hart frequently discussed the feeling that they had to "do something about the Bank."[7] There was a distinct sense that the Bank of Montreal was "not doing the things" it needed to do to continue to prosper.[8] The existing reporting relationships prevented a clear view of how people were getting on in their positions and how the Bank itself was faring.

The only flow of reliable information to senior decision-makers in Montreal was through the Bank's corps of inspectors, who wrote annual reports on how branch and regional management were doing. The inspectorate wielded tremendous power: up to the mid-1960s, the major determinant of a branch manager's career – promotion or demotion – rested on the recommendations of the inspectors at the end of the annual inspection.[9]

A single, static, annual picture of how specific managers were faring across the Bank's territory was increasingly unequal to the types of information flows required to make the right kinds of strategic decisions. In fact, one observer lamented that, in effect, nobody had a good handle on what mangers were doing, how good they were, and whether they were better deployed elsewhere. The inspector, for example, was in an individual branch for only two or three days. "How could he get a real feel for what these guys were doing?" one executive asked.[10]

The Little Bang

Until the mid-1960s at least, a large part of the problem was that Canadian banking as a whole had evolved into more of a comfortable club than a system where individual banks competed for business. By and large, the banks charged the same interest, serviced similar customers, and operated along similar lines. The Bank Act of 1967, however, liberalized loan provisions as well as introduced conventional mortgages as a major new possibility for the chartered banks (though the original liberalizations on mortgages were made in the 1954 revision of the Bank Act).[11] As one executive of the era recalled, "it was very comfortable up to that point. Then people started to get uncomfortable because it all changed. We weren't going to charge the same. We don't go to each other's cocktail parties any more, which we used to do. Oh, very clubby – awfully clubby!"[12] The noblesse oblige of the time also included a gentleman's agreement to not "steal" anybody else's customers "because the guy might give you crap at the next cocktail party!"[13] The noblesse also extended to executives moving between banks. If one was truly motivated to change employment, as one executive recalled, "you had to resign and then go and hope you got a job."[14]

By the mid-1960s, the Bank had become, in the words of one observer, "bound by tradition and paternalistic. You didn't join an organization: instead you became a member of the bank family."[15] This was a strength and a weakness. Bank of Montreal bankers were brilliant at the business of banking, including having first-class internal training systems to make bankers. That was the strength. The Bank would also take care of you in return for loyalty and longevity. The potential danger in this arrangement was an increasing immunity to new ideas and that might hinder the Bank from understanding and acting upon the evolving context of the market.

What was management training like on the eve of McKinsey? In 1964, a new managerial recruit would undertake a forty-eight-month training program in the Bank. This called for continuing to do your job while doing some prescribed reading and taking periodic tests. The "branch accountant" would then meet with you every three months to review your progress and evaluate the tests. The training was essentially a banking apprenticeship heavily focused on the technical aspects of branch banking matters.[16] While the internal systems for training were first class, management and administrative training left something to be desired. Outside training in this scenario was seriously lacking.[17]

What was missing, and posed a great challenge to include, were the support systems that encompassed financial information, financial control practice, service marketing, human resource management, and other functions.[18] As one executive later put it, "the management style had up to that point been more experience based, rather than reliant on the evolving principles of management science."[19] "In the 1960s," the senior banker recalled, "managers essentially supervised activities and executives made decisions – both based primarily on their experience and knowledge of 'how things worked in the past.' Few managers or executives had university education."[20] Technological change and a changing competitive environment would demand that executives be equipped with a broad set of analytical skills and advanced education as well as experience.[21]

Most of the major Canadian banks found themselves in this predicament in the 1960s. Their senior management tended to comprise a well-connected social and banking elite. In the case of the Bank of Montreal, the roll call of Canadian business was impressive. As one director later recalled, the board at least represented the "sons of the Montreal establishment" perhaps chosen more for social connection than business acumen.[22] "They were lovely people, but they weren't equipped to handle the terrific revolution, I can only call it that, in the business world that took place after the Second World War … where we moved heavily to professional management."[23]

The managerial culture at the Bank tended to be hierarchical and deferential to authority. "You served your time and then you moved up the ranks," one senior executive of the era recalled. Significantly, the metaphor that is frequently cited is the military one – "I guess the army's probably about the easiest example I could give," one contemporary-era official suggested. "You were not encouraged to speak out if you disagreed because obviously the boss knew best as you went on."[24]

A good example of the paternalism typical of the banking of the era was the power of managers over marriage plans. Subordinates in the bank had to ask for permission to be married since, among other things, it affected the bank's ability to deploy personnel in various places. One young branch manager in the late 1950s, for example, not only sought permission from his manager, but had to get his future father-in-law to "vouch for me."[25] That military-style system was ripe for change.

As we saw in Part Five, the legacy of the 1930s and 1940s, particularly the reorientation of the Bank away from its quasi-governmental functions and toward personal and commercial banking, involved a major transition. The post-war economic boom had made the transition that much less urgent, since growth was the order of the day and personal banking experienced a significant growth. Indeed, in 1946, the Bank reported 1.5 million accounts on its books. By 1954, that number had reached nearly 2.1 million, and by 1961 had touched the 3 million mark.[26] However, when the Canadian economic engine slowed down in the mid-1960s, BMO's disadvantaged position vis-à-vis its competitors became increasingly obvious.

The Bank was falling behind in almost all areas: domestic banking (branch presence, share of business, service offerings), international banking (share of foreign currency exchange, correspondent banks, international relations), personnel (training and retention), growth (in the increasingly competitive market), and organization (lack of communication, unclear chain of command, excessive bureaucracy).

Against this background of systemic problems, Hart and his management team called on McKinsey, which was given the mandate to figure out how the Bank of Montreal could return to a more competitive position. McKinsey's approach was an up-close examination of distinct areas of the Bank of Montreal's business, in hopes of drawing lessons that could be applied to the organization at large.

The Findings and Recommendations

The studies piloted by McKinsey looked into a number of aspects of the Bank, chief among them the domestic banking system and, specifically, the question of human capital and talent. One of the major findings of the McKinsey studies was that the system of reporting was particularly in need of major reform. One bank manager of the day recalled that McKinsey was "unable to find any organization charts that I'm aware of, and I don't think they found any, either ... So we just sort of reported, in a loose sort of way, up the system."[27] Managers were compelled to report on some matters to different departments, but there was little cohesion or system to the way things were done.

Another major McKinsey recommendation that the Bank almost immediately adopted was the reorganization of the head office functions into staff and line functions. Departments or divisions were created in the areas of personnel, marketing, credit, and administration, with line functions reporting to branch managers, district managers, regional vice-presidents, and a senior vice-president.[28] Prior to the change, the domestic banking function had become a "true fiefdom" of area superintendents with expertise in administration and credit in the "old school way" – and typically far removed from more contemporary notions of leadership and new management practices.[29]

The fundamental restructuring of the domestic banking system represented an epochal change in the organization of the bank – in effect, the first major one since the Great War. A new series of geographic divisions were established, each with thirty or thirty-five branches overseen by a district manager. Importantly, at the divisional level, a series of streams was established, divided into what made the most sense – credit expertise, marketing expertise, human resources, and administration.

In retrospect, the focus on the domestic organization was well placed. Up to the 1960s, as one seasoned executive later recalled, "the bank was the branches and the branches were the bank. There wasn't much else."[30] The head office function was powerful, but relatively small. The biggest credits would be handled by the head office, but in the mid-twentieth century, a branch banking system meant that the bulk of the organization and banking took place at the branches. Virtually everything was posted at the branch – so the key to transformation was the individual branch.

Organizational changes are not exactly the most exciting developments in the life of an institution, but these could be the exception – at least from the perspective of their dramatic effect. The changes described here enabled the Bank to "restock" its key executive and senior management posts with a host of more specialized personnel whose talent, training, leadership qualities, and temperament fit the demands of the day in business building, marketing, human resources, and administration.[31] That in itself also had a long-term effect on bringing the customer into greater focus. Where once credit was king – in terms of organizational preoccupation – now, customer satisfaction was emerging as a clearly articulated strategic objective. The organizational changes, for example, gave district managers a credit line for the first time – typically $50,000 – to look after the needs of small businesses and individuals in the region. That new freedom – a degree of decentralization of decision-making – proved to be key to the emergence of the contemporary customer-focus of the bank.

Another element that transformed the Bank of Montreal's approach to banking was the implementation of performance measures and evaluations. These are a ubiquitous part of corporate life in the twenty-first century, but in the late 1960s, they were virtually unknown. Until then, divisional executives would be charged with assessing managerial abilities, and those were typically not tied to customer satisfaction, but rather to credit line handling and the performance of their loan portfolio. One observer of the process described the role of the customer as secondary: if the customers weren't too happy, they at least were "lucky to have a bank to deal with!"[32]

The Special Development Program, 1965

The McKinsey studies underscored the conviction that the Bank's long-term success could only be guaranteed by the recruitment, training, and retention of strong personnel across all branches and divisions, but especially in management.[33] The Special Development Program, developed by McKinsey and the Bank of Montreal in 1965, was the response. The program was designed to strengthen recruitment, training, and development of personnel through a combination of new and improved training programs as well as competitive compensation packages that rewarded performance and innovation.

In preparation for the new development program, McKinsey had examined a variety of measures, including the Bank's personnel records and retention rates. The results were troubling, to say the least: "of male employees with less than one year's experience, more than 40% of the total employed resigned in 1965 ... This compares with a one out of four resignation ratio in 1965 for male personnel in the 1–2 year category and one out of three ratio in the 2–5 years group."[34] Turnover among male personnel with over five years of experience had more than doubled since 1960: "the actual number resigning in 1965 is up approximately two and a half times over 1960."[35] McKinsey's study revealed that the main reasons for this high turnover rate were inadequate salary scales, the desire to pursue further education, and, most troubling, the lack of clearly defined development plans within the Bank.

It was clear that these levels of resignation were a problem and would pose a threat to the Bank maintaining talent pools of necessary qualified personnel in years to come. They estimated that between 1 May 1966 and 31 December 1971, the Bank would need a minimum of 509 new branch managers.[36] At existing turnover rates, this would be nearly impossible to achieve.

Something had to be done, and that "something" was the Special Development Program (SDP). McKinsey and the Bank designed this program specifically to reduce high employee turnover and to address the Bank's urgent need

Table 15.1 | Stages of the Bank of Montreal Special Development Program

Phase	Stage	Duration
1	Concentrated experience in bank routine (basic training)	6 months
2	Responsibilities of accountancy	6 months
3	Preparation for appointment as accountant	12 months
4	Branch credit responsibilities	12 months
5	Head office and divisional orientation	1 month
6	Divisional assignment in one of the following specialty areas: • Credit • Administration • Marketing • Personnel • Securities • International banking • Foreign exchange	3 months
7	Divisional credit or selected main branch or large branch experience	8 months
8	Appointment as assistant branch manager	12 months

for qualified managerial personnel. More specifically, the program sought to develop well-qualified non-graduate bank personnel as well as university graduates to the position of branch manager within five years. The training program was designed to eliminate the desire on the part of employees to pursue education elsewhere by offering a clear development program internally. Also, the problem of salary scales would subsequently be adjusted to be competitive with other banks, businesses, and active recruiters in the Canadian marketplace.[37]

The SDP capitalized on the Bank of Montreal's existing training infrastructure and complemented the Standard Training Programme and the Accelerated Training Programme that were already in place.[38] In fact, the SDP relied on the Accelerated Training Programme to supply a number of high potential participants.[39]

In its final incarnation, the McKinsey's Special Development Program consisted of eight distinct phases, spanning a total of five years (see table 15.1):

The combination of the SDP with more competitive salary packages, purposeful training, and clear developmental direction was intended to both limit employee turnover and meet the Bank's urgent need for management personnel in the long term.

A New Generation Rises

McKinsey's various studies and reports – their tenor, their assumptions, and their recommendations – reflected the spirit of the age. As the Bank began to implement the recommendations in technology, organization, and especially personnel from the late 1960s onward, the leadership and people of the Bank of Montreal began a remarkable and durable transformation that would vary in speed and direction, but never quite come to rest.

Nowhere was this more felt that in the rush of a young, new generation of men and women entering the Bank in the late 1960s – the same generation that would go on to lead the Bank in the 1980s and 1990s. The Special Development Program's most dramatic effect was in the kind of people it brought into the Bank. For the first time, young people – men, but increasingly also women – with undergraduate degrees in commerce or the liberal arts, master of business administration degrees (at a time when they were rare and highly prized), and other academic qualifications were flowing into the precincts of the Bank. Combined with new opportunities, new technologies, and new organization, new positions were created across the company, and filled by a new breed of BMO banker. By the mid-1960s, the Bank was leading the pack in university recruiting. "I wouldn't say we were the first guys to go to campuses to recruit," one 1960s-era human resources executive suggested, "but we were the first guys to be really aggressive. People knew that the Bank of Montreal was on campus. They knew that we had a good program." The Bank's reputation as a prestige Canadian financial institution also helped in light of the developing job shortage in the country. The university recruitment program involved not only personnel people but also line managers. It offered important insight as to "what was out there in the way of talent" and was structured in a way that protected the newly hired university graduates from being treated as "nonentities" or "people to be criticized."[40] That was an important consideration, not least because what once took forty-eight months to reach – a managerial position – would take these new recruits a single year.[41]

The effect was almost immediate. In 1968, for example, a group of eight MBAs were hired by the Bank in Montreal, put into a "great big bullpen," as one of them later recalled, and assigned to a particular department of the Bank. Areas of specialization included corporate planning, systems analysis, "manpower planning," and international banking.[42]

This group flourished under the leadership of Hartland "Hart" Molson MacDougall. MacDougall was the scion of two prominent Montreal business families. His maternal grandfather was Molson, of brewery fame, and his paternal grandfather's uncle had founded the Montreal brokerage firm MacDougall,

MacDougall & MacTier Inc. His grandfather, Hartland Brydges MacDougall, briefly worked for the Bank of Montreal in the early twentieth century before rising to fame as a hockey player for the Montreal Victorias, later becoming a successful stockbroker. As the *Globe and Mail* put it in his obituary: "with a name like Hartland Molson MacDougall, it is perhaps apt he became one of Canada's premier bankers."[43]

Hart MacDougall followed in his grandfather's footsteps when he joined the Bank of Montreal as a teller in 1953, thereafter serving in various posts in the branch network, and then in progressively more responsible executive positions by the late 1960s. In 1970, he became executive vice-president resident in Toronto.[44] This new group fanned out across the head office organizations to document and "flow chart" the functions, identifying potential savings, where mechanization could assist, and how the information flows could be improved.[45]

The managers also cast their recruiting nets to Britain, where progress through the ranks in UK banks proceeded at a glacial pace. The Bank of Montreal could offer an accelerated trajectory for ambitious bankers in their late twenties and thirties.[46] The old apprentice system of banking was beginning to fade into history as a new spirit animated the managerial ranks at the Bank.

Dawn of the Woman Banker

The face of the Bank was beginning to change in other ways as well. In Canada, the participation of women in paid work nearly doubled from 21.6 per cent in 1950 to 39.8 per cent by 1970.[47] At the Bank of Montreal, by the 1940s, women outnumbered men in the total staff complement; by the early 1960s, this was the case by a significant margin (see table 15.2).

Women who were traditionally confined to teller positions and the occasional branch manager's position in the early 1960s were beginning to filter into the organization as a direct consequence of the new approaches of the era. Of course, there were exceptions, with some women being hired directly into the computer department as early as 1966.[48] One executive recalled that in the early 1970s, the Bank of Montreal was among the first ones to hire females for the [management] training program out of university and give them relatively senior positions at the time."[49] In certain areas of the Bank, such as the trading floors, the questions began – slowly – to shift from "who are you?" to "can you make us money?"[50] In one case in 1969, the Bank hired a female MBA from McGill University in what was quite possibly the first such case in the annals of the Bank of Montreal. If that star recruit could not yet symbolize the completed project of the Bank's reformers in the late 1960s, she certainly would have captured the hoped-for sign of things to come.

Table 15.2 | Men and women staff, Bank of Montreal, selected years 1920–61

Year	Men	Women	Total Staff	Number of Offices
1920	2,414	1,502	3,916	312
1940	3,623	2,003	5,626	511
1950	3,735	5,286	9,021	564
1956	4,255	7,159	11,414	694
1958	4,624	7,557	12,181	761
1961	5,181	8,334	13,515	882

Source: BMOA, "Career Opportunities at Canada's First Bank," 1962.

Taken together, these changes to the corporate culture of the Bank would constitute the single-most determining factor in the Bank's transition to the contemporary era.

Montreal Branch Case Study, 1967

McKinsey's mandate went beyond the Bank's human resources. It was extended to investigating the Bank's financial standing and future. As the Canadian economy contracted and the Bank of Montreal's deteriorating position vis-à-vis other banks became more visible, the managers wished to play on the Bank's strengths. To this end, McKinsey assessed the Montreal Branch. In 1967, the Montreal Branch was the largest and most profitable branch in the Bank's domestic banking system. However, after a few years of declining numbers, Bank of Montreal management was growing worried. McKinsey was tasked to evaluate exactly why the Montreal Branch had been so successful and how future success could be ensured. While the Montreal Branch was a special example, it was hoped that lessons learned there could be fruitfully applied to other branches as well.

The Montreal Branch was chosen because it was an important barometer of the overall health of the branch network. It generated over 4 per cent of domestic banking's total revenue and almost 10 per cent of its profit. In fact, it generated more profit at a higher rate of return than the next four central office branches combined. Almost a third of the Montreal Division's revenue, and close to half its profits, were derived from the Montreal Branch.[51]

The McKinsey report concluded that the Montreal Branch had achieved this prominent position for a couple of reasons. First, less than 1 per cent of the branch loan accounts (14 accounts) generated 48 per cent of its total Canadian dollar loans. Second, less than 2 per cent of the branch's deposit accounts (228 accounts) generated 75 per cent of its deposits.[52] The Montreal Branch was thus clearly advantaged by a few large loans and a few large accounts, each of which generated a lot of money at comparatively little servicing cost.

The position of the Montreal Branch, however, was not assured. The branch had acquired only two loan accounts of over $1 million since 1964. Moreover, its net deposit position had declined from 1962 to 1966. Its return on revenue declined from 52.2 per cent in 1966 to 39.2 per cent in the first six months of 1967.[53] Therefore, the challenges of the Montreal branch in some ways mirrored the broader renewal-focused issues surrounding the Bank in the 1960s.

McKinsey's Solutions

McKinsey determined that there were three factors that determined branch growth and success. These applied to Montreal Branch as much as any other branch in the Bank of Montreal network:

Meeting the needs of extremely large commercial loan and deposit accounts.

Centering branch decision-making around an integrated data-gathering, analysis, and control system that provides timely, accurate information.

Utilizing available manpower.[54]

The report found major opportunities for improvement at the Montreal Branch in account management, data gathering and analysis, and "manpower utilization."[55] The report further recommended organizational and structural changes at the Montreal Branch to ensure that the reforms could be implemented,[56] and urged implementation of these changes as soon as possible. It also recommended a trial period of at least two to three months at the Montreal Branch before applying any changes to other branches.

The Montreal case study got to the heart of the matter of challenges facing the branch system. In 1969, McKinsey's Donald Clifford reported that the Toronto-area operations were in similar need of reform and that "the time may well be right for a hard look at the Ontario operations and what has taken place there."[57] Clifford's team, which included Bob Manning and J.D. Fisher, identified four serious issues confronting the Toronto branch network. The Bank's head office provided no clear policy direction; its organization had too many layers of bureaucracy; unlike its competitors the Royal

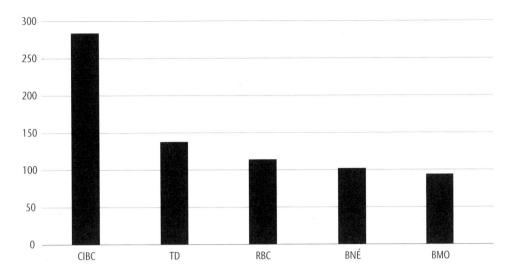

Figure 15.1 | Bank branches in Toronto area, 1969

Source: BMOA, Strategic Planning, "Memorandum from Donald K. Clifford Jr to J. Leonard Walker," 1 May 1969, 1.

and the Toronto-Dominion, the Bank of Montreal had no branch-level profit planning; and finally, the branches suffered from "very low morale."

The report went on to highlight some of the critical differences between the Bank of Montreal and its Canadian competitors, especially pointing out some of the programs that other major banks used to attract customers. The Bank offered no mutual funds or overdraft protection and was slow to get into the credit card game. From loans to savings to chequing, there were minor irritations that put the Bank in a suboptimal position.

By far the biggest problem, however, was the relative lack of branches. In the Toronto area, Fisher pointed out, BMO had fewer branches than any of its major competitors (see figure 15.1).

The report also highlighted the continuing structural challenges that the Bank faced. The system of regional offices and district managers (a system suggested by McKinsey in earlier studies) was "one factor in the time lag between changes of policy at Head Office and changes of policy at the Branch counter."[58]

Finally, employee training retention, as set out in the Special Development Program of 1965, was not hitting its mark at the branch level. The report team spoke with several university graduates who had worked at the Bank of Montreal for two or three years and "who [were] apparently still interested in pursuing banking careers. They have all left the B of M and are apparently very critical of the B of M organization and management."[59] In other words, the retention policy needed a second look. The reports from the branch front were not always encouraging; however, they provided a powerful, detailed, and actionable basis on which to move forward.

The Strategic Plan, 1970–74

In 1969, president Leonard Walker unveiled the Bank's four-year strategic plan for 1970–74. It sought to address four main issues: branch extension, personnel/training, mechanization, and international banking. This strategic plan would prove to be the blueprint for the transformation of the Bank of Montreal.

Branch Extension

Studies had shown that the Golden Horseshoe (the area around Toronto) would continue to grow at a much faster rate than other parts of Canada.[60] The Bank had a much lower proportion of branches in this area than its competitors. The strategic plan proposed to drastically increase the Bank's presence there. Of the 245 branches that the Bank planned to open nationwide between 1970 and 1974, half (122 branches) would be in the Golden Horseshoe. Because none of the 41 closures planned during the same period would be in this area, 60 per cent of the net increase of branch openings would be in the Golden Horseshoe.

Personnel and Personnel Training[61]

Like the problems the Bank faced in 1965, massive branch expansion would put tremendous strain on the Bank's resources of qualified management personnel. An accelerated training program was required. The focus would be on technical aids and the development of "people management" personnel training would be emphasized across all departments. The Personnel Department was tasked with ensuring that human resources were adequate to meet the goals of the 1970–74 timeline. In addition to new and improved training programs, the Bank would step up recruitment.

Mechanization[62]

To increase efficiency, reduce operating costs, and improve management information, the Bank embarked on a broad and ambitious plan of mechanizing its operations. Mechanization would also provide computer services to customers. Trained personnel were required to work with new computers and technologies, so plans were also made to meet the demand for technical personnel.[63]

Accelerated Development of International Banking[64]

International expansion had been the Bank's largest growth area for much of the post-war period. By the 1960s, however, the Bank was losing momentum in this critical area. The challenges of domestic banking had overshadowed paying greater attention to international banking opportunities. Therefore, the plan for 1970–74 was to concentrate on strengthening correspondent relationships by adding personnel servicing specific areas of the world and by ensuring that service to correspondents and foreign customers, in general, was of the highest standard. The Bank's relationship with 260 correspondent banks would likewise be restructured for speed, efficiency, and cost reduction.[65] Here, too, special recruitment and personnel development plans had to be established for international operations to be successful.

Marketing

Marketing was not an official part of the strategic planning document, but it was given considerable attention all the same. McKinsey's report on the reorganization of the Marketing Department investigated its role both at head office and in divisional offices. The conclusion, perhaps not surprisingly, was that marketing would be an important strategic element of the future of the Bank in three ways. First, marketing professionals could identify and analyze priority markets for branch development, high-potential customers and prospect groups, new service opportunities, and the effectiveness of current programs.

Second, marketing professionals could be instrumental in proposing a line of profitable competitive services, effective advertising and promotion programs, locations and types of branches, and programs for preparing Bank personnel to capitalize on the potential service areas.

Finally, marketing professionals could provide leadership in implementing, with the line banking and other staff functions, approved recommendations in three areas requiring the Marketing Department's direction: service area development, advertising and promotion, and introduction of new services.

Through these three services, the Marketing Department could assist in the Bank's transformation across the board – in analyzing the size of and trends in banking markets, developing guidelines, measuring effectiveness, recommending new services, building a customer database, and ensuring that regional differences were accounted for in the market.[66]

The Mark of Change

In 1967, the Bank unveiled a new logo: the M-Bar. The logo was the brainchild of Hans Kleefeld of Stewart & Morrison Ltd of Toronto, though it may have been more than a passing coincidence that Fred McNeil's ranch in Granum, Alberta, was called the "M-Bar Ranch."[67] The logo was accompanied by a new official colour: First Bank Blue. In time, the new symbol became one of the most enduring emblems in Canadian enterprise.

The M-Bar very much symbolized the coming transformation in the Bank of Montreal. The logo embodied the modernity that the Bank's leadership clearly envisioned as its future. It captured that balance between form and dynamism: solid, confident, yet fluid in movement. It emerged at a time of impatience with the status quo, virtually at the beginning of a generational change within the Bank. The aspirations of the generation of the 1960s followed on that impatience with the way things were, looking to renewal, vitality, and rededication to excellence. The M-Bar would represent those hoped-for defining qualities. In the years to come, as a sign and as a brand, the new logo would come to signify the remaking of the Bank of Montreal as its leaders and people adapted to the powerful forces of change.

The leadership of the 1960s responded to an increasingly complex operating environment by mobilizing personnel and resources to identify, understand, and analyze the scale of the challenges before them. At the beginning, Bank of Montreal bankers shrewdly brought in people and firms from the outside to provide independent advice. Managers also hired change agents such as Fred McNeil and others to establish a beachhead for the coming cultural transformation of the Bank. That transformation sought not only modernization but also, perhaps more importantly, a new equilibrium between dynamism and form. The post-war period, and arguably the period before then, had tilted the Bank toward form – and the structures that endured. By the 1960s, the Bank was in marked need of an injection of dynamism and renewal. The bureaucratic forms that had served a previous generation and time had become rigid and less able to meet the evolving needs of customers and of strategic vision. Organizational structures that had once facilitated long-distance flows and decision-making were now slowing the Bank's machinery and, most importantly, its ability to adapt to change.

In some ways, the complexity of renewal for some institutions like banks can be compared to a matryoshka doll – it's never one challenge or issue but many, enfolding and being enfolded by others. In any large, mature organization, responding to what needs changing and what needs preserving is a constant challenge. Organizational behaviour, bureaucratic practice, incentive structure, and divergent interests and objectives can help or hinder how well an organization can respond to changes within its environment. In banking, the challenge is even greater. In the Canadian banking system, the challenge to achieve that balance between dynamism and form is made more acute because of banking's role as guardian and guarantor of the financial system of a peripheral North Atlantic economy. As mentioned earlier, the Bank of Montreal's specific institutional inheritance also played its part: organizational structure and values cemented in place from an era when it functioned as a quasi-governmental institution and avatar of Canadian finance abroad. The mentalities, mindsets, and modes of getting things done left a vibrant legacy of high reputation, prestige, and professionalism. Yet, over time, the duty of each generation is to push and pull the institution they serve into dynamic renewal. In this situation, the challenges and the stakes involved in overhauling the culture, mindset, and organization of the Bank should not be underestimated.

With the help of McKinsey, substantial and far-reaching changes in the acquisition of human capital within the ranks of the Bank began to create a sustained momentum to redress that balance. A university-trained managerial class emerged – one that would be able to implement the kind of technological and organizational transformation strategies that executives wanted, customers expected, and the times demanded. By the mid-1970s, the task of transformation was well underway, but in some ways, had only just begun.

CHAPTER SIXTEEN

The [Digital] Conversion of St James [Street]

This chapter is about the Bank of Montreal's response in dealing with technological innovation in the post-war period. By the late 1950s, technological change – especially in banking systems – offered a way for North American financial institutions to overhaul their creaky, antiquated, and often increasingly problematic systems. Automation, mechanization, and computerization also offered potential opportunities to translate technological innovation into a greater customer focus.

Technological transformation and banking in contemporary times exist in very close relationship. Since the dawn of the digital age in the 1960s, technological change has slowly but inexorably moved to occupy centre stage in the managerial mind at the Bank of Montreal. The capital outlays on technology alone would make it a key topic of discussion in senior executive councils, but eye-watering dollar figures are only part of the story: the long-term effects on corporate objectives are of equal, if not greater, importance.

In the twenty-first century, banks and financial institutions that are too slow to implement technological innovation and adapt to evolving customer demands for instantaneity and simplicity will find themselves losing market share. One recent account of Canadian banks and their relationship with technology argued that not only were Canadian banks laggards in the field but also breathlessly announced that "without a super-fast, information-rich payments system, Canada's productivity will sag under the burden of inefficient, paper-based invoices and payments."[1] In this world view, not only are markets endangered but also national competitiveness. There is a chorus of observers, casual and otherwise, who echo the refrain that if institutions don't embrace technology, they will wither and die. The subject is also popular grist for the mill. "On any given day," one US bank auditor quipped, "you can pick up any periodical and the chances are 10 to 1 that somewhere there will be an article dealing with the subject of electronics or information. This flood of information has resulted in the subject's becoming the most popular since sex was invented."[2]

Each era has had its share of prophets of the digital age – in the 1960s, in the 1980s, the early 2000s, and in the 2020s. Often, however, the wrong ultimatum – along the lines of "embrace technology or die" – is being laid down. Most institutions understand all too well the need to modernize technology. The challenge is to answer how technological change can be deployed, how it is shaped by an organization's strategy and structure, and how technologies will in turn influence strategy and transform structure.

This chapter examines how Bank of Montreal management grappled with the demands of technological change, what push and pull factors were in play, how technology connected to strategy and performance, and to what extent management succeeded in balancing competing interests between organizations, groups, lines of business, and regions.

Management Styles and the Digital Transformation

Looking at the long-run experience of the bank into the 1990s, if we ask three fundamental questions about technology and banking at BMO, we will begin to understand the extent to which technology has transformed what economist Andrew Tylcote called "styles of management." His three areas of attention focus on whether technological change has altered the way things are made or the way things are done; the way organizations are structured and evolve over time; and, finally, how people optimized work and generated profits as a result of these changes.[3]

The Bank of Montreal's experience with technological transformation did not fundamentally alter the way that the Bank operated – at first. The early innovations did, however, herald a long-term fundamental change in what the Bank could deliver in terms of products and services, how they were delivered, and the evolutionary path of Canadian banking.[4] Innovations in Information and Communication Technology (ICT) that began in the 1960s transformed the way Bank of Montreal conducted business and operations. However, think of it as a long wave that saw Bank executives adopt and incorporate technology when it made sense and the cost was justified. Sometimes they were among the first to do so in the industry; other times, different priorities took precedence in the managerial mind of Montreal bankers.

There is no doubt that technological transformation has become a major challenge and a central preoccupation of contemporary senior management. It is also incontrovertible that Canadian banks have been hard-wired for stability, and that aggressive innovation in forms and styles is a process not usually associated with Canadian financial institutions. As a premier Canadian financial institution, the Bank of Montreal also had other institutional imperatives. Decision-makers had to consider its multi-faceted role: in maintaining system stability; in preserving the integrity of its vast information network of millions of individual and business accounts; and in maintaining the confidence and trust established by its fame and its reputation since the beginning of the Canadian financial system. That meant getting technological transformation "right" was critical for trust-driven institutions, especially those that handled people's money.

Yet, the actual long-run experience of the Canadian banks can be instructive and can offer a more nuanced perspective. Indeed, the rhetoric about the Information Age has been with us for more than a generation. The US bank auditor made his remarks about Canada's productivity in 1955 – but they could have easily (with some style differences and perhaps an emoji or two) been printed in 2020. As Joseph Schumpeter instructed in 1939, before we draw any inference at all from the behaviour of time series, "it is always of the utmost importance for us to be thoroughly masters of the economic history of the time, the country or the industry, sometimes even of the individual firm in question."[5]

The Bank of Montreal: A Different Story to Tell

As in other areas, the Bank of Montreal has a different story to tell: its experience with technological transformation after 1960 was extraordinary, albeit uneven. It did not quite fit the stereotypical conservative, risk-averse mould of banking. Indeed, BMO's approach to technological transformation was in some ways more complex than the straightforward accounts of technological change in other banks.

One of the key features of BMO's adoption of information and communication technology was that it followed an incremental adoption curve. As James Cortada notes about the financial, telecommunications, media, and entertainment industries, it was only over time that the "accumulated uses and transformations" occasioned by millions of individual adoptions together constituted a massive transformation.[6] That transformation did not, however, come in the form of a revolution. The story of the Bank of Montreal's early adoption of ICT provides us with an insight into how Bank managers perceived technological change, and how that change occurred over time. In time, not only did managers shape technological adoption in the Bank but also technology began to change the managerial approach to banking.

The North Atlantic Banking Experience

James Cortada reminds us in *The Digital Hand* that there are few industries where ICT made a more dramatic impact than in banking. "At the start of the second half of the twentieth century, not a single bank used a computer; by the end of the century, what banks did, what services and products they provided, and how they competed and worked were deeply influenced by computing."[7] When it came to technological innovation, banks outspent manufacturing and retail companies by 200 per cent in the 1960s and 1970s. By the 1970s and 1980s, banks were utilizing technological advances in processing power and information processing to empower a more customer-driven or customer-centric approach to banking. The advent of automated teller machines (ATMs), online banking, 24/7 banking, and the widening spectrum of services on offer to BMO customers anywhere in the world could scarcely have been imagined immediately after the Second World War. The development of credit and debit cards, and their pervasiveness, has led to a cashless economy in the twenty-first century. In many ways, the insight may be true that contemporary bankers are not so much in the business of handling money as managing information about money.[8]

A Massive Information and Intelligence Network

The vast, transformative potential of ICT in banking was predicated on the fact that the banker's central task was information and control processing. For the Bank of Montreal, for example, the task of gathering, storing, transmitting, analyzing, and acting on information was a central concern since its establishment in 1817. The nature of the information also crossed the spectrum. The processing of day-to-day information on accounts, deposits, interests, loans, audits, inspections, and the like filled rooms with ledger books and account information. The control processing challenge of coordinating a large transcontinental branch network demanded not only small armies of clerks and personnel but also the evolution of an elaborate set of circulars, rules, regulations, and codes of conduct and behaviour that fundamentally shaped the character of banking in the nineteenth and twentieth centuries. Technological transformation touched virtually every category, including financial data, market information, intelligence gleaned from networks of financial intelligence in key markets of the North Atlantic world, information on creditworthiness of individuals, the health of individual industries and regional economics, information on regulation and public policy, competitors, and market conditions.

The processing power of computers in those key categories of collection, sorting, management, and display of information would have a powerful long-term effect on banking.[9] At first, the effects were in dramatically increasing information processing capacity – in other words, to do what banks did, but in a fraction of the time and at a fraction of the cost. Later, an expanded array of services and innovations and lower operating costs emerged as another powerful set of benefits. An expanded range of customer services and convenience in the 1970s and 1980s changed the banking value proposition, often in unforeseen ways. The power of computing, when combined with the power of deregulation of the financial sector, made it possible for banks to operate in insurance and brokerage, and vice versa.[10] Technological change was one of a number of major forces of change that pulsed through the financial services sector in the North Atlantic world.

The story of the technological transformation of banking, and in this case, Bank of Montreal banking, is therefore a complex one. It is complex because ICT has ushered in long-term transformations in a number of areas: information processing, expansion of financial products, customer experience, scale and scope of banking activity, and of course in the changing nature of employment and the evolution of human resources. Indeed, information and telecommunications technologies "did more to change the nature of work and who did it than possibly any other technologies had in the history of the nation."[11]

The Bank of Montreal's first forays into technological transformations followed a classic pattern. Managers in the 1960s looked to technology to improve the way they handled banking operations. Improvements in productivity and lower operating costs, or even the avoidance of future expenses, were classic objectives of Bank of Montreal bankers through the decades. They started, sensibly, with what is frequently referred to as the bank office – not least because that's where the lion's share of the work took place. The circulatory system of money and financial instruments was a labour- and information- intensive enterprise within a bank, let alone between banks. The simple matter of keeping bank balances accurate also constituted a significant and ongoing task over time.

Cheques and Balances

"No single activity of banking generated more discussion over more decades than check handling," James Cortada noted in his overview of technology in financial institutions. "No single function stimulated more speculation and wishful thinking about the 'checkless society' or e-money."[12] Indeed, this is how the Bank of Montreal entered the technological innovation game in the late 1950s. A day in the life of a cheque, for example, would involve writing, sending, cashing, recording, sorting, and sending back through the banking system to the original bank that issued the cheque.

By the 1950s, the US banking industry was on the brink of a control processing crisis. The use of cheques had doubled between 1943 and 1952, with the industry predicting they would be processing a billion cheques per year by 1955.[13] The RAND Corporation concluded in the 1960s that, with the exception of the US government, "the commercial banking system is the largest processor of paper" with 15 billion cheques handled "in addition to its other financial transactions."[14] The cheque and chequing accounts were convenient, but generated massive challenges for information processing. Bankers in the United States attempted to divert payments into other instruments, but were never completely successful in killing the paper cheque.[15]

Bank of America (BOA) in the United States was a pioneer in responding to the challenge of information processing by examining the problem as early as 1950. By the mid-1950s, it sought the consensus of the US banking industry to pilot the Magnetic Ink Character Recognition MICR sorting solution, which it obtained in 1957.[16] The BOA's industry-leading Electronic Recording Machine–Accounting (ERMA) followed, and went live in 1960–61. With the assistance of General Electric, thirty-two computers would service 2.3 million checking accounts across 238 branch offices.[17] That was only the beginning, with millions of savings accounts being integrated into the system. It came, of course, at a cost of multiple millions of dollars, but the computer had arrived in the world of US banking, with cheque processing as the principal and most important digital application. Other applications relating to deposits, loans, and mortgages followed.

Banks in Canada faced the same problem. The remarkable growth in new accounts in the post-war period – at the Bank of Montreal, accounts swelled from 1.5 million in 1946 to 3 million in 1961 – constituted a powerful push factor to look at new forms of automation.[18] New accounts and new services would put an increasing strain on the legacy systems. If the Bank was to grow without collapsing from the weight of accounting and bookkeeping, new ways would have to be found. The systems would also have to respond to the principal risks inherent in banking –interest rate fluctuation, credit, and liquidity. Only later would the idea of offering new services to customers take root, beginning with faster cheque posting, inter-branch banking, credit cards, and bank machines.

The Bank of Montreal's adoption of technology to transform its systems from the 1960s onwards was said to be ahead of its main competitors among the Canadian chartered banks. Compared with other sectors, however, the managerial caste at the Bank could afford to take its time to implement new information and communications technologies. The reason was simple: the old technologies – the pre-IT suite of calculators, adding machines, tabulators, and the like – worked well enough.[19] Some observers have noted that the "prior commitment to and use of existing technologies served as both a braking mechanism and confidence builder while their managers looked at the potential of the computer."[20] There was one very powerful incentive for Canadian banks to remain with the status quo: the post-war period was one of growth and prosperity. Compared to the hard scrabble of the 1930s and the sacrifice of wartime banking in the 1940s, post-war Canada must have seemed like the promised land.

In the case of the Bank of Montreal in the 1960s and 1970s, that was not quite the case. The management had plunged into the renewal of systems with enthusiasm, though not without a little trepidation (It's costing how much? Will it work?). As we saw in the last chapter, the incentives for the Bank of Montreal to take the risk of changing operations had more to do with internal strategic developments than exogenous factors. In the 1970s, however, the equation changed. Inflationary pressures, rising wages, an oil crisis, and skyrocketing interest rates drove bankers to improve marketing and operational efficiencies.[21]

Overview: Going Digital

Let's begin with an overview of the Bank's technology story in the post-war period to the mid-1980s.

The post-war years, as we have seen, had been prosperous ones for Canada and the North Atlantic world. From 1945 to 1973, industrialized nations across the world went through a period of prolonged economic prosperity; industrial production was up, and many countries, including Canada, experienced a great baby boom. Years of austerity in Canada were left behind: pent-up consumer demand was unleashed upon the economy. Between 1946 and 1956, the average annual income of manufacturing workers in Canada more than doubled, and spending rose accordingly.[22]

Banking in Canada became more universal, accessible, and popular. Substantial increases in consumer spending meant that banks had to process many more transactions. *Staff*, the Bank of Montreal staff magazine, noted in 1962 that the main problem facing the bank was that "Canadians like to write lots of cheques. In fact, they write more per capita than any other people in the world."[23] Moreover, the magazine added, between 1952 and 1962, the number of cheques that the bank had to clear more than doubled. Technological innovation was hailed as the way for banks to deal with this increased volume. As described earlier, the proliferation of cheques, especially in the US banking system, had become a serious headache for the major banks.

The first technological innovations at the Bank of Montreal came as the solution to a specific problem. Data processing was a way to deal with the increased volume of banking transactions, and especially cheque clearing. In the late 1950s, for example, the Bank installed electronic punch card machines as well as semi-automatic bookkeeping machines to help post transactions more quickly and more accurately. It was the technological watershed for the Bank of Montreal, and Canadian banking in general.

After the installation of "back of house" computer technology to streamline and accelerate transaction processing, the Bank embarked on a much more ambitious program: to transform its methods of accounting and banking from fully manual to almost entirely electronic. The first step took place with the establishment of the Montreal GENIE centre in June 1963. GENIE was "the first Canadian application of a fully integrated data processing operation, proving deposits, sorting and clearing cheques to their destinations and posting all current and personal checking accounts entries on magnetic tape."[24]

GENIE would prove to be the most significant innovation in the Bank of Montreal's immediate post-war history. It provided an important technological foundation, with the implementation of electronic data processing setting the course for further technological innovation and mechanization. Indeed, today's Bank of Montreal would not exist without GENIE. Its technologies, while frequently updated with the latest hardware, would form the backbone of further mechanization plans for the bank for a generation to come.

With individual branches now outfitted with electronic data processing capabilities, the logical next step would be to connect the individual branches to one another, creating a truly national banking network. In the late-1960s, the Bank began a feasibility study to this end. In the 1969 Annual Report, the Bank unveiled a five-year plan to bring all branches "on-line."[25] The Bank Mechanization project, or MECH as it became known, would finally roll out in the mid-1970s. As we have seen, MECH made possible major new services, including Master Charge in 1973, Multi-Branch Banking (MBB) in 1979, PINs in 1984, and CIRRUS in 1985.

The Bank's motivations for technology adoption were not atypical of the wider North American banking industry. President Fred H. McNeil, speaking in 1973, recalled that "when the Bank embarked on its mechanization program, some major assumptions were made. These were, first, that the volume of paper handled, of accounting entries, and of calculations, would grow enormously; second, that the cost of doing these things manually, or semi-manually, would accelerate rapidly, while the cost of doing them by computer would decline."[26]

The massive investment in mechanization was not without risk. "It was not an easy decision at that time," McNeil added, "to undertake a program that would not begin to pay off for more than five years from its inception, and that would, in the interim, require the assembling and commitment of a large group of highly skilled people, to say nothing of the very substantial sums of money."[27] Nevertheless, as McNeil aptly described, there was a post-war optimism and faith in technology that penetrated even the highest echelons of Canadian banking. The Bank of Montreal, along with other Canadian banks, set out on a race for competitive advantage. The result, in the span of about two decades, was that Canadian banking moved from being conducted largely manually to largely electronically.

Post-Tronic Machines

Mechanization and electronic data processing at the Bank of Montreal began in earnest in March 1958 when four Post-Tronic posting machines were installed at the head office in Montreal. This put the Bank in the lead in the field of semi-electronic bookkeeping.[28] As the Annual Report of 1958 noted, the machines represented "a major advance in modern, high-speed posting procedure, clearing cheques and posting current accounts speedily and accurately."[29]

Automation provided the bank with advantages of speed and efficiency over its competitors: "The machines complete posting and checking operations of current accounts in less than half the time needed under former methods."[30] The machines posted ledger and statement simultaneously by using an identifying account number inscribed on all cheques and deposits, permitting verification. This greatly reduced human error associated with non-electronic machines. "All the operator has to do," one report suggested, "is to press the appropriate keys to designate the number of the account involved, and the amount of cheques or deposits to be recorded." The machines automatically completed the new calculation and recording.[31]

The Post-Tronic Machines "read" cheques and deposit slips by means of Magnetic Ink Character Recognition (MICR) numerals, printed in ink containing iron oxide particles. The numerals could therefore be magnetized as they entered the sorting equipment, and then acted as signal switches for rapid reading. The preparations to deploy this technology involved converting thousands of chequing accounts to the new system, which in its turn involved "many thousands of small individual printing runs to conform to common standards established by the Canadian Bankers' Association."[32] By October 1958, the Bank of Montreal had installed similar machines in Toronto, adding four more in Calgary in early 1959.[33]

The technological leap forward in the late 1950s was accompanied by a new Montreal head office building, which opened in 1960. As the Annual Report of that year noted: "Modern 'wonders' in advanced technology have been utilized in the new air-conditioned building to speed business for both visitors and staff, and to make conditions more comfortable and pleasant for everyone working in or entering the Head Office. From the high-speed automatic elevators that whisk workers to their jobs and visitors to their destinations in second, to the latest developments in telecommunications that speed more than a thousand messages daily through the Telegraph Department, the new Head Office is designed to provide greater efficiency in all departments."[34] Modern buildings were only the beginning of the transformation as some minds turned to ideas of a more ambitious technological transformation of the Bank's systems and structures.

GENIE

Five years after the introduction of the Post-Tronic machines, the Bank of Montreal introduced what was arguably its biggest technological investment: GENIE, which stood for *Gen*erates *I*nformation *E*lectronically. It gave the Bank of Montreal Canada's first fully integrated, automated banking system. Claiming another "first" crown was a point of pride for Bank of Montreal bankers. The system, comprised of state-of-the-art IBM computers and sorter readers, "deposits, sorts and clears cheques to their destination and posts all current and personal chequing account entries on magnetic tape" with incredible speed and efficiency.[35]

As with the Post-Tronic machines, GENIE was targeted to increase worker efficiency and accuracy, reduce costs, and lighten the workload so employees could be redeployed to other tasks – among them, serving customers. Up until that point, "the bulk of clerical effort involved in providing banking services" was devoted to "keeping accurate records of the myriad transactions taking place each day: calculating interest in charges for services, and prepare reports and providing information to managements and to customers."[36] As President R.D. Mulholland put it in 1963, "as automated banking spreads across the country, it will free branch staff from much routine and provide them with more interesting and rewarding work. The Bank has given the undertaking that no jobs will be lost through automation; customers will profit by more efficient and personalized service."[37]

The hopes for GENIE and for the technological future the system heralded were focused on the liberation of labour and on productivity. As the *Toronto Stock Exchange Review* put it in late 1963: "The Bank of Montreal is confident that the "genie," the genial, wonder-working giant, will help to lighten the burden of paperwork that was threatening to engulf it." Automated banking would, in time, result in faster and more efficient service, it was hoped. The Bank also announced that it was "planning a broad range of other applications for its versatile computers over the next few years" in areas such as "installment personal records, the bank payroll, travelers cheques, money orders, settlements and drafts."[38]

The labour-saving component of GENIE was, by any measure, a remarkable improvement. Compared to manual labour, GENIE's speed was nothing short of astounding: it could post 3,000 banking transactions a minute and read 800 punch cards. Its reels could store 1.5 million bank accounts, and its printers could print up to 1,200 full lines of figures every minute. In addition, GENIE's IBM 1419 Magnetic Character Reader was capable of sorting more than 1,600 cheques a minute.[39]

GENIE was launched on a staggered rollout, an approach that the Bank of Montreal would use in the future to introduce most of its new technological services. In early 1963, eighty-five branches in the Montreal Clearing House area were outfitted with GENIE computers, followed in quick succession by another thirty in the greater Montreal area.[40] "Within the next few months," the Annual Report noted, "'GENIE' will introduce its electronic wizardry to branches in the Toronto area, and similar installations will follow at other major Canadian centres in quick succession."[41] R.D. Mulholland summed up the Bank's progress for 1963 as follows: "Last year, I mentioned that we had opened our first 'GENIE Centre' or computer facility, in Montreal, for the handling of centralized clearing operations and demand deposit accounting. In recent months, we have opened similar centres in Toronto and Vancouver and now have a total of 5 computers in operation in the 3 locations. Conversion of branches to the new system has been effected in Montreal and has been nearly completed in Toronto and the system is now being extended to include branches in the surrounding areas. Some 60 branches in and around Vancouver will be brought into the system during the coming months."[42]

The rollout of GENIE provided customers with faster and more efficient service and, hoped Mulholland, would enable "the bank to keep abreast of demands for service into the foreseeable future."[43] The transition from a manual to an electronic system of accounting did present some oddities and stop-gap measures. Within a few weeks of coming online, the GENIE centre in Montreal was working around the clock. However, lacking a method of transmitting the necessary information between branches, checks, deposit slips, statements, and other documents had to be travel between branches by automobile.

The Bank updated its GENIE computer system within two years of the first rollout. Initially, GENIE ran on an IBM 1402 system, but by 1965, a switch to the more sophisticated IBM 69 was underway. By the mid-1960s, momentum clearly favoured technological expansion. The Bank's technology investments were continually in next-generation computers with greater processing power. Moreover, the aim of the technology was not merely to solve old problems but also to enable new applications and services that could be facilitated through the power of the computer.[44]

A year later, in 1966, the Annual Report provided an update on the state of mechanization, underlining the fact that the Bank of Montreal was the first bank in the country to place "such advanced equipment in daily use." Continuous technology rollouts of new or next-generation computers were occurring across the country's major urban centres. "Development work has been carried forward on several new computer applications which are expected to be phased into operations during the coming year," Mulholland reported in 1966. "The Account Reconciliation Plan, which speeds cheque reconciliation procedures; provides improved accuracy and reduces costs for customers, has been well received. Other computer services are under development."[45]

This first encounter with major technological change convinced a younger managerial cadre that technological transformation would be an important part of the Bank's competitive future. The Final Management Report on Bank Mechanization captured this aptly: "We can be first! We will be first! And we can make a lot of money and have a more pleasant environment while we do it. But we must now add another dimension to our effort, and gain the violent, enthusiastic and dedicated support of all persons in the bank. Under these conditions magnificent success could be anticipated; without it, a mediocre advance, and in different economics for all that we should expect."[46]

However, the implementation of the new technologies was not without its shadow side. The fear of technology-induced unemployment, or "machines taking over our jobs," was paramount. During the introduction of GENIE, the concerns were addressed head-on:

> One important question which is going to arise in a lot of people's minds at this stage is, "What about my job with all these changes?" The answer is a simple one and quite straightforward. The bank has given a definite undertaking that no member of the staff will ever lose his or her job as a result of automation, and, fast as they are, the machines will still need trained operators to run them. Some relocation will be necessary ... after adequate training, some staff members may find themselves performing work rather different from that they are doing now, but no one will be out of a job. As a matter of fact, the automation program will go a long way to making a lot of jobs more interesting for, by and large, the machines will relieve people of much monotonous routine, freeing them for more interesting, more rewarding work, performing the essential

"brain-power" functions that machines can never take over. Altogether, it's an exciting and stimulating prospect ... and undertaking which will benefit all of us, as well as all our customers.[47]

Bank of Montreal management neatly parried this concern with a pledge that no jobs would be lost due to automation. The early technologies at least, GENIE and its counterparts, would be retailed as technologies of liberation. The guarantee of no job loss proved to be both credible and easily accomplished.[48] But there was something more at stake – the implicit social covenant between banking staff and the Bank that favoured long-term commitment to the Bank in exchange for employment stability. The nature of the work might change, the Bank's communications subtly suggested. "The B of M automation programme will replace routine with more rewarding work and create a lot of interesting jobs. (And as you already know, the Bank has given an undertaking that no member of the staff will ever lose his or her job on account of automation)," the *Staff* magazine noted in 1963.[49]

Beyond these assurances, the Bank went to some length to make the technology seem friendly, approachable, and, above all, controllable. One of the main ways of doing this was by giving the staff a sense of control over the new technology.[50] This was partly achieved through a naming contest that gave people a symbolic sense of agency.[51] Staff members submitted 1,849 entries.[52] The winning GENIE name came from Dick Filliter, manager of the Yarmouth, Nova Scotia, branch.[53]

Traditional banking had been the repository of millions of accounts or, if you will, millions of pieces of the most sensitive kind of private data: financial. Therefore, privacy and security concerns were bound to surface. A pre-launch inspection in May 1963 noted that "the prime concern is that no one person should have sufficient control to originate a document and process the data contained therein through the system, or to introduce unauthorized data through the console of the computer."[54] As a solution, a strict separation was maintained between the computer room (data processing) and the branches where the documents originate. Access to the computer room was limited to authorized personnel. Strict sign-in procedures became a normal feature. Data security has been a concern for better than half a century.

MECH: Bringing the Bank of Montreal Online

GENIE's automated banking system was just the start. In the late-1960s, the Bank embarked on what was arguably its biggest post-war endeavour. Once branches were fully automated, the logical next step was to connect the individual computer systems to create a truly transcontinental, integrated, online banking network. The Bank set out to do this through the Bank Mechaniza-tion Project, better known as MECH. Based on employment trends, records, and assumptions in the late 1960s, it was predicted that, once fully imple-mented, MECH could save the Bank $18 million to $20 million per year.[55]

The move to online banking and computerization in the late-1960s was a sensible and necessary one. The Pre-survey Study for online banking in 1968 noted: "Increasing requirements for information relative to Bank operations appear to have placed excessive work-load demands on branch staff and per-sonnel; existing methods and systems are stretched to their limits, and faster and more economic data handling approaches are required."[56] Increased vol-umes of data processing were only the beginning: "The introduction of new customer services has accelerated, and is not only burdensome on branch personnel, but the scope of such new services is limited by the increased workload so generated; more economical and timely data handling means appear necessary to cope with this new trend."[57]

In any event, labour shortages meant that some other means would have to be found to meet consumer demand for expanded banking services. "The increasing demand for new customer services, and the rapid growth of bank-ing in Canada," one report suggested, "may result in a need for so many addi-tional staff that our available manpower resources could prove inadequate; salary costs are climbing at an unprecedented rate. New and economical methods are needed to permit the profitable expansion of our business, con-sistent with the manpower resources now available, and likely to be available, in coming years."[58]

The technological transformation of the Bank of Montreal, even in the late 1960s, was beginning to have some effect on the scope and structure of banking in the institution. One 1968 report suggested that "new informa-tion handling approaches appear capable of influencing existing branch organizations in the branch network structure itself; the extent to which a 'satellite' branch organization, for example, is desirable, and the need for changes in internal branch routines as a consequence of available tech-nology and new marketing trends, cannot be fully explored without the development of a more comprehensive policy with respect to mechaniz-ation."[59] In the coming years, that would only be the tip of the iceberg in terms of changing structures.

The learning curve of Bank of Montreal personnel, combined with the pace of implementation, sometimes generated the impression that a coher-ent policy was not being followed. "A lack of understanding with respect to the scope, implication, and economic consequences of a mechanization pro-gram," one report concluded, "has been evidenced by the Bank's disjointed approach toward an automated operation."[60]

The lack of operational knowledge about the degree of required mechanization was also a challenge to technological "reformers" of the late 1960s. As one report suggested, "the bank does not know the factors relating to the bank and its environment which must be considered to enable it to decide whether, or to what degree, it should mechanize."[61] Here again, the learning curve seemed steep in places, and shows the contingent and indeterminate character of implementing this scale of technological change in such a large organization. In the event, by the mid-1960s, the Bank began looking to fill its ranks with university graduates, thus opening a human capital pipeline that would, in the late 1960s, add a new and formal dimension to the professionalization of the workforce. The Bank was also on the eve of hiring an ever-increasing number of graduates who would handle the computer and electronic-related dimensions of a technologically evolving bank.

Part of the problem facing the Bank was the steep learning curve posed by advanced data processing applications, a completely understandable state of affairs in 1968. "Recent technological developments have made practicable a broad range of advanced data processing applications which have not adequately been explored by management,"[62] one pre-mechanization report concluded, but the issue could be resolved by putting those "broad range of data processing applications" on the radar of senior managers as they planned future strategy.

It was increasingly understood and accepted that "although at this time the timing of the various developments cannot be specified with any degree of certainty," it was indeed likely that "the 'bank of the future' will operate more or less in an 'On-Line' environment."[63] GENIE had shown BMO managers that computer technology was more than up to the task of information and control processing of truly vast amounts of data – and could store it at relatively low cost, retrievable at a moment's notice "if suitably indexed."[64] The only bottleneck for GENIE resided not in the technology, but in the input speeds of the workers.

This problem was solved by connecting multiple input and output devices (like card readers and printers) to a single computer so the processors could obtain faster completion times. "It is clearly a short conceptual step from locating many of these devices in the computer room itself," one report noted, "to their eventual dissemination to other offices where they would be more convenient to the computer room's users or customers." The possibility of telecommunications and computers working together was especially attractive: the connection of devices "similar to type writers or teletype machines, and connecting these, over telephone lines, to a very large central computer" would be the prelude to the development of nationwide networks. That way "a user in, say, Vancouver, can make essentially the same use of a Montreal based computer as can, for example, a Head Office programmer or analyst."[65]

Although the pre-mechanization survey of 1968 put it in relatively straight-forward terms, MECH's mandate was enormous. Once fully implemented, the system was to be "one of the most powerful, advanced and complex" computer systems ever assembled. It would be expensive, too, requiring an up-front investment of $80 million, and an estimated annual operating budget in excess of $40 million, which amounted to about 10 per cent of the bank's total operating expenses.[66]

Directors of the Bank believed the high cost of the mechanization project was more than justified. MECH would bring the Bank of Montreal into the Space Age and make it future-ready. The article *The Bank of Montreal Strode into the Forefront of the Space-Age of Banking*, published in the 1969 Annual Report, highlights the hopes vested in the new technology. About 1,100 branches would be equipped with terminals: one teller terminal for every two tellers and one administrative terminal in each branch. The terminals were to be linked to a giant computer in Toronto that was to process "all transactions for all branches, maintain all records, including customer accounts, for the entire bank system, and handle management information which will be processed and transmitted over the administrative terminals."[67]

The implications for personnel and customers was game changing. The volume of routine bookkeeping, records, reports, and information processing was estimated to "clog itself in a decade under current methods and procedures." Simultaneously, as already mentioned, the expansion of the Bank's branches, services, and offerings was adding further pressure to the system.

The transition from using computer processing power for certain aspects of banking operations – such as cheque sorting and clearing, demand deposit accounting, some management information, and, to a limited extent in some banks, for online savings – to a broader, universal application was on its way. "Our plan," the Bank announced, "which is a total computer system for the entire operation, will eliminate just about all of the manual bookkeeping and routine chores that exist today and free personnel to devote themselves to the prime role of serving the customer in a more personal and rewarding way than time permits at present. It will provide a capacity to offer an entire new range of banking services."[68]

As President J. Leonard Walker suggested in 1969, MECH "promises to have more far-reaching effects on the Bank's operations than any other single development in our history. Within approximately five years' time, we expect to have all but a few of our branches linked to central computers and we expect to have the largest and most advanced integrated terminal on-line banking system in the world."[69] Moreover, the timeline in which the directors wanted MECH implemented was mind-boggling. Although pre-implementation studies only commenced in late 1968, the board wished to "develop

... and fully install a 'mechanized banking' system by or about December 31, 1974, and, most importantly, to achieve the cash-flow targets set at that time."[70] Wheels were turning as well on expansion of other services. Notably, at this point the Bank's directors were already toying with the idea of "Any Branch Banking," something that would finally be implemented in the early 1980s under the moniker "Multi-Branch Banking" (MBB).[71]

MECH passed into the design and implementation phase in late 1969. That involved ordering of equipment, writing computer programs, testing, personnel training, and the development of a detailed implementation plan. The whole project demanded a large group of personnel. To that end, the Bank established a special school to train those who would develop and install the system. AGT Data Systems and IBM Canada were also important partners in the project.[72] "The heart of the operation is in Montreal's Place Bonaventure," one observer reported, "where the Organization, Research, and Systems Department, together with the Montreal computer facility, has moved into the colorful new quarters." There, Bank of Montreal personnel and computer specialists were figuring out ways to "apply computer technology to banking operations on a massive scale." But it was in the branches, districts, and divisional organizations where the real data would have to be provided and where the testing would meet its greatest challenges. The Bank estimated two years before beta-testing would be available. "In the end," one article suggested, "it will be a mammoth, intricate, and efficient system substantially created by Bank of Montreal people and designed to serve people – those who run the Bank and the customers they serve."[73]

Mirroring GENIE, before nationwide rollout of MECH, a pilot program involved the initial "mechanization" of a select number of stores. This approach allowed the directors to check in regularly and halt the program if unsatisfactory results were found. After extensive testing of all aspects of MECH, the actual rollout commenced with the mechanization of one store. The converted store would operate as normal, with MECH fully implemented, for a period of several months. "During this period the performance of the system will be evaluated against the set of predefined acceptance criteria," an internal report revealed."[74] If successful, more branches would be converted thereafter.

In mid-1976 – a two-and-a-half-year delay on the delivery date estimated in the late-1960s – the Bank announced that it had "recently successfully converted 12 branches to Release 1 of the MECH system and is seeking permission from the senior officials of the day to proceed to the conversion of a further 41. These 53 branches will constitute the 'first plateau' at which time a decision will be made by the Bank to continue a 'second plateau' of approximately 300 branches. Ultimately it is planned to convert approximately 1200 branches to MECH."[75] This objective was completed by 1979.

MECH: Far-Reaching Consequences

At the outset, Bank of Montreal directors hoped that the Mechanization Project would increase efficiency, reduce costs, and allow the bank to offer new services to its customers.[76] However, MECH's far-reaching consequences and benefits were hardly known. One internal report put the challenges smartly and succinctly:

> It is not particularly clear at this time what effect an On-Line Banking System would or should have on the organizational structure of the Bank, and, of course, attention should eventually be directed toward the various possibilities. Conceptually, the changes in operation of the Bank could be profound. Customers, in effect, could do business with the Bank of Montreal rather than with a specific Branch, because all customer files will likely be located centrally and could be accessible by any Branch. Thus, the present concept of "Branch Banking" could change. Changes in the concepts of centralization and decentralization could also result, and the scope of our role in the business community could be vastly extended. From the point of view of the Branches, much of the behind-the-counter work will be eliminated, and more time will be available for concentrating on directly servicing the customer. Not only this, but we could anticipate being able to eventually provide an array of computer-based analytical tools which would be used from the Branch terminals.[77]

The savings that the program promised were derived almost entirely from the mechanized processing of customer transactions. Aside from freeing up personnel, this offered additional benefits such as accurate, inter-branch exchange of information. In this regard, MECH found a solution to a problem the Bank had struggled with for decades.

In the nineteenth century, the Bank of Montreal Character Book provided a standardized procedure for every conceivable aspect of business within the bank, from the duration of book loans from branch libraries to the appropriate margins for office communications and memos. The book included a combination of letters and numbers that branches used to relay complex information about customers quickly and efficiently in an age when communication over long distances was slow and often cumbersome.

Client information included creditworthiness, character, assets, and any other information that might be considered relevant, and each branch recorded and kept this in the so-called Reference Book. Any changes were immediately communicated to the head office and other branches. A century later, MECH offered

> a system of central "files" which consists of detailed records of all cus-
> tomer accounts, Branch operating records (G/L, personnel, premises,
> etc.), an "external" data bank, and an extensive customer data file (per-
> sonal and corporate data). This system of central "files" can be regarded
> as being "continuously" updated, "immediately" accessible by any
> Branch or Division of Head Office Group (except for confidential data),
> and the data could be at the "ultimate" level of detail (i.e. in terms of
> individual transactions). A Management system which would provide
> all levels of management (Head Office, Division, District, Branch) with
> data and information, in the form in which they require it, for plan-
> ning, organizing, directing, and controlling ... operations.[78]

The traditional difficulties associated with obtaining and synthesizing data from the network of branches for "management information purposes, it was hoped, would be largely eliminated, and, presumably, control of our vast net-work of Branches would be a more practicable task."[79] In other words, the reporting system offered the potential for "a very powerful and sophisticated management information system."[80] It was, as it were, the Character Book for the twentieth century.

In addition, as with previous automation efforts, the system was expected to liberate human resources, which would not only improve customer service but also lead to a substantial savings by reducing routine costs.

The opportunities for cost reduction would prove too compelling to pass up. "At the branch level," one report suggested, "these could amount to as much as $15,000,000 to $20,000,000 annually, or more, plus, perhaps, from $650,000–$1,000,000 annually in Head Office and the Divisions."[81] An "On-Line banking system" that handled virtually all types of routine branch transactions "appears capable of achieving the above gross savings."[82] One report concluded that the "potential net annual operating savings appear, therefore, to range from $4 million–$12 million."[83]

Other impacts of technology were less immediate. By the early 1980s, new information technologies and data processing had progressed to such an extent that it no longer made sense to base the Bank's corporate and govern-ance structure on geography. Instead, the Bank of Montreal would be organ-ized around the type of client served. "The need to integrate information," one banking observer noted, "overrode the importance of geography and even political boundaries. Time and the advantages of real-time computer operations had had a decisive impact."[84]

Tuning the Machine

New technologies allowed banks to offer new services, increased convenience, and provide faster service. Although MECH offered massive advantages
for the Bank of Montreal both in cost savings and more efficient and accurate
services, it also promised significant benefits to the customers. More so than
GENIE, which was limited to the back-of-house operations, MECH offered the
opportunity to change the customer experience in a substantial way. As Fred
McNeil put it in his address in the 1973 Annual Report: "More than four years
ago, when the Bank embarked on its mechanization program, some major
assumptions were made. These were, first, that the volume of paper handled, of accounting entries, and of calculations, would grow enormously;
second, that the cost of doing these things manually, or semi-manually,
would accelerate rapidly, while the cost of doing them by computer would
decline; and third, that, as educational standards rose, our people would
be less inclined to find job satisfaction in doing what they considered to be
dull, repetitive work that could be done much faster and more accurately
by modern technology."[85]

McNeil emphasized that the decisions taken were not easy ones for
management, especially "to undertake a program that would not begin to pay
off for more than five years from its inception," and that would "require the
assembling and commitment of a large group of highly skilled people, to say
nothing of the very substantial sums of money."[86] The risk, however, paid off:
"Not only have the original assumptions proved valid," he remarked, "but the
projections of the growth of transactions and the cost of handling them manually have already been exceeded by a considerable margin. We are, therefore,
more than ever convinced of the soundness of the course adopted."[87]

The complexity of the system was one of the greatest challenges facing the
programmers. The volume and variety of banking transactions had to first
be programmed into the system – then tested, then evaluated. "Myriads of
programmes had to be written, programmes delineating a multitude of individual transactions, each of which had to be inter-related," McNeil told the
annual general meeting in 1974.[88] The plan was to be online by 31 December
1974.[89] "When installation has been completed," he concluded, "this system
will be the most modern and efficient of its kind in the world. It will also
enable the Bank to offer more and better services to the public."[90]

Those "more and better services" enabled by data processing were also favourable to the Bank's bottom line. Payroll services for companies, for example,
were beginning to be competitively offered by the banks – and the Bank of
Montreal had the wherewithal to compete to win. The TD, Royal, and Commerce were already implementing payroll packages.[91] The data processing

systems were also defensive – in the midst of the possible loss of banking business, the power to answer competitors in this space was important.[92]

In offering data processing services to its customers, the Bank set out three clear goals: a depository or safekeeping function; a money transfer function; and a credit providing or capital mobilizing function.[93] The services would have to provide a "cost-reduction opportunity for the customer."[94]

Building on MECH's Foundations: New Services

MECH and the development of online banking allowed the Bank to offer many new services for its customers. Major milestones were the introduction of Multi-Branch Banking (1979) and PINs (1984), CIRRUS (1985), and Master Charge (1973). All of these services relied on a network of computers established by GENIE and MECH.

Multi-Branch Banking and Personal Identification Numbers

MECH was finally delivering meaningful results by the mid-1980s, showing the tremendous foresight of BMO's directors, who had initiated the project in the late-1960s. It could facilitate transactions at branches by processing credits, debits, customer information, and enquiries in real time. Eventually, it would also offer other services, including financial triggers, calculating interest, overdraft interest, and service charges without human input and updating account records accordingly.[95]

Because the files were centrally available, customers could, in theory, access their accounts from anywhere. As envisaged in 1968: "On-Line Banking can be regarded as providing each Branch with its own large computer, while simultaneously making all operating records in the Bank immediately available to a central Bank computer for analysis and reporting purposes. Clearly, the potentialities are immense, the possibilities are exciting, and since the evolution is more or less inevitable, all modern Banks will have to devote increasing attention to the patterns which are emerging."[96]

The Bank finally acted on these new possibilities in 1979, with the introduction of Multi-Branch Banking (MBB). "For the first time, any customer of the bank of Montreal will be able to go into any online branch in Canada, make deposits and withdrawals and obtained a balance on his account just as if he were in his own branch."[97]

MBB was a significant step in customer convenience and, as R.D. Mulholland pointed out, unique to the Bank of Montreal, at least at that moment. Use of the Multi-Branch Technology in this way had been envisioned almost a decade prior, in 1968, when a pre-mechanization study noted that, "with centrally located files, the up to date record of any customer account would be available to all branches. Customers could thus transact business at any Branch of the Bank – anywhere in Canada – essentially as it simultaneously and instantaneously up-dated ledger cards were somehow made available for every account in every branch."[98]

A few years later, the advent of the Personal Identification Number (PIN) and debit cards took this technology even further. Contemporary observers, perhaps with the condescension of posterity, might see this as a small, incremental change in the technology. But at the time, this development was hailed as a revolution in customer convenience. In 1984, the Bank unveiled the MBB card and PIN, enabling customers to access their accounts through the automatic teller machines.[99] Customers could, for the first time, conduct most banking transactions on their own, "such as cash withdrawals, making deposits, checking account balances, paying utility bills, transferring funds, and getting cash advances."[100]

The introduction of MBB and PIN also allowed for vastly more capable Instabank terminals, which had been introduced on a trial basis in 1975, but were now able to deliver services more quickly, easily, and securely.[101]

CIRRUS

After MBB, the next logical step was to integrate more banks into one network. CIRRUS was a new service made possible by the introduction of new technologies. According to accounts of the time, the network was designed to enable its cardholders to withdraw cash from their savings or chequing accounts or access a line of credit using the automated teller machines of other CIRRUS member institutions in the United States and Canada.[102] The network was formed in mid-1982, and its first interstate transaction was completed in January 1983. In 1985, the Bank of Montreal joined the CIRRUS network of banking and financial institutions. By 1986, CIRRUS had 2,347 members in forty-nine US states and 4 members in Canada. By the end of the first quarter of 1986, CIRRUS had nearly 11,000 machines available to more than 45 million cardholders."[103]

Al Bates, senior vice-president BMO and deputy group executive of domestic banking, speaking on 22 July 1985 at the announcement of BMO joining CIRRUS saw the following expansion of convenience for customers of the Bank:

> As of today, the Bank of Montreal Instabank customers will be able to withdraw cash from their chequing accounts as they travel throughout the United States... It means that our Bank of Montreal customers will be able to withdraw cash from their accounts in 7,500 automated

banking machines in forty-seven states throughout the continental United States. It will be available to our customers wherever the CIRRUS logo is shown in the ATM's [sic] of our member banks in the United States. You know, it wasn't that long ago that hand operated calculators such as the one I have right here in front of me were in common use within the banking industry. It was a time when you could only withdraw cash from your bank and at your branch. And it was very difficult sometimes to even do that if you weren't known. We have evolved from there. We introduced not too long ago the multiple branch banking system which allowed you access to your accounts at any branch of the Bank of Montreal.[104]

The network development and connectivity between BMO and the other banks was a source of some contention. RBC had signed up with PLUS – an interbank network similar to CIRRUS founded in 1982. In 1984, the four VISA banks (CIBC, TD, RBC, and Scotia) announced they were going to merge automated banking operations.[105] This system was acquired by VISA in 1987.[106] The interconnectivity among the other banks elicited press interest, since it seemed to have momentum: "The project starts with 250 high-traffic locations next year, then goes to about 2,000 machines coast-to-coast after that and then, likely, international." The union of the other four banks meant to some that "the days of the debit card, or payment card, are closer than any of us expected" since the banking system would allow access to your bank account with your own bank card from any machine. The odd bank out at the time would be the Bank of Montreal, which was said to "cling to MasterCard" when VISA was making such remarkable inroads.[107]

The problem was partially solved with the creation of the Interac Association, formed in November 1984 by Canadian Imperial Bank of Commerce, La Confédération des caisses populaires et d'économie Desjardins du Québec, Bank of Nova Scotia, Royal Bank of Canada, and Toronto-Dominion Bank. Coming together increased customer convenience by allowing equal access to any automated banking machine (ABM) of any institution. The Bank of Montreal joined the year after Interac's establishment.[108]

The push toward interconnectivity between banks was not always an easy road as the banks sometimes disagreed about how to proceed. But the ultimate benefits were too strong to pass up as ATMs began to proliferate across the country.[109] The Bank of Montreal was late to the party, announcing participation only when "the Interac network now links 2,500 ABMs across Canada. Bank of Montreal will add its machines and provide its customers access to the network in mid-June [1986]."[110] The plain fact was that BMO was committed to its own network, CIRCUIT. CIRCUIT was a Canada-wide, multi-bank expansion of its own Instabank/MBB network, so the Bank had a vested interest in seeing this system prevail.[111] However, BMO joined Interac when it was clear that its rival network could not compete.

Master Charge

The Bank's entrance into the world of credit cards followed a similar line. The concept of the credit card really took root in the immediate post-war period, expanding from a limited retail presence in stores and gas stations to the development of third-party universal cards. The first to appear in the United States was the Diners Club credit card in 1949, which later prompted American Express, Hilton Hotels, Bank of America, and Chase Manhattan Bank to offer their own cards in 1958.[112]

Canada's reception of this new credit technology came in 1968 through Chargex (BankAmericard), now familiar as VISA. Indeed, the Chargex (BankAmericard) was the only major credit card available in the Canadian market in the early 1970s. It had 3.2 million cardholders and 50,000 participating merchants in the country at that point. It was only in 1973 that the Bank of Montreal entered the credit card business through a partnership with Master Charge, the major competitor of Chargex (BankAmericard). Bank management suggested at the time that Master Charge was "the world's best known and accepted all-purpose bank charge card."[113] Canadian financial institutions, however, opted to join the VISA consortium. The Bank of Montreal and the Provincial Bank of Canada were the only two Canadian banks to offer Master Charge.[114]

President McNeil explained that Master Charge would compete directly with Chargex (BankAmericard), which was operated by five banks. Though the Bank of Montreal and the Provincial Bank had been invited to join Chargex (BankAmericard), they had decided to introduce their own competitive card.[115] Why? There were several reasons. The Master Charge system was part of the Interbank Card Association, a non-profit consortium of banks established to provide credit card interchange. Interbank had members in Europe, North and South America, and Japan. Worldwide, the number of Master Charge holders topped 31 million, with 1.3 million merchant outlets recognizing the card – fewer than VISA, but competitive all the same.[116] In any event, the Bank reckoned that the "current tendency is for about 30 per cent of charge cardholders to carry two separate cards, giving them a choice and flexibility in stores, restaurants and hotels."[117]

BMO rolled out Master Charge across Canada in the summer and fall of 1973. Again, the Bank used a staggered rollout system, first introducing the new product/service in large urban centres before radiating out to smaller communities.[118] The launch involved hiring and training over 350 people and construction of a computer-based authorization and processing system based in the Bank's MECH program. It included a major advertising and promotion effort and required the enrolment of tens of thousands of merchants and hundreds of thousands of cardholders.[119] In 1984, the Master Charge lineup was expanded with the introduction of the Mastercard Gold Card, geared toward "higher income, status-oriented professionals."[120]

Analysis: Technology Takes Command

This chapter has provided a detailed overview of how Bank of Montreal bankers responded to the sweeping technological and market changes in the first generation of the Digital Age. The historical events surrounding GENIE, mechanization, and the advent of credit cards in the 1960s and 1970s make this more than a technology story; for the first time, banking strategy and operations placed technology centre stage as a key driver. It is also a story about technology facilitating the transformation of how work was organized in the Bank. The technology wave began in the back offices, but soon embraced retail bank branches and ultimately the entire banking system of the globe.[121] The nature of work and the nature of the customer experience changed fundamentally over time. The workforce at the Bank of Montreal in 1930, 1960, and 1990 reflected the transformations wrought by information technology. Technology, in other words, shaped the nature of work as much as it shaped the business of banking. For an extreme but illustrative example of this, one need only refer to the retail bank branch experience in 1945, 1985, and contemporary times. Over time, the architecture of banks slowly came to favour an open layout. The progressive march of technology enabled the handling of massive volumes of transactions, while ATMs altered the relationship between customer and banker by transferring the work of the teller to the consumer. The Internet, in its turn, is completing the revolution in technology, and along with it bringing further changes to the relationship between bankers and customers. Those transformations began with a crisis in cheque clearing and the emergence of credit cards, but then grew from there, to solving specific organizational and informational challenges, and proposing expanded services. In other words, the technology platform the Bank built to address specific problems created a springboard for future innovation and expansion.[122]

The world beyond batch processing beckoned, especially when computers and telecommunications merged to form powerful real-time information networks.[123] At first national, then continental, then global transactions were being considered through organizations such as the Society for Worldwide

Interbank Financial Telecommunication (SWIFT).[124] Later, the advent of more powerful mainframe computers and decentralized networks ushered in the dawn of personal computers and processors, and that, in its turn, had a profound effect both on the nature of work and the customer experience. The payments system almost all of us take for granted – essentially, with an Internet connection or small plastic card, you can pay for any good or service virtually anywhere in the developed world – was a revolution that occurred in banking systems as well as in individual financial institutions like the Bank of Montreal.[125] It was the product individually and collectively of complex managerial decisions and processes, processes of adoption, and the introduction of a whole new set of system dynamics.[126]

The history of technological transformation at the Bank of Montreal – the roughly two decades after 1960 – is also a story of managers making decisions about massive investments and outlays on matters they knew rather less about than anyone cared to admit. They relied on a cadre of experts and information networks to determine the path forward. Sometimes this worked out well (GENIE, MECH); sometimes results were not optimal (Master Charge). There is no doubt, however, that the Bank of Montreal management of the 1960s successfully prepared the institution to face the future with the tools and platforms the times demanded. If the BMO bankers of 1958 were of the analog variety, by the 1970s, through experience and successful execution, they were fully certified digital bankers.

PART SIX

The Road of Return, 1974–1989

There is a tide in the affairs of men.
Which, taken at the flood, leads on to fortune;
Omitted, all the voyage of their life
Is bound in shallows and in miseries.
On such a full sea are we now afloat,
And we must take the current when it serves,
Or lose our ventures.
William Shakespeare, *Julius Caesar*,
Act 4, Scene 3

The wisest are most annoyed at the loss of time.
Dante, *Purgatorio* III. 78

A compass… [will] point you true north from where you're
standing, but it's got no advice about the swamps and deserts
and chasms that you'll encounter along the way. If in pursuit
of your destination, you plunge ahead, heedless of obstacles,
and achieve nothing more than to sink in a swamp… [then]
what's the use of knowing true north?
Lincoln (2012), quoted in John Lewis Gaddis,
On Grand Strategy[1]

The greater the difficulty, the more glory in surmounting it. Skillful
pilots gain their reputation from storms and tempests.
Epictetus

This final section of the scholarly part of this book examines the Bank of Montreal's experience from the mid-1970s to the end of the 1980s. Part Five provided an account of the path of the post-war Bank – in particular, how it handled the opportunities generated by a surging Canadian economy and the challenges encountered in renewing a remarkable organization. By the mid-to-late 1960s, the leadership was beginning to size up the massive scale of the work ahead to push and pull Canada's first bank into a more competitive position.

By the mid-1970s, the leadership understood that the work had merely begun. The Bank's most astute executives and directors knew it, and some were in a position to do something about it. To remain relevant and retain its status as an active, central player in Canadian banking, the Bank was being called to a thoroughgoing transformation of its operations and strategy. As we saw in Part Five, elements of that transformation – the deployment and renewal of human and technological capital – were already making their mark on the institutional life of the Bank. Moreover, in terms of performance and operations, there were important and far-reaching initiatives, not to mention a younger generation – a ginger group – of bankers in the works who were already making their presence felt. After 1990, that generation would take the helm.

Without major strategic change, Canada's first bank would have struggled to remain relevant in its domestic market and international presence. When it did decide to move, the Bank could rely on multiple strengths. The Bank of Montreal had the material and human resources, as well as the technology and sufficient internal capabilities, to mount a meaningful comeback. It also had sufficient numbers of executives who understood what the issues were, what the stakes were, and how urgent the problem had become. The Bank also had another, more intangible set of advantages: a resilient culture and legacy forged in over a century and a half of banking from which its leaders could, possibly, draw inspiration and connection. That legacy and the importance of upholding the highest reputational standards of Canadian banking and banking professionalism were never far from the minds of Bank executives. In addition, the Bank of Montreal was a high-trust institution whose networks ran deep and wide.

More tangibly, the network of professional bankers and leaders of Canadian enterprise with local, regional, and national roles and responsibilities across Canada and the North Atlantic world constituted an inimitable advantage for the Bank of Montreal. Added to that were its powerful, industry-leading capabilities in specific areas, such as project finance and commercial banking. Not least, by the mid-1970s, the Bank had over 3 million customers – 3 million relationships based upon reputation, service, and loyalty.

What the Bank did need was a leader – a grand strategist – who would be able to align an ambitious set of aspirations with a defined set of capabilities.

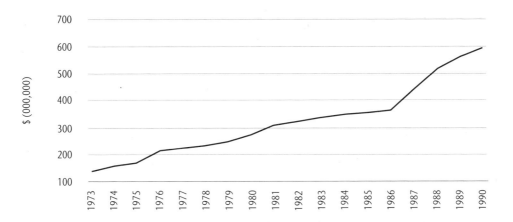

Figure VI1.1 | Canada's gross domestic product (GDP), 1973–90

Source: "GDP ($US, Current), Canada 1973–1990," World Development Indicators, The World Bank, www.worldbank.org/ (accessed 24 July 2018).

The leadership of the 1960s and 1970s, through the administration of Arnold Hart and then Fred McNeil, was able to identify certain elements that needed the most urgent attention and to respond. The 1970s and 1980s required nothing less than a cadre of transformational leaders to take the helm and put the Bank firmly on the road of return, if not to its former primacy, then certainly to a greater competitiveness, purpose, and performance. To make matters more interesting, this period – from about 1975 to 1990 – was also characterized by the end of the fabulous run of relatively easy prosperity in the North Atlantic world. The oil crisis of 1973 and the slowdown of growth in western economies combined with serious inflationary pressures on prices and wages threw economies, including Canada's, into turmoil.

Where the years 1945–73 saw the world's greatest economic boom ever, the period 1974–90 saw more turbulence and greater economic challenge. While Canada's gross domestic product generally grew over this period, it did so more slowly than before (see figure VII.1). Furthermore, the period was marked by major economic downturns in 1974–75, 1980, and 1981–82. Although there were intermittent periods of growth and optimism, 1974 was the beginning of a roughly thirty-year period during which Canada experienced very high interest rates and high unemployment, and the federal government ran massive budget deficits. These factors led to the rejection of the Liberal government in 1984 and the overwhelming rejection of the Progressive Conservative Party in 1993. It was not until 1996, under Liberal Prime Minister Jean Chrétien, that Canada returned to a budget surplus.[2]

Fifteen Tumultuous Years

The post-war economic boom came to a crashing halt across the western world in 1973–74. The 1973 oil crisis, followed shortly thereafter by the collapse of the Franklin National Bank – at the time the largest bank failure in US history – resulted in a significant economic downturn in the United States.[3] Predictably, Canadian exports to the United States fell drastically, with Canada's GDP barely eking out a small gain in 1974.[4] And that was only due to the fact that the economic downturn did not affect all areas of industry equally. While housing and the automobile industry fell sharply, other sectors were unaffected. Energy, metals, and other raw materials even saw prices soar.[5] By the spring of 1975, the market bounced back, although inflation continued to accelerate throughout the late-1970s and into the 1980s.

Hoping to stabilize the situation, the Carter administration introduced credit controls in the United States in 1980.[6] This resulted in a sharp drop in the Canadian housing market, automobile exports, and a weakened GDP. This recession resembled that of 1974–75 in its unequal effect on the Canadian economy, leaving certain areas completely unaffected.[7] Interest rates continued to soar, however, rising above 20 per cent in both the United States and Canada.[8] This resulted in a severely weakened economy, with both industrial output and employment falling steadily in 1981–82. Although the economy recovered starting in about 1983, unemployment remained stubbornly high throughout the rest of the decade.[9]

The Canadian economy softened again starting in 1989, when sharp cutbacks in manufacturing negatively impacted GDP growth. Unemployment levels soon followed, beginning a steady rise starting in the middle of the 1990s. The contraction was worsened by the Gulf War, which broke out in August 1990, and by the Goods and Services Tax, which the federal government introduced in January 1991. Both considerably depressed consumer spending.[10]

Because of its size, position, prestige, reputation, and importance, the Bank of Montreal was destined to be a key player in the unfolding of Canada's economic fortunes, and those of the Canadian banking sector, in this period. In other words, what happened at the Bank of Montreal was of extraordinary consequence to Canadian banking and the broader economic life of the country. By 1974–75, the question was whether the Bank would be able take on the scale of the internal changes required – in organization, behaviour, and strategy – to meet the multiple challenges posed by a more volatile set of market and economic circumstances.

These fifteen years in the life of the Bank of Montreal were some of the more momentous in its two centuries of existence. One big reason was that its leadership was simply running out of time to regain its organizational and strategic balance. The countless experiences and events of this period reflected and refracted the zeitgeist of time and the changes in Canadian and global banking, and involved simultaneous transformations of human, social, and reputational capital. The persistence of an unpredictable and volatile economic environment made everything much more difficult. Since an examination of the Bank's myriad experiences is not possible, the three chapters in Part Six focus on the heart of the history.

Chapter 17 offers a general overview of the 1975 to 1989 period – an analysis of the leadership, the cultural and organizational transformations, the strategies deployed, and the performance of the Bank. In the interests of time and focus, I have deliberately shortened the story of the deep, bureaucratic inner workings of the Bank, hoping that may be the subject of future monographs and articles on the evolution of communications, marketing, and a host of flourishing new services in that period.

Chapters 18 and 19 concentrate on two of the pivotal undertakings of the era: the acquisition of Harris Bank of Chicago in 1984 and the international operations of the Bank of Montreal, respectively. Both are key to understanding the strategy of the Bank in this period, in ways seen and unseen. Each in its own way had a marked effect on the subsequent fortunes of the Bank and its path into the contemporary era.

CHAPTER SEVENTEEN

The Saviour General and the Two-Front War, 1975–1989

*I am mindful of human weakness, and I reflect upon
the might of Fortune and know that everything we do is
exposed to a thousand chances.*
Scipio Africanus in *Livy, Books XXVIII–XXX*,
Book 30, Chapter 31

This chapter traces the experience of the Bank of Montreal from 1975 to 1989, taking us to the perimeter of this scholarly history. These roughly fifteen years are particularly vital ones for understanding the flight path of the Bank to that point, and the trajectory of its future growth. In other words, the circumstances in which the leadership and people found themselves in the mid-1970s was borne on the powerful currents of the Bank's culture and the decisions of its leadership in the post-war period. Equally, the actions taken after the 1970s would fundamentally shape the position of the Bank for decades to come, but with one big difference. If the Bank of Montreal obtained outcomes in the 1970s and 1980s similar in scope and effect to those of the 1950s and 1960s, there was a good chance that it would not survive the subsequent decades. In this period's more troublesome and turbulent economic and geopolitical circumstances, strategy and leadership would not only "matter," as the contemporary chorus of management writers constantly admonish, it would make a determining difference. In the three post-war decades to the mid-1970s, unprecedented material prosperity in the North Atlantic world meant that protected, regulated oligopolistic financial institutions (such as Canadian banks) that fell behind could do so in a genteel manner. The circumstances and realities of the following generation of the 1970s and 1980s would not be so accommodating. Banking was changing from a technological and market perspective. Large parts of it were going global. The end of relatively easy post-war prosperity and the onset of serious inflationary pressures put Canadian banks squarely in the political crosshairs. Demographic and labour-force changes were raising questions about how employees were organized and how institutions were making a place for women in the workforce.

The Two-Front War and the Power of One

Before we begin our examination of the Bank's journey through the 1970s and the 1980s, there are two things to keep in mind: one dealing with the nature of the challenge, and one dealing with the nature of the leadership response to that challenge.

First, in an important sense, the Bank of Montreal of the mid-1970s was facing a battle on two fronts: an internal one centred on renovation, renewal, and transformation; and an external one defined by a complex, changing environment for financial institutions. The danger of being consigned to progressively marginal relevance was real: it might have meant relegation way down the league tables, or obliteration through death by a thousand cuts, or incorporation into a big merger. The Bank of Montreal of the 1960s and early 1970s had begun to respond to the challenges confronting it, but there were still much bigger issues to tackle in strategy, vision, and execution.

Second, in the history of the Bank of Montreal, there were times when the leadership of single individuals may not have been urgent or determining – the nature of the Canadian chartered banking environment gave precedence to the calm, steady hand. Yet, there were also times where forceful and bold acts of leadership altered the Bank's course for the better. The power of individuals is too often forgotten in the "anonymous age of high technology and massive bureaucracies."[1] If you are tempted to think that events transpire as a result of purely impersonal forces – "almost without human agency," as classicist Victor Davis Hanson has suggested – think about how often on the battlefield or in corporate life much has hinged on the abilities of just a few rare people of genius.[2] The success of Apple, Microsoft, and Tesla were predicated on the singularity of a Steve Jobs, a Bill Gates, and an Elon Musk.[3] In the military sense, on occasion, there are people who can still make a difference – who can still matter more than the "inanimate forces" that are said to drive the history of institutions. These rare individuals in the theatre of war, from ancient times to the twenty-first century, Hanson calls "saviour generals," who by training, character, temperament, and strategic insight are able to reverse a tide or turn back an impending loss. These "firemen," as Hanson describes them, "are asked to distinguish the conflagration that others, of typically superior rank and prestige, have ignited."[4] The qualities required of a leader faced with the challenge of turning the tide and galvanizing a dispirited and unfocused organization – special strategic knowledge and insight, outspokenness, individualism, eccentricity, and bluntness – were exactly the ones that incited incomprehension, suspicion, and spite.[5] They were often seen as "suspect outsiders," who even after their successes, in retirement did not enjoy the acclaim their achievements may have called for, ending up "caricatures of their brilliant selves," with people were more likely to remember the style or the eccentricity, and the defeats, rather than the victories.[6]

For the generation of the 1970s and 1980s at the Bank of Montreal, I argue that that individual – that pivotal player – was William David Mulholland Jr. In an important historical sense, Mulholland was the Bank of Montreal's saviour general – the executive, the recovery artist, who transformed the Bank of Montreal. He did so incompletely, and imperfectly – as successive generations of leadership would amply attest to – but what he did was enough to turn the tide and put the Bank of Montreal on the road to return.

By the key markers, Bill Mulholland fits the profile of the saviour general. In 1975, he confronted a situation in urgent need of reforms, a new strategy, and a new attitude. He was an outsider and a contrarian. He demonstrated the latter in many ways – socially and professionally, in ways well documented and better yet remembered by that generation of bankers. He understood that uncertain strategies, tactics, and dangerously outdated operations had led the Bank of Montreal into the predicament it found itself in.

Mulholland had an independence of mind and an eccentric and often abrasive, dismissive style of leadership, though it never strayed into unorthodoxy. His unconventional personality – likely innate rather than merely acquired – was also critical to his rejection of past conventional thinking about the Bank's strategy. Beyond that, Mulholland was not a career banker. He had come to BMO from an investment banking career that included working at Morgan Stanley, and serving in other increasingly prominent but non-bank-related positions. As a result, Mulholland was a "bothersome outsider" absolutely willing to implement change. The fact that those who knew him often remember him as having the mien of a "Marine Corps general" is a telling indication of the kind of executive he was. Indeed, of all the descriptions that were used in public, in the press, and in private correspondence, the comparison of Mulholland to a soldier was almost universal.[7] Some meant it as an epithet, while others used it as a term of admiration. Consciously or not, those that drew the parallel were surely on to something.

The Bank of Montreal's saviour general Bill Mulholland and his small group of executives had three main roles in this period. The first was the same as every other chief executive before or since: to keep the ship steaming forward and to ensure its safety and the safety of its millions of customers. In Canada's oligopolistic and highly regulated banking system, there are multiple safeguards against the most serious dangers that might befall the largest chartered banks. The conservative culture of Canadian banking and the professional training of bankers offered an important backstop as well.

In their second role, Mulholland and his general staff, in their management of a large, complex institution, had to deal with the short-term challenges posed and opportunities offered by the times. This involved the day-to-day operations, responding to demographic change, answering the opportunities of the market, and assessing the risk and the reward inherent in a changing national and global marketplace as well as in the regulatory realm. This was a somewhat more challenging role than the first since it involved questions of renewal and strategic thinking. But here again, the Bank showed itself capable of rising to the occasion.

The third, more historical and consequential, role was long term, strategic, and unique: to fight and win that two-front war that featured internal reorganization and mastering a changing external reality. Writ large, it would be to restore the Bank of Montreal, to set it on the road of return: a return to fighting form, to gain back what was lost in the post-war period; a return to a clear vision of leadership, both inside the organization and beyond it; a return to strategic and competitive advantage through bold leadership and a clear program that would transform the culture of the Bank before the point of *no* return. Mulholland's main mission was to turn around the sagging fortunes of the Bank of Montreal in the eleventh hour.

The emphasis on Mulholland does not, of course, imply that he did it all. He led a large and complex contemporary North American financial institution known nationally and internationally for its professional and capable bankers. Canada's first bank had a remarkable history at the centre of the financial life of the country with one of the greatest and most effective financial and information networks. Organizations are run by elaborate teams of decision-makers, executives, managers, and employees doing their jobs. Mulholland also relied on an executive team that shared, and would be able to execute, his strategic vision – and perhaps at times keep his more egregious tendencies in check. The emphasis within the press, and within the bank in later years, on the legendary stories of interminable waits for meetings and his dressing down of subordinates, calling senior executives on the carpet, and sometimes exasperating a major client or two, were all part of the Mulholland mystique. However, what Mulholland did for the Bank of Montreal was as simple as it was powerful – he gave it a clear vision, a fearless strategy, and a force of will, powered by an imperturbable personality, to see it through. If fortune favoured the bold, it would, for the first time in a while, also favour the Bank of Montreal, in spite of the mistakes and missteps along the way.

This chapter's story of the Bank in the 1970s and 1980s begins with a look at its leadership, strategies, and initiatives, including root-and-branch reform of the corporate organization. It examines the players, the stakes, the environment, and the strategy of the Bank of Montreal in the Mulholland years. The chapter also focuses on the main highlights of the period, such as the Domestic Development Program, the bank's participation in the public sphere, its involvement in Dome Petroleum Ltd, and the acquisition of Nesbitt Thomson. As already mentioned, chapters 18 and 19 focus on more epochal themes: the acquisition of the Harris Bank of Chicago and the international operations of the Bank. This chapter ends as the Mulholland years draw to a close: the main battle had been won; a new set of challenges, and the times themselves, called for a new approach and a new leadership to confront a changed competitive environment.

This chapter cannot hope to cover all the developments in the life of the Bank of Montreal in this period. The lived experience of the hundreds of branches and thousands of employees, the banking divisions and particular lines of business, the specific deals, and the thousands of stories and experiences that make for a vibrant and interesting institution are an important part of the history of the Bank. At the same time, the limitations of time and space require that choices be made. The big story in this period is clear: how the Bank of Montreal confronted the big challenges before it, inside and outside, foreign and domestic.

Mulholland and His General Staff

We begin with a closer look at the leadership of this vital period in the life of the Bank of Montreal, starting with a closer look at the man at the top. William David Mulholland Jr was born on 16 June 1926 in Albany, New York, where his father worked as the director of lands and forests for the Empire State.[8] He was educated at the Christian Brothers Academy, a private Catholic military college and preparatory high school in his native Albany. He completed his studies in 1944 and immediately enlisted into the United States Army (Serial Number 42123994), though he needed his parents' permission since he was just shy of the required age of majority.

Mulholland was commissioned in the infantry as a company commander and participated in the Philippines Campaign of 1944–45 under the command of Admiral Chester W. Nimitz and Admiral William F. Halsey Jr.[9] On 20 October 1944, General Douglas MacArthur's Allied forces took the island of Leyte, signalling the beginning of the end for the Japanese occupation of the Philippines. Young Mulholland toyed with the possibility of accepting a commission in Chiang Kai-shek's army, but evidently thought better of it. The connection with China and the Asia Pacific region must have run deep for him to consider joining the Kuomintang – to say nothing of his later relationships, as the Bank's chief executive officer, with China's Communist regime.[10]

Mulholland was discharged in 1946. Thereafter, he worked as a policeman to make enough money to put himself through Harvard University, where he earned his Bachelor of Arts (cum laude) in 1951.[11] In 1952, he completed his Master of Business Administration at Harvard Business School. The Harvard Business School was not only a pioneer in business education but also held an "undisputed number one rating" among the six US business schools that offered pure "graduate professional" studies at a tuition of $800 annually.[12] The school, under Dean Donald K. David (1942–55), became a globally recognized institution with an outstanding reputation.[13] Moreover, Harvard MBAs were few and far between and set the gold standard for executive training. Mulholland's post-graduate career began at Morgan Stanley in New York, a global investment bank created in 1935 in the wake of the Glass-Steagall Act that separated investment banking and commercial banking businesses. During Mulholland's years with Morgan Stanley, the firm's speciality lay in the area of public financing, managing loans for some of the world's largest companies.[14]

In 1962, he became a general partner and became directly involved in the public financing of what has been described as the "largest-ever sale of corporate securities to finance construction of the Churchill Falls hydro-electric project in Labrador."[15] Mulholland's involvement in the financially complex and politically sensitive file throughout the 1960s involved Hydro-Québec, the government of Newfoundland and Labrador, the Quebec government, and the British Newfoundland Corporation Ltd (BRINCO).[16] Mulholland's first job was to find a way to get Quebec and Newfoundland leaders to co-operate on such a contentious issue. Mulholland's skill lay in his ability to handle the wiliness and cunning of men such as Quebec premiers Jean Lesage and Daniel Johnson, Newfoundland premier Joey Smallwood, and a host of canny politicians, including René Lévesque, and other officials within the Canadian government. Mulholland's "other" job was to find the financing, which turned out to be, at $500 million, the "largest private loan ever arranged" to that point and an audacious tour de force.[17] What is often skipped over in the standard Mulholland biographies is just how fraught the issue was, entangled as it was in one of the most protracted disputes over boundaries, rights, and the commercial terms of the product itself – electricity – including price, length of contract, completion guarantees, and the like.[18] The complexity of the networks and relationships involved, as well as the fine negotiating skills required, fundamentally honed and shaped Mulholland's style and approach. His involvement in the Churchill Falls project would come to define much of his career for almost two decades, into the 1970s.[19]

Mulholland's involvement in BRINCO took a dramatic turn on 11 November 1969 when the BRINCO corporate jet crashed, killing all aboard, including six corporate executives. To fill the void, on 1 January 1970, Mulholland became president and chief executive officer of the company, the animating force behind the construction of the project – one of the largest of its kind in the world at the time. The project was hailed by the Canadian prime minister Pierre Trudeau as begging "comparison with the pyramids, but with a usefulness that begs comparison with the Nile."[20] Just a month after the BRINCO appointment, in February 1970, Mulholland also took a seat on the board of directors at the Bank of Montreal, one of the main financiers of the Churchill Falls project.[21]

Just five years after that, on New Year's Day 1975, Bill Mulholland became president of the Bank of Montreal, a role he would serve in until 30 June 1981. On 15 January 1979, he was appointed chief executive officer, serving in this position until 30 June 1989. He was also chairman of the board between 1 July 1981 and 15 January 1990.[22] Between 1975 and 1979, of course, Mulholland served under Fred H. McNeil, deputy chairman and chief executive officer, who had distinguished himself in the 1960s as having the vision and foresight to understand at least part of what needed to be done. At various times, the Mulholland's senior leadership team would feature, in various capacities, some remarkable bankers: Stan Davison (the banker's banker who joined the Bank of Montreal in 1947 at Kelowna, B.C., and worked his way up to vice-chairman and senior officer in Western Canada), Jake H. Warren (the former deputy minister of trade and commerce, and vice-chairman of the Bank of Montreal between 1979 and 1986), W.E. Bradford (accountant and former BRINCO colleague who became Mulholland's general manager of domestic banking and eventually deputy chairman), J.A. Whitney (a Yukon-born career banker who oversaw credit policy in the Mulholland era), and R.H. Call (the canny strategist).[23] L.R. "Dick" O'Hagan, a vice-president, was not a banker, but a brilliant communicator whose talents would often be called upon as the Bank strove to transform itself. By the mid-1980s, others came into the magic circle, perhaps most notably Grant L. Reuber. Reuber was a distinguished economist and public servant who joined the Bank of Montreal in 1978 as senior vice-president and chief economist, eventually becoming deputy chief executive in 1981 and president in 1983.[24] Also joining were Keith O. Dorricott (a laser-sharp chief financial officer and in a later period, vice-chair), W.B. "Bill" Bateman (corporate and government banking, another talented US import), G.E. Neal (treasurer), Matthew W.

Barrett (*le dauphin* and head of domestic banking), K.E. Palmer (commercial), G.W. Hopkins (operations and systems), and Donald Munford (a plain-spoken English banker and martinet overseeing credit and risk).[25]

Strikes the Eleventh Hour[26]

"Shock, dismay, and perhaps even a little sadness are being felt in the invest-ment community following the announcement by the Bank of Montreal of its balance revenue after tax for the third-quarter," the *Globe and Mail* reported in August 1974.[27] Bank officials attributed the issue to a narrowing of interest rate margins and higher expenditures for both the Master Charge and mech-anization programs. Others, however, pointed to a more fundamental prob-lem. As one analyst suggested, "the essential problem is not a sharp increase in costs associated with the Master Charge and mechanization programs. It is a failure to increase net interest earnings and other operating revenue at rates adequate to finance these programs.[28] The broader indicators were also negative – for example, the Bank's balance of revenue per average asset was thirty-four cents, compared to the earnings of the other chartered banks that were registering in the fifty- to sixty-three-cent range.

As Don Munford, a Mulholland-era senior executive recalled, there was also a serious accountability problem. "It was felt that some of the things that happened to us were Acts of God as opposed to Acts of Management." Mun-ford conceded that it "would have been only a matter of time before the bank sank beyond reach had it continued along that trajectory."[29]

At one board meeting in 1974, Mulholland took control of the meeting after they had been informed that the Bank had just lost substantial sums on a foreign trading position. Hart and McNeil were paying close attention to the young Mulholland; it is said that his performance at that meeting tipped the scales in favour of breaking with tradition and appointing an outsider to the Bank's top role.

When the opportunity presented itself, McNeil made his move. As he told the press in 1974, "we had lots of problems at that time, and I kind of felt I was sinking under them." Mulholland became the Bank's president in November of that year, with the official appointment coming on New Year's Day 1975. Mulholland later quipped, "I swear to you, [Bank of Montreal] is the last place I expected to be. It's hard to conceive of coming into this business at this level from the outside."[30] Yet that was precisely what the Bank at that moment re-quired – an outsider absolutely willing to do what was necessary to turn the ship around.

There was no shortage of raised eyebrows that Canada's first bank would appoint an American to lead it. "Have we really reached the point," asked

Canadian historian Peter Neary in *The Canadian Forum*, "where no citizen of this country could be found to lead one of our largest banks?"[31] The answer to Professor Neary's question was evidently "no," but the question raised did reflect the protective nationalist impulse that was a feature of the mid-1970s.

The General Takes Command

News of the appointment of Mulholland was met with some excitement and anticipation. In the words of one banker there at the dawn of the era: "My sense was here was a man with huge vision as to what he wanted the bank to do, and his vision was Morgan Guaranty. BMO was to be the Canadian Morgan Guaranty. We would be global in status. We would go after the top echelons of corporate business, and understand that he came from Morgan Stanley. So he was a corporate – an investment banker that was running a bank that was largely retail and still is."[32] The Mulholland vision directly spoke to a weakness in the Bank itself – that it ought to focus on the corporate wholesale business and "we needed more attention, more aggressive management of that." This was over a decade before the purchase of an investment bank was even contemplated or, indeed, allowed. As one observer put it: "he was way ahead of the block then, and his vision was far different to any of the other Canadian banks."[33]

Mulholland moved on the personnel front fairly quickly, making "a pretty clean sweep of the old guard" and "putting some younger, newer, often more capable, knowledgeable people in their place."[34] To the observers and executives of the day, the Bank seemed to exist as a "number of separate banks as opposed to one bank," where the corporate and institutional financial services arms were distinct from, and felt superior to, the personal and commercial divisions of the bank.[35]

Mulholland's "outsider" persona also asserted itself quickly, if symbolically, at the executive levels. The long lunches of executives and the proverbial banker's hours came to an end. As Don Munford recalled with perhaps only slight exaggeration, "the gentlemen's club ended overnight."[36] One press account suggested that the incoming president "worked such long hours that his chauffeurs would change shift while waiting for him to call it a day." Others speculated that the Montreal head office was renovated to accommodate sleeping quarters for him – a story that migrated to Toronto's First Canadian Place when the Bank moved most of its senior executives there in the late 1970s.[37] Some of Mulholland's older children would make appointments at the Bank in order to see their father.[38]

Mulholland took swift action across all fronts. As one era-executive recalled, upon arrival, he decreed that there would be "no more alcohol. No more guns. No more fooling around." He continued: "I remember going downstairs in

Manulife Centre and just mindlessly buying a bottle of wine and bringing it back up to my office and suddenly realizing that I had alcohol in my office. Well, of course that wasn't really what he was after, but I was so scared that I had already violated a rule of the bank and that I was going to get fired for having a bottle of wine."[39]

Another bank official recalled the atmosphere as getting much more serious: "I think he brought a huge positive shot in the arm to the bank in terms of 'We're a bank. We're not a social club.' His own work ethic – he would often get between three and four hours sleep a night, and much of his home hours were spent poring over bank business – was legendary."[40] Mulholland fully traded on his emergent persona and his powerful presence within the bank: people often feared him and with reason: "he demanded so much. He didn't suffer fools gladly. A lot of people weren't comfortable with that, and rightly so. And I think a lot of people left because they didn't like that, but they needed to go, frankly. I mean, it wasn't a popularity contest and he knew that. I think he focused on a lot of things that were important. I think he brought a lot of his interest in world politics and world economics to the bank, he thought we should be punching above our weight."[41]

One of Mulholland's many challenges was to turn around the Bank's reputation in the corporate market that it had become a laggard, in spite of its size and the clout it could wield. Its nature, according to one veteran senior executive, was "more like an English bank: Highly bureaucratic, highly centralized, and, [in time] through the personality of Bill Mulholland, totally dominated by one man."[42] The Bank in this period was also in some ways a very old school institution: "you joined the bank like you went into the priesthood: You did what you were told, you went where they sent you, but you always had a job."[43]

The External Environment of the Mulholland Era

Overall, the 1970s and 1980s in both Bank of Montreal banking and the broader sector of Canadian banking was about technological change, legislative change, and changing market influences.[44] In combination, these forces unleashed a remarkable response that included an expanding array of banking products and services. Contemporary readers would be astonished at how restricted that range was before the major liberalizations of the 1970s and especially the 1980s. Household lending, personal wealth management, and the entry into securities markets were but three of the major areas of expansion newly permitted by Canadian regulation in the era. Then came trust, mutual fund and retail brokerage, even insurance.[45] Since the mid-1960s to the end of the Mulholland era, observers have argued that the Canadian banking industry was very competitive.[46] It only grew more competitive after 1980 as a result of the Bank Act changes discussed elsewhere.

Throughout the 1970s, inflationary pressures, the question of interest rates, and bank prime rates became a significant political question. The Canadian left, in particular, focused on the control of the chartered banks not only over the banking system but also "over the largest corporations of this country."[47] The inflationary pressures of the day were clearly creating political problems: "[when] the cost of living is increasing by 9 percent, we find that the assets and profits of the banks have been increasing month by month and year by year at well beyond that rate."[48] The representations made in the late 1970s in anticipation of Bank Act revisions, for example, included numerous briefs filed by associations dealing with everything from expanding competition to the eternal question of bank fees and account charges.[49] As MP Bob Rae suggested in the debate over the 1980 Bank Act revisions, the "fact remains that the banks are taking systematic advantage of those Canadian who choose to pay off their loans early because of the way in which they calculate payments of interest ... Some will rob you with a six-gun and some rob you with a fountain pen, Mr Speaker."[50]

The expansion of the role of banks as financial institutions offered tremendous opportunities – if the banks could harness their existing capabilities in credit and risk management and cross over into the new areas of financial services that were being offered. The traditional field of banking involved business lending, deposit taking, and payment services. The other three pillars of the Canadian system were trust and mortgage loan companies, life and health insurance companies, and securities dealers.[51] By the 1970s, that world was fading; by the 1980s and 1990s, that world was replaced by a new set of realities ushered in by globalization, technological innovation, rising wealth, and interest rate volatility.[52]

Progressively liberal changes in the regulatory landscape through the Bank Act permitted banks to take advantage of the broader changes in the banking landscape. First, mortgage loans were allowed – without interest ceilings (1967). Then banks were allowed to use their mortgage-loan subsidiaries to remain exempt from reserve requirements, as well as to enter the field of factoring and leasing through subsidiaries (1980). Those changes in particular were said to increase what was considered an already-competitive industry.[53] The 1987 Bank Act revisions allowed banks to buy securities dealer subsidiaries.[54] Those changes were called "The Little Bang" and followed on the heels of a royal commission chaired by Justice Willard Z. Estey and the failure of two western Canadian banks, as well as a strong lobbying campaign on the part of the Big Six banks to be allowed to enter the securities business under certain conditions and restrictions.[55]

The General and His Strategy

After his initial debut, Mulholland quickly went about getting to know the organization, touring its seven divisions and some of its 1,200 branches. As he later suggested, the most serious problem he perceived had to do with people: the morale of the Bank had reached a dangerous low. His first job was to convince "people that they really could do it and that they really weren't Clark Kents, but Supermen."[56]

The Mulholland strategy was predicated on installing a younger generation of bankers and putting them in charge. "The difference," one executive recalled, "was he also gave you accountability along with responsibility. And if you couldn't take that, then you were in trouble. And in my view, younger people were able to do it because you didn't know different."[57] This was part of Mulholland's realization of the changing nature of banking, and especially the fact that the Bank of Montreal would have to move from "a process lending-type business into a market-driven, market competitive, market making business. Ergo, he started to expand his relationships with international people."[58] His chosen instrument in this was to look to the treasury function in particular to implement these changes. Treasury operations assumed responsibility for the liability side of the balance sheet, and Mulholland increased the responsibility of the treasury accordingly.[59]

His first managerial order of business was to manage the balance sheet more forcefully and carefully than had been done in a long time. Asset management and interpretation of results were Mulholland's real strengths, reported one analyst, and he was determined that it become the Bank's strength as well.[60] The funds management side was critical for Mulholland. Specifically, he addressed the problem of the Bank's low capital-to-assets ratio (the lowest in the industry) by reducing the assets that were in the most rapidly growing category and causing a significant problem: the lowest-yielding assets.

One area that concerned Mulholland was the risk function in the bank – attempting to build a culture "that from a risk standpoint was very strong." The troubled experience of the early 1970s in this area reinforced the push into a greater and more robust risk culture.[61] One executive who worked with Mulholland made it clear that Mulholland's approach from early on was to understand the details of each department – "every function, every cost" – in order to get a firm grasp of what exactly he was dealing with. "The first thing we did was functionally and financially took apart headquarters and he used me a lot of times to communicate in more detail. We eliminated a lot of waste and a lot of talk because the Bank of Montreal he inherited was a bureaucracy in every sense of the word. It was conservative; it was traditional; it was credit-driven. Nothing wrong with that. It was credit-centric. Nothing wrong with that in the banking business. But it sort of dominated all the other professional functions."[62]

Mulholland perceived that domination quickly and moved to staff human resources, information technology, marketing, corporate communications, and the like with first-class people. "He professionalized, modernized and fundamentally transformed the Bank of Montreal single-handedly into a business [bringing] accountability and performance expectations into a company that had none – a company that was underperforming."[63]

Addressing the dysfunctions in the corporate culture was vital, especially given the complexity of the task and the pressure to change. The three main cultures at the bank – the corporate, the personal and commercial, and the branch culture – were often in conflict with one another. Complicating matters was the paternalistic attitude that was a legacy of generations past and, not least, a lack of accountability in the branch culture.[64]

The Mulholland administration also moved to improve the nature and quality of assessments, especially in terms of profitability. As an executive involved in this effort recalled,

> I spent a good portion of my time developing a profitability assessment information system. We talked about corporate relationship management. We had no idea what relationships, or what parts of a relationship, were profitable. We had no idea what we were earning or where we were earning. Therefore we could not effectively manage a relationship. We simply didn't know – for example was the relationship with Bell Canada profitable? Was it not profitable? What areas were profitable? What business were we doing with a client? What business was the branch in Vancouver doing with them? What were they doing down in Montreal?[65]

The Bank deployed a team to develop a profitability system so senior executives could determine what the bank was earning in terms of return on assets, return on capital employed, and "what business were we even doing, so that in the end we had a system that you could go to your PC and say, 'This is our relationship and this is what we're earning and from its component parts.'"[66]

These were but opening gambits in the larger battle for deliverance of the Bank. Mulholland's strategy would revolve around several axes in the years to come. First, he focused on the ambitious but necessary project of the complete reorganization of the Bank – to put it on a sound competitive footing and to specifically take aim at processes and systems that slowed things down. The Bank would also be reorganized along functional, not just purely geographical, lines.[67] Second, he would push aggressively into new markets and competitive areas, which included a major expansion into global banking, especially banking in the United States. Each of these epochal themes forms the subject of the two thematic chapters that follow.

Project Financing

The Bank had become particularly noted for financing of major projects. In the first few months of Mulholland's tenure, the Bank established the Project Financing Group, which specialized in arranging financing for major undertakings across the globe. Because of the increasing size of "the developments being funded, the financing arrangements [were] necessarily complex and it has become increasingly difficult to serve major clients through traditional banking practices," as the Annual Report of 1975 stated.[68] By 1980, the announcement came that "on November 1 of this year, following two years of study, the Bank implemented a series of changes, the principal feature of which was the establishment of World Corporate Banking Group. The new group was created to serve international and transnational markets, specifically larger multinationals, foreign governments and foreign banks, and those industries such as petroleum whose essential nature is international."[69] It would be headquartered in Toronto with offices in financial centres around the world. Its objective was to serve "larger multi-national companies, foreign governments, the petroleum industry and a network of correspondent banks that ensure Bank of Montreal is a presence in virtually every country of the world." The World Corporate Banking Group was one of two corporate banking groups at the Bank of Montreal, along with the North American Corporate Banking Group, which looked after corporate and government clients in Canada and the United States.[70] From the spring of 1975 onward, several offices were opened, including ones in Singapore (the centre of the Asian dollar market) and Frankfurt, West Germany.[71]

Training and Recruitment

Mulholland and his team also saw the area of training and development as a strategic priority – and for good reason, given the significant changes happening in banking and the need for Bank personnel to be up to speed on those. One of Mulholland's first tasks was to establish First Bank College, in downtown Montreal, providing under one roof meeting rooms of various sizes, a library, a simulated branch, an audiovisual centre, and living accommodation for personnel on course. As the 1975 Annual Report commented, "it is already proving very effective in our many and varied training programs."[72]

The training and development component of the Bank's employer value proposition was not lost on new recruitments. "Coming in, I was very impressed by the training they gave to the employees. That was very important to me, just coming out of university that you weren't just sort of thrown into the deep end of things."[73] What helped immeasurably was the strong *esprit de corps* of the local branches as well as the intensely social nature of their interaction. That counterbalanced somewhat the rules-based nature of 1970s banking: "This is the way things were done, and you did it and you didn't deviate, and you got into big, serious trouble if you deviated from the practices."[74] Some observers go further in arguing that Mulholland's most important contribution was to set up a Management Development Programme and systematically recruiting MBAs and placing them into special training programs.[75]

As a result of recruitment and training thrusts, the profile of management became younger, more dynamic, and better prepared – not to mention more diverse, "both in terms of educational background and gender – you name it."[76] The additional result for the Bank of Montreal was what many who lived through it identified as a dramatic and accelerated change.

Dawn of the Woman Banker

In a sign of things to come, concerns about the treatment and representation of women grew increasingly prominent at Canada's Big Five banks.[77] In 1976 at the RBC's annual meeting, chairman W. Earle McLaughlin, in response to a question as to why no women were on the board of directors, claimed that there were "none qualified for the role," continuing on to ask Ruth Bell, the challenger, "Why don't you be a nice girl and let me exercise your ballot?"[78] The reaction was understandably strong. MP for Vancouver Kingsway, Simma Holt responded in February 1977 in a speech in the House of Commons during debate of the Bank Act:

> When that gold-plated bank president, W. Earle McLaughlin, made his infamous statement he was not speaking in isolation. He was not unique. He was the voice of the thousands and thousands of men who run this country ... The pictures that appear of executives – and until recently of cabinets – are always of men. Where are the women? In the annual reports of banks or big companies the women are usually standing by the filing cabinet. Even now, when women are wearing long skirts and pant suits, these pictures still show the women in short skirts because it tittles – it gives men pleasure. These big bank, big company annual reports are the cheap businessman's *Playboy*. It is not even well done.[79]

The Bank of Montreal responded in no uncertain terms and, over the course of the 1980s, established something of a competitive advantage in this area – a lead that it has consistently maintained since. By 1986, the Bank of Montreal saw an increase of 14 per cent in the number of women in middle management positions. As one contemporary (and pioneering) woman executive, Betsy Wright, suggested in 1986: "There are several factors responsible for the more prominent contributions women are making. Pre-eminent among these is that more women are getting their MBAs than ever before." Wright noted that the proportion of women receiving MBAs in Canada had risen from 2.5 per cent to 29 per cent of total enrolments.[80] "The Bank is a prime illustration of a progressive organization that has accommodated such aspirations," she concluded, citing that the management of the bank featured 7 per cent of managerial positions occupied by women in 1970, compared to 45 per cent in 1985, with women holding about 8 per cent of senior management positions, "more than a five-fold increase since the beginning of this decade [1980]."[81]

In 1970, 3 per cent to 4 per cent of BMO's total management structure were female. That number rose to 11.2 per cent in 1972 and to 30.1 per cent in 1980. In the same year, 2,307 women at BMO occupied managerial positions. The Bank used a series of job grades between 1 and 14 – from entry level to the most senior – and in 1980, 510 women were in job grades 5 or higher; stated another way: 11 per cent of the jobs in grades 5 or higher were filled by women. In the most senior positions, grades 10 to 14, there were 17 women (or 2 per cent of total senior management) in 1980. This was an increase of 8 women from 1978.[82]

Other currents from the broader cultural environment flowed through the Bank in the 1970s and 1980s, including efforts by some bank employees to organize for collective bargaining. The moves were not particularly welcomed by management, who sought to blunt the collective bargaining drive by offering more generous packages of wages and benefits, especially at the branch level, by the Retail Clerks International Union. "Our policy regarding unionism is naturally to abide by the law," Fred McNeil commented in 1980. "We have in fact, twelve branches certified, six contracts and we had twelve branches which were certified and by mutual consent of the parties involved withdrew the certification."[83]

The Transformation of Technology

As was discussed in detail in chapter 16, technological transformation marked this period as much as any other force in banking. By the mid 1970s, mechanization began to really make its mark. "As recently as October, the Bank of Montreal had only five branches converted to mechanical operations from manual – a low number compared with that for other major banks or even some of the smaller banks," the Annual Report of 1976 noted. "Now, there are around 165 Bank of Montreal branches online and the system is functioning very well."[84] The situation represented a "a very welcome turn of events for Bank of Montreal officials," the press reported, especially since reports of problems seemed to dominate coverage after 1974.[85]

But technological innovation reached further. The Bank also involved itself in several pioneering projects, like the initiative undertaken in Winnipeg whereby the main branch would be "directly linked into a spacious underground concourse – FirstBank Square. In this square, the Bank installed a 'first' for Western Canadian convenient banking services: television tellers."[86] As one executive recalled, "every year we'd make very big investments in technology. We'd have a huge array of very interesting projects that we would work on. New business ventures that we want to go in on the business side of it. And of course, we correspondingly would want to make investments in technology to support that."[87]

In 1976, in concert with most of the major banks in North America and Western Europe, the Bank of Montreal introduced SWIFT, a new electronic message switching system. It represented the first step toward international electronic banking, allowing members to exchange private and confidential messages as well as transfer funds and confirm financial information.[88] "Seven Canadian banks will make international payments through an electronic funds transfer system from Jan. 31, 1977," the *Globe and Mail* enthusiastically announced, "marking a substantial improvement in speed over tradition mail and Telex methods."[89]

Of more significance to the Bank of Montreal was the launch of MBB. Truly a first for Canadian banks, the system was based on a centralized computer network that spanned five time zones from Atlantic to Pacific. It allowed customers with an account at any "'on-line' branch to make deposits and withdrawals at any of the nearly 1,050 branches on the network."[90] Other banks chose to wait and see if the system worked and was popular. It did and it was. The Bank spent $2 million on advertising and promotion of this important new service, indicating "how much importance [the Bank] attached to [MBB] – and the success it expects it will be."[91]

As a logical next step, BMO joined its bank machines to the CIRRUS automated banking machine network in the United States and underwrote CIRCUIT, a Canadian version, in the mid-1980s.[92] The Bank initially resisted joining other Canadian chartered banks in forming the Interac network, participating only belatedly after it dawned on executives that the latter system would prevail."[93] Innovations such as MoneyTrac[94] (enabling customers to obtain account information at terminals), point-of-sale terminals,[95] and other incremental improvements kept the Bank very much in the technology game.

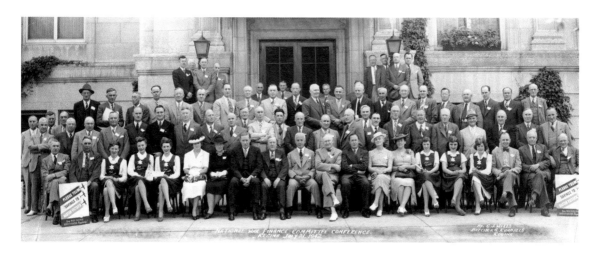

(*above*) Under the leadership of G.W. Spinney, the National War Finance Committee oversaw the successful sale of Victory Loan Bonds, a critical component in financing the Canadian war effort. This group photo of the committee was taken in Regina, Saskatchewan, on 21 July. Spinney is in the centre of the photograph, seated in the front row. 1942. G.J. Wells, Butcher & Runnals, Regina.

(*below*) This photograph shows new immigrants arriving in Canada from the Netherlands. Bank officials in Quebec City were given permission to board their vessel, the SS *Waterman*, in order to create a floating branch. Effectively this allowed the newcomers to exchange their cheques and drafts for Canadian currency before the ship eventually arrived in Montreal. The entire operation lasted twenty-four hours. 1947.

With new technology, transcontinental integration and communication between the Bank's branches from coast to coast became easier and quicker. This advertisement boasts of the fast, convenient, and secure "private wires" (telegraph lines) that made truly national banking in Canada a reality. ca. 1950.

She's done her Banking!

She has saved herself an hour's trip to town and back—time she can spend in giving her garden that extra care it needs . . . in doing over Junior's shirt . . . or just relaxing on the porch before starting dinner.

Smart housewives, who live out of town, do their banking by mail. They save time and inconvenience, and lengthen their day at home.

If you live in a newly-settled or outlying district, you will enjoy that convenient, time-saving method of handling your money —banking by mail. You'll find the welcome mat out at the B of M when you drop in to ask about this service . . . but if you can't get in for a while, why not write today for our folder, "How to Bank by Mail"? With it, you can open your account without even a visit.

"MY BANK"
TO A MILLION CANADIANS
B of M

BANK OF MONTREAL

WORKING WITH CANADIANS IN EVERY WALK OF LIFE SINCE 1817
SO47

This advertisement speaks to the increasing post-war consumer boom and the suburbanization of Canada's middle class. "Smart housewives, who live out of town," the advertisement reads, "do their banking by mail. They save time and inconvenience and lengthen their day at home." 1950.

TWENTIETH
CENTURY
TOTEMS...

SYMBOLS OF
BRITISH COLUMBIA'S
CENTURY OF PROGRESS

BRITISH COLUMBIA'S
FIRST PERMANENT BANK
1887

Bank of Montreal
Canada's First Bank
FOUNDED IN 1817

(*above*) This photo of the Vancouver Main Branch shows a bustling workplace. The location was at the heart of the Bank of Montreal's expansion in British Columbia. 1952. Steffens Colmer Ltd, Vancouver.

(*opposite*) This advertisement, part of the Bank of Montreal's "Canada's First Bank" slogan series, celebrates British Columbia's "Century of Progress" (1858–1958). While the depiction of a "twentieth-century totem" is considered culturally insensitive today, it reflected attitudes of the time. The totem portrays logging, mining, fishing, and other industries that crucially contributed to British Columbia's – and Canada's – economic development in the preceding century. At the totem's foundation is the Bank of Montreal, which first permanently established itself in British Columbia in 1887. 1950.

AGAMEMNON M. McMUMMY (Archaeology '53)

says: *"The longer you can keep something, the more interest it gains."*

... The same thing happens to your money

in "MY BANK"

BANK OF MONTREAL
Canada's First Bank

WORKING WITH CANADIANS IN EVERY WALK OF LIFE SINCE 1817
U2-52

This advertisement was part of a series designed for university student newspapers by Doug Wright . It focuses on archaeology and reads: "The longer you can keep something, the more interest it gains." with the tagline ... The same thing happens to your money in My Bank [Bank of Montreal]. ca. 1953.

This advertisement highlights the benefits of Bank of Montreal's branch banking system, which kept the big national bank very local- and community-oriented. "We try to keep constantly in mind that the Bank is not primarily an impressive row of figures or an imposing building," the ad reads. "We think rather of the Bank as the local manager and his staff, on whom our customers can always call for friendly counsel and service. Our branch banking system is founded upon this relationship." 1953.

The Bank of Montreal booth in the Queen Elizabeth Building at the 1956 Canadian National Exhibition in Toronto. Here, a visitor operates a question box that, when buttons are pressed, flashes answers about a new Bank of Montreal product: home-improvement loans. 1956. Bridgens Ltd.

Sous la bonne terre du Québec

un trésor illimité !

QUÉBEC. Ses forêts sont une verdoyante splendeur. De gras troupeaux laitiers y paissent de fertiles pâturages. Les lacs abondent en poisson et le flot pressé des rivières déborde d'énergie.

Et au coeur profond de la bonne terre du Québec repose un trésor — vastes et éblouissants gisements de richesses minérales !

Au nord, à l'est, au sud et à l'ouest, les mines du Québec donnent rapidement les minéraux essentiels à la prospérité de la Province et à la sécurité du Canada. Minerai de fer de l'Ungava... cuivre de la région de Rouyn... plomb et zinc dans l'Île de Colomb... or dans la partie occidentale... amiante, argent, mica, oxyde de titane.

La bonne vieille terre du Québec recèle des trésors tels que, même avec 80 p. 100 de son territoire encore inexploré, avec un potentiel minier à peine entamé, le Québec émerge rapidement comme le nouveau géant industriel du Canada.

AU SERVICE DU QUÉBEC DEPUIS 140 ANNÉES...

Depuis qu'elle a ouvert son premier petit bureau, rue St-Paul, à Montréal, le 3 novembre 1817 et sa première succursale à Québec, deux semaines plus tard, la Banque de Montréal a joué son rôle dans le développement et la prospérité de la Province, en offrant ses services partout où le besoin d'une banque se faisait sentir. Aujourd'hui, la B de M met au service du Québec pas moins de 134 succursales installées aux endroits stratégiques. De son imposant siège social au coeur du district financier de Montréal, à sa modeste succursale de Sept-Iles — le premier bureau de banque régulier au seuil de l'Ungava — la Banque de Montréal continue de travailler avec la population du Québec... pionnière auprès des pionniers... soutien des établissements plus anciens... collaboratrice de tous et partout pour la grandeur du Québec de demain.

BANQUE DE MONTRÉAL

La Première Banque au Canada

AU SERVICE DES CANADIENS DANS TOUTES LES SPHÈRES DE LA VIE DEPUIS 1817

This French-language advertisement of the 1950s highlights the enormous resources and potential of the province of Quebec, and situates the Bank of Montreal as the best-positioned institution to help the Québécois develop this potential. 1957.

The Bank of Montreal is a truly national bank, with branches from sea to sea to sea. Here, two men stand in front of a Bank of Montreal building in the Canadian Arctic. 1960. ©Library and Archives Canada. Reproduced with the permission of Library and Archives Canada.Library and Archives Canada/Credit: Rosemary Gilliat Eaton/Rosemary Gilliat Eaton fonds/e010799974.

A man is setting up a Bank of Montreal sign in the Canadian Arctic. 1960. ©Library and Archives Canada. Reproduced with the permission of Library and Archives Canada. Library and Archives Canada/Credit: Rosemary Gilliat Eaton/Rosemary Gilliat Eaton fonds/ e010799987.

Many of Canada's most senior business and political leaders attended the opening of the Bank of Montreal's new head office building in December 1960. Pictured here, from left to right, are: BMO president G. Arnold Hart, Montreal mayor Jean Drapeau, Quebec premier Jean Lesage, and postmaster general William McLean Hamilton. 1960. Canada Wide Photo.

This staged photograph was taken for the Bank's *Staff Magazine* to promote the Bank of Montreal's new technologies, including cheque encoders and the GENIE machine. Shown is Joan Walker encoding cheques on one of the new machines. 1962. Graetz Bros. Ltd.

In the 1960s, the Bank of Montreal considerably expanded its California operations. This photograph was taken at the opening of the Los Angeles office. Pictured, from left to right, are: Malcolm Allan, president of Bank of Montreal (California); J.L. Walker; Harold S. Foley; Frank Southee, senior V-P Bank of Montreal (California); G. Arnold Hart; and George Patterson, Canadian consul general in Los Angeles George Patterson. 1963.

Newfoundland premier Joey Smallwood delivers a speech at the opening of the new premises for BMO's Corner Brook Branch. Seated behind him, from left to right, are: Thomas R. Francis, general manager for the Atlantic provinces; F. John Edwards, branch manager; J. Leonard Walker, general manager of the Bank of Montreal, and W.J. Lundrigan, contractor for the building. 1965.

oil AND
gas
MAP OF CANADA

OIL FIELDS

GAS FIELDS

PIPE LINES

REFINERIES

CANADA'S FIRST BANK

Covers Canada...Spans the World

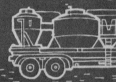

BANK OF MONTREAL
OIL AND GAS DEPARTMENT
CALGARY, ALBERTA

(*above*) This image, published in *Staff Magazine*, shows the Bank of Montreal's float at Charlottetown's Gold Cup and Saucer Parade. Standing on the float, promoting the Bank's new Bancardchek, are Maureen Callaghan (*left*) and Sharon Butler (*right*). 1968.

(*opposite*) The Bank of Montreal made serious efforts to dramatically expand its operations in western Canada starting in the 1960s. This advertisement, created by the Bank's Oil and Gas Department in Calgary, Alberta, highlights the rich natural resources of that province and the tremendous opportunities for economic development they represent. 1966–67.

(*above*) When the Bank of Montreal and the Bank of London and South America ended their BOLAM partnership in 1970, the Bank of Montreal retained former BOLAM operations in Jamaica and The Bahamas. Shown here is one such rebranded location in Kingston, Jamaica. 1971. Raymond Ryder Photographer, Quebec.

(*opposite*) This image, from the Bank's 1968 Annual Report, shows the enormous growth in senior leadership. Membership would be reduced in later years. 1968.

(*above*) "Instabank ... The little bank that's always open." With these words, the Bank of Montreal announced Instabank in the 1974 Annual Report, with terminals to be rolled out on a trial basis in 1975. "Instabank is an unmanned banking station which does almost everything a full branch can do ... it can perform up to 98% of all basic banking transactions at any time of the day or night," the Annual Report explained. 1974.

(*opposite*) This image from the 1975 Annual Report shows three generations of chief executive officers, from left to right: G. Arnold Hart (CEO 1959–74), W.D. Mulholland (CEO 1979–89), and Fred McNeil (CEO 1974–79). 1975.

(*above*) Bank of Montreal president W.D. Mulholland with Mexican president José López Portillo and Mexican officials at the official signing of the 1980 loan agreement. 1980. (*opposite*) The MECH program introduced many new machines and computers into Bank of Montreal branches in the 1970s. This image, published in the Bank's *Concordia* magazine in 1976, shows Cora Trimm, a teller at the Bank of Montreal's Front and Yonge branch, operating a new terminal. 1976.

Photograph of W.D. Mulholland and Fred McNeil watching a military parade in Mexico City from a balcony high above reviewing stands at the edge of the road. (Undated, but likely taken at the directors' meeting in 1981.)

Technological investments also made possible the introduction of such innovations as daily interest savings accounts – with the Bank of Montreal being the first of the major chartered banks to introduce the service in August 1979. As suggested in its Annual Report that year, "to our minds, the introduction of our new technology is, in itself, one of the most fundamental and exciting changes we have ever made in our banking operations."[96]

The Early Results

Under Mulholland's leadership, change at the Bank of Montreal unfolded rapidly. "In less than five years," a feature article on him in *Canadian Business* enthused, "Mulholland has transformed Canada's First Bank, turning from what one analyst described as 'the worst-performing bank since the 1967 Bank Act' into a lean, innovative organization, whose earnings and asset growth are the envy of the industry." The writer went on to say that it was likely "one of the quickest, most impressive turnarounds in the history of Canadian banking."[97]

It was indeed a quick and remarkable turnaround. Assets grew from $17.6 billion in 1974 to $27.6 billion by mid-1978. Mulholland used the growth in assets not only to indicate that things were on track but also to stimulate executives into realizing "the pace at which this organization has to change to accommodate it."[98] The rate of change suggested that within a few years, a $30-billion bank would become a $60-billion bank. Mulholland insisted that this was the trajectory – and whatever the Bank needed in the way of management resources, systems, the whole apparatus would have to be ready.[99]

Mulholland's early success attracted more than the usual interest from other banks, including the Chase Manhattan, which had made overtures in mid-1978 to see if they could coax Mulholland onto American soil once again.[100]

Organizations in Time

The central priority of Mulholland's tenure was the complete reorganization of the bank "so it would behave less like a bureaucracy and more like a competitive business."[101] In the first year or two, Mulholland's plans included strengthening administration and finance divisions. He allowed greater autonomy to the divisions, while at the same time implementing more rigorous controls and information systems to gauge performance. New groups were established to supervise large corporate accounts. Commercial loans and banking were expanded and reorganized. The reforms were intended to strip out layers of bureaucracy so that the line officers in, for example, retail marketing, would be able to get the kind of staff, analytical, and marketing support they needed without waiting, in many cases, months and months for supplies and resources to arrive. "The result is," he told the press in 1978, "our guys are doing better – the same guys, mostly. They've got the tools to do the job. They don't have to go running for permission for every bloody paper clip they want to buy. And they don't have to process all their loans through head office."[102]

Another move involved a strong reorientation to the west, to Calgary, where vice-chairman Stan Davison was moved to head western operations. In addition, the Bank announced the construction of a $150-million twin-tower office and commercial complex in that city. These were signs of its commitment to Western Canada and, in part, its recognition, in the words of F.H. McNeil, that "the relative growth rates in Canada are shifting, most particularly in energy."[103]

The Context

In a nutshell, the Bank of the mid-1970s, as we have seen, was in need of a major transformation. As one internal document soberly put it:

> Profitability was low. Liability management was nonexistent and there were money market and foreign exchange problems. The Bank had undertaken a major expansion in computerizing its network of 1,300 branches and this had proven extremely costly. The Bank's stock price was depressed, and its market share of personal deposits was lower than it had been for years. The Bank could not identify which branches or services were profitable. Turnover among clerical personnel exceeded fifty percent, management trainee turnover was in the 40 to 50 percent range, and management turnover was fifteen to seventeen percent.[104]

To Mulholland, many of these problems stemmed from the Bank's structure, which in the mid-1970s was still oriented around geography. This had made sense in the nineteenth century, when operations were spread from the Atlantic to the Pacific and cross-country communication was slow. As the Bank expanded internationally, the same approach held, with segregation between domestic banking and international banking. The type of customer (e.g., individuals, small- and medium-sized companies, and large corporate businesses) was not factored into the structure. As a result, the Bank could not easily respond to specialized markets and, for the sake of geographic consistency, could only offer a relatively small number of products and services. McKinsey & Company had pointedly raised the latter in the late 1960s as a particular problem hurting the Bank of Montreal's competitiveness.[105]

As we've seen, Mulholland had three aims with the restructuring: to enable the Bank to better compete in the Canadian market, to make it more agile in an increasingly global and competitive world, and to set it on a course toward increased foreign expansion. A special committee, appointed in 1976, advised that the best way to address the Bank's problems was to split its retail and commercial divisions, allowing each segment to provide the best service possible to its clientele. Mulholland, however, did not think the Bank was ready for such a major move. Instead, he proceeded piecemeal, making relatively smaller changes over the next five years to get the Bank of Montreal ready for the larger split between retail and commercial.

The first step in Mulholland's make-over program came in 1976, when the Corporate Banking Group was established. It served large national and international companies within Canada.[106] Instead of making the national/international division, the Bank now had a department that dealt with a specific type of customer, and could therefore meet that customer's needs more quickly and efficiently. Next, Mulholland established a globally integrated treasury function, whose job it was to manage cash, assets, and liabilities for the Bank as a whole. "By 1982," one internal document reported, "the Treasury Division had developed to the point where the Bank reconciled global positions daily, maintained a 22-hour a day active dealing capability, and monitored open positions on a 24-hour basis."[107] In 1984, Grant Reuber could report that "we have according to an independent survey, perhaps the best Treasury operations of any bank in Canada. In operating capability, we are, some say, the best of any bank in Canada. We are the only bank with a complete operating capacity in both Canada and the US. We have the highest level of liquidity in recent memory – enough in fact to support a very large growth in loans without impairing our capital ratios."[108]

Mulholland then established the Domestic Operations and Systems Division, a worldwide integrated, electronic data processing department. Building on the technology developed as part of MECH, this department increased the speed of processing and increased managerial control by providing a clear overview of the financial well-being of the bank in near-real time. By 1982, the entire domestic network was active and online, linking eight regional data centres and over 5,000 branch terminals, ATMs, and customer terminals with two central computing centres.[109]

With this degree of managerial oversight and control, Mulholland was now ready to tackle larger organizational problems.[110] In 1981, he created the World Corporate Banking Group, serving large international clients, multinational corporations, foreign governments, and foreign banks. The new group had a worldwide network of accountants and managers located in important financial centres around the world, allowing the Bank to respond to local needs.[111] Meanwhile, the Canadian Corporate Banking Group established in 1976 had its mandate expanded to include the United States, creating a base for a large, North American banking structure. This structure laid the foundation of a truly North American bank, something the Bank of Montreal would truly achieve when it acquired Harris Bank in 1984. As Professor James C. Rush put it, "the Bank was no longer a Canadian bank with some international operations. It was an international bank with a Canadian base."[112] That was hyperbolic, but it certainly fit the Mulholland narrative.

With the realignments between 1976 and 1981, Mulholland sought to "achieve three objectives: a focus on principal market segments, improved opportunities for the professional development of officers and staff, and improvement in the quality of service."[113] With these changes made and objectives achieved, Mulholland and his team believed the Bank was primed for the next big step: the Domestic Development Program.

Domestic Development Program (DDP)

By 1982, Mulholland felt that the Bank was ready to accept the original recommendation made by the special committee in 1976 and split the Domestic Banking Group in two: retail and commercial. It turned out to be one of the most controversial decisions of the Mulholland era.

The Domestic Banking Group was the largest, most important component of the Bank of Montreal's business, comprising over 1,300 branches across Canada and providing daily banking services to millions of Canadians. The branches, moreover, provided "transaction processing and other services to the other bank Groups; the Treasury Group, Corporate and Government Banking, and International Banking."[114] Over an eighteen-month period, the Domestic Banking Group was fully split into two separate functions: retail (now called Domestic Banking) and commercial (now called Commercial Banking). This affected the jobs of 20,000 employees, involved the physical reorganization of most of the bank's Canadian branches, and required massive organizational and administrative support.[115]

The goal of the Domestic Development Program was to allow the Bank of Montreal to compete in the Canadian market, make it more agile in an increasingly global and competitive world, and set in on the course towards increased growth and expansion, both foreign and domestic. After some initial hiccups and transitional pains, customer satisfaction was up by 1986, and some parts of the Bank's network reported increasing their business by substantial margins.

The retail branches, now labelled the Domestic Banking Group, ran the existing branches and provided daily banking services to Canadians across the country.[116] The new Commercial Banking Group was henceforth responsible for serving the Bank's "independent and mid-sized business and agricultural enterprises, offering commercial credit and non-credit services."[117] The new departments were physically separated. If they existed within the same branch – as was often the case – walls separated them.[118] In addition to these shared branches, the Commercial Banking Group also operated a "new coast-to-coast network of 98 Commercial Banking Units (CBUs)," which were solely devoted to serving commercial clients and offered no retail banking services.[119]

Executives at the Bank of Montreal hoped that this new, segregated set-up, approved by Mulholland in late 1982, and division of labour would "increase market share and profitability by giving the Bank of Montreal a competitive advantage over other banks which were still operating under the old comprehensive branch banking system."[120] So convinced were they of its merits, they wasted no time, approving implementation starting 1 November 1982. It was hoped that it would take no more than two years to change over the banking structure in its entirety.

Transitioning Employees and Customers

Given the scale and size of the changes, the Bank of Montreal took extra effort in guiding its staff and customers through the process. The bank printed booklets that informed its customers of exactly what they could expect:

> For Personal Banking Customers:
> There will be no change in the way they do their day-to-day banking at their Bank of Montreal branch except a perceptible improvement in the degree of professional banking service and advice they will receive from customer service personnel and the manager. The managers, freed from the tasks of commercial banking and personal lending, will have more time to devote to personal banking customers. Personal loans will be handled through a personal lending officer, located in the branch or nearby.

> For Commercial Customers:
> With specialist account managers handling their account, business and agricultural customers can look to increased expertise by the Bank in the handling of their banking business, from the point of view of credit services and non-credit services such as cash management. Freed from the day-to-day branch activities, commercial account managers now have more time to manage and to advise clients.[121]

For its own staff, the Bank took an original approach to coaching and development. In 1982, the Bank released a cartoon entitled "Domestic Development Man." The cartoon was about a fictional branch in Smalltown, Canada.

Each page featured an episode where a customer was unhappy with the service he or she received. Domestic Development Man then came to the rescue, explaining to the staff how the new DDP was designed to help them navigate and solve these problems. "These materials were well received by bank personnel although some managers complained that Domestic Development Man was inconsistent with the conservative image of the bank."[122]

Results May Vary

The goal of the DDP was to improve the Bank of Montreal's market position among stiff competition and to make the Bank more agile and responsive to changing trends. The retailing branches were reorganized to be able to respond better to customer service needs, while the more commercial functions were transferred to the relevant business units.[123] The initial results were promising: the Atlantic Region saw a massive spike in new loan business, rising from $500,000 before the DDP to over $7,000,000 in 1985.[124] While this was the best result nationally, other regions also experienced progress.[125]

As can be expected with an endeavour of this magnitude, though, there were a few glitches, and the Customer Test of Service confirmed that the initial implementation of DDP had a "negative impact on customers' perception of branch service."[126] Indeed, as the Domestic Development Man cartoon alluded to, there was plenty of opportunity for confusion and misunderstanding between staff and customers. However, it appears that things soon smoothed out and that the dip in customer satisfaction was temporary; satisfaction levels soon rose beyond pre-DDP levels.[127]

The Commercial Banking Division experienced more growing pains. Part of the problem was that small- and medium-sized businesses were transferred to a division that hitherto was used to dealing only with large commercial clients. The commercial bankers did not have the experience or knowledge to handle high-volume (and relatively low-value) transactions. Furthermore, the Domestic Banking Division, now isolated from colleagues in commercial banking, often forgot about this component of the business and did not think to refer potential commercial business to the CBUs. Finally, as the DDP coincided with an economic downturn, the CBUs were concerned from the outset about the quality of their commercial loans. Account managers spent more of their time worrying about their existing loans, turning their attention inward rather than toward developing new business. As a result, as one internal memo conceded, "the Bank's share of the commercial loan volume market continued to drop throughout the DDP conversion period and for some time thereafter. As a consequence of the resulting pressures, many employees in the Commercial Banking Division were very concerned about their performance and their future in the Bank."[128]

Although things reportedly became more stable in the late-1980s, as economic conditions in both Canada and the United States improved, the fabled results of increased profitability and market share promised by the DDP remained ambiguous. (Ultimately, however, the results of the DDP were deemed so disappointing that Mulholland's successor, Matthew Barrett, reversed many of the changes virtually as his first act as CEO.)

The DDP represented the kind of major surgery that the Mulholland team felt unavoidable from a cultural and organizational perspective. It worked in the sense that layers of non-performing management were washed away. But it is also fair to say that the entire program was detested at the branch and operations level. The unintended side effects were major. One legacy of the DDP was internal rivalry – frankly, retail against commercial. As one Mulholland-era banker recounts: "the competition bec[a]me internal, whereas the competition, folks is across the street right? But these decisions that we made [rendered] the competition internal, [and] broke up the concept of a functioning team."[129]

Other observers broadly concurred. The separation of personal and commercial banking meant separate organization of processes and functions – systems and credit, to name two. One of the biggest faults of the reforms was the difficulty in servicing small independent businesses: "The independent business sector, small business sector, a lot of the dealings that these business people undertake are prettÆy much intertwined with their individual dealings. They're very much coupled. And they were used to dealing with the branch manager on both sides of the ledger, if you want. And that was a fundamental error in structuring this thing and setting it up. So you had an error on where that market should have been placed and then you had all the difficulties that for sure went into the execution of the thing."[130] The lack of coordination between personal and commercial banking was the biggest challenge. When the DDP divided personal and commercial, "they didn't make it in the best interests of the individual to actually coordinate with each other in order to make it happen, so the franchise dried up on commercial because where do small businesses go? They go to branches. Branches didn't care about that. They were only interested in their personal business."[131]

Communication across retail and commercial was virtually non-existent. Regrettably, the problem was recognized, but as one executive lamented, "we had no will or no way, maybe no desire at that time to actually do anything about it, right? ... We were still caught up in this, 'Where do we make the money?' thing, right? ... And then ... it became a productivity nightmare, okay? Because everybody wanted to win this game now, right? ... We're trying to make all these investments and it's always a money game, right?"[132]

One of the key ways "to win ... a money game" without growing is to cut expenses. As a DDP veteran acknowledged: "And we would cut expense ... oh, man. We had rightsizing. We had downsizing. We had reengineering. You know, as an area manager, once I had 32 severance packages in my desk drawer. I was waiting every day for someone to phone me and tell me how many people I could fire. And it wasn't a matter of whether I can afford to fire the people, it was a matter of we have to take the costs out because we want to be – we want to win this thing. We want to be the most efficient line of business."[133]

The consequences of that unintended policy outcome affected recruiting and reputation. At that moment, recalls one regional manager, "we were probably the furthest thing from an employer of choice, and that was the other side of our responsibilities, of course. When you manage anything, you're responsible for getting those critical jobs staffed so you can make the money so you can show return to shareholders, etc., etc."[134] He concluded that they were "terrible times – and the reputation – our reputational risk was, you had to be so careful how you – or tried to. We were trying to manage the reputation risk of the bank on our own, individuals, you know?"[135]

The DDP was a key initiative of the Mulholland era: ambitious, far-reaching, and necessary. However, its design flaws and its execution rendered an ambiguous legacy. That said, in the long term, even if it was a blunt instrument, the program produced some positive results. But it simply went against the natural weave of the organization. It produced its share of dysfunction and more than its share of resentment. By the late 1980s, it had become a liability and a distraction.

The Bank in the Public Sphere

The Bank of Montreal's presence in the public sphere in the 1970s and 1980s involved several important interventions on everything from regulatory matters and the Bank Act to the social, political, and economic issues facing the Canadian polity. In an era of inflationary pressures, high interest rates, stalled growth, recession, controversial public policy over energy and oil pricing, and the threat of Quebec secession from Canada, there was no shortage of issues to handle. Indeed, the Bank Act was the least of the industry's worries.

A new Bank Act was passed in 1980, after an extension of the older Act in 1977. The Canadian banking picture was expected to "change substantially" with the entry of new banks as a result of the conversion of foreign bank subsidiaries to chartered institutions. As the *Globe and Mail* reported in December 1980: "Passage of the new Bank Act will remove the uncertainty that has been hanging over the banks since 1976 and should help their profit grow by about 20 per cent in fiscal 1981 ... The Bank Act will be positive because it will increase the bank's financing flexibility ... They will be able to offer convertible preferred shares and convertible debentures, and to offer debentures in foreign currencies."[136]

The Bank's 1982 appearance at the hearings on bank profits before the House of Commons Standing Committee on Finance, Trade, and Economic Affairs on 3 June 1982 offers a glimpse of where Mulholland positioned the Bank of Montreal in the midst of the challenges facing Canada in various sectors.

Mulholland faced questions about the Bank of Montreal's priorities, preference for big business, and inconsideration toward consumers and farmers. On the thorny question of consumer lending, Mulholland highlighted the balancing act that the Bank had to perform, both allowing liberal lending policies to encourage growth and investment, while at the same time not putting customers in potentially precarious financial situations. He insisted that the Bank had offered "flexible financing arrangements, such as consolidation of outstanding debt and rescheduling, so that the payment schedule does not hamper ... cash flow."[137]

When asked what BMO was doing to help customers who faced the possibility of defaulting on their mortgages, Mulholland answered that BMO was helping them obtain the benefits of the Canada Mortgage Renewal Plan, which offered subsidies of up to $250 for people who had to pay more than 30 per cent of their income on debt servicing. Between the introduction of this program in September 1981 and the testimony (in June 1982), BMO renewed 20,000 mortgages, and only thirty-four people had applied for assistance under the government program.[138]

Mulholland emphasized that BMO reviewed difficult mortgages that did not qualify for the Mortgage Renewal Plan on a case-by-case basis, offering a variety of options to provide debt relief, including interest deferrals, acceptance of interest-only payments, extended amortization periods, and special counselling. Finally, Mulholland emphasized that BMO was the only of the Big Five to offer the full range of standard mortgage options, from one-year open to five-year closed.[139]

The same charge of inconsideration was levied against BMO vis-à-vis Canada's farmers. Farms had been hit especially hard by the economic downturn of the early 1980s. Mulholland once again took the occasion to talk about some of the things that the Bank had done to help farmers, both nationally and in Ontario, including creating special credit review committees and participating in the Ontario Farm Adjustment Assistance Programme (OFAAP) to ease credit. The OFAAP was a $60-million program created by the Canadian Bankers Association and the Ontario Department of Agriculture to help farmers obtain the maximum credits and benefits to which they were entitled. Mulholland further noted that the Bank also placed special emphasis on being informed about all aspects of farming and the agricultural industry. It had created regional advisory panels consisting of farmers to get the straight story from those on the front line, and had hired fourteen agrologists internally to provide specialist advice. By June 1982, these teams had worked with seventy accounts comprising about $55 million in loans.[140]

BMO's historic preference for large, corporate businesses was also questioned. When asked about the differential rates between loans for small business and large businesses, Mulholland explained that this difference was due to administrative costs: "The Bank of Montreal charges, on average, about one percent more on its loans to small business than on those to large corporations. This premium is attributable to the higher credit risk associated with the average small business, as well as to higher administrative costs. It does not, however, fully cover the extra costs we incur. We make less on a small business loan than we do on a loan to a large corporation."[141]

Mulholland further underscored the Bank's commitment to small business by highlighting its publication of "Small Business Problem Solver" booklets (producing roughly 200,000 in 1982) to provide small businesses with advice.[142]

When asked about the size and power of Canada's chartered banks, Mulholland predictably did not think Canadian banks were too big or too powerful. He underscored that the Bank of Montreal competed with between 50 and 200 major competitors in various markets and argued that large Canadian banks remained large precisely because they had first-rate reputations and offered reliability and service that smaller competitors could not match. The Big Five made use of "economies of scale" which, according to Mulholland (and, later, economists studying the era), served the Canadian banking industry (among the stronger in the world) well.

Mulholland also stressed the fact that BMO (and other Canadian banks) were obligated to keep statutory reserves at the Bank of Canada. As of 1982, reserves were in the order of $7 billion for the Canadian banking industry. Assuming a prime of 17 per cent, this represented an earnings loss of $1.2 billion for the Canadian banking industry (compared to total earnings of $1.7 billion).[143]

Foreign Lending Policies

At the hearings, Mulholland was also asked about the Bank's policies regarding foreign lending, especially in South Africa and Chile. Although the apartheid regime of institutionalized racism in South Africa had been in place since 1948, by the late-1970s calls for a boycott of South Africa and for banks to cease investments in the country grew louder and louder. In Chile, the overthrow of the Allende regime in 1973 and the installation of a military dictatorship under Augusto Pinochet likewise raised questions about the morality of continued investment in the country. Mulholland underscored that when issuing foreign loans, the Bank took ethical, political, social, and economic factors into consideration, and would not lend for purposes that would support repression in any form, including discriminatory racial policies or the purchase of arms.[144] This represented a public shift from earlier positions that permitted loans to South Africa and Chile. As recently as 1977, Fred McNeil had stated that he believed the Bank should not cease investments in either South Africa or Chile because this would be morally inconsistent, as "man's inhumanity to man is unhappily almost universal."[145] It was yet another sign of how much BMO had changed under the leadership of Mulholland.

The Bank of Montreal in Quebec

On sensitive topics much closer to home, the Bank of Montreal, as a Montreal institution, was asked to express itself on the issue of Quebec sovereignty, something which often seemed akin to touching the electrified third rail in a subway system. While the Bank's approach to the question of Quebec's secession from Canada was to not intervene officially in the public square, there were a few exceptions. On 20 May 1980, as the results of the referendum in Quebec rolled in and it became clear that the federalist option would prevail, Mulholland expressed relief at the outcome, suggesting that Quebec had "chosen wisely." He elaborated by saying that the outcome of the referendum provided a beginning and a foundation for a discussion about "a stronger, more united, and more rewarding Canada."[146]

On the more fraught question of the move of head office functions from Montreal to Toronto, the Bank chose to emphasize the westward trend of economic development. Fred McNeil emphasized this line in 1979 in an important speech in Edmonton on the matter. Soon after, in November, Mulholland argued that technological innovation allowed BMO to "decentralize" and keep in touch with local markets more effectively. As he put it, technological innovations had allowed BMO "to defy the law of corporate gravity ... a law that seems to have been formulated jointly by Newton and Kafka. The law states that the larger the corporation, the greater its mass, the stronger its attraction to the center."[147] Technological innovation, however, had allowed BMO to have "substantial management headquarters" in Montreal, London (European division), and Singapore (Asian division). These offices had a substantial degree of authority and responsibility, but computers allowed head office to "keep pretty good track of what's going on [and allowed it to] intervene."[148]

Mulholland's remarks at the 162nd Annual Meeting in Montreal on 14 January 1980 more directly addressed what might happen to BMO headquarters if the Quebec referendum of 1980 resulted in secession from Canada. He noted that the law required the head office to be located in Canada.[149] More unambiguously, he concluded that "we are proud to bear the name of Canada's fairest city – Montreal. We are grateful for its 162 years of gracious hospitality and we hope to enjoy many more. We are in Montreal because we choose to be, not because we have to be. However, this institution belongs to Canada, and it supports, unreservedly, a united Canada."[150]

The fact was, however, that the Montreal connection of the Bank of Montreal was proving to be a growing reputational hazard. Therefore, in the late 1970s, the Bank had begun to move a number of departments to Toronto and, with them, executive office jobs.[151] The other regrettable fact was that, by the late 1970s, potential Bank of Montreal bankers did not want to move to Montreal for a variety of reasons.[152]

By the early 1980s, the relocation of the head office, at least unofficially, concluded with the move of the CEO and chair to Toronto. As one francophone banker observed:

Well that moved quite rapidly with some stealth if you want. But he couldn't move ... you know, initially they say, "Well yes, I'm going there because we have all these operations in Toronto. It's now becoming the centre of business, whatnot, but I still have my office down here." And he did come once a week initially and as they all did initially for, you know, six months, whatever, then after that it doesn't make any sense. I mean, they've got so much to do, they can't say, "Well today is my day in Montreal and I do all my operations from Montreal but I'm on the phone in Toronto." Or whatever. So you play that made-up game for a while, make believe, and then, actually, gradually, you just don't do it anymore.[153]

The westward movement of head offices in the 1970s – from Montreal to Toronto, principally – was partly the result of Quebec's political environment and partly the attraction of Toronto itself, which had reached an undisputed status as the financial capital of the country. Some institutions, like Sun Life, either chose or were compelled to move formally, officially, and irrevocably, while others preferred a less pyrotechnic solution.

The Economic State We're In

The deteriorating economy of the late 1970s and early 1980s and a turbulent international political economy provided a troubling backdrop for the conduct of banking. It also drew Mulholland more and more into the public policy sphere. In response to the worsening economic conditions, both McNeil and Mulholland outlined what Canada could do to weather the storm. Both underscored the importance of developing Canada's natural resources, for which they called the potential "second to none." In an address to the Canadian Club in Montreal in April 1980, Mulholland put it as follows:

> I believe that there is a promising approach to mitigating the negative effects of international economic pressures on our economy. Canada stands on the verge of a series of major developments which will permit us to recover our economic momentum through the eighties. To what projects do I refer? Most of them are well known to you. We have already done much of the planning for full-scale development of the oil sands, for heavy oil, for the gas pipeline, for the oil pipeline, for the Lower Churchill Falls, for the east of Montreal gas pipeline, and for a succession of further developments in the James Bay region. This package might be called a Resources Independence Program for the Eighties. It invites the acronym R-I-P-E, RIPE.[154]

Indeed, the Bank championed the energy sector as a way out of Canada's economic malaise, and also a way to secure Canada's energy independence. As Fred McNeil told the annual meeting audience in 1980, "Canada must be among the most fortunate of developed countries. We have enough conventional oil resources to give us the time to develop [a] new supply from our unconventional sources – the oil sands, the heavy oil deposits and frontier development. But this can only be done provided Canada's domestic oil prices are allowed to escalate quickly to, at a minimum, the Chicago price level, and ultimately to the world level."[155]

The Bank's leadership throughout the late 1970s and early 1980s argued for a more defined industrial policy in other areas as well, including the mineral industry. The theme was consistent, with Mulholland and McNeil arguing that Canada needed to take the lead in responsibly developing its resources as a key aspect of its economic growth and development.

In Mulholland's view, a mineral industry policy had become even more critical in light of geopolitical developments in the late-1970s, referring to the Iranian Revolution (January 1979) and the Soviet invasion of Afghanistan (December 1979). As he put it:

> Security considerations become extremely significant in the North American context if current international tensions give further isolationist tinge to a potential American consensus centered around

increased military spending and increased protection for American industry. If the postwar trend toward trade liberalization should be interrupted by renewed protectionism, or neo-mercantilism as it is called, Canada will be forced into the only trade bloc which geography has bestowed on her: a north American common market. I am not advocating such a development. I simply suggest that these possibilities underline the importance of our dealing from whatever strengths we possess. One of these strengths we possess is mineral resources. We need a mineral industrial policy to ensure that we have the fullest possible knowledge of the extent of these resources and that we have in the private sector companies who can bring them on stream with minimal lead times at competitive prices.[156]

The Bank's interventions in the public square throughout the late 1970s and the 1980s were generally meant not only to advocate for the Bank's own interests but also to provide elements of leadership on specific questions of national economic development. In tone and substance, those interventions generally stayed within the prescribed lines – a sensible approach, considering the traditional suspicion with which large sections of the public perceived the Canadian chartered banks.

A Historic Acquisition

In 1986, the Bank established a new Capital Markets Group with offices in London, Sydney, Singapore, Toronto, Tokyo, and New York, but its big move into capital markets came in 1987.[157] In August of that year, late in the term of the Mulholland ascendancy, the Bank of Montreal announced that it had acquired Nesbitt Thomson Corp. Inc., Canada's fifth-largest brokerage firm.[158] The purchase was made possible by regulatory reforms to the Bank Act earlier that year, which allowed banks for the first time to purchase investment houses. The deal was historic: the Bank of Montreal was the first Canadian bank to purchase a Canadian brokerage firm, putting it ahead of its competitors and positioning it to deliver new services across the country.[159]

On 12 August 1987, the Bank of Montreal signed an agreement with the shareholders of Nesbitt Thomson wherein the Bank, through its wholly owned subsidiary Bank of Montreal Securities Canada Limited, would take over Nesbitt Thomson by purchasing the brokerage firm's shares for $22 per share.[160] The offer was good for about six weeks – until 29 September. At that point, the Bank announced that it had obtained "12,104,437 Class A Shares tendered under the Offer, representing approximately 99% of the Class A shares outstanding."[161] It obtained the remaining Class A shares by

December of that year. In the end, the Bank of Montreal paid approximately $292.4 million for a 75 per cent stake in the company, with Nesbitt Thomson's employees holding the remaining 25 per cent.[162]

The BMO-Nesbitt Thomson deal was made possible by changes to the Bank Act and to Ontario legislation, which together "effectively eliminated the Canadian equivalent of the US Glass-Steagall Act, which had previously kept banks out of much of the securities business."[163] The revisions were Canada's response to the waves of deregulation washing over the financial world in the 1980s, and the changing trends in the international financial markets. Increasingly, large companies would use market borrowing (the issuing of debt and equity), instead of bank lending, to raise funds. This kept banks from competing in a large and growing market segment, but at the same time, securities dealers were not always able to generate the large amounts of money needed for these transactions.[164] As an internal briefing note put it, these legislative constraints limited the Bank of Montreal and other Canadian banks: "Banks had the capital necessary to underwrite large corporate deals but were prohibited by law from doing so in Canada; investment houses had the expertise and distribution networks but lacked the capital to compete with large international players. The net result was loss of business for the Canadian financial industry, as large Canadian issuers and investors alike turned to offshore merchant and investment banks to satisfy their needs."[165]

The Federal and Ontario governments responded to these concerns by deregulating the industry, allowing "banks, trusts, investment houses and insurance companies to participate in financial activities formerly exclusive to each."[166] The legislation was introduced on 30 June 1987 and was to take complete effect exactly a year later. As a result of the legislative changes, the major Canadian chartered banks went on an acquisition frenzy. In addition to the Bank of Montreal acquiring Nesbitt Thomson, the Canadian Imperial Bank of Commerce took over Wood Gundy, the Bank of Nova Scotia acquired McLeod Young Weir, Toronto-Dominion took ownership of Gardiner Group, and the Royal Bank of Canada obtained a share of Dominion Securities.[167,168] In all, Canada's largest chartered banks bought five of the Big Eight investment companies between 1987 and 1988.[169]

The 1987 deregulation finally allowed Canadian banks to more fully compete with foreign banks, whose entry into the Canadian marketplace had been made easier by revisions to the Bank Act in 1980.[170] Mulholland praised the deregulated financial environment, claiming that the 1987 legislative changes were a milestone in the history of the Bank of Montreal: "'By establishing this relationship with a mature, respected securities firm with first class leadership and professional talent, and an excellent track record, we have,' said Mr Mulholland, 'added significantly to the Bank's capacity to provide immediately a broader range of services to our existing customers."[171] Mulholland further observed that by the mid-1980s, it had "'become apparent that, with the opening of the Canadian market to foreign-based financial institutions, Canadian firms and especially the chartered banks would be required to act, not only to secure their competitive position at home but also to strengthen their capacity to fulfill their traditional role of supporting Canadian commercial and trading interests in the United States and elsewhere in the world."[172]

Nesbitt Thomson's chairman, Jon Brian Aune, echoed Mulholland's sentiment: "With the Canadian market being entered by very large, well-capitalized, foreign securities firms, we felt it important ... to prepare ourselves to meet their powerful competition. In the circumstance, we regarded the reinforcement of our capital base as absolutely essential. After considering various alternatives, we concluded that an alliance with a major Canadian chartered bank made the most sense for us. The exploratory talks that were initiated with the Bank of Montreal led to serious negotiations with today's highly positive outcome."[173]

"Not Entering through the Back Door"

"The Bank of Montreal hasn't entered the brokerage business through the back door," journalist Philippe Dubuisson wrote in August 1987.[174] Indeed, the $292.4-million acquisition was a bold move, characteristic of the Bank of Montreal under Mulholland's leadership. At the time of the takeover, Nesbitt Thomson had "55 branches across Canada, in the United States, Germany, France, Switzerland, England, Argentina, and Venezuela ... employ[ed] over 2,000 people, of whom 650 [were] account executives, [and] ... ha[d] operated profitably in each of the 108 consecutive months end[ing] July 31, 1987."[175] Second only to the takeover of Harris Bankcorp, Inc. three years prior, the Nesbitt Thomson acquisition was significant, and a critical move for the future of the Bank of Montreal itself. William Bradford, deputy chairman of the Bank of Montreal, underscored this in an interview in 1987:

> I don't think there's any question [that we have an advantage over other chartered banks]. There isn't another chartered "A" bank in Canada today that will have a full-service securities operation, complete with corporate debt, corporate underwriting, corporate finance, mergers and acquisitions, private placements, all at their disposal on day one. Some will have a discount brokerage. Some of them will have made a modest entry into the corporate debt and equity underwriting field, but here is a firm of 600 professionals ready to work for Bank of Montreal

customers. I don't think that there's any question that we should be able to get a leg up on our competitors, in that respect.[176]

"Our customer base," he added in another interview later in the week, "includes large multinational corporations who require not only traditional banking services, but also the services of brokerage houses. To remain competitive on international markets, we have to position ourselves in such a way as to offer a full range of products and services to our clients. If we don't do it, others will do it in our place ... In the short run, the entry into the brokerage industry by the Bank of Montreal is a defense measure, aimed at protecting its business. In the longer term it forms part of an offensive strategy aimed at broadening the activities of this institution."[177]

Francophone Tensions

Not everyone was happy about the merger, or the way it was presented to the public. As the merger between two companies headquartered in Montreal, some French Canadians were unhappy that the major announcement of the merger was made in Toronto. Concerns were first raised by journalist Richard du Paul, and repeated by Jean-Guy Dubuc in an editorial for *La Presse,* where he angrily observed:

Thursday, an important business deal was announced: the Bank of Montreal, second largest in Canada [*sic*], took control [*sic*] of Nesbitt Thompson, Inc. [*sic*], fifth largest brokerage firm in the country. A "historic and mutually beneficial transaction," they said. Bravo! The financial earth moved. We know that the head offices of these two important institutions are located in Montreal. This permits the Bank of Montreal and Nesbitt Thompson [*sic*] to issue shares that can take advantage of the Quebec Stock Savings Plan. Nonetheless, this announcement of the deal between these two Montreal businesses was made at a news conference held exclusively in Toronto. Montreal journalists summoned to witness this "historic" event were gathered into a room on the second floor of the Bank of Montreal on Saint James Street, "with nothing more than a four-inch speaker as a link – one way – with Toronto, to listen to the proceedings..." ... When these Torontonians were asked why they elected to hold a news conference in Toronto rather than in Montreal, Deputy Chairman William E. Bradford, responded: "We didn't have time [to do otherwise]. It was easier for us to do it here..." ... There's the problem: not only do they ignore Montreal, but they also don't see the need to explain. Is it the widely-held attitude of superiority amongst the Toronto business community towards those in Montreal that moves them to act this way? Or is it the disdain held by some Anglophones for francophones, even in Montreal, which convinces them that the only white language is English?[178]

The Bank of Montreal was concerned about this reception in Quebec. Senior Vice-president Dick O'Hagan wrote to Chairman William E. Bradford shortly after the publication of the article, stating: "Unfortunately Editor Jean-Guy Dubuc chose to reiterate Mr du Paul's concerns on the editorial of today's *La Presse* ... As a result of this unfavourable attention, we might consider reinforcing the significant and longstanding Quebec presence of both these institutions by planning an official signing ceremony in Montreal when the acquisition is complete."[179] The signing ceremonies were indeed held in Montreal several months later. But the writing was on the wall, and had been for some time: power had flowed largely to Toronto. In subsequent years, BMO's Montreal leadership would have to work hard to maintain its rightful place in the Bank's structures. In this situation, the nature and quality would be critical.

"A Powerhouse from Day One": BMO Nesbitt Burns

The rest of the capital markets story happens on the other side of the 1980s. In 1994, the Bank of Montreal doubled down on its move into the full-service brokerage market with the purchase of Burns Fry. As the *Financial Post* announced on 19 July: "The bank ended intense speculation yesterday with the announcement it will spend $403 million to purchase Burns Fry and create Canada's largest brokerage firm by merging it with subsidiary Nesbitt Thomson. The new company, to be called Nesbitt Burns, will have assets of $28 billion, combined capital of $600 million and 3,700 employees across the country."[180]

Burns Fry was one of only three Canadian brokerage firms that had not been swallowed up by one of the Big Five Canadian banks by 1994. Burns Fry CEO John MacNaughton commented that the firm had been approached several times over the years, but that "only B of M outlined a strategic future for Burns that interested senior managers. 'Until Steck came along and explained his vision, nothing caught our imagination,' MacNaughton said. 'This is a powerhouse from day one.'"[181]

Burns Fry was 75 per cent owned by its employees and 24 per cent owned by San Francisco–based BankAmerica Corp. The latter announced on 18 July that it would sell its stake for $100 million cash.[182] "Under the terms of the merger agreement, Burns Fry shareholders [would] receive stock exchangeable over four years into a maximum of approximately 5 million Bank of Montreal common shares, and $283 million in cash. At their option, Burns

Fry shareholders [could] elect to receive up to $30 million of the cash payment in additional exchangeable stock. At current market prices for Bank of Montreal common shares, and depending on the extent to which exchange rights are exercised, the value of the transaction [would] be no more than $403 million, or two times book."[183]

While analysts questioned paying twice book for Burns Fry, there was no doubt that this move put the Bank of Montreal firmly ahead of the competition and created the largest brokerage firm in Canada. Size was not everything, however, and critics questioned "how the new company [could] compete in the areas in which neither firm is a market leader, including corporate and government debt operations."[184] Brian Steck, chairman and chief executive officer, Nesbitt Thomson, noted that "we will be able to provide to clients a full range of top-quality investment banking services to meet all their needs. The new firm will have expertise, scale, and distribution capacity that are second to none. As well, this merger will sharply accelerate our ability to expand our US strengths in research, institutional equity operations, fixed income and other investment banking activities. It will be a Canadian firm headquartered in Canada with truly North American capabilities. This will provide clients with coverage on both sides of the border."[185]

In terms of US presence, the move was in line with a strategy pursued by the Bank of Montreal since at least 1984. "Steck said the new organization will focus on building a greater US presence. Nesbitt has already been shopping for a US stock brokerage retail operation, he said, but is close to a deal."[186] The merger of Nesbitt Thomson and Burns Fry consolidated the Bank of Montreal's holdings in the United States, and formed the basis for expansion throughout the subsequent two decades.

Nesbitt and Burns in the Lens

As was the case with Harris, the Nesbitt Thomson operations were run as a separate and distinct division of the Bank – not surprisingly, since bankers and investment dealers could not have been more culturally, operationally, and temperamentally different. As one senior investment dealer recalled, Brian Aune "kept Nesbitt Thomson and then Nesbitt Burns kind of away from the bank. So none of us, I mean, until I started working directly at the bank in 1999, I didn't have much contact with the rest of the bank. Like, we were the brokerage arm. That's what we did. So we didn't have a lot of contact."[187]

The contemporary practice of the institution transmitting a single message and vision – whether that be through an individual employee or a newly acquired firm – did not exist when BMO took over Nesbitt Thomson in the 1980s or Burns Fry in the 1990s. As one investment executive recalled:

Meanwhile, down in the trenches, people were just staking their ground ... There was all this tussling for the first, I would say, twelve to 18 months, and then it became socially unacceptable to be seen as not on the same page. Then it just went underground for a while, to a stage where we're at now, where people hardly talk about it anymore. [Today,] who can remember who came from Nesbitt and who came from Burns? But at the time, this notion that we were, you know, a match made in heaven and everybody was so happy and all that kind of stuff, the reality of it for a period of time was that, it was very much everybody trying to defend their way of doing things, defend their territory. There were still situations where they had the co-head thing going on, somebody was going to lose their job, and there's all that posturing that goes on when that sort of thing is happening.[188]

As another senior executive commented: "It was big time clash of cultures. You had the Nesbitt people, who were interested pretty well only in their next deal and how much bonus it would generate, and they didn't care what they did along the way – or that's how it came across – or they would present some outlandish explanation that also didn't go down very well within the bank."[189]

In other words, acquisition did not mean integration. As one bank official recalled: "It's their [Nesbitt Thomson's] culture, it's our culture and boy oh boy, you know, trying to, in the early days, mix cultures between a bank and an investment bank, it was tremendously difficult."[190] What made matters even more difficult, or perhaps impossible in the next decade, were the highly prescriptive individual employment contracts that were worked out between Mulholland, Bill Bradford, Brian Steck, and Morgan Stanley. When the Bank's next administration started to study those contracts, in the words of the executive deputized to bring the divisions closer,

my God, we just – our jaws just dropped. I mean, I give Brian Steck an awful lot of credit. He wrote – he must have spent thousands of hours of his own time looking at every line of this contract because it really gave him total control over what he was going to do. The employment contracts were I think five years and there were big payouts at the end of five years based on a formula. If Nesbitt didn't like what we were doing to them or if we wanted to make some kind of change in the way we were operating with them – and remember, they still had 25% ownership – we only had 75% at the beginning – they could veto that and if it came to a push versus shove, they could exercise their right to cash in and get out. You know, the employee owners.[191]

The arrangements were as much an expression of the diverse cultures of the organizations as they were a serious display of negotiating prowess on the part of the Nesbitt Thomson folks. For Mulholland, the important thing was to get in the game – and the players could be sorted out at a later date.

The Dome Affair

One of the most public episodes in the story of the Mulholland years was the Bank's involvement in oil patch loans, specifically with Dome Petroleum, one of Canada's foremost oil and gas companies of the 1980s. When the company ran into financial trouble amid falling oil prices and rising interest rates, the Bank of Montreal led the charge for Dome's creditors to be paid what they were owed. What followed was one of the most audacious and high-stakes financial episodes in the Bank's recent history.

Dome Petroleum Ltd was founded in 1950 by Jack Gallagher, a bold and charming businessman from Winnipeg, Manitoba.[192] Gallagher was intensely interested in northern oil exploration and filed for a position in the Canadian Arctic in 1959.[193] Just two years later, in 1961, Dome Petroleum became the first company to drill in the Canadian Arctic, beginning a decades-long search for oil in the high North. In 1974, Jean Chrétien, then minister of northern affairs, asked Gallagher if Dome was interested in oil exploration in the Beaufort Sea. After securing major tax breaks from Ottawa, Dome enthusiastically agreed and, by 1976, conducted the first oil exploration there.[194] Over the next few years, Dome assembled a fleet of driller platforms and icebreakers to search for oil in the Beaufort Sea, striking a number of sizable finds but "none large enough to warrant the enormous expense of developing them."[195]

By the late-1970s, Dome Petroleum seemed to be on top of the world. In response to the oil shocks in 1973 and 1979, the Canadian government energetically pursued a national policy to reassert domestic control over Canadian national resources, and especially oil. Pushed by Ottawa, Canadian banks were encouraged to support this nationalization effort.[196] Dome took this opportunity to secure almost $7 billion from foreign and domestic lenders to fund Dome's ambitious expansion plans, building it into one of the foremost Canadian oil and gas companies. Backed by huge amounts of credit, Dome acquired Siebens Oil and Gas for $400 million – almost all of it on credit – from Hudson's Bay Oil and Gas Company in 1979.[197] It then went on to buy up billions of dollars' worth of properties belonging to Kaiser Resources, TransCanada Pipelines, and Mesa Petroleum.[198] In 1981, Dome acquired Hudson's Bay Oil and Gas Company, paying US$1.7 billion for a controlling interest of just over 50 per cent.[199]

By now, Dome's debt load was so significant that even minor market fluctuations could bring it down. Just a day after the deal with Hudson's Bay Oil and Gas closed, Dome was struck by a one-two punch: oil prices plummeted as demand slacked and interest rates skyrocketed to 23 per cent. The combination was lethal: Dome owed creditors billions of dollars but had no cash stream to pay for it. The federal government in Ottawa sprang into the fray in 1982, offering Dome Petroleum $500 million "to prevent the company from collapsing and hauling its lenders down with it."[200]

Ottawa's intervention did not prevent long-term turmoil for the company. Its debts were staggering, with four of the Big Five Canadian chartered banks having loaned significant amounts of money to Dome. The Canadian Imperial Bank of Commerce, the largest Canadian lender, was owed $910 million. The Bank of Montreal, Dome's second-largest Canadian lender, was owed $850 million. Also in were the Toronto-Dominion Bank, for $730 million, and the Royal Bank of Canada, for $240 million.[201] Dome also owed money to a series of international lenders, including a consortium of banks led by Citibank, that were collectively owed $1.4 billion.[202] In all, the company owed creditors over $6.5 billion – a position from which it was almost impossible to recover. Between 1982 and 1987, Dome paid its lenders $3.54 billion in interest payments alone.[203]

The banks were unwilling to let Dome collapse because of the huge amounts of money involved. In 1983, Dome's creditors agreed to a debt restructuring arrangement. In 1985, the lenders signed a new restructuring plan to extend the repayment terms through to 1995. The following year, after Dome failed to meet its obligations, the lenders agreed to an interim plan to 30 June 1987.[204] This was just another move to stave off – rather than avoid – bankruptcy. Dome, and its chairman J. Howard Macdonald, knew the company's only hope was a buyout. To that end, Dome set up a private office in New York City and approached select corporations about a potential sale.[205] Dome had a lot to offer: while its debts were enormous, it also had rights on some of the most lucrative oil and gas lands in Western Canada.[206] The New York office saw visits from Imperial Oil, TransCanada Pipelines, and Amoco Petroleum Ltd.[207] Amoco Canada, the Canadian subsidiary of Amoco Petroleum, was particularly keen. Amoco was already the fifth-largest petroleum company in the United States. With the potential acquisition of Dome, it would become the largest natural gas producer on the continent.[208] Thus, it was not surprising that on 10 April 1987, Amoco Canada made an offer to purchase Dome Petroleum for $5.1 billion.

Amoco's offer was about $1 billion less than Dome Petroleum owed its creditors. Furthermore, Amoco's offer only provided around $200 million in cash, with the rest made up on Amoco Canada notes, the value of which depended on the future price of oil.[209] Although Dome had also received other offers – including a \$4.3 billion offer from TransCanada Pipelines Ltd, which already owned 12.5 per cent of the company – it went with Amoco's offer.[210] As Dome explained, "the reason we chose Amoco was a rather basic one. For all our constituents, to us it was the best offer."[211] On 18 April 1987, Dome announced that it had accepted Amoco's offer. However, Dome's final sale was conditional on acceptance by its creditors, who were owed \$6.3 billion, and its shareholders, whose stock verged on worthlessness.

Dome's creditors were, predictably, not happy with the deal. Under the terms, the secured lenders – of which the Bank of Montreal was one – would receive between 86 cents and 89 cents on the dollar, depending on the price of oil. Unsecured lenders would receive about 35 cents on the dollar.[212] This amounted to significant losses for the creditors, including the Bank of Montreal, the Toronto-Dominion Bank, and the Royal Bank of Canada. All publicly stated their opposition to the deal.[213] The Bank of Montreal was among Dome's best-secured lenders, with all loans made to Dome "secured by assets ... valued by independent reports at more than two and one-half times the value of the money loaned."[214] Yet, under the terms of the Amoco offer, the Bank of Montreal still stood to lose about \$105 million – this in addition to the \$135 million the Bank had already written off.[215] In fact, approximately half of all the Bank's non-accrual loan balances in 1987 were accounted for by Dome Petroleum.[216] To add insult to injury, the Amoco offer forbade Dome from soliciting competing bids or providing information that would assist competing bidders.

On 22 April 1987, Bill Mulholland wrote to Howard Macdonald personally requesting copies of certain documents respecting the proposed sale.[217] The Bank believed that Amoco's offer was low and wanted more insight into the details. Mulholland's request was denied, and the Bank of Montreal started legal proceedings in the Court of Queen's Bench of Alberta to get the confidentiality clause of the Dome-Amoco deal revoked.[218] Chief Justice William Moore sided with Dome and Amoco, and prevented the Bank of Montreal from receiving further details about the Amoco offer, or the competing offers from TransCanada Pipelines and Imperial Oil, until 14 May 1987.[219]

Undeterred, the Bank of Montreal sued again in early July. This time, the Bank wanted to get the "no shop, lock up" clause revoked and to open the deal to other bidders. Then, in an unexpected turn of events, Amoco Petroleum and the Canadian Imperial Bank of Commerce threatened legal action against the Bank of Montreal. Lawyers for the companies argued that if the Bank of Montreal was successful in getting the court to reopen the deal, "then the bank should be financially responsible for any subsequent losses to creditors."[220] Dome lawyer Cliff O'Brien also pointed out the hypocrisy in the Bank of Montreal's move, reminding people in the *Calgary Herald* that "the Bank of Montreal has no right to force Dome Petroleum to consider more offers … because the bank itself blocked competing offers when it bought [Harris Bankcorp, Inc.] in 1984."[221] Lawyers for the Canadian Imperial Bank of Commerce echoed Dome's sentiments, stating that BMO "would be held liable for damages suffered by [CIBC] if any new offers made for the company weren't as good as the Amoco bid."[222] Many were surprised to see CIBC side with Dome, despite the latter owing the former nearly a billion dollars. CBC suggested that this "marvellous alliance" was because "if Amoco is successful in buying Dome th[e]n the Commerce will be lending them the money to do it."[223]

The spectacle of suit and countersuit between the banks was met with consternation in Ottawa. Federal energy minister Marcel Masse stated that "Dome Petroleum is deteriorating from a pressing national issue to a spectator sport."[224] Undisturbed, the Bank of Montreal kept pushing for better terms. If no other offers could be solicited, then perhaps the best option was to let Dome go bankrupt and sell off its assets. After all, loans made to Dome had been secured by assets valued at more than twice the loan amount.[225] However, Ottawa strongly objected to letting Dome go under, with Marcel Masse reiterating that

> the Bank of Montreal says its not being offered enough money for Dome by Amoco Canada. That's fine, it's the banks [sic] money. The Bank of Montreal is entitled to conduct its affairs any way it wants. However, that isn't all the Bank of Montreal has said. The bank has stated that putting Dome into bankruptcy and selling it off piece by piece might fetch more money than Amoco is presently offering. Perhaps this is true. The question is, what are the other costs going to be? A Dome bankruptcy would torpedo the oil industry's recovery. In a western Canadian oil patch, Dome Petroleum is almost everywhere. Besides employing close to 4000 people directly, its activities employ thousands more. But it's even bigger than that. Dome is involved in nearly one out of five of the deals done in the western Canadian oil patch. If Dome dies, it'll take a good chunk of the oil industry with it.[226]

Dome's bankruptcy would have been the largest bankruptcy in Canadian corporate history.[227] Moreover, Dome was responsible for hundreds of smaller companies and thousands of workers in Canada, and Ottawa was hesitant to let this go bust. In a charge that had been levied against Canada's big banks before, people accused the Bank of Montreal, as a central Canadian institution, of being out of touch with the needs of Western Canada. Calgary oil analyst Ian Doig suggested in the press that "if the banks of central Canada are truly interested in the economy of western Canada, and are truly interested in the resurrection of the oil business, then they would not delay [approving the Dome-Amoco deal]."[228]

The Bank of Montreal's lawsuit to overturn the Amoco purchase was thrown out of court on 28 August. Justice Gregory Forsyth stated that there was no reason to overturn the Amoco purchase, given that either party could withdraw legally from the arrangement after 30 November.[229] Nevertheless, there was little indication that Dome's creditors would be any more supportive of the deal by then.[230] In response, Amoco restructured its offer, in effect offering the Canadian banks an extra $100 million. As the *Toronto Star* explained:

> The apparent act of magic is the result of a deal hammered out last week between Amoco and Placer Dome Inc., the mining company formed by the recent merger of Dome Mines, Placer Development, and Campbell Red Lake ... Under the terms of Amoco's deal with Placer Dome, which owns roughly 20 per cent of Dome Petroleum, Placer Dome will forgo the $99.8 million it would receive if Amoco bought Dome Petroleum. Amoco in turn would turn the money over to the four Canadian banks. The deal between Amoco and Placer Dome doesn't increase the amount of Amoco's offer for Calgary-based Dome, but rather redistributes the cash available, Amoco spokesman Don Smith said yesterday.[231]

The increased cash did nothing to persuade any of the banks to support Amoco's offer.

Desperate to secure support before the 30 November deadline, Amoco tried to lure at least one of the banks into endorsing the deal. Amoco offered the Citibank syndicate, which was collectively owed $1.4 billion, an extra three cents for every dollar owed. Other lenders were not extended this offer. The increase added about $30 million to the final purchase price – a very small amount in a $5.1-billion deal. "A similar increase granted to all of Dome's 56 lenders, collectively owed $6.3 billion," the *Toronto Star* reported, "would add more than $180 million to the final price tag."[232] That same month, a report commissioned by twenty-five of Dome's unsecured lenders was released, adding even more pressure on Amoco to up its offer. The report, conducted by Lancaster Financial Inc., claimed that Dome should have been paid at least $5.7 billion and possibly as much as $6.2 billion, and that "Amoco drove a hard bargain last April by convincing Dome to accept its $5.2-billion takeover plan."[233] This report echoed statements made by a Wood Gundy analyst on 23 May 1987, who stated that Dome was worth about $800 million more than the Amoco offer.[234]

Finally, just days before the 30 November 1987 deadline after which either Dome or Amoco could walk away from the offer made in April, Amoco raised its offer by another $400 million, to $5.5 billion. The "new package," the *Toronto Star* noted, "has met with approval from most ... banks and they have signed agreements indicating support."[235] The following June, Dome's shareholders also fell in line, agreeing – though barely – to the takeover by Amoco. With this, the largest corporate takeover in Canada's history up until that point was completed. In the final arrangement, Amoco paid $5.5 billion, gaining both Dome's huge oil and gas assets (including holdings in the Beaufort Sea and the Arctic islands) as well as its debts.[236] The Bank of Montreal, in turn, was rewarded for its efforts: recovery of the full principal amount in "cash and indebtedness of Amoco" with the new Amoco obligations carried on an accrual basis.[237] The Dome affair, one of the last major episodes of the Mulholland years, showed the strength of the Bank's negotiating abilities.

The Lion in Winter: The Late 1980s and the Yearning for a New Day

By at least the early 1980s, Mulholland's reputation for arrogance, impatience, and toughness fundamentally shaped his public image. As a then-former executive of the Bank remarked to one magazine: "There's no question he frustrates people. Someone must have a high level of frustration absorption to be able to work with him."[238] It was a role and a persona he seemed to relish, though by the later 1980s some speculated that his tough-guy style drove away executive talent.[239] The stories of his making people wait for hours on end for meetings were legendary in the era and thereafter. As one BMO employee recalled, "he'll keep 30 or 40 people, each making at least $150,000 a year, in a room for 2½ hours, just to show that he's the king, to show his power. Then he arrives, announces an executive change for 20 seconds, and leaves."[240] Another suggested more temperately, perhaps, that "people either respond to Bill's specific type of leadership or ease themselves out," while others suggested he was very demanding but fair.[241]

From the directors' point of view, the reviews were also mixed – again, not so much on the strategy front, but rather focusing on their influence in the Mulholland bank and the way things were done. As one Mulholland-era director explained:

> The directors received absolutely nothing in advance of a board meeting, including the agenda. They never got anything ... But the fact of the matter was that when the material was put together, I mean, staff would work all night to be ready for a board meeting the next day. And they didn't have agenda books and organized tabs and things like that. They handed a director, when he came in, a bundle with an elastic around it. Some pages were 8½" x 11" sheets; others were legal

size. And they had no time to go through it because they would arrive maybe five minutes before the meeting. They might thumb through but you couldn't read a pile of paper like this in that period of time.[242]

This is perhaps one reason that sweeping changes to the workings of the board of directors were in the works after Mulholland retired in 1990.

The Canadian financial press found Mulholland's persona irresistible.[243] "King Bill's" brilliance and intellect combined with his personality made for a scintillating narrative in the usually staid reportage of Canadian banking. "The boss from hell," for example, was a popular term. Yet in most accounts, journalists acknowledged that Mulholland's skills and temperament were suited to turning the bank around – suited for major change. Furthermore, Mulholland's inescapable emphasis on principled banking and ethical behaviour was noted both inside and outside the Bank – a signal as much of the man's character as it was of the indelible mark his family and early education had on him.

As a "master change agent," however, the charge from those who left the bank during this period was that Mulholland "was unsuited to the methodical job of overseeing and building a complex organization over the long term."[244] Scores of amateur psychologists in print and disaffected former executives eager to offer views lined up to discuss the perils of perfectionism and why having good emotional intelligence was key to the success of a functioning organization, not to mention offering their views on what the compulsion to have people wait hours upon hours to see him could mean, beyond the obvious indifference to courtesy.

In the closing years of his administration, Mulholland's less commendable qualities were all more sharply noticed, especially his progressively serious inability to inspire loyalty among executives who would not put up with the working environment that he had created. "The cumulative effect of all this on bank performance," one observer suggested, "is lamentable because staff spend too much time worrying about internal problems and not enough worrying about their customers."[245] While the bank had indeed been put on a strong foundation and had turned around, so to speak, by the late 1980s, there were enough problems in the performance of the bank to suggest the time had come for William D. Mulholland to leave the stage.

One executive of the era reminisced that Mulholland "was one of the brightest men I have ever met. He was super smart ... But Bill Mulholland couldn't spell 'people skills.' He had absolutely no understanding, no comprehension of how he was treating people."[246] Yet, this director conceded, "the guy was – he was brilliant. Big balls; really big balls. There hasn't been a CEO of the Bank of Montreal ever whose balls would be half the size of Bill's. But Mulholland had the balls and he was brilliant and the story was – and I believe it – that the credit approval program/plan/policies that he put into effect at the Bank of Montreal were the absolute best in Canada by a substantial margin ... But the way he treated people was ghastly, absolutely ghastly, and he didn't know he was doing it. As a matter of fact, if he ever tried to be nice it was horrible."[247]

The inside story was more nuanced. Other observers suggested that Mulholland's real gift was not only that he was brilliant but also that "he could see around corners. That's what people used to say about him. He could anticipate things. And he would let you work out your own problems. In other words, he wouldn't solve your problems for you ... He wasn't Mr Friendly. He was brilliant and he was totally supportive. But if he didn't respect you then he had no time for you."[248]

The fact is that the Bank of Montreal's saviour general was attempting to save the Bank, and attempting a general change in the culture of the bank. "I would say that he struggled with an organization that had a comfortable legacy," one colleague noted.

> So I don't mean just the organization was comfortable but things had gone well and the world was changing and he had to approach change in a dramatic fashion. I mean, he had to – he really had to – ... engage in disruptive strategies, to disrupt the status quo in order to make change. And so everything from automation, going to online banking nationwide ... The Bank of Montreal was a pioneer in that area, pioneer, first bank to employ automated bank machines. He knew these changes were coming and he also knew that we needed to open up to global financial markets so our initial foray into the Euro dollar market, into LDC lending, all of these things were really part of his disruption of the status quo. A dramatic and rapid modernization of the bank. And I think there are people who would give him credit for saving the bank from just basically sailing off into a quiet oblivion.[249]

Mulholland's eccentricities were not just about interpersonal relations. He attempted to, enigmatically, put the executives who worked for him to the test, as this official recounted about a trip to Brazil: "I remember a trip to Brazil, where he was going to see a minister of finance and he always would have to have some submission to the minister every time he went in. And there's three of us, all went through the same sort of process, like on the flight down where he'd say, 'Right, here's what I want to talk to the minister of finance about.' And it would be complex. You'd then have to spend the rest of the trip trying to sort out exactly what he meant, and then you had to try and write it out for him, and he would either toss it out or he would just – give you another couple of hints and you'd start again."[250]

By 1989, the year of Mulholland's retirement, the focus on his controversial personality came to dominate the public view of this remarkable executive. As one *Maclean's* article reported, "he has become legendary for public humiliations of even the most senior executives, and many critics blame him for the steady exodus of top talent from the Bank of Montreal since he became president in 1975."[251] Those who joined the exodus included such BMO stalwarts as Hartland "Hart" Molson McDougall, who left to head up Royal Trustco Ltd in 1984, and John D. McNeil, who departed in 1979 for Sun Life of Canada, where he would become chief executive officer. The loss of executives such as Dale Parker, Bill Harker, and Ed Mercaldo – all superb bankers – was neither casual nor collateral. As one of the ex-BMO bankers suggested: "They were not presidential contenders, but they were key parts of the fabric of the bank."[252] As many as 300 executives and managers joined the exodus in the Mulholland years. As one columnist suggested at Mulholland's departure, "there are more former executives of the Bank of Montreal in Canada than of any other bank in the country, and most of them readily tell tales of their plight under Mulholland."[253]

"Mein Erbe num nehm'ich zu eigen"[254]

Mulholland's reputed plan was to retire at age sixty-two, in 1988, but one last campaign beckoned: the acquisition of Nesbitt Thomson. In the end, he retired in late 1989 and relinquished the chairmanship on 15 January 1990 to Matthew W. Barrett, his hand-picked successor and a banker who could not possibly have been more of a contrast to the outgoing general.

The contemporary verdicts at Mulholland's retirement were decidedly mixed – along the lines that he imposed order when it was needed but also eliminated a generation of management talent. In an essay on the retirement of Mulholland for the *Financial Times* in February 1989, author Ann Shortell wrote that he would be remembered "as the man who imposed discipline and order on the unwieldy bank. He accomplished this task so effectively that within a decade people had forgotten just how bad the bank had really been when he arrived."[255] The shadow side of the Mulholland years, however – how relationships were handled, how entire levels of management were eliminated, and how fear was used as a managerial tool – resulted in an embarrassingly high turnover at the bank. The *Toronto Star* proclaimed "Bad boy Bill Mulholland to quit Bank of Montreal" with a reputation "unequalled in corporate circles."[256] The rapid turnover of executives, especially veterans in the early 1980s, meant that a "younger breed" of executives were set to take the helm, something that pleased Mulholland – and besides, he suggested, "the old ones are getting tired." [257] The saviour general acknowledged that the "demographic gap in the bank's personnel complement" would be an issue for the incoming administration.[258]

As for his record, considering the acquisition of Harris, the less-developed country (LDC) loans, Dome, and the rest, Mulholland himself suggested that he deserved "a C plus maybe, gentleman's grades."[259] The consensus was aptly summed up by a young Terence Corcoran of the *Financial Post* who suggested that Mulholland took definitive charge of the Bank, led it forcefully and effectively and positioned it well for what was to come. "The Bank of Montreal is not the most profitable, the most successful, or the best-run bank. But compared with its sorry state in 1975, it is now in a powerful position to become a leading national and international bank."[260]

His successor perfectly summed up the Mulholland era within the Bank – perhaps one of two or three contemporaries who can claim to have been eyewitnesses at close quarters to the unfolding of this remarkable period. Matthew W. Barrett viewed the Mulholland era at the Bank in this way:

> And because they weren't schooled and skilled in modern management sciences, his predecessors, when Bill came in, he was looking at what must have frightened the hell out of him, it was chaos. So the metaphor I use because it was often true – funny enough, when I went to Barclays, I thought, "Oh, Bill, you must be smiling down on me now" – is it's like you're appointed to run a big-name hotel and get the number of guests up and the occupancy rate and get them eating and drinking more and make more money and you come in and you find the toilets don't flush, the wiring needs to be completely changed, there's rot in the basement and in the foundations, the roof needs repair, blah blah blah. So before you can go on any scheme to be a world-class resort, you've got to fix all these things. Being in a position like that is a completely thankless position because once you've done it, nobody knows what it was like beforehand and it is invisible work. And Bill Mulholland did all that so he put in modern management systems, he put in professionals who were skilled in their disciplines, he injected some really good talent to the bank etc. etc. so the plumbing – he rewired a 747 in flight, you know, which is a tricky thing. But there's no thanks for it.[261]

Barrett's remarkable tribute to his predecessor – and his acknowledgement not only of the remarkable accomplishments but also of the thanklessness of the task nicely captures the realities of being the Bank's saviour general, the turnaround artist who ensured that the Barrett generation would be able to guide and upgrade the organization and move it in a strategically ambitious direction.

The Bank that Bill Mulholland handed over to the next generation led by Matthew Barrett was, in almost every sense, ready for a change of pace and rhythm. The remarkable burst of enthusiasm, excitement, and energy released in the early 1990s was a testament to this fact. That enthusiasm, excitement, and energy – and the arrival of an immensely charismatic and popular peacetime general in the form of Matt Barrett and his second-in-command Anthony Comper – was only made possible by the campaigns waged and victories secured by the Bank of Montreal's saviour general. As one senior executive recalled, Mulholland "brought [a] sort of vision and a conviction, he knew what he wanted to do and his vision was to not be bounded by the Canadian borders and he wanted to have more of a North American presence because he thought that would be important to the future of the bank."[262] He promoted a whole generation of young executives, and eliminated a generation of other executives – many of whom would go on to great careers elsewhere, but who were not suited to the Mulholland bank – by order of the general himself.

Whether Mulholland should have left earlier – timing is always difficult – is debatable. For a bank desperate for leadership – visible leadership – he provided it. In fact, Mulholland became the voice of the bank. As a senior communication executive recalled: "None of our executives, generally speaking, were ever quoted in the paper. There was very little communicating going on that didn't come from official communication under a press release or something."[263] That began to change in the last years of the Mulholland administration however.

There were shadow sides, too, on the road to return. The culture needed reform, but the pace of change was exhausting, especially near the end of the Mulholland era. As one official recalled:

It was a really tough culture. It was a tough culture going through the '80s. The recruiting campaign that Mulholland had gone through, by the mid- and late '80s it was starting to fracture a little bit. People were not able to keep up the pace; keep up the pace both physically – it was a great era in which machismo to try and keep up with the chairman was what everyone did. So "I'm going to fly to Australia and I'm just going to have a shave and I'm going to my first meeting," because that's exactly what Bill would do. And I'd done it with him. He and I would take a ten-hour flight to Brazil on a Saturday night, and on Sunday morning he'd expect the whole of our Brazil team to be on parade, ready to meet us. On a Sunday morning in a Catholic country. They would be told, "Fine. Go to church early in the morning and get to the office by midday because Rayfield and I are going to be there."[264]

That culture and that pace could not be maintained indefinitely. The team spirit was flagging. The time had come, finally, perhaps belatedly, for a changing of the guard. Yet even there, Bill Mulholland had shrewdly and strategically chosen his successors, as the following years would reveal.

The Verdict

Evaluating the Mulholland years is a great deal more complex an undertaking than meets the eye. One can begin with the most straightforward story: what do the statistics say? The Bank's performance under Mulholland's command in the 1980s in comparison with other banks is shown in the series of graphs (see figures 17.1–17.5). During the 1980s, the Bank returned to a generally more competitive posture in several categories. Its book value per common share and dividends registered second among the big chartered Canadian banks. Its revenue also posted a strong performance, generally registering a third place – though for a time it was second among the Canadian banks in this category. It is a similar story with assets, where the Bank rose to third, then second, before finishing the decade in fourth place.

Of course, the financial results both enlighten and obscure a great and re-markable story of transformation of the Bank of Montreal in this period. In his first years as president and then as chief executive officer, Mulholland fought a two-front war – internally as the great challenger of the status quo, and externally as the grand strategist determined to leverage the full power, reputation, and reach of the Bank in Canadian and international fields.

Under his command, the Bank of Montreal underwent a thoroughgoing transformation, both internally and in the national and international markets in which it participated. He attempted, and largely succeeded, in matching the aspirations of that generation of managers with the growing capabilities of the bank. He continued the aggressive push in technological transform-ation. He completely reoriented the organization to build capabilities in personal and commercial banking. Mulholland's sometimes ruthless out-sider approach ensured a comprehensive disruption of the executive ranks in terms of quality and what was expected of them, getting rid of some and promoting scores of promising juniors. His capacity building in merchant banking and project finance created centres of excellence where professional bankers flourished and could compete with the best that national and inter-national banking could offer. In the memorable metaphor of Matt Barrett, Bill Mulholland was able to successfully rewire a 747 in flight.

Mulholland's long-range vision inspired him to pursue some of the most generation-defining campaigns of the Bank's twentieth-century history: the acquisition of Harris Bank of Chicago, the multi-pronged expansion into

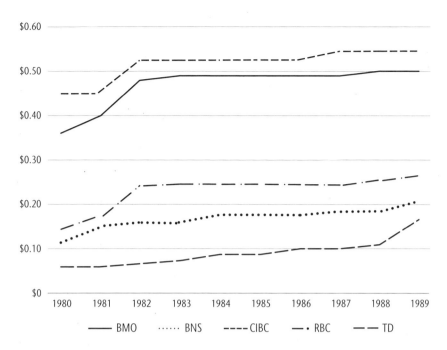

Figure 17.1 | Dividend per share, Big Five banks, 1980–89
Source: Data provided by Thomson Reuters.

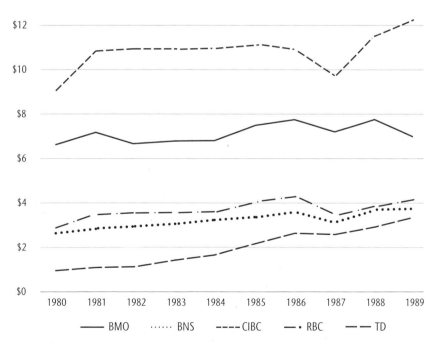

Figure 17.2 | Book value per common share, Big Five banks, 1980–89
Source: Data provided by Thomson Reuters.

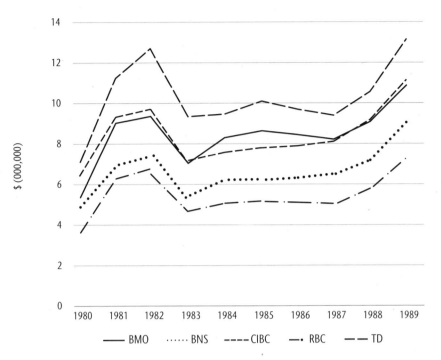

Figure 17.3 | Revenue, Big Five banks, 1980–89

Source: Data provided by Thomson Reuters.

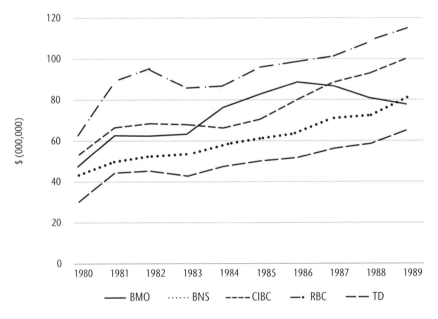

Figure 17.4 | Assets, Big Five banks, 1980–89

Source: Data provided by Thomson Reuters.

THE ROAD OF RETURN, 1974–1989

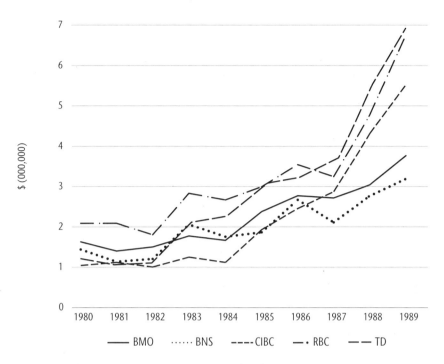

Figure 17.5 | Market capitalization, Big Five banks, 1980–89
Source: Data provided by Thomson Reuters.

international financial markets, and the absorption of Nesbitt Thomson are of varying but undeniably central importance to the making of the Bank of Montreal. His strategy, especially in the first years, combined a sense of the whole vision of where the Bank could go, while revealing the significance of its respective parts.[265]

Mulholland seemed to find the right flows both within the Bank itself and in the opportunities that emerged in Canadian and international finance – controlling some factors, aligning himself with others, and all the while relating everything to his central vision of first restoring the Bank of Montreal into a force to be reckoned with, and then connecting the full power, organization, legacy, and capabilities of Canada's first bank to the aspirations its greatest leaders had for their institution.

Over time, however, Mulholland tried, as it were, to control the flows themselves, much like the elder Pericles commanding Athens: "inner-directed and outwardly oblivious."[266] Focused only on the central vision, without considering the punishing pace and what it would take to inspire the organization to greater heights, he failed, in a sense, to respect the limits of the kind of change the organization could handle. The no-compromise approach not only defies its own environments but also sets its own directions, anticipates no obstacles, and makes no accommodations. As Shakespeare writes in *Troilus and Cressida*: "It *sequentially* consumes its surroundings and ultimately itself."[267] The approach of the lone, brilliant, eccentric outsider was urgently needed in the 1970s and into the 1980s. By the later 1980s, as the Bank's fortunes were once again on sure foundations, a new, more stable hand was required.

Mulholland's record was not without its disappointments and unfinished business, as we have seen throughout this period. His international ambitions were frustrated time and again by circumstance. The acquisition of Harris Bank was a generationally significant move, but for whatever reason, the years of salutary neglect and either the unwillingness or inability to integrate the two organizations would be a major piece of unfinished business. The Domestic Development Program may have been necessary, but it was also bitter medicine whose details and execution left a legacy that, in large part, had to be unravelled by successors. The ambitions to become a major player in sovereign debt were fulfilled (a subject covered in chapter 19), but also created some seriously tricky situations. These details mattered, but they often seemed sacrificed to the grander vision. "I never really, truly understood why we weren't doing better than we were actually doing," confessed one era executive. "I felt we had the capacity to do it, but we weren't getting there."[268] On the other hand, many had not realized just how far the bank had come in such a short time.

In later years, Mulholland seemed almost to revel in his larger-than-life persona. At the very least, it certainly did not seem to bother him. The problem, however, was that his leadership style, his exigent approach to subordinates, and his driven nature had, by the late 1980s, pushed the organization to the breaking point. The gathering, breathless, and sometimes even gothic reportage of autocratic decisions, spurned executives waiting hours for meetings, overworked chauffeurs, and nonplussed directors were exquisite grist for the mill of the financial press. And also a clear indication that the saviour general's moment had passed, that the torch would pass to a new generation that he had shaped and promoted.

The response to the end of the Age of Mulholland was a perfect indication of the victories and unfinished business at the Bank of Montreal. From virtually the moment Matthew W. Barrett and his team arrived, it was as if a dam had burst. The Bank almost viscerally responded to the youth, charisma, and personality of the new CEO – and, importantly, the strong message that the Bank's leadership would come together *as* a team. "It was a marvel to me," one director reflected as he looked back on that moment of transition, "when Matt took over from Mulholland, to watch the impact of leadership on how he brought the rest of the team up. He took exactly the same team that had been cowering under Mulholland. He didn't add a single person and he just lit a fire under them on the strength of his personality, his intellect, [and] his knowledge of the bank."[269] What is more, the Bank got not only Matthew Barrett but also Tony Comper. As one executive put it, "they were the Odd Couple, but I think they were perfect for each other so that Matt could go fix the ego of firm, while [Tony] would fix the operations of the firm and make sure that the kind of stuff that needs to happen is going to happen."[270] On the threshold of the 1990s, the Bank of Montreal needed a brand of leadership that could mobilize the organization to new heights. The torch, and the needs of the organization, passed from the saviour general's command and the battles of the 5,479-day "war" to the optimism and aspirations of peacetime opportunity: new approaches, a new sense of purpose, and an *esprit de corps* galvanized by a new style of leadership and a new level of focus on the customer experience.

None of this would have been remotely possible without the organizational and strategic successes of the 1970s and 1980s under W.D. Mulholland. They were achieved by virtue of his strategic vision, his unshakeable loyalty to mission, and his unwavering ambition to reform and recreate a great institution that had, in an important sense, lost its way. His strategy and vision may not have always produced victory. But he did unequivocally offer something more fundamental: deliverance at a pivotal moment in the Bank's history. Thriving on the thrust of market manoeuvres and ignoring criticism, resentment, and envy, Mulholland pushed through the far-reaching transformations required to secure the Bank's place as a vital institution in the North Atlantic world. He may have, as Matthew Barrett once declared, received no real thanks for it: the moments of glory were passing and, by the late 1980s, few and far between. Yet, subsequent generations of the leadership and people of the Bank owe the saviour general a debt of gratitude for doing the improbable and setting the Bank of Montreal on the road to return.

CHAPTER EIGHTEEN

The Day the *BMO* Universe Changed

This chapter focuses on the lead-up to and the acquisition and immediate aftermath of the Bank of Montreal's acquisition of the Harris Bank of Chicago in 1984. The significance of this acquisition to the subsequent history of the Bank provides a rare opportunity: it is, if you will, a close-up of the Mulholland bank at the height of its strategic powers, in a time and a place where its actions and tactical moves could very well determine the long-term future of the Bank itself, let alone its presence in the United States. Between 1977 and the late 1980s, the story was only beginning, but it was precisely in this period that some of the permanent features of the BMO-Harris relationship were established and entrenched.

If seen from the contemporary rear-view mirror, the acquisition of Harris Bankcorp, Inc. represents a singular strategic triumph of the Bank under the leadership of W.D. Mulholland. In the 2017 Annual Report, for example, the Bank's diversified business in the United States contributed about 25 per cent of adjusted earnings.[1] It has also emerged as a central inheritance from the previous generation to the current management. More than any other single acquisition, event, or initiative, the purchase of the Harris Bank of Chicago has been seen as the kind of big move that many banks and bankers are called to aspire to, but that few actually have the opportunity to realize.

To the twenty-first-century Bank of Montreal, the acquisition of the Harris Bank is seen as an uncontested positive, conferring competitive advantage and giving force, shape, and authority to the Bank's status as a North American bank. As we complete the second decade of the century, the cross-border nature of the acquisition and the increasing interdependence of the continental economy over the last three decades in terms of trade and exchange seem to have made the acquisition of Harris Bank a model and example of successful long-range strategic intent.

The origins and development of the BMO-Harris relationship in its first decade or so tells a somewhat different and more complex story – a story that was rather more indeterminate and contingent than this century's result might suggest. The Bank's acquisition was but the first, albeit brilliant, step in a long and often ambiguous process that each subsequent administration of BMO bankers had to confront, understand, and act upon. The potential of the relationship was in some ways commensurate with the challenges the "special relationship" presented in terms of strategy, culture, and performance.

In other words, the long-term success of the BMO-Harris story was by no means straightforward. From the retrospective gaze of a current generation, clean lines appear to connect action and result, cause and effect, obscuring the difficulties and reversals of those early years. That experience in the crucial first decade of the relationship can teach us a great deal about how BMO, as an organization, responded to opportunity and challenge posed in the wake of the acquisition. It is a story that underlines the importance of culture and highlights just how complicated it is to change and align to strategic goals.

The BMO-Harris story is much more than the ultimate, twenty-first-century triumph of continental banking. The founding story can tell us a lot about what worked and what did not work, sometimes for years. In the wake of the acquisition and in the years that followed, the romance of the 1984 moment gave way to more prosaic but no less important tasks such as integration and strategic alignment. Also, BMO executives of the era were by no means agreed on whether the expansion into the United States was warranted in the first place, and then when it was a reality, whether it was a good long-term move. Indeed, it was in these first formative years that the attitudes, actions, and approaches of the Mulholland bank would leave some major challenges and lost opportunities for the subsequent generation.

The Rear-View Mirror

Looking in the rear-view mirror, the long-range importance of the Bank's acquisition of a major Chicago bank is indisputable. In short, it gave BMO an opportunity to establish itself as a North American bank with a powerful anchor in a key market in the United States: the Midwest. In the two decades since the acquisition, the Bank of Montreal's management has become increasingly continental, with deep capabilities on both sides of the border.

Its executives and emissaries eventually felt as at home in the banking markets of Chicago and the corridors of influence in Springfield, Madison, and Washington, D.C., as they had for 175 years in Montreal, Toronto, and Ottawa. Further acquisitions in the United States, such as Marshall & Ilsley in 2011, have powerfully extended the range and influence of the Bank of Montreal south of the border. As the 2020s approach and the long process of integration makes increasingly profound inroads, the Bank has reached an inflection point in the transformation of a Canadian bank into a North American bank. For this reason 4 September 1984 – the day the deal was signed – can be seen as the day the BMO universe changed. Of course, the speed and direction of change, and how, exactly, it has changed, is also an important part of the story.

Project Park

In early 1983, Bill Mulholland and a small team of his closest executives, including president Grant Reuber and deputy chairman Bill Bradford, made the momentous strategic decision to attempt to purchase Harris Bankcorp, Inc. The preliminary approaches between Bill Mulholland and Charles Bliss, head of the Harris, were made in February 1983 through the offices of Morgan Stanley.[2] After the usual approvals, "Project Park," the code name given to the operation, was put into effect to move the Bank of Montreal through the required phases of the acquisition.

The move was part of a larger strategy of the Mulholland bank to open the organization to the world, as discussed in chapter 19. Expansion into the United States was a natural extension of existing operations in New York, San Francisco, and (at least historically) Chicago. Mulholland's gaze came to rest on Chicago, and on one of its largest banks, the Harris. From a geographical perspective, the deal also made eminent sense toward establishing a foothold in the strategically important Midwestern-Great Lakes region. As soon as the green light was given, a small, specialized team drawn from the Bank's senior executive cadre augmented by a group of hand-chosen experts sprang into action to examine the acquisition target and make recommendations.

Harris Bank had been founded as an investment-banking firm in 1882 to engage in the underwriting of municipal, public utility, and corporate securities. In 1907, Harris bankers added a general banking business and incorporated as such under the banking laws of the State of Illinois. Following passage of the US Banking Act of 1933 that prohibited bank participation in the business of underwriting and distribution of public utility and corporate securities, Harris expanded its commercial banking activities while continuing its traditional business of underwriting and distribution of municipal securities.[3] "Park [Harris] can be characterized essentially as a full-service 'trust and trading' bank with this mainline business supplemented by a substantial, but more specialized, regional and national corporate banking business, some retail banking (representing approx. 25% of loan portfolio)," one internal project report offered. It also mentioned that the Harris had engaged in "a minor amount of international banking (representing approx. 14% of income)."[4] The bank's business was organized very simply, with three major departments: the banking department, the trust department, and the investment department.[5]

The Harris managed approximately 6,000 trust accounts, with some $20 billion in trust assets under management.[6] By the end of 1981, the Harris ranked ninth among banks and trust companies in terms of discretionary assets under management.[7] Its investment department also distinguished itself as one of America's major nationwide underwriters and dealers in municipal and US government securities, and the bank was known nationally as a dealer in "Federal Funds and other Money Market instruments."[8] The Bank of Montreal team reported that Harris was an inherently "operations intensive" and required "a substantial commitment of systems and human resources to 'operational underpinnings.'" In this regard, over the previous ten years, Park's substantial growth in revenue from increased business had been offset by substantial growth in operating expense.[9] The bank had invested heavily in automation, both designing its own and buying systems.

Harris also had a significant international foothold. International banking services represented about 14 per cent of Harris's income, and included foreign loans, letters of credit, foreign exchange, and Eurocurrency dealings. In addition to Chicago headquarters, the bank also had branches in London, Nassau, and Singapore; representative offices in Mexico, Brazil, and Japan; an Edge Act bank in New York; and an I.B.F. in Chicago.[10] Furthermore, the Harris's international banking structure included minority equity positions in an Australian merchant bank (40 per cent) and a Brazilian investment bank.[11] In addition, Harris's loan portfolio was 16.5 per cent internationally oriented (see table 18.1).

After the team reviewed Harris's business profile, including assets (see table 18.2), international operations, and loan spread, it came to the preliminary conclusion in early 1983 that Harris "compete[d] as a leading full-service trust and trading institution," but that the Bank of Montreal planned "to be more specialized in [their] approach."[12] There was more to Harris than its financial position, however.

There was no question that Harris Bank was firmly rooted in the Chicago community. Indeed, A.W. Harris had founded the Chicago Community Trust in 1915, so the pedigree ran very deep. In the 1960s and 1970s, Harris's public image was particularly strong, bolstered by the success of a media

Table 18.1 | Harris Bank international loan portfolio, as at
31 December 1982, totalling $662.4 million, representing
16.5 per cent of Harris's total loan portfolio

Geographic Distribution (by domicile of obligor)	%
Continental Europe	29
Middle East and Africa	6
Pacific and Far East	11
UK and Ireland	6
Western Hemisphere (excl. US)	36
US	12
	100

Source: BMOA, Harris Bank, Pre-purchase "Blue Book" + Information on
Harris + BMO fit, "Status Report as at 21 April 1983: Description of Park," 14.

Table 18.2 | Harris Bank assets, as at 31 December 1982

Assets	Value $(000,000)
Cash & Due from Banks	746.7
Deposits with Banks	916.0
Investment Portfolio	488.4
Trading Securities	262.9
Domestic Money Market Assets	127.8
Loans	4,019.9
Allowances for Possible Credit Losses	(35.0)
Acceptances	335.6
Premises and Equipment	116.0
Other	158.5
Total	7,136.8

Source: BMOA, Harris Bank, Pre-purchase "Blue Book" + Information on
Harris + BMO fit, "Status Report as at 21 April 1983: Description of Park,"
15–16.

and advertising campaign featuring Hubert, an adorable and very popular
talking lion.[13] The Bank's commitment to the inner city in the 1970s, and
its involvement with minority enterprises was also a standout aspect of its
operations in the 1970s.[14]

Harris's human resources record was the subject of some additional scrutiny. In 1974, the feminist advocacy organization Women Employed filed

charges against the bank for discriminatory practices.[15] In December 1977, the United States Department of Labor issued an administrative complaint "alleging discriminatory employment practices by Park resulting in affected classes of female and minority employees."[16] On 30 January 1981, a Department of Labor administrative law judge recommended to the Secretary of Labor that government contracts be cancelled until certain conditions were met. The recommendation included a payment of approximately $12 million as back pay for affected classes. "Management continues to believe that it does not engage in discriminatory employment practices," the internal BMO report concluded.[17] Years later, in January 1989, Harris paid another $14-million settlement to its female and minority employees, without admitting fault. At the time, it was "the largest settlement to date between the Department of Labor and a private employer."[18]

In spite of the issues and some of its challenges, the Harris Bank was a rather typical Midwestern Chicago bank. That meant that it had a certain culture, a certain kind of organization with some well-defined characteristics: professional, tightly knit, well regarded, and conservative are adjectives that come to mind. As one long-time Harris executive revealed about the bank before 1984: "We were a strong Midwestern bank. We had clients outside of the Midwest but our base was there. And of course the Chicago area was a big part of it. And in those days we pursued the large companies too. I think now they're handled by the investment banking unit, which we didn't really have at that point. We were a conservative bank. The culture was conservative. It was strongly suggested – you got the word that you should wear a hat to work but it wasn't mandatory like the Northern Trust."[19]

Another Harris employee in the pre-Bank-of-Montreal days adds that the Harris was a very collegial institution.

> You know, and the world has changed a ton. Back when I joined there, I mean, everybody sort of – the common thing was you get into work. At 9:30 it was coffee break until 10:00. Everybody and their brother went to the cafeteria. And, again, it was pre-email, pre-cell phones, etc. So you actually did a lot of business and a lot of networking and stuff happened in those instances, and so if there's somebody you needed to catch up with, he would be there. You could grab them. Then everybody did lunch 12:00 to 1:00 … Then everyone went to coffee at kind of 3:00, 3:30. On Wednesdays they had – Wednesdays was ice cream sundae afternoon, so every afternoon there were ice cream sundaes for the world. So it was a kinder, gentler world a little bit back then, but it was a very collegial organization. Not a command-and-control environment at all. I honestly can say I enjoyed working with just about everybody I met there.[20]

These statements also seem to capture in some ways the strengths and weaknesses of the Harris Bank from the point of view of the mid-1980s. Focused as it was on tight-knit networks and relationships, it had perhaps lost a competitive edge in the process.

Greenwich Research Associates, a research firm contracted by BMO to report on Harris, concluded in 1982 that the Harris had a great reputation and was "perceived as a quality bank by those corporations using it as a principal bank." The report, however, suggested that "there were clear signs that the quality of services provided deteriorated (on a relative basis) somewhat over the past four to five years." The Greenwich study referred to the fact that for banks generally, "account officers' failure to follow-up promptly and effectively is not only the most serious mistake, but is also the mistake that most often causes the loss of business." Harris appeared to have a problem here, as evidenced by the declining percentage of their clients expressing satisfaction with their follow-up capability. From other analysis in this review, "it would [also] appear that internal operational problems are possibly a major contributing factor to this declining level of client satisfaction."[21]

BMO's investigation also suggested that the bank's "current ability to generate sufficient capital internally to support continued asset growth is not very strong" – at only 6 per cent.[22] The historical performance of Harris – on issues such as net interest margin, return assets (ROA), and return on equity (ROE) – compared to its peer group – Bank of New York, Irving Trust Co., Republic Bank Corporation, Continental Illinois Corp., First Chicago Corp., Mellon National Corp., and The Northern Trust – was also a significant issue.[23] The Montreal bankers concluded that the Harris "appears to have been managed less aggressively than its peer group and as a result, performance has lagged although asset quality has remained high. Additionally, Park appears to have faced difficulty controlling non-interest expenses."[24]

The thorough examination of the Harris continued a detailed and useful picture of what the Bank of Montreal was getting into. The consensus at this point was positive, and strongly in favour of continuing. However, if the Bank of Montreal were to proceed, some decisions needed to be made about its existing US operations. As the report outlined, certain "restrictions imposed on interstate and international banking" meant that BMO would have to "de-bank" its bank subsidiaries in California and New York prior to "consummating the acquisition of Harris."[25] "If after the acquisition BMO wants a branch in the United States with full deposit taking powers ... it can establish such a branch in – but only in – Illinois ... the Illinois branch could be chartered either as an Illinois State branch or as a Federal branch."[26] However, if BMO wished to, "it could establish non-banking subsidiaries of the types permissible of bank holding companies."[27] There were no interstate restrictions on these entities and the activities in which they could engage included consumer and commercial finance, leasing, factoring, discount brokerage, trust services, loan servicing, and certain financial advisory services. BMO could also establish agencies and limited branches in states other than Illinois. It could establish a so-called investment company under Article XII of the New York Banking Law, which could make loans and accept credit balances in New York. BMO could also establish one or more Edge Act banks to conduct international activities, which could branch on an interstate basis. Finally, BMO could acquire a bank in any state that enacts legislation permitting out-of-state bank holding companies to acquire banks in that state, such as South Dakota or Delaware.[28]

Those were the details. In the eyes of BMO's leadership, they added up to significant synergies between the two organizations. "Conceptually," one report suggested, "acquisition of Park by Bank of Montreal would blend together nicely in broad functional terms, the Trust and Trading strength of Park with the Account Management and Operations strength of Bank of Montreal."[29] In terms of presence and international identity, the US strength of Harris combined with the Canadian and international strength of the Bank of Montreal was also a strong positive. Moreover, in terms of funding, Harris's US capital base would assist Bank of Montreal's Canadian capital base.[30]

In addition, Harris Bank's size would "appear ideal for Bank of Montreal – large enough to make a very material difference, yet small enough to 'get our arms' around to ensure potential synergies are exploited and realized."[31] These positive elements would counteract some of the difficulties the Chicago bank was encountering on the operations side and the problem of declining customer satisfaction.[32]

There were other pull factors for the Canadians in terms of Harris Bank's US cash management capability, the funding of US domestic loans, and the possibility that the Chicago bank would enhance BMO's capabilities in the US money market, foreign exchange, and bond trading and underwriting. The Bank of Montreal's growing international presence would position it well to exploit Harris's US-based trust skills on a worldwide basis. Even early on in the process, Bank of Montreal analysts argued that it was important for the Harris to maintain its own identity as a pure US bank. The reasons were understandable, and focused on the perceived impact of foreign ownership of Harris on its customer base and on potential loss of retail and wholesale business. Retention of key employees was another motive.[33] This idea, as we shall see, attained the status of untouchable orthodoxy.

The Harris, of course, was not the only bank in the United States that would be a good fit for BMO. In line with market trends, it had eyed other US banks In fact, BMO's acquisition of the Harris Bank of Chicago came at a time when mergers and acquisitions in the US banking industry were on the rise.

For example, by 1983, there were 432 mergers with $43 billion in acquired assets.[34] Back in 1978, BMO had entered into talks with Bankers Trust of New York about the "possible takeover of 89 Bankers Trust retail banking offices in the New York area."[35] The *Globe and Mail* noted that this deal "would fit in a strategy [an analyst] sees Canadian banks taking of emphasis on expansion of their international operations."[36] Bankers Trust parent company, Bankers Trust New York Corp., was too big for the Bank of Montreal to acquire – being of roughly equal size in terms of assets.[37] The size of the Harris was more appropriate to BMO's ambitions. The final nudge came when Stanley G. Harris Jr retired in 1980, ending family participation in the management of the bank. The stars were aligning, and the Mulholland bank saw the main chance.

The Hour Approaches

The Bank of Montreal had prepared well for the possibility of purchase, and had a clear understanding of exactly what it was getting into. In preparing for the reality of acquisition, one senior auditor recalled an intense flurry of activity:

> In 198[4] the bank bought Harris. My first indication of this – I was still chief auditor at the time and I was just summoned to a meeting one night, and this was to do due diligence. BMO President Grant Reuber was in charge of this due diligence process. There were about a dozen of us in the room and he says – and we weren't even told the name of the company, there were code words – "We've got to go in for a week, and we've got to go in and do this and this. You're responsible for this area, you're responsible for this area, you're responsible for this area." This was sort of the extent of our instructions. We'd never done this before. "And there's an area that we don't have in the bank: Trust accounting. We don't do that here, so [name], you do that one too." I spent the next 24 hours talking to somebody who knew something about trust accounting to get myself up to speed ... Mulholland gave strict instructions: "Hands off Harris. Don't try to change Harris." He says, "Why would you buy a dog and then bark for it?"[38]

There were other possible angles. As another banker suggested, "I mean, looking back at it, the one thing – and I think Mulholland said this at one time. Somebody asked him why he bought a bank that had such a low return on assets and low return on equity and that kind of thing, and he said, 'Because it's important that we're in the United States and I want to sleep at night.'"[39]

The Offer

Project Park then moved to the offer phase, which staked its claim and provided some clear outline of what the value proposition was believed to be. It also gave a broader public the idea of exactly how the Bank of Montreal would handle the acquisition. The offer certainly emphasized the win-win nature of the transaction to the US Federal Reserve. BMO viewed the Harris "as an attractive means of establishing a substantial presence in the United States, an essential long-term strategic objective for an international bank headquartered in North America."[40]

In the final offer, the Bank of Montreal paid out $82 per share for 100 per cent of Harris's common shares (6.66 million shares), for a total purchase price of $547 million.[41] These numbers satisfied the Harris family, who insisted on two conditions: "the tender offer had to be for all shares of stock, and the price had to be at least 1.6 times book value."[42] In addition, as part of the deal, the Bank of Montreal pledged to "transfer more than $1 billion in US loans to its new subsidiary during the next three years ... Mr Mulholland ... said [the loan transfer] represents a substantial portion of Harris' projected growth for the coming years."[43] The Harris's growth would be further aided by significant cash injections that the Bank of Montreal was to make over the coming years, investing over $76 million 1984 alone.[44] Finally, and importantly, BMO pledged that the Harris would not really be integrated into the larger entity. As one of the key offer documents suggested, "BMO does not contemplate any significant changes in the Harris management structure nor personnel. Harris bears a distinguished name in United States banking, and BMO intends that, if this transaction is consummated, it shall continue to operate under the Harris name."[45] The offer satisfied the Harris board of directors, who agreed on 5 October 1983, and the shareholders, who gave their assent on 18 January 1984.[46] Now the wait was for regulatory approval.

The offer suggested, presciently, that Canada–US co-operation and trade would be key to the future success of the acquisition, and that the deal would position both entities to take advantage of emergent conditions. The advantages that the Canadian bank possessed in project financing (since the 1820s) were a particularly compelling point. In addition, the Bank could point to strengths in commercial real estate ($2.6 billion in loans), agribusiness (a market share of 21 per cent), retail banking (1,200 branches, mortgage portfolio of $4.2 billion, personal deposit base of $17.9 billion, and personal loans outstanding of $3.1 billion), and cash management (one of the world's great banks in this area).[47]

One of the potential showstoppers for the Bank of Montreal in the regulatory approvals process was the problem of capital adequacy. The Federal

Reserve did not view the Canadian banks – BMO included – with great favour in this important category. The Fed, under its chairman, Paul Volcker, believed that Canadian banks were undercapitalized. The Bank argued, ultimately successfully, that the Canadian banking market was so structurally different from the US market as to make application of US guidelines to the Bank of Montreal inappropriate. "Unlike many American banks," one brief to the Fed argued, "the Canadian banks are not dependent on the economy of a particular sector of the country but have a broad source of funding which has remained at a relatively stable and high level over the years."[48] The Bank was able to match the re-pricing of assets and liabilities closely and did not have a large portfolio of long-term, fixed-rate mortgage loans or other fixed-rate assets that could not be funded on a matching basis.

What is more, at that time, Canadian mortgages were generally for twenty-five years with the rate being adjusted not less frequently than every five years. The Bank's $5 billion mortgage portfolio had an average term to rate adjustment of only 1.6 years (the higher the adjustment frequency, the higher the chances for default) with less than 1 per cent of the mortgages having a rate maturity date of more than five years. The portfolio was held in a subsidiary of the Bank and was funded by the subsidiary on a matching basis. Thus, it could be argued that one should exclude the $5 billion from the asset base since there was very little exposure to interest rate fluctuations, and the average annual loss record in the portfolio over the past five years was less than 0.003 per cent.[49] The Bank would suggest to the Federal Reserve that it should look at the capital of the institution to be acquired in the United States to determine that the capital of that institution is adequate and, if necessary, strengthened by the acquisition. The proposed acquisition would not cause the capital level of Park to be diminished. "It is important that the foreign institution be a source of strength to the US bank that is proposed to be acquired." This should not be determined on the basis of ratios alone, the report concluded, but should be looked at in terms of overall performance, size, and ability of the foreign institution.[50]

The arguments were persuasive enough for the Federal Reserve and so one of the biggest deals in Canadian or American banking history proceeded to its final phase. On 25 July 1984, the Federal Reserve Board announced its approval of the acquisition, which was received in Harris's Chicago headquarters early on the morning of 26 July (with handwriting over it that said "mixed emotions").[51] The deal closed at 11 a.m. on 4 September 1984 in Chicago, after a year and a half of preparation, analysis, and due diligence. When Mulholland returned to Canada and was asked by Canada Customs whether he had purchased anything while in the United States, he quipped, "Yes, a bank."

The End Game

The 1983 Harris Annual Report hailed the Bank of Montreal's acquisition, which at that time was awaiting regulatory approval. The report emphasized the main driver of the deal: size, "both in terms of revenue generation and in unit cost containment."[52] At the time of the acquisition, Harris was an awkwardly sized bank. As the Annual Report pointed out, the bank had a lending limit of $40 million, below the "entry level for us to participate in many large national and international corporate credits."[53] The Bank of Montreal's assistance would open up opportunities to participate more actively in energy, real estate, and transportation, which demanded greater size and capacity. Additionally, the acquisition would bring a solution to other awkward-sized problems, too. One of the other areas of "increasing concern" to Harris executives in the early 1980s was the rapid escalation in systems development and programming costs. "The Harris has sometimes seemed to be an awkward size – too large to acquire electronic data processing products from the outside, but too small to develop and maintain those resources internally on a cost-effective basis."[54]

The acquisition came not a moment too soon, it would seem, since the Harris's 1983 financial performance was "disappointing," with a 13 per cent decline from profits of 1982 and a return on assets of 0.41 per cent and a return on equity of 8.02 per cent.[55] Harris CEO Ken West concluded his note to the shareholders by looking "to the future with renewed enthusiasm and optimizing concerning our ability to service our customers, to provide opportunities for our employees and to become an integral part of one of the world's leading financial institutions."[56] As the brochure produced for the big announcement proclaimed, "it is apparent ... that we will become a qualitatively different and better institution, not just a bigger one. The most important differences will be greater access to opportunities – for our customers, for our organization and for each of us as individuals."[57]

Press reaction to the deal was mixed but had something for everyone. Newspapers enthusiastically hailed the $547-million acquisition, "the second largest merger of its kind in US history."[58] The *Chicago Tribune* reported that the Federal Reserve had approved the acquisition in spite of some misgivings about the Bank of Montreal's low primary capital ratio, something the *Globe and Mail* of Toronto neglected to mention. Rather, the *Globe* focused on the fact that the Harris would be managed as a "self-sufficient organization" and that "no significant changes in Harris management structure or personnel [were] contemplated."[59] The *Harris Herald,* the in-house publication for employees, underlined the idea that this acquisition was a matter of "two healthy institutions coming together in pursuit of superior growth opportunities," especially in Metro Chicago and the corporate middle markets throughout the Midwest.[60]

Post-Merger Integration

However complex the eighteen-month acquisition process proved to be, the bigger questions would be how the Bank of Montreal would harness the Harris's strengths and capabilities, and how far the Bank would go to take advantage of an integrated approach? In a speech entitled "The Harris Connection" to the Canadian branch of the Association for Corporate Growth in March 1985, Deputy Chairman W.E. Bradford explained: "We needed Harris to expand our growth opportunities, and to help us compete with the world's best and biggest banks, not only in the United States and the major financial centers of the world, but also in our home market, right here in Canada."[61] Bradford focused on globalization in finance as the main driver, as well as the need to develop a "substantial US presence" to provide the most effective service to the Bank's North American customers. The Harris provided a quality bank, a well-managed bank, and a bank that was "big enough to give [the Bank of Montreal] a competitive position in the US corporate banking market, but not one that would be too larger or too awkward to supervise"[62] Bradford also explained that the Bank of Montreal would maintain the Harris identity, its own management, and its own board.[63] The Harris's sterling reputation, the quality of its management, and its market presence and customer relationships were all key to the acquisition, so the Bank of Montreal saw no reason to change it. In fact, "having paid commensurately for these important assets, we had no intention of diluting them."[64] BMO would maintain oversight, but the management team was "left in place with instructions to manage – and we stay out of the way."[65] For Harris bankers, this was the best of all possible worlds.[66]

In 1986, two years after the acquisition, the *Harris Herald* published a special issue looking at the merger and its effects on both institutions. "Our life has changed in many ways," Ed Banker [*sic*], senior VP of banking at Harris and the principal liaison between the two organizations, stated, "we are seeing many positive effects of these changes come to fruition."[67] He was right. Banker could point to a strengthening of the bank's position in the large corporate market. In the short years since the Bank of Montreal acquisition, Harris was now considering $200-million loans, where a few years prior, $60 million had been the frontier.[68] The Bank of Montreal connection was also important in other respects. In 1984, the BMO put over $76 million into Harris to help finance operations. The following year, it invested another $50 million to help finance the purchase of the First National Bank of Arlington.[69] From a monetary perspective, the acquisition was a good thing: by 1986, the Harris achieved record levels in net income and assets.[70] By 1993, almost a decade after the merger, the Harris had "tripled its number of retail and small business customers to more than 800,000 ... and ... its book equity value ha[d] increased from US$434 million to US$1.8 billion."[71]

One of the most crucial aspects for the Harris, however, was that its independence had been maintained. CEO Ken West pointed out that the Harris had "retained [its] autonomy in just about every sense of the definition."[72] As Phil Delaney added, the BMO-Harris deal was not a merger, it was a marriage: "you don't merge into one person; what you do is learn how to make your styles work together."[73] This was the big advantage of the deal, as Delany elaborated: "They [Harris and BMO] don't have to merge; in fact I think at Harris we have retained our culture and enriched it. Bank of Montreal has not tried to make us become something we are not, they are not, they have not tried to change us. We really have learned from each other."[74]

This approach was maintained throughout the 1980s. Only in the 1990s would the two banks slowly begin integration, a trend that intensified over the course of the 2000s and 2010s. A major milestone in this process came in 2005, when the name Harris Bankcorp, Inc. was officially retired and all US branches were renamed BMO-Harris.

In part, the slow integration between the two banks was because the Bank of Montreal itself required serious attention.[75] As a BMO executive of the day suggested, "BMO started to have its own issues ... Their problems were such that they couldn't worry about Harris so basically they said, 'Leave Harris alone.'"[76] The later 1980s provided plenty of matters requiring urgent attention – less-developed country debt; substantial write-offs in 1984, 1987, and 1989; and other serious issues. "So there was quite a period of time," one executive recalled, "when I would say that we were occupied with dealing with those kind of issues."[77]

The other reason was Mulholland's long-term vision for the Harris and for the North American ambitions of the Bank of Montreal itself. As another executive recalled: "we bought Harris Bank and we weren't allowed to touch it. We weren't allowed to go anywhere near it. I mean, if you went down to Chicago and you walked into Harris Bank and someone saw you there, you would have been shot. I mean, he just didn't want anybody touching Harris Bank."[78] As a different executive remembered, "when [BMO] took over the Harris, there was nobody here from the Bank of Montreal for – I would say at least a year. Nobody. Literally. And so the word was, 'Keep your hands off Harris Bank.'"[79] As Mullholland suggested years later, the object was "not to have a Canadian bank in the United States. The object [was] to have a well-managed successful American bank in the United States, a solid nucleus from which we can branch out."[80]

Many suspected that Harris independence was also preserved by the fact that Mulholland believed that most Bank of Montreal bankers did not quite grasp what was happening in the United States, that BMO bankers were excessively Canadian in their outlook and perspective. He understood the cultural differences between the BMO bankers and the Harris bankers. One era executive recalled that the cultural differences between Canada and the United States were much more profound than they would become, for example, post-NAFTA: cultural differences, differences in banking style, in systems, in markets, in regulatory environment, in accounting regimes, and more.[81] The cultural differences extended to other interesting points of contrast. For one, BMO was used to doing things on a large scale – to have an impact on markets and strategy. Harris's attitude, as an executive recalled, was: "don't go up against the big guys, right? Work in your own little corner of the world and don't [try] … because if you go up against Continental or [First National Bank of] Chicago, they'll crucify you. Well BMO didn't have that attitude."[82] For another, there were national cultural characteristics: Americans were seen as more gregarious and outgoing than typical Canadians. "We [Americans] are more outgoing. Americans will tell you what they think, good, bad or indifferent. Canadians are a little bit more reserved. But I think Canadians can be more tolerant. They seem more tolerant and so when I was there, I interfaced with and met a lot of different people and I was brought in on things very easily."[83]

Thus, it is perhaps unsurprising that, for many years, the culture at Harris Bank was reluctant to accept that a Canadian bank had taken over this Chicago institution. One veteran of the BMO-Harris experience recalled that more than a few Harris executives of the era seemed to "resent being acquired and resentful that [BMO] was going to manage them."[84] The banker continued:

> I think the mistake we made early on was trying to be way too nice, in
> terms of "Well, they're doing a good job, a credible job. Let them stay
> entrenched. Let them go." But I think the disservice that they paid to
> us in return was that they tried to ignore us and in some ways tried to
> get our clients to ignore us – or their clients to ignore us. We'd try to
> integrate products and they would resist. I think what actually brought
> them around, at least in the corporate banking activity is over time
> they realized that we could bring more to the table than they could
> and we could do things for their client that they couldn't do and if they
> didn't do, would lose the client eventually as they outgrew them.[85]

Another Harris banker recalled that a group of Montreal bankers "came down one day and wanted to go up and look at our trading area, our … foreign exchange area, which was a big, big business for us. And we had a sort of a mediocre office and mediocre material up there. I mean, we didn't have the money to put a first-class operation in. And [Harris] management said, 'No, you can't go up and see that.' So they went up to the twelfth floor or something, or whatever floor, and put in a brand-new – they brought their business from New York, put it here in Chicago. And they had been treated that way by senior management."[86] As another BMO executive echoed, Harris bankers had, mostly jokingly, called Canadian visitors "AFCs, which stood for Another [expletive] Canadian," which shows that even bankers can have a sharp sense of humour.[87] These remarkable stories illustrate just how deeply this kind of thing can take root in a short period of time. As one executive put it:

> The other big question mark on that was it's a foreign bank. So culturally, what's this going to mean? And everybody liked the Harris Bank culture who worked at Harris Bank. They tried to hang on to that forever. So the biggest thing: they were all kind of upset about. "Really?" What was this going to mean about the culture? Now, obviously, the more senior you were, the more you worried about what it meant from a job impact, but as you know, there was not a lot of head cutting, etc. So I'm sure people lost sleep and worried and gnashed their teeth a lot about it, but that was misplaced because nothing ever happened about it. The cultural part, that became a battle for a lot of years. Harris wanted to maintain its culture obviously, and Mulholland made the mistake of saying, "We're going to keep the 800-pound gorilla off your back" sort of thing, and so they did kind of leave it hands-off for a long time, and as a result you never really got any of the synergies or the benefit in any big way.[88]

These feelings were perhaps another reason why the Bank of Montreal left the Harris largely independent throughout the 1980s and into the 1990s. As one executive argued, BMO left Harris "alone for so long that they [didn't] even think that they're part of us other than we remind them every once in a while that they're owned by a Canadian bank. And I've had instances where I've reported to people in Harris, and they're in Canada, and they actually think that Harris bought BMO. [That was] the story they like to portray. Because how could a Canadian bank from somewhere buy a US bank? It doesn't make sense to them. So I think we left them alone for so long and they've kept that Harris identity and whatever."[89]

That said, the reason for the continued independence might have been as much regulatory as cultural. There were, and still are, tremendous differences between Canadian and American banking laws and regulatory regimes. This made integration an even greater challenge – even if the institutions had been ordered to come together. One banker with major responsibility for North American banking at BMO expressed the frustration: "I'll just absolutely tell you I failed at it, but it's very hard to run a North American bank across borders where the countries and the banking systems are so different, and the markets and the competitors are so different. And so, my job, frankly, was to facilitate that cross-border understanding. I never really got it done right. I tried but I didn't do a very good job at it."[90] In reality, however, this cannot have been the responsibility of one person or team – the organizational culture and environment was too resistant to change.

Challenges aside, there was cultural resistance to the BMO takeover both from within the Bank of Montreal and the Harris Bank. The younger generation of Harris bankers were perhaps more open to the idea of joining a bigger bank than their older peers: "Somebody like me – if you'd been there for five years or less, you're still a little bit naive and you're not in any kind of senior role where you're worried about 'Oh my God, the BMO guy is going to come and get my job,' or – so from my perspective and guys around my age – there were two things that were water cooler chatter: one was looking at it from the opportunities of 'Geez, well, a bigger bank. This has got to be good for us, right? Because we're young. There's got to be more opportunities potentially coming at us. Bigger balance sheet, can take more risk; things like that' – that all seemed positive."[91]

But many older generations voiced more negative reactions – reactions not limited only to the Harris Bank. There was plenty of resistance within the Bank of Montreal. One BMO banker recalled that many were "very negative on the transaction." Some felt that the Bank had overpaid for the Harris, and that it was somehow a "disaster." Indeed, these feelings might have been so prominent that they dissuaded Mulholland from doing more acquisitions. "I had always perceived that his vision was that Harris was just step one and that more would follow," one former Harris executive recalled, "but I think he was probably quite surprised at the kind of negative reaction that he got, and we didn't do anything strategically with Harris for the longest period of time, and that's kind of unfortunate. The funny thing is, the valuations subsequent to our deal – actually, they crept up and they dipped again when we had the recession late '80s/early '90s, and then through the '90s, in the boom period, the valuations just shot through the roof. At that point, everybody said what a genius Mulholland was to have acquired Harris when he did."[92]

The Verdict: Strategic Triumph and Missed Opportunity?

Whatever the prevailing opinion at the time, the BMO-Harris connection and the relationship between the two banks constitutes a defining feature of the contemporary Bank of Montreal experience. This goes far beyond the bottom line. From the 1980s to contemporary times, the Harris has been the vessel into which the continental dreams of Montreal bankers were poured. It was seen as a key strategic complement, a way to reform and revitalize the parent Bank as globalization and trade flows generated fresh opportunities in the 1980s and 1990s. Moreover, the Harris conferred a distinct and undeniable competitive advantage over the other Canadian chartered banks in the United States, and signalled the Bank of Montreal's return to form. The Harris positioned the broader bank in a way that other chartered banks could only envy. The Mulholland generation foresaw greater continental integration and understood the capabilities and the bench strength the Bank needed to develop in order to deliver for customers and to participate in major project financing. It is also worth remembering that BMO acquired the Harris in an era before the decades of trade liberalization enshrined by the continental free trade deals of the 1980s and 1990s.

As one retrospective banker suggested, the Harris acquisition was "genius" and "ahead of its time" in many ways. Unfortunately, the same banker reflected, BMO missed an opportunity in the aftermath of the acquisition: "I think that BMO had the opportunity of being there in a way that no other bank was, and didn't take advantage of that ... Which goes back to the other problem [the Bank of Montreal's conservatism]. But also, I think there is the whole issue of Canadian corporations knowing how to succeed in the United States. It's a very complicated history of failure across the industry. And so I personally believe that the opportunity for BMO to have done something with Harris that was not done was an opportunity that was missed."[93]

This was an inescapable conclusion of the historical record of the first few years, and one that Mulholland perhaps tried to guard against by delaying the integration.

Post-acquisition decisions are key in the success or failure of any merger enterprise. Strategies that develop collective competence and learn from their experiences are the ones that will flourish in the long term.[94] In the case of BMO-Harris, the complexity of the situation at the acquiring bank has to be taken into consideration. The information and assumptions surrounding actions and outcomes can be a big problem because they are so difficult to assess. One scholarly observer has pointed to a specific risk in these situations: superstitious learning. In this concept, the accumulation of experience can produce "more confidence in the managers' own competence than actual competence."[95] As a result, experiential learning can become "superstitious" because the "subjective experience of learning is compelling, but the connections between actions and outcomes are misspecified."[96] As Maurizio Zollo puts it, "firms do not really know what they think they know, despite (and even because of) the accumulation of experience."[97] The strong idea here, derived from previous experience, is that the Bank of Montreal management, in spite of its due diligence and its excellent analysis, underestimated the cultural impact of not acting. In retrospect, the ordinance that the "Harris should have been left alone and not integrated" need not have been respected for so long.

Whatever the explanation, the Bank's pattern of dealing with its Harris acquisition led to avoidance of greater integration for many years. In the process, the Bank also missed a golden opportunity to fully exploit the advantages of such an acquisition. When integration was eventually begun in the 1990s and 2000s, BMO bankers had to confront an entrenched and change-resistant corporate culture and administrative apparatus that would draw human and material resources better deployed elsewhere. BMO's own conservative and risk-averse culture played a defining part. Leadership, at least initially, was convinced that its own institution was simply not ready for the cross-border challenges that this new relationship represented.

Scholars studying post-merger integration suggest that initial integration is inevitably suboptimal and that, as a result, acquisitive growth decreases an acquirer's performance, eventually forcing it to engage in organizational restructuring to more fully unlock the synergistic potential. In addition, firms gain experience in integration that they can implement.[98] Even considering these insights, the integration of the two organizations took a great deal longer than anyone would have originally supposed.

There is, of course, mitigation: this was the first time that the Bank of Montreal faced questions of integration in the contemporary era. But if this critical chapter in the experience of the Bank of Montreal contains lessons, they would have to begin with the supreme importance of addressing questions and challenges of culture and organizational behaviour. The Harris acquisition was a strategic masterstroke whose force was blunted by decisions taken at the outset – for better or for worse – by an acquiring organization that was neither culturally nor organizationally ready for the opportunity and by an acquired organization that was content to be left alone.

Afterword

There is a scene in Steven Spielberg film *Lincoln* (2012) that features the titular president explaining how he could reconcile the praiseworthy goal of passing the Thirteenth Amendment abolishing slavery and involuntary servitude with the, say, extraordinary *realpolitik* methods of passing that amendment through Congress: "A compass ... [will] point you true north from where you're standing, but it's got no advice about the swamps and deserts and chasms that you'll encounter along the way. If in pursuit of your destination, you plunge ahead, heedless of obstacles, and achieve nothing more than to sink in a swamp ... [then] what's the use of knowing true north?"[99]

That relationship – between strategy and execution, between the noble goal and knowing how to get there – was the balance in play during the first, critical years of BMO's relationship with the Chicago bank. The Mulholland bank excelled at the first element – finding true north in strategic terms – and left the second, more prosaic element – dealing with the "swamps and deserts and chasms" that needed to be overcome if the strategy was to be truly successful – to subsequent generations of leadership. It was under the leadership of Alan McNally (1993–2002), Frank Techar (2002–06), and Ellen Costello (2006–10) that the legacies of the BMO-Harris nexus were truly dealt with.

The BMO universe not only changed on 4 September 1984 but also expanded. The initial decades of the Bank's Canada-US banking relationship are perhaps analogous to the timescale for cosmological change to unfold as it should – a very long time. Yet the contemporary result suggests that one can finally see the Northern Lights over Chicago.[100]

CHAPTER NINETEEN

The Far Journey: The Bank in the World

F ew of the Bank of Montreal's post-war involvements have been the subject of more inherited assumptions than operations beyond Canada and the United States, outside the Bank's traditional territory. Views about that experience are a kind of Rorschach inkblot test. Shown an ambiguous image, a person's mind works hard at defining its meaning and, in the process, reveals how they see the world.[1] For some, the Bank's operations in the Caribbean, Central and South America, China, and the Asia Pacific are all about seizing opportunity and maintaining competitiveness in an era of globalization. For others, the story revolves around long-term commitment to strategy. Still others view the Bank's record through the unyielding lens of short-term profit and loss as the natural and inescapable indicators of whether to stay or leave. In some ways, those assumptions and legends of past experience are treated as the conventional wisdom of BMO bankers – and treated respectfully, because legends are made by the collective in the moment and thereafter, while histories are generally written by one scholar.[2]

These various perspectives have all been represented around the Bank's Executive Committee table down the decades, each the product of professional training, specific banking realities, or initiation into the banking world (merchant banker, accountant, auditor, investor, commercial or personal banker). There was, and continues to be, one additional seat at that table, occupied by the institutional memory and culture of the Bank. As in every organization or institution of a certain age, tradition can be seen as "democracy of the dead," as G.K. Chesterton so memorably put it.[3] Consciously or not, the perspectives of the Bank's life beyond Canada and the United States have made their mark on the institutional memory and strategic context of operations into the contemporary era. The balance between these forces constituted what it meant to be the Bank of Montreal in the world. It is, therefore, important to define that experience, to give shape to that institutional memory that exercises its influence on how the Bank has viewed its activities abroad.

This chapter examines the Bank of Montreal's international operations (excepting the United States) to the late 1980s. It cannot hope to capture the entire breadth and the rich personal experiences of those endeavours – the relationships, meetings, deals, triumphs, and reversals that constitute the life of Canadian bankers abroad. That would require a separate and fascinating book – if it were even allowed to be published! The goal is, however, to give a coherent overview of those operations and how they fit into the larger story of the Bank's late twentieth-century experience.

The Bank of Montreal's international operations began early in the twentieth century – and well before, if you count its London presence. So why does it belong so late in this book, in this section on the 1970s and 1980s? For several reasons. If anyone deserved the title of champion of international banking beyond Canada and the United States, it was Bill Mulholland, though his predecessor Arnold Hart could give him a real run for his renminbi. The Bank's international involvement predated Mulholland's arrival, of course, and was a feature of overall bank strategy long after he departed the field. Indeed, in the late 1950s and 1960s, the Bank looked abroad to expand. In many ways, however, it was mainly during Mulholland's tenure that it most aggressively experimented with the banking world abroad as it sought to define a more coherent international presence and personality. For example, between 1976 and 1982, the Bank of Montreal's international business grew the most rapidly of the five major Canadian banks – an average of 34 per cent in comparison with the 25 per cent average growth of the four other banks combined.[4] The prestige, reputation, and stability of the Bank of Montreal and its growing expertise in mega-project financing in the resources and utilities sectors poised it for potential global success.[5] The need to diversify geographically was also a factor pulling the Mulholland bank into the international arena.

There was another, intriguing reason for Mulholland to become the internationalist he became. In the words of one senior banker, it was to disrupt the status quo: "He knew changes [in the banking world] were coming and he also knew that we needed to open up to global financial markets so our initial foray into the Euro dollar market, into LDC lending, all of these things were really part of his disruption of the status quo. A dramatic and rapid modernization of the bank. And I think there are people who would give him credit for saving the bank from just basically sailing off into a quiet oblivion."[6]

The Bank's experience abroad had ebbed and flowed according to the demands of corporate strategy, internal requirements, and the domestic market environment. When it came to the world of banking beyond Canada, the Bank's vision had traditionally focused on London and the United States, to maintain its presence in the North Atlantic's major capital markets.[7] Only in later years did the Bank systematically contemplate extending its strengths and capabilities in specific international fields. Those pursuits – including the triumphs and challenges – tell us a great deal about the aspirations, commitments, and needs of the Bank, and also how BMO used its international operations to move faster down the road of return. This chapter sets the context for the Bank's international operations, which come to a climax in the 1970s, with a special focus on its operations in Mexico, the Caribbean, and in the Asia Pacific. A final section analyzes the Bank's involvement in international sovereign loans.

Defining the Context

To understand the longer-run context of international banking with respect to the Bank of Montreal's experience, some background is in order. Between 1890 and 1931, the emergence of international banking mirrored the first phase of the internationalization of a worldwide and interdependent economy.[8] In this period, multiplying trade volumes, bigger capital requirements of public finance, and the emergence of new industrial enterprises provided a major impetus for finance to cross borders and continents. Communications technology – the telegraph and telephone in particular – facilitated greater flows of information and the opportunities for control required by management.[9] The rules of the international monetary system provided an environment especially hospitable to the internationalization of finance. In the case of the Bank of Montreal in this early stage, its flag followed trade: the arrival of Canadian business in countries like Mexico prompted expansion of bank activities there. Think of it as gravitational pull created by Canadian enterprise. In general, however, British, French, and German banks dominated this first expansion of multinational banking, which came to an abrupt end with the abandonment of the gold standard and systemic collapse of the international banking structure in 1931.

The second major era of international banking came in the wake of the Second World War, during what has been called the golden age of Western capitalism ("les trente glorieuses" in Part Five). Banks looking to the global market after 1945 faced an over-regulated sector in almost every country worth banking in, especially after the reforms of the 1930s and 1940s, which placed a range of constraints on monetary policy, discriminatory credit allocation, and capital-to-asset ratios.[10] Initially at least, transnational expansion was not an attractive option for the Bank of Montreal, which demonstrated a scarce enthusiasm for foreign adventures (with a few obvious exceptions discussed later in this chapter.) Yet, by the late 1960s and early 1970s, trade and foreign investment increased the demand for banking services, which spurred a strong expansion in the international banking scene.

Other developments added to the impetus: a long-term relaxation of foreign exchange controls (after 1958), the emergence of the Eurodollar market, and the development of a money market for time deposits in foreign currencies were major factors.[11] The financial integration of major OECD (Organisation for Economic Co-operation and Development) countries as a result of these changes made for a more attractive climate for international banking in all its manifestations (such as inter-bank dealings, foreign currency markets, and so forth). The emergence of banking multinationalization also offered opportunities for banks to expand their relationships with corporate customers with global activities (sometimes referred to as a "follow-the-customer" strategy).[12]

The story of the Bank of Montreal's late-twentieth-century experience in international banking should be understood against the broad experience of Canadian banks abroad in this period. In the fifteen years between 1965 and 1980, Canadian banks acquired "more than 160 primarily foreign banks and companies," either in whole or in part.[13] Furthermore, the trend was to move from retail banking to wholesale banking services in this period. Canada's big banks also doubled their share of foreign assets from 20 per cent to 40 per cent between 1965 and 1980. Yet, the share of assets in foreign currencies dwindled from 15 per cent in 1960 to about 6 per cent in 1980. International banks from the United States, Japan, Europe, and elsewhere proved to be aggressive and innovative competition for Canadian banks, especially in handling international cash positions, interest, and foreign exchange volatility.[14] As James Darroch notes, electronic-based, transnational Euromarkets changed the nature of international banking – and fundamentally so. Here again, technology played a central part in developments: superior information flows not only drove transaction costs down but also made banking services less important for large firms. If a large multinational like IBM or General Motors could go directly to the market for funds, why use a bank intermediary?[15] This "disintermediation" and "deregulation" blew that market wide open.

Moreover, in the 1970s, the Canadian domestic banking market pushed banks to consider international fields, particularly in the wake of federal legislation designed to limit inflation and prices in the mid-1970s.[16] That led several of them, including the Bank of Montreal, to push more aggressively into international banking, including sovereign and less-developed country loans. The search for profitability was a key driver in this evolving strategy. At the Bank of

Montreal, Bill Mulholland led the charge into these international fields. By the late 1980s, however, the factors pushing and pulling the Canadian banks onto the global banking terrain had all but vanished: complexities and disillusionment in some of the Bank's major markets prompted a return to North America and the more promising and stable fields of retail banking.

Projecting Montreal onto the Global Stage

As earlier chapters chronicled, the Bank of Montreal had a long presence in international banking, at least in the North Atlantic world, having established offices in New York (1859), Chicago (1861), and London (1870). However, a significant international expansion would not happen until the twentieth century. The Bank expanded to Mexico in 1906 and continental Europe (Paris) in 1919, and opened then a second branch in London. In 1918, it also acquired the Bank of British North America, thus gaining a foothold in California. While international activities were severely curtailed during the Great Depression – the Bank shut down its operations in Mexico and continental Europe – a reconsideration of international operations and expansion followed the Second World War.

Between 1950 and 1980, the Bank opened new offices throughout the United States, re-established a presence in Mexico, and opened offices in France, Germany, Italy, and Spain. Major new investments were also made in Asia, where the Bank opened offices in prominent financial capitals like Tokyo, Hong Kong, and Seoul, before entering the mainland Chinese market in 1983 with an office in Beijing. The most substantial international presence of the period, however, was the Bank of Montreal's partnership with the Bank of London and South America (BOLSA) and Barclays DCO: the Bank of London and Montreal (BOLAM). Started by BMO and BOLSA in 1958, before being joined by Barclays six years later, BOLAM was a significant player in the Caribbean and Latin America, with branches in The Bahamas, Colombia, Ecuador, El Salvador, Guatemala, Honduras, Jamaica, Nicaragua, Panama, and Trinidad. BMO's involvement in this part of the world was entirely through BOLAM. In 1970, the Bank of Montreal withdrew from BOLAM, taking with it BOLAM's branches in The Bahamas and Jamaica.[17]

It is important to make a careful distinction between branches, agencies, and representative offices. Branches offer full retail service banking, while agencies are small permanent deposit branches. Representative offices – BMO's most prominent form of international representation outside of BOLAM in this period – conduct marketing, establish international connections, and are generally only involved in non-transactional operations. For the Bank of Montreal, representative offices often served as a general liaison between the host country and the head offices in Canada. By 1972 (after the partnership with BOLAM, which had branches throughout Latin America and the Caribbean), the Bank of Montreal only had ten branches outside of Canada – in United States (five), United Kingdom (two), Germany (two), and Grand Cayman (one).[18] The vast majority of BMO's international presence was comprised of representative offices. In the mid-1970s, its number of branches placed the Bank of Montreal second-last among its competitors, behind the Royal Bank of Canada (85 non-Canadian branches), Bank of Nova Scotia (69), and the Canadian Imperial Bank of Commerce (57).[19] It was only ahead of Toronto-Dominion Bank, with four non-Canadian branches.

This relative disadvantage internationally vis-à-vis other Canadian competitors lay behind the major reorganization in the 1980s, and was cited as one of the reasons BMO ceased business in The Bahamas and maintained or intensified its focus on China. The acquisition of Harris Bank in Chicago in 1984 accelerated both withdrawal from and reorganization of international operations. California operations were scaled back considerably, and the Bank shut down offices in Europe and Asia. By 1990, BMO's retail banking services were largely limited to Canada (BMO) and the United States (Harris), while the remaining international presence was through representative offices, offering financial services to corporate clients and governments (after 2006, BMO Capital Markets).

The Bank of Montreal's global presence in the twentieth century is therefore marked by tentative expansion, followed by a return to home territory. After a period of international expansion between 1950 and 1970, when the Bank entered new markets almost annually, the strategy after 1970 took a different orientation while maintaining some continuity. Under Mulholland's leadership, international operations were reappraised and reorganized. His vision for the Bank of greater involvement in global financial markets was matched by an impatience for results. The Bank entered the 1990s as a much leaner institution with a more carefully appraised international presence and portfolio.

In addition to a physical presence around the world, the Bank of Montreal entered into affiliations and partnerships with various banks and organizations, further enhancing BMO's international reach. Table 19.1 highlights some of the largest and most significant in the 1945–90 period.

A Southern Exposure: The Bank of London and Montreal

The Bank of London and Montreal remains one of the most interesting chapters in BMO's post-war international experience. Created as a joint venture between Bank of Montreal and the Bank of London and South America (BOLSA) in 1958, it was an exceedingly good match at the time.[20] The two banks needed each other. Bank of Montreal needed BOLSA (and its branch system)

Table 19.1 | Bank of Montreal international affiliations and partnerships, 1970

Affiliation/partnership	Date	Description
Australian International Finance Corporation (AIFC)	1970	The AIFC was a partnership between the Australia and New Zealand Banking Group (40%), Bank of Montreal (20%), Irving Trust Company (20%), and Mitsubishi Bank (20%).[1]
Hochelaga Holdings N.V.	1970	The Bank of Montreal established this offshore subsidiary company to hold its ownership stakes in Banque Transatlantique, Joh. Berenberg, Gossler & Co., Nacional Finaciera S.A., and Mass Containers Limited.[2] At the time Hochelaga Holdings Inc. was created, the combined value of the companies it held was about $1.5 million.[3]
Joh. Berenberg, Gossler & Co.	1968	Joh. Berenberg, Gossler & Co. was a leading private bank headquartered in Hamburg, West Germany.[4] The Bank of Montreal obtained a 9% share interest in 1968.[5] The Bank's shares were transferred to Hochelaga Holdings N.V. in 1970.
Banque Transatlantique	1968	Banque Transatlantique was a French bank and an important member of the influential Crédit Industriel et Commercial banking group, the largest non-nationalized banking organization in France. BMO obtained an interest share of 10% in 1968. Headquartered in Paris, Banque Transatlantique also held significant subsidiaries in Morocco and Tunisia. R.D. Mulholland, president of the Bank of Montreal, was elected to the board of Banque Transatlantique.[6] BMO's holdings in Banque Transatlantique were transferred to Hochelaga Holdings N.V. in 1970.

/continued

to expand its presence in Latin America, and the joint venture came at a particularly opportune moment since the volume of trade between Canada and Latin America had increased substantially during the 1950s. BOLSA, on its part, was eager to enter into an agreement with a prominent North American banking institution that had the fiscal solvency and operative know-how to underwrite such a venture.

In late 1957 and early 1958, BOLSA approached the Bank of Montreal about the possibility of a joint venture. It was BOLSA's first choice in the hemisphere because "the Bank of Montreal has an unparalleled record of sound conservative yet progressive banking and reputation second to none."[21] Secondly, BOLSA saw the two banks as "complementary and not competitive [with each other.]"[22] The Bank's impeccable reputation had generated substantial

Table 19.1 | *continued*

Affiliation/partnership	Date	Description
Montfield Trust Co. (Bermuda)	1968	Montfield Trust Co. was a trust company set up in Bermuda in 1968 as a partnership between the Bank of Montreal and the Bank of N.T. Butterfield & Sons Limited.[7] The Bank of Montreal provided 40% of the capital, and held a 40% ownership stake.[8]
Private Investment Co. for Asia (PICA)	1968	PICA was a private investment company in which the Bank of Montreal held a 50% ownership stake.[9] PICA, incorporated in Panama in 1968, was headquartered in Tokyo, Japan. The board of directors was comprised of representatives from Australia, Canada, Italy, Switzerland, West Germany, Japan, and the United States.

Sources:

1 Michael T. Skully, "Financial Institutions and Markets in Australia," in *Financial Institutions and Markets in the Southwest Pacific: A Study of Australia, Fiji, New Zealand, and Papua New Guinea,* edited by Michael T. Skully (London: MacMillan, 1985), 32.

2 BMOA, Bank of Montreal Annual Report, 1970.

3 Bank of Montreal, Executive Committee of the Board Minutes, 13 January 1970.

4 BMOA, Bank of Montreal Annual Report, 1968.

5 Wallace Clement, *Continental Corporate Power: Economic Elite Linkages between Canada and the United States* (Toronto: McClelland and Stewart, 1977), 313.

6 "Bank of Montreal acquires interest in French banking group, plans to expand foreign business," *Globe and Mail,* 27 March 1968.

7 BMOA, Bank of Montreal, Executive Committee of the Board Minutes, 20 July 1969.

8 BMOA, Bank of Montreal, Executive Committee of the Board Minutes, 23 December 1969.

9 Wallace Clement, *Continental Corporate Power: Economic Elite Linkages between Canada and the United States* (Toronto: McClelland and Stewart, 1977), 313.

dividends in precisely offers such as this: "There is a long tradition of friendship between the Bank of Montreal and the City of London (for example, during the last war the Bank of Montreal was of great assistance to the Bank of England)."[23]

One curious reputational consideration for BOLSA was the Bank's home city: BOLSA was concerned that Montreal had lost ground to Toronto as an international financial centre, though it remained "a great capital city [*sic*]."[24] Still, for international deals such as this potential one, "the disadvantage of being too closely identified with the Province of Quebec is a factor," which nonetheless "need not enter into any serious consideration of a proposal to form a partnership to expand Anglo-Canadian banking in the Latin American continent."[25] This was perhaps a portent of things to come for the Bank's domicile city in terms of metropolitan rivalry with Toronto.

The Bank's president Gordon Ball commissioned a report on the possible venture in early 1958; the investigation was chaired by B.C. Gardner and involved John Walters, assistant ceneral manager, E.R. Ernst, superintendent of the International Department, and Fraser Cliff, assistant chief accountant. Characteristically for Bank mandarins of the era, the approach was careful, but positive:

> The proposal has considerable merit if it is approached, not from the view of enlarging our figures, but as a constructive venture into the foreign field with a good, reputable and experienced partner, and with reasonable expectation of profit and expansion, which, while advantageous in themselves, will aid us considerably in the domestic field. We obtain entry into six foreign markets with a population of 30 million people, and to do this without experience might well be a costly matter ... I think it is right to emphasize that the present proposal may be only a first step and that it should be kept firmly in mind that the prospects for growth and enlargement of our interest in South America and other parts – on a 50-50 basis – should be taken into calculations.[26]

The Bank proceeded with the venture. The new bank, the Bank of London and Montreal (BOLAM), had an initial nominal capitalization of CA$20 million. The board of BOLAM consisted of six members from BMO and six members from BOLSA. Chairmanship was rotated between the two annually, with management in the hands of BOLSA personnel for the first three years.

Under the terms of the joint venture, BOLSA contributed to BOLAM existing BOLSA branches in six Caribbean and South American countries (see table 19.2). The value of existing BOLSA assets and business that was to be merged into BOLAM was calculated at CA$4,400,900.[27] The Bank of Montreal contributed an equal amount in cash. Additional capital would be equally split between BMO and BOLSA. Under the initially proposed contract, management of BOLAM would reside in London, but this arrangement meant that BOLAM's entire earnings would be liable to UK income tax and profit taxes. The Internal Revenue Act of the United Kingdom held that if a collaboration was in any way directed from London (as it would be through BOLSA), UK income tax was payable. For this reason, Montreal bankers proposed that the administration and incorporation of the new bank to be in The Bahamas. Thus, BOLAM's head office – which for tax reasons was an active company with administrative staff of its own – was set up in Nassau.

The partnership with BOLSA in the creation of BOLAM promised to be a valuable acquisition for the Bank of Montreal. In 1956, Canada had purchased oil, coffee, and other products valued at $240 million from the countries in which BOLAM now had offices. In the same period, Canada had sold manufactured

Table 19.2 | BOLAM branches on opening day, 1958

Country	Branches
Colombia	• Barranquilla
	• Bogota
	• Cali
	• Medelin
Ecuador	• Guayaquil
	• Quito
El Salvador	• San Miguel (Agency)
	• San Salvador
	• Santa Ana (Agency)
Guatemala	• Guatemala City
Nicaragua	• Managua
Venezuela	• Caracas
	• Caracas East (Agency)

goods, including newsprint, valued at $63 million. The volume of trade between Canada and the BOLAM area had increased substantially in the years leading up to the joint venture.[28] However, despite these promising figures, management did have some concerns about the political instability of the region into which the Bank was about to expand. They were placated when the due diligence report confirmed that while revolutions "are rather common, [they] rarely seriously affect the economic stability of a country; in fact, they often result in much needed but sometimes short-lived reforms in political and economic spheres."[29] That judgment would be put to the test in the 1960s and 1970s.

BOLAM's Early Development

The first report on BOLAM reached the Bank of Montreal board on 16 December 1958. It noted that the thirteen offices continued to operate under the BOLSA name until legal transfers into BOLAM were completed.[30] Nicaragua had already approved the transfer, with Ecuador expected to follow suit. No complications were expected, although the legal process, especially in Guatemala and Venezuela, was expected to take longer. It would only be a few months until the first branch expansions were announced: in Kingston, Jamaica (March 1959), and Port of Spain, Trinidad (autumn 1959).[31]

BOLAM's performance in the early 1960s was both positive and promising. By late 1963, BOLAM chairman Sir George Bolton was actively searching for new acquisition targets. That autumn, he reported his intention "to explore with Inversiones Mendoza the possibility of merging the operations of the Bank of Venezuela with Banco La Guaria, 60% of the capital stock of which is controlled by Inversiones Mendoza, the balance being in the hands of the public."[32] A meeting was held in New York on 25 October with members of the Mendoza Group, with the suggestion that "the venture be put together on a 60% Venezuelan and 40% Anglo-Canadian participation basis, it being generally conceded that it would be necessary for the Anglo-Canadian participants to contribute more capital to the operation."[33] In due course, the executive committee agreed, and the venture proporal was sent for approval to the boards of the parent banks.

In the mid-1960s, new opportunities presented themselves when Barclays DCO (Dominion, Colony, Overseas) expressed an interest in partnership in the Caribbean. Its African business was being increasingly affected by Africanization programs across the continent, so Julian Crossley, of Barclays' international division, looked to "expand into new territories" and "acquire a foothold in South America in particular, where DCO was almost absent, and to limit competition of BOLAM in the Caribbean."[34] As BOLAM and DCO were competitors, Crossley initially wanted BOLAM to take a stake in DCO to prevent expansion of BOLAM into DCO territory. This idea was rejected because BOLSA did not want to have any responsibility for Barclays' African holdings (which ownership in DCO would do). As George Bolton (BOLSA) explained to Julian Crossley (DCO) in a letter on 20 February 1959:

> I have given a lot of thought to the proposal that BOLAM might acquire a share interest in DCO, but I do not feel that this helps to achieve our objective, nor do I feel it good policy for BOLAM to be directly associated with your tremendous activities in Africa. This also applies to suggestions I have made that Barclays might take an interest in BOLSA. I would therefore like you to consider more specifically a proposal that was touched upon in an earlier conversation for the whole of DCO operations in the West Indies to be hived off into a separate organization with its head office and management resident, for argument sake, in Barbados. If something of this kind could be arranged, Barclays West Indies would retain its own identity and continue to carry out its existing operations. BOLAM would concentrate on the non-English speaking areas, using its manpower and financial resources to expand not only in the territories where it already has branches, but also in places like Mexico, Honduras, Costa Rica, and Cuba. The two banks, so organized, with some agreed areas of activity, could then have a substantial interchange of capital – Barclays West Indies having a holding of BOLAM shares and vice versa.[35]

The orderly development and management of the retail banking between the two top players was tempting, as it would allow resources to be focused on the development of services and potentially greater profitability.

Crossley was opposed to the idea of merging Barclays West Indies locations with BOLAM as part of the deal. Instead, he counter-proposed a deal that gave Barclays a one-third ownership in BOLAM and prevented BOLAM expansion into DCO territory. That prospective deal occupied Arnold Hart and George Bolton in extensive discussion about the pros and cons of a partnership with Barclays DCO. On the negative side, the deal contemplated the cessation of competition between Barclays West Indies and BOLAM branches, effectively limiting BOLAM's ability to expand into territories where Barclays West Indies had a significant foothold. The Bank of Montreal, in particular, was concerned about three-way ownership, with two-thirds landing in British hands and putting Canadian interests at a disadvantage. On the positive side, however, Crossley and Bolton recognized that "certainly in banking it is more than ever the day of Big Units; a small concern, however well managed, simply does not have resources to make policies effective."[36] A second powerful reason was to provide a bulwark against American expansion: "it seems an important British and Canadian interest to be able to run a strong and efficient banking organization in an area which otherwise might be left wide open to the American banks."[37] Old ties die hard: the Bank of Montreal leadership as a matter of course identified strongly with their colleagues in the City of London. The partnership proceeded in 1964, with Barclays DCO becoming a full and equal partner in BOLAM. Each of the three partners would be able to nominate up to five directors on the BOLAM board as representatives of their respective bank.[38]

The three-way partnership did not last long. A short few years after the deal with Barclays, in early 1970, the Bank of Montreal decided it wanted out. There were several reasons for this decision. With two-thirds of BOLAM owned by British interests, BMO's Canadian interests were always in the minority. On top of that, the Canadian government changed its foreign investment policies: in light of these changes, "it ha[d] become more evident that the Bank of Montreal's contribution to growth and the development in the area, particularly Canadian identity, has not come up to our expectations through the BOLAM vehicle."[39] Negotiations between the Bank of Montreal and BOLSA on the terms of the separation carried on throughout January 1970. As the executive committee of the board minutes noted: "Negotiations have been carried out in Montreal for the past two weeks with two senior officers of BOLSA acting on behalf of that bank and Barclays, and several of our executive officers."[40]

Shortly thereafter, the Bank of Montreal exchanged its BOLAM stock for that of BOLSA, and then bought from BOLSA the BOLAM branches located in Trinidad, Jamaica, and the Bahamas, with certain exceptions. The 715,000 shares of BOLAM were valued at £3,375,000 sterling to be paid in BOLSA shares valued at CA$8,690,625. The book value of the Bank's BOLAM holdings was CA $7,720,597.[41] The branches that the Bank desired would cost $1.1 million in Bahamian dollars (B$) and would not carry on domestic retail banking business at all.[42] Thus, in March 1970, the Caribbean operations of the Bank of Montreal were incorporated as the Bank of Montreal (Bahamas & Caribbean) Limited with an authorized capital of B$25 million of which B$3 million was to be issued and paid up.[43]

At the same time, the Bank went through the necessary bureaucracy of transferring BOLAM's banking licences to the Bank of Montreal. The Trinidadian government took the opportunity to kick out what it saw as a hold-over of British influence. The government announced that it would be taking over the BOLAM bank branch in Port of Spain, intending to use it as the headquarters of a proposed National Bank of Trinidad and Tobago.[44] As the *Globe and Mail* reported on 24 March 1970: "The Bank of Montreal announced recently that it intends to acquire 100 per cent ownership of the Bank of London and Montreal through a share exchange. The Trinidadian Prime Minister, Eric Williams, took to the airwaves to announce it, partially in response to 'Black Power' demands for economic independence for Trinidad and Tobago."[45] After the announcement, the Bank of Montreal had no other choice than to withdraw its intent to take over BOLAM's Trinidad branch, removing BOLSA from any contractual obligation. As the Bank of Montreal's Annual Report later reflected: "In Trinidad ... before we could take over the operation, the government decided to acquire the BOLAM office to start a government owned bank."[46] Instead, the Bank of Montreal exercised its option to acquire two branch banks in Jamaica and two in the Bahamas.[47]

After the resistance met in Trinidad, Bank of Montreal executive responsible for the line of business, Peter R. Shaddick, moved to assure the Bank's leadership that the takeover plans in Jamaica and the Bahamas were proceeding according to plan. Speaking with reporters in March 1970, he stated that "the governments of Jamaica and the Bahamas have given verbal approval to the proposed transfer for banking licenses in the two countries from the Bank of London and Montreal to the Canadian bank."[48]

The branch in Kingston, Jamaica, was one of the oldest in the BOLAM system, opening in March 1959. Like Trinidad, Jamaica had obtained independence from the United Kingdom in 1962, but here the Bank of Montreal was able to transfer BOLAM's banking licences to its new Jamaican operation, the Bank of Montreal (Jamaica) Ltd. In the spring of 1970, the Bank of Montreal (Jamaica) Ltd commenced operations with a capitalization of CA$2 million, "offering 51 per cent of its equity to Jamaican investors," no doubt in an attempt to placate local resentment of foreign influence and avoid what had happened in Trinidad.[49] However, by early 1977, the nationalization impulse began to take root in Jamaica with the election of a new government. In January 1977, Jamaican prime minister Michael Manley announced that his government intended "to take over control of three commercial banks on the island." He also said "the Government intends to take a 51 per cent interest in Radio Jamaica, which [was] owned by non-Jamaican interests, and control of Caribbean Cement Co."[50]

The Caribbean was increasingly a less hospitable place for Canadian capital. After the Bank of Montreal was forced to sell its holdings on the island to the Jamaican government, the latter converted the old Bank of Montreal branches in Kingston and Half Way Tree to branches of the newly minted government-owned Bank of Surrey. Mirroring Trinidad, it was intended to be a new national bank for Jamaica. However, by the summer of 1978, the Bank of Surrey had ceased all operations.[51]

The third and most successful of the Bank of Montreal's post-BOLAM Caribbean operations was in The Bahamas where, on 15 July 1970, the Bank of Montreal (Bahamas & Caribbean) Limited commenced operations.[52] Back in February 1970, Peter R. Shaddick had sent an application to Carleton E. Francis, The Bahamas' minister of finance, to establish a retail banking subsidiary in the island country, laying out in detail the Bank's plans. Shaddick informed Francis that the Bank's hopes to become a prominent presence in The Bahamas and in the Caribbean through BOLAM were being frustrated because of government policy and economic trends and had "led the Bank of Montreal to conclude that it wishes to bank in the islands under its own organizational set-up; this organization being a Bank of Montreal subsidiary, incorporated in Nassau, working in partnership with local shareholders."[53] Given that decision, the Bank signalled its intention to sell its BOLAM shares to the remaining BOLAM partners, and to receive certain options to acquire branches in the territory. "In essence, the Bank of Montreal will withdraw from the Central and South American branches and BOLSA and DCO will withdraw from the Island branches."[54]

The Bank of Montreal (Bahamas & Caribbean) Limited was the largest of BMO's Caribbean subsidiaries and was incorporated with an authorized capital of B$25 million and a paid-up capital of B$3 million.[55] This was unsurprising. The Bahamas was key to the Bank of Montreal's long-term strategy for the area. Just like BOLAM, the Bank of Montreal intended to headquarter a new, larger Caribbean operation in Nassau. Under the proposal submitted to the Bahamian finance minister in February 1970, the Bank proposed to open at least eight branches in The Bahamas and to make the Bank of Montreal (Bahamas & Caribbean) Limited a key part of a bigger initiative, called the Canadian Caribbean Banking Corporation, which was to be established

Table 19.3 | Intended branches for the Bank of Montreal's
proposed Canadian Caribbean Banking Corporation

Country	Number of Branches
Barbados	3
Jamaica	8
Guyana	8
Bahamas	8
Trinidad	6
Guadeloupe and Martinique	4
Leeward and Windward Islands	3
Total	40

Source: BMOA, Bank of Bahamas, "Presentation to the Government of
The Bahamas by Bank of Montreal Re: Canadian Caribbean Banking
Corporation – The Canadian Caribbean Banking Corporation Organization
Structure – 1975," 16 February 1970.

Table 19.4 | Banks and their number of branches in
The Bahamas, 1985

Bank	Number of Branches	
	New Providence	Freeport
Royal Bank of Canada	8	1
Bank of Nova Scotia	6	1
Canadian Imperial Bank of Commerce	5	2
Barclays Bank	5	1
Bank of Montreal Bahamas Ltd	2	1
Chase	1	1
Citibank	1	0
Subtotal	28	7
Total	35	

Source: BMOA, Bank of Bahamas, "Review Bank of Montreal Bahamas Ltd,
Bank of Montreal Bahamas Corporate Planning, 1985.

by 1975.[56] The Canadian Caribbean Banking Corporation was intended to
become a major player in the area with a presence across the Caribbean
(see table 19.3); however, that envisaged expansion did not materialize. No
new branches were opened, and by 1977, the Bank of Montreal had lost its

holdings in Jamaica, leaving the Bank with branches only in The Bahamas and no presence on other Caribbean islands. Reflecting the new reality, the Bank's name was changed in 1983 to Bank of Montreal Bahamas Ltd.[57]

By 1985, the Bank of Montreal Bahamas Ltd operated only three branches in the Bahamas: two in Nassau and one in Freeport. It was one of seven commercial banks on the island serving the local market and, thus, faced stiff competition (see table 19.4). Market share was dominated by three other Canadian banks – the Royal Bank of Canada, the Bank of Nova Scotia, and the Canadian Imperial Bank of Commerce – which, together, held about 75 per cent of the loan/deposit base on the island. With its measly 6 to 8 per cent, the Bank of Montreal was a very small player.[58]

In the wake of the international reorganizations that followed the purchase of Harris Bankcorp, Inc. in 1984, Bank of Montreal leadership faced a decision about the fate of the Bank of Montreal Bahamas Ltd. In 1985, the Bank of Montreal Bahamas Corporate Planning Department conducted an in-depth review. The process gives us a good glimpse into the thinking and decision-making process of the Bank of the era as leadership considered the following five options: (1) continue as is – no investment in either automation or branches other than that already planned; (2) revert to a branch structure; (3) continue with changes – (a) reduce the infrastructure, (b) reduce capital to a "minimum level", and (c) make the "defensive investments" felt necessary to even maintain current market share; (4) sell Bank of Montreal Bahamas; or (5) liquidate.[59]

In the end, the Bank decided to go with option number 4, to sell the Bank of Montreal Bahamas. The reasons were multiple, but deteriorating financial results were prominent in the thinking. The Corporate Planning Department projected that, over time, the local loan base in The Bahamas would decrease and that foreign currency deposits were anticipated to decline at a rate of CA$5 million per year. Under this scenario, net interest income would fall by 11 per cent by 1989 while expenses would rise by 5 per cent. This would put the Bank of Montreal Bahamas in the red by 1989.[60] What is more, because the Bank of Montreal Bahamas was third smallest in the market with very few branches, it simply could not compete as a full-service retail banking operations, especially if it was unwilling to make investments to increase market share.[61] The Bank was also unwilling to invest in the processes required to automate the back office and match competitor service offerings. A minimum of two new branches were required to keep up with possible demand. That would involve expenditures in the $2-million range in a twenty-four-month period, which would have a serious impact on an already declining bottom line.[62] At any rate, even this investment "would be based on defensive considerations with poor prospects to increase market share in view of the stronghold position of Royal, CIBC, and Bank of Nova Scotia who would continue to be much larger operations with important scale of volume advantages," the report concluded.[63]

Another consideration that factored into the Bank's decision was the stability of The Bahamas itself. Although The Bahamas had a stable government, it had been in power for many years and was said to be plagued by corruption at all levels. The Bank was especially concerned about the government's involvement in the massively profitable drug trade. Furthermore, the Corporate Planning Department was worried that the elections of 1987 came with risk of local upheaval.[64] The economic outlook, to complete the picture, was also not especially rosy, with high unemployment (20 per cent to 30 per cent), endemic drug use, and crime dominating the picture.[65] Besides, the Bank was looking to Chicago and Harris Bank as the strategic lodestar of its future, not the Caribbean.

But those official reasons were not the only motivations. As one Bank of Montreal executive involved in the operations at the time suggested, Mulholland became much more sensitive to being above board in dealings with the regulatory authorities in the United States in the wake of the acquisition of Harris Bank. "I think it's making a nice profit … it's doing well," he recalled Mulholland saying, "You've done a good job. But I think the time has passed. We should get rid of it because I don't want to sacrifice that big investment in the Harris Bank and run the risk that we may be caught unwittingly as part of something that [Colombian drug lord Pablo] Escobar and these guys are pulling off on the Bahamas."[66]

That, if anything, was an understatement. As a senior auditor sent over to the Bahamian operations recalled, the money sloshing around the island was affecting Bank behaviour and organization. On one trip, his team entered the vault and saw there was a huge pile of moneybags in the corner. One would expect such a thing in a bank vault, but these were overflowing. Asked for an explanation, the manager of the branch said: "That's the money we can't fit in the safe." The money was uncounted, so the auditor and his team had to count it, without the benefit of a counting machine – a job that ended up taking virtually the whole night. The next morning, the rest of the audit continued:

> We sat behind the teller line, because as an auditor, you didn't have a desk … So I sat and was just watching [the teller line], ticking away, doing my job of watching the teller line, and I saw a teller take a deposit from a customer, stamp all her things, do her things, and take the deposit slip and the cash and put it in her purse. Which – I thought, "Hm. Not the normal thing to happen. It's supposed to go in your drawer." So I went to the manager and said … "Yeah. So I think you'd better get her in the office and tell her to bring her purse." So we get her

in there, we open the purse, dump it out, and here's deposit slips and money and whatever. And we sort of said, like, "What are you doing?" And she goes, "Well, why shouldn't I do it? Everybody else does it too." And I think it was part of the drug money culture, that if it was a small amount, nobody's going to complain about – that they were taking it. So then we had to have her fired and, you know, then watch everybody else, what they were doing.[67]

Considering the Bank's reputation for probity and professionalism, this was a hair-raising state of affairs.

So, without an ability to leverage the Bank's automation capabilities, with no access to the large corporate market, without a link for the global corporate funds management network, and not being part of the North American strategy, as well as to avoid anything to do with the drug trade, the bank's Bahamian presence was coming to an inevitable end.[68] In the end, the Corporate Planning Department concluded that: "As a relatively small competitor in the Bahamian market, the bank cannot as easily justify capital investments in automation as its larger competitors. Without these investments, though, a deterioration in market share in a highly competitive environment is likely. This and the parent's global strategy in which the Bank of Montreal Bahamas Ltd does not have a significant role are the reasons why the Bank of Montreal would like to divest itself of its subsidiary."[69]

The Treasury Group Management of the Bank of Montreal concurred, adding: "Bank of Montreal Bahamas Ltd is not strategically important to the Bank in an international customer delivery network. Future prospects for sustaining historic levels of earnings on a stand-alone basis are not good beyond 1986 at best. The Treasury Group should therefore obtain Senior Executive approval to actively and immediately pursue a commercial sale of Bank of Montreal Bahamas Limited. The expediency of such a course of action is critical to maximize sale price prior to serious profit deterioration and/or the avoidance of further capital expenditure."[70]

The Final Boarding Process

In 1988, the Bank of Montreal reached a deal with the Government of the Commonwealth of The Bahamas and the Euro Canadian Bank to sell the Bank of Montreal Bahamas Ltd. The government agreed to "a purchase price of US$5 million cash for the domestic business; BMO to keep the retained earnings and the general reserves totaling about $8 million, as well as the foreign currency term deposits totaling about US$90 million. This means a cash takeout of roughly US$13 million."[71] The deal was finalized in September

1988, and by October, the Bank of Montreal Bahamas Ltd closed for business, bringing to an end the Bank of Montreal's retail banking venture in the Caribbean and Latin America that had begun with the BOLAM partnership exactly thirty years prior, in 1958. For the time being, the Bank of Montreal continued "to offer foreign currency term deposit services in Nassau through its wholly owned subsidiary, Bank of Montreal International Limited, but ... cease[d] to be engaged in local retail banking."[72] The deal created the National Bank of The Bahamas, a full-service retail bank with branches in Nassau and Freeport. Under terms of the deal, the National Bank of The Bahamas was jointly owned (49/51) by the Euro Canadian Bank and the Government of the Commonwealth of The Bahamas.[73]

The Caribbean experience presented the Bank of Montreal's leadership with a set of challenges that in some ways transcended the business of banking or the specific proximate causes of its departure from the field. One of those challenges was central to all long-range strategy: a clear vision as to why the Bank was there and a commitment to that vision in the long term. Stay or go, give or withhold, hesitate or leap: the "condescension of posterity" is not presented with the facts and exigencies of the moment. The reasons for leaving seem compelling and logical, but at the same time point toward the fundamental issue of the international operations of the period – the seeming lack of a long-term commitment to the Bank's international presence.

Banking in Mexico

The Bank of Montreal has a long history in Mexico, making attempts to establish a permanent presence there no less than three times between 1906 and 2001. The Bank's objectives in Mexico were driven by the same careful, pragmatic approach that characterized its other international operations. When political or economic turmoil caused a downturn in the Mexican market, BMO pulled out. Conversely, when opportunities for expansion presented themselves, BMO seized the moment and made substantial investments into its presence there.

The Bank of Montreal first entered the Mexican market in 1906, opening a branch office in Mexico City. In 1910, the country collapsed in revolution and civil war that officially lasted until a new constitution was signed in 1917, although violence continued until 1920. However, according to BMO records, the year 1917 "may be taken as the beginning of our operations after the revolutionary period," as Mexico returned to the gold standard and relative economic stability was achieved.[74]

During the revolutionary turmoil, though, the Bank operated at a loss. Internal records estimate that between 1911 and 1915, the Mexico City branch lost between US$50,000 and US$100,000 per year. It was not until after 1917 that the branch began turning a profit. As the effects of the revolution sub-sided, BMO's Mexican business boomed in the 1920s. The bank significantly expanded, opening up a number of new branches: Veracruz (1922), Puebla (1923), Guadalajara (1924), Monterrey (1924), Tampico (1926), and a second Mexico City office (1926). At its post-war peak, BMO operated seven offices in Mexico. Following the collapse of world markets in 1929, business turned sour. In the immediate aftermath and during the Great Depression, BMO grad-ually exited the Mexican market. Most of the branches ceased operations by 1934–35; however, it appears to have taken until 1938 for BMO's main Mexico City branch to close down, and for Mexican legal authorities to finalize the closure of all BMO branches.

The period after the Second World War stirred renewed interest in a possible return to Mexico. In January 1945, the general manager reported that Bank officers familiar with the area had made a recommendation that the Bank open a representative office in Mexico City to promote business development in the Republic of Mexico and throughout Central America. Unlike the pre-1935 Mex-ican branches, the new representative office would not conduct regular bank-ing business, but would keep in close touch with banking correspondents and provide "a useful service to Canadian firms trading in those areas, and a similar service to companies in Mexico and Central America which export goods to Canada."[75]

The idea must have gained some traction, since George Spinney offered further reflections in 1946 about the possibility of reopening branches in Mexico at an undisclosed future date. "Should it be decided to reopen a branch in Mexico City," Spinney suggested, "consideration might be given to the desirability of forming a separate corporation similar to San Francisco ... If this were done it is assumed we would be on an equal footing with local banks as regards to all operations. This would also get away from any liability the Bank of Montreal [would be exposed to] in Canada by way of suits, et cetera, which would have to be instituted against the local bank."[76] The latter was a considerable issue after the Bank's removal from the country in the 1930s, and showed that BMO had learned from its earlier mistakes.

BMO's Second Mexican Adventure

The Bank of Montreal formally re-entered the Mexican market in 1963. As had been suggested back in 1945, the Bank intended its new Mexican operations to be a "source of commercial and credit information for Can-adians doing business in Mexico." Being the only Canadian banking office in Mexico (the other Canadian banks had also withdrawn from the country in the 1930s), it would facilitate trade and other business ties between Canada and Mexico and "help Canadian businessmen develop their Mexican interests."[77] The Mexico City representative office was the Bank's nineteenth location outside of Canada, not including the BOLAM offices, and it quickly grew to become an important part of its international presence. Business was booming throughout the 1960s and into the 1970s with the representative office loaning money to Mexican businesses and providing opportunities for Canadian businesses abroad. As one article of the era suggested, "foreign capital was pouring in, thanks to hot construction and energy industries. BMO had dozens of people in [Mexico City], arranging corporate loans for commercial ventures."[78]

But as in the 1920s and 1930s, the good times did not last. To finance rapid industrialization, Mexico – along with other Latin American countries, notably Brazil and Argentina – had borrowed heavily. When interest rates rose in the aftermath of the 1979 oil crisis, Mexico struggled to make payments, precipitating the country's worst economic crisis in fifty years: foreign capital stopped flowing in, loan portfolios were closed, investors were called home, and foreign banks, including the Bank of Montreal, curtailed their operations drastically. The Mexican government was left to find a way out of the financial disaster and stave off bankruptcy.[79] Partly because of the economic downturn and partly because of the reorganization within Mulholland's bank in the mid-1980s, BMO cashed in its Brady bonds (issued in the early 1980s as part of an international rescue package) and completely shuttered its Mexican operations for a second time.[80]

It was not until the mid-1990s that the Bank of Montreal re-established a presence in Mexico, this time not through branches or a representative office, but through an ownership stake in a Mexican bank: Bancomer. The details of this story lie beyond the scope of this chapter and are explored in more detail in Part Seven. Suffice to say here, the Bank's third Mexican adventure, like the previous two, also ended in a complete withdrawal, in 2001. Taken together, the three Mexican forays demonstrate the Bank's continual conservative and careful approach to banking, being quick to withdraw from an unprofitable market to avoid calamitous losses.

China and the Asia Pacific

This final section focuses on the Bank of Montreal's involvement in the Asia Pacific region. If its other international operations outside the United States had a temporary or expendable feel to them, China was a notable exception. The Bank has had a special connection with the People's Republic of China (PRC) that has been consistently developed, nurtured, and handed down faithfully since the leadership of Arnold Hart, to Fred McNeil, to Bill

Mulholland, and to his successors. China has been, in effect, an article of faith in Bank of Montreal banking: it inspired endurance and the commitment that seemed lacking in other markets (or at least was not accorded to other markets.)

The market potential for banking in China stirred the imaginations of the Bank of Montreal leadership. As early as 1928, the Bank pondered expansion of its services into this country and into the Pacific region more generally. At the 1928 Annual Meeting, General Manager Sir Frederick Williams-Taylor reported that "the extension of Canada's overseas markets had made it necessary for the Bank to provide special facilities for the financing of trade with many countries, particularly in the Far East."[81] A special delegation of Bank of Montreal bankers was sent to Asia, where they visited China and Japan, to investigate the possibility of establishing a permanent physical presence. A.S. Minnion, manager of the Bank's Foreign Department, was among the delegates, and he recommended that "in the event of extension of our activities to the Far East, Shanghai, which is the principle port in North China (in fact, in all China), should be selected as the first point of entry."[82] Minnion thought that by opening a representative office in Shanghai, the Bank could capitalize on the lack of intimate knowledge in China of Canadian banking practice.[83] The Bank of Montreal then officially applied to open a representative office in Shanghai in 1929.[84] However, with the Great Depression, the Second World War, and finally the Chinese Communist Revolution, nothing came of the Bank's plans.

In 1945, General Manager B.C. Gardner told shareholders that the Bank had undertaken "an extensive survey of its foreign banking arrangements with a view to facilitating the trading operations of its customers, and was considering surveying other areas, particularly the Far East." And at the Annual Meeting in 1953, General Manager Arthur C. Jensen reported that two of the Bank's senior officers were at that time "visiting correspondent banks and others in a number of countries in the Far East."[85] When the Bank once again set its eyes on the Far East, China and Shanghai were no longer its preferred first choice. Instead, the Bank opted for Tokyo, where it opened a representative office in 1962. Nevertheless, the Bank of Montreal was an exception among banks in that it continued to finance trade transactions with China throughout the 1960s. Moreover, in 1963, the Bank established a full correspondent banking relationship with the head office of the Bank of China. This was a major step as it preceded official diplomatic relations between Canada and the People's Republic of China by seven years.[86]

In 1971, the Bank of China officially invited BMO chairman G. Arnold Hart to China. The Bank jumped at the opportunity "to help cement our business relationship with them and to gain some first-hand knowledge of the country," especially in view of Canada's official recognition of China the previous year.[87] Over the ensuing years, Hart would be a central figure in the development of the Bank of Montreal's relationship with China – its government and, in particular, its bank (Bank of China). This was a natural fit. Hart had a special connection to Asia Pacific. As special head office representative in 1953, he accompanied Edward R. Ernst, superintendent of the Foreign Department, on a three-month tour of the region – visiting Japan, Hong Kong, the Philippines, India, Pakistan, Ceylon, Singapore, and Indonesia. At that time, it was the "most extensive trip ever to be undertaken by representatives of a Canadian bank," the 1954 Annual Report noted, "and their itinerary carried them over 35,000 miles by air."[88] Hart the banker must have seen the inherent possibilities in the region; Hart the cultural observer must have seen how the Chinese measured relationships in decades and centuries.

Hart was the first Canadian bank chairman to receive an official invitation from the Chinese, a strategic advantage that would be pressed to the full in the subsequent years. The move was significant not only for the Bank but also for its major clients, such as Canadian Forest Products Limited, which had closed the first commercial transaction since the Government of Canada recognized China with the sale of 12,000 tons of wood pulp. The required letter of credit was opened by the Bank of China through the Bank of Montreal.[89]

The chairman's visit in June 1971 was a highly coordinated affair, with assistance from the Canadian Trade Commissioner in Hong Kong as well as the Canadian High Commission in Malaysia. Arnold Hart recorded the crossover from Hong Kong into China in considerable detail, including the fact that he had neglected to bring his vaccination certificate to show Chinese border authorities. "This presented no problem because there immediately appeared a Chinese doctor dressed in white, including a white cap with a gauze over his nose and mouth, [who] proceeded to vaccinate me."[90] The delegation reached Beijing that same day and in the coming days was treated to extensive tours of The Forbidden City and the Great Wall, which included events such as Red Detachment of Women: A Modern Revolutionary Dance Drama.[91] The tour also included visiting other major cities, travelling by air. In one instance, "after being airborne for nearly three hours," the pilot announced that the "plane is bad" and there would have to be a forced landing at Changsha. Hart and company spent a few hours at a Chinese air base waiting for a replacement airplane, and admiring the Russian MiG fighters and their Chinese equivalents take off on patrol.[92]

Hart's reportage to the board about the visit was extensive and took the form of a travelogue. His discussions of China as a country of "sharp contrast – from the large cities teeming with people to the peaceful and beautiful country-side to the almost breathtaking and magnificent legacies of Ming and Ching Dynasties" obviously made an impression on him.[93] His description of Beijing was also both detailed and fascinating. "Everyone seems to bustle and work hard, be it in the cities or in the country."[94] The Hart delegation's visits to the People's Bank of China were in some ways intended as a tutorial on the Chinese banking system and its role in the central planning function of the PRC itself. The sub-banks such as the Construction Bank and the Bank of Communication specialized in the provision of long-term funds for capital projects.[95]

The main point of the visit, apart from familiarization, was to continue building a strong relationship. "Good relations with the Bank of China are especially important because its monopoly position as the sole foreign banking organization in China allows it to direct substantial business to those correspondents in favour," one report from the Hong Kong office emphasized.[96] If anything, that reminder was an understatement. As we have seen, the Bank of Montreal's relationship with the Bank of China began in 1958, when the latter began directing business to BMO. Formal agency arrangements were established in 1965, and in February and March 1970, the Bank of China's Hong Kong and Beijing branches opened accounts with the Bank of Montreal.[97] The initial overdraft line afforded to the Bank of China was CA$5 million. Further agreements in August 1970 facilitated trade transactions between Canada and China that could be handled in renminbi (the Chinese currency). The Bank of China, in turn, maintained fixed deposits in various currencies, which could reach substantial figures – at times CA$19 million, £3 million, and DM10 million. The sub-banks (such as the Bank of Communication) held separate accounts with the Bank of Montreal as well.[98]

Hart well understood the need as chief executive officer to be personally involved in these transactions – CEO to CEO, so to speak. Personal contact was the best and most effective way of cementing and strengthening the relationship. Bank of Montreal business was, of course, top of mind in the discussions and exchanges with the Bank of China, including clarifying interest rates on loans and other areas that required further explanation. In view of China's possible future needs for US trade, the Bank's delegation was also intent on putting forward the case for Chinese trade with Canadian subsidiaries of US corporations, where possible. "We impressed upon [our ambassador] that we consider it imperative that this limitation of Sino-Canadian trade be removed as early as possible," Hartmann suggested.[99] Hart further noted that the United States would jump into China trade much sooner than it was originally thought (he was right on the money, as it were!) and intended for Canadian subsidiaries to get in on the action before the US parent companies did, or else the Americans would "want the business for their own plants resulting in a trade loss to Canada and proportionately to our Bank."[100] The

1971 visit thus represented a golden opportunity to reinforce relationships and put Bank of Montreal front and centre as a facilitator of banking and a bridge to the Western world. The Bank's reputation as a trade bank was most apparent in its list of priorities for the visit, which included, prominently, how the Bank could help in developing trade, particularly through its trade and finance group.

The 1975 Visit

In May 1975, Chairman Hart visited China a second time, "prompted by the desirability of maintaining close contact with the Bank of China, and having in mind the activities of our competitors."[101] As before, Hart's recounting of the visit was both informative and entertaining.[102] The visit was again closely coordinated with the Government of Canada, especially as regarded the state of China-Canada trade. That trade was characterized by three main elements, as the acting general director of the Department of International Trade suggested: "(a) the oft-repeated friendliness of Chinese authorities toward Canada, (b) the fast growth of two-way trade accompanied by an increasing trade surplus in our favour, and (c) the slow-growth of our exports of manu-factured products."[103]

Hart's discussions with Bank of China officials focused on bank business, like credit line extensions beyond CA$50 million. Interestingly, Hart reported the incident of a telex message about a loan that the Toronto-Dominion Bank had been copied on (by mistake), and that "the mere mention of that bank is like waving a red flag in front of a bull."[104] The PRC had terminated its relationship with the TD for unknown reasons, and Hart added that the bank officials were clearly "rankled" and it seemed apparent "that as long as a proper explanation was not given, these occurrences could well stand in the way of the further development of our friendship."[105] These errors were liable to be interpreted as unfriendly acts, instead of genuine errors, Hart warned, and as the matter was investigated via telephone, "it appeared that we had not made any actual mistake and that in both cases others had been to blame."[106] He concluded that the Bank's "relationship with the Bank of China would appear to be on solid ground. Nevertheless, it is one that we must continue to cultivate assiduously."[107]

Hart speculated that from a competitive point of view, BMO was ahead of the Royal Bank in terms of business in China. The Bank of British Columbia and the Bank of Nova Scotia also trailed behind. The Canadian Imperial Bank of Commerce was in China around the same time, leading Hart to conclude that "there is no doubt ... that our competitors are continuing to pay close attention to the PRC and we would be well advised to have a senior official from Head Office visit Peking and Shanghai at least once every two years – and hopefully the ground could be covered in between by our senior officer in Hong Kong."[108] Hart was convinced – rightly – that the PRC would become a "power to be reckoned with increasingly in the world of trade and finance."[109]

Throughout the 1970s, the Bank kept a close watch on developments in China, not least through its Economics Department studies of current trends in politics, economics, and foreign trade.[110] In 1979, Chairman McNeil continued the relationship with another "state visit" to China.[111] In turn, Bill Mulholland continued and amplified the Bank's connection with the PRC, opening up a representative office in 1983 in the Jianguo Hotel in Beijing.[112] By that time, only forty-one other foreign banks had received approval to operate in China, with four of them being Canadian.[113] In 1985, Mulholland led a team for another visit, this time to the Three Gorges Dam hydroelectric power site and the Gezhouba hydroelectric project in Yichang. That trip enabled the Bank's senior management to extend Canadian hydroelectric expertise – something Mulholland had from his previous Churchill Falls development experience.[114]

The Bank's reputation in China was carefully cultivated by BMO executives throughout the 1980s, and honours such as being offered speaking roles at exclusive Chinese conferences reflected BMO's standing. At the Beijing '87 International Marketing Conference, organized to promote international trade with China, BMO deputy chairman William E. Bradford got the nod to represent the only Western bank.[115] As Bradford suggested after the conference, "China is not a place where profit comes easily or quickly. The Chinese people are very cautious and you have to work hard to win their confidence. It takes a long time to establish a solid business relationship."[116] Bradford noted that this patience had paid off: the Bank had served as lead manager and underwriter in the $427 million credit for a thermal power plant in Shenzhen, Guangdong Province, and as co-lead manager in a $210 million loan to the Pan Zhi Hua Iron and Steel Company [sic].[117] He indicated in 1987 that there were "at least 10 more projects of that same magnitude in China's current 7-year plan."[118] The secret, Bradford suggested, was "striving for a special relationship."[119]

The strong, consistent, and expanding presence of the Bank in China under the Mulholland administration paved the way for his successors to take the relationship to yet higher levels – and every subsequent chief executive did. There were several motivations for the Bank of Montreal to involve itself in banking in Asia Pacific. However, as one seasoned Bank veteran put it, a principal reason was "primarily the syndicated loan business, where the balance sheets of all of the Canadian banks were so under-utilized in terms of the world's banks, it gave them enormous advantage when places like the countries of Asia started to demand or need these large-scale US dollar loans."[120]

The Canadian banks had a significant advantage: their balance sheets. The Bank of Montreal went after the Asian business in a particularly strong way, not least because they had bankers, hired from the United States, who knew the business intimately and could make a difference – people like Eddie McCullough. "We got ourselves in some pickles, especially in South America," one executive recalled, "but by and large in Asia, [we had] a different mentality. When an Asian borrows money from you, he pays it back, particularly the countries that we were strong in." However, when the syndicated loan business began to diminish over the years, the business declined correspondingly.

> We didn't really know – we didn't really have the contacts to do anything but that. We had been doing it very, very well, but when it went away, we didn't have a head start. We didn't have any step up on anybody. We didn't have the resources. We largely had representative offices in Asia, whereas the Royal, the Scotia in particular, they had branches. They had operating entities, whereas we only had a branch in Singapore, we had a branch in Korea, and we had a branch in Tokyo and Hong Kong. Three of those four were the pillars of Asia, but we didn't have any, we had no representation certainly in Malaysia – we had a rep office in Indonesia. We didn't have an operating entity in other than those four, in those four countries. And without an operating entity in, like, a branch, you couldn't do the foreign exchange business. You couldn't do the trade finance business. You couldn't do the letters of credit business. You could do it through somebody else, but you couldn't do it yourself, and that's the way the business turned. And if you didn't have the engine in the car, you couldn't run the car. You couldn't get in that race. And I think that's what happened. By the time we understood that, it was too expensive or the bank couldn't afford to go out and buy or develop an operating entity in some of these countries, whereas Scotia, they had little joint ventures, they had little branches in some pretty "out" outposts.[121]

Hong Kong

Before serious inroads were made into China, the Bank of Montreal established its second Asian location, a representative office in Hong Kong in 1969 (this became a full-service branch in 1978).[122] "Hong Kong, of course, was the 'gateway to China,'" J. Leonard Walker noted at the Bank's Annual Meeting in

1970. Peter Shaddick, executive vice-president international, added: "Hong Kong is Canada's second largest trading partner in south-east Asia, while the Pacific rim as a whole is becoming increasingly important to Canada's economy. Representation in Hong Kong means the B of M can take better advantage of the outstanding trading potential of the area." Shaddick was right. The Hong Kong office was instrumental in financing Canada-China trade after Canada and China established diplomatic relations in 1970.[123] To further facilitate and encourage trade between the two countries, the Bank of Montreal opened an account in China's national currency, the renminbi, at the Bank of China that year. "It was among the first foreign banks to do so. In return, the Bank of China opened a Canadian dollar account at the Bank of Montreal's Head Office in 1970, and a US dollar account in 1973."[124]

The Hong Kong office served other purposes as well and, like the other contemporaneous representative offices (e.g., Dusseldorf, Paris, Milan, and Tokyo), was designed to promote general banking interests, corporate financing, and the forging of new business opportunities and contacts for the Bank of Montreal in Asia. Under the leadership of H.C. "Hal" Hartmann, the office was opened to promote general banking and business development interests through close liaison with other BMO offices throughout the world and to serve as a two-way information centre for businessmen both in Southeast Asia and in Canada.

In 1984, the political landscape upon which Hong Kong's financial security and prosperity was predicated shifted. The Thatcher government in Great Britain reached an agreement with Deng Xiaoping's government in mainland China to hand back Hong Kong to China in 1997 upon the expiry of Britain's ninety-year lease of Hong Kong and the New Territories. In response to the deal and in the face of increased uncertainty, the Bank of Montreal drastically scaled back its Hong Kong operations in 1988, focusing more on high-net-worth individuals and those wishing to immigrate to Canada.[125] The Hong Kong office further focused on shipping and real estate – as one executive put it, "deal[ing] with what's available at the moment and where the demand is coming from." As the new kid on the block, BMO would have to take a bit more of what was available on the margins, since the established banks had the core business. That also meant handling riskier ventures – which meant some early losses in shipping for the Bank in Hong Kong. The real estate market was more promising, but since the Bank did not have "the experience of being abroad a long time, to know that this roller coaster would go back up again ... So we sort of jumped off the roller coaster at that point ... [retrenching] until about 1996."[126]

For the first two decades of its operations, the representative office served as an outpost for the Bank of Montreal in Asia and forged business relations between Canada and Southeast Asia. The expansion into Hong Kong proved to be a profitable enterprise and prompted the Bank of Montreal to open branch offices in Hong Kong and Seoul; representative offices in Taipei, Guangzhou, Beijing, and Sydney; and treasury operations in Singapore and Tokyo. Over the years, the Bank's Asia-Pacific strategy closed operations in Singapore, India, Japan, and South Korea, hoping to focus first on North America, before discovering China anew. Here, Mulholland's imprint is clear: he travelled several times to China "and was quite excited about [it]" even in the 1980s, when the Bank opened a representative office in Beijing.[127]

The LDC Crisis: Brazil

In the 1960s and 1970s, Latin American economies (especially in Argentina, Brazil, and Mexico) were booming. Because of their soaring economies, they had easy access to credit, and many countries borrowed heavily to invest in infrastructure and other projects. Initially, these loans were obtained through the World Bank, but after 1973, private banks also joined, extending substantial loans to countries in Latin America. As a result of the 1979 oil crisis, Latin America was hit with a financial crisis in the early-1980s. Investment ceased, world trade declined, debt exceeded earning power, and countries were no longer able to meet obligations. After financial restructuring in 1982 and 1983, the Brazilian economy once again saw growth, starting in 1985. It had a trade surplus in 1985 and 1986, and "both local and foreign bankers had predicted that Brazil would soon resume normal borrowing operations."[128] As a BMO banker of the era suggested, "you know, there was LDC debt, was a significant, significant overhang of that for our company. We were the largest exposed of the Canadian banks in terms of Lesser Developed Country debt, particularly Mexico and some of the others, taking substantial write-offs in '84, '87, '89. So there was quite a period of time when I would say that we were occupied with dealing with those kind of issues."[129] By the mid-1980s, the Bank realized that lending to countries was "not necessarily a smart thing because the only revenue base countries had was tax," as one banker put it. "There was no – countries didn't produce anything per se that they got revenues from. So you basically were lending against a tax base, and that has limited capacity and has lots of cyclicality."[130]

A price freeze increased purchasing power and stimulated a boom in consumer spending. The country's foreign exchange reserves then nose-dived as Brazil imported many of the desired goods. This brought on a debt crisis in early 1987. On 20 February 1987, the Brazilian government announced an open-ended moratorium on interest on its debt to foreign banks. This shook the banking world. Brazil was the largest debtor in the developing world, owing a total of US$108 billion, about US$81 billion of it owed to private banks.[131] The Bank of Montreal's share of this was US$1.3 billion. As one senior bank auditor, put it, the Bank and international finance with it was entering deep waters "because there were billions of dollars outstanding to Brazil and Mexico and all these countries, and all the banks had them. It was huge, it was obvious, I mean, it just broke all the rules. The number-one rule when you make a decision to lend somebody money is, 'Do you think they can repay?' 'Well, countries never default on their debt.' That was the prevailing theory. Countries do default on their debt, and it was billions and billions of dollars. That was one of the big things I got heavily involved in. I remember meetings with all the banks' CEOs and CFOs, and the Superintendent of Financial Institutions trying to work out how to resolve this."[132]

After the Brazilian government announcement in February 1987, the Bank of Montreal, one of the government's largest private debtors, acted quickly. In the spring of 1987, BMO president Bill Mulholland released a plan to turn US$100 million of the US$1.3 billion debt into equity investments in the Brazilian economy. Mulholland envisioned the US$100 million converted into shares in a fund that would purchase shares in Brazilian businesses in the form of minority participation (under Canadian law, BMO was expressly forbidden to own any part of the Brazilian government/economy outright; thus, a fund had to be set up first). The Bank of Scotland had entered a similar arrangement with the Brazilian government, where US$12.5 million of the US$50 million debt was covered by a 28 per cent ownership in a state-owned Brazilian paper and pulp company.[133] In a public statement, Mulholland said that the initiative served to demonstrate that creditor banks and Brazil share a common interest in restoring healthy growth in Brazil. To the extent that other banks are prepared to undertake similar initiatives, Mulholland said, it will further the process of restoring stability and encouraging growth.[134]

Pedro Leitão de Cunha, chairman of the Banco de Montreal Investimento S.A., a subsidiary of BMO, applied for the necessary approvals for this deal on 2 April 1987. This was undoubtedly a very difficult time for the Bank and for all internationally involved banks. As one analyst of the era recalled, the Bank and its American counterparts got hit because of the substantial exposure to Mexico, Brazil, and Argentina debt – a situation that in some ways would repeat itself decades later with the creditworthiness crisis of Greece, Spain, and Portugal. "Countries got ahead of themselves. They got overextended. Banks ended up holding a bunch of sovereign debt and I don't think it's exactly the same now, but it's similar."[135]

In order to convert US$100 million in debt to equity and accommodate Canadian law under the Bank Act, the Bank established a subsidiary in Barbados to hold interests in various investment vehicles in Brazil. It applied to the Securities and Exchange Commission of Brazil to establish an investment portfolio in Brazil and obtained the necessary approvals from the Brazilian central bank. Under the act, BMO was expressly forbidden to deal, directly or indirectly, in goods, wares, and merchandise that were not strictly banking related.[136] This meant that conversion of Brazilian debt into local equity had to go through (wholly owned) subsidiaries. In light of the barriers thrown up by the Bank Act, BMO advocated for amendments to accommodate foreign debt conversions in connection with the resolution of sovereign loans that were in default. For the time being, however, BMO designated Banco de Montreal Investimento to manage the Bank's Brazilian investments, which would include high-grade securities listed on Brazilian stock exchanges and direct investments in Brazilian assets and enterprises.[137] Banco de Montreal Investimento had managed mutual funds in Brazil since 1967. It had been one of BMO's most successful endeavours in Latin America, delivering impressive results. For example, the Montrealbank Fund, a leading Brazilian investment fund managed by Banco de Montreal Investimento enjoyed a US-dollar-based rate of return of 11.5 per cent from 1975 to 1987.[138]

The Bank of Montreal used the Brazilian affair to boost its international reputation and heavily promoted its activities in the Brazilian market. The promotional objective of the debt-to-equity conversion plan was "to receive broad, favourable public exposure in Brazil" and "to explain the plan carefully to customers and shareholders, primarily in Canada, in order to avoid misunderstandings that might negatively influence the Bank's stock."[139] BMO launched a press tour with Bill Mulholland giving press conferences in Brasilia and New York, which received favourable coverage internationally. President Mulholland's speeches and interviews stressed the institution's humanitarian qualities, presenting the deal with Brazil as a pragmatic and mutually advantageous offer on behalf of the Bank. Mulholland proclaimed that it was "important *to me* that Brazil has a healthy economic growth, not just *to Brazil*. I don't regard these as two conflicting objectives." But of course, the bottom line also mattered. When Mulholland looked at Brazil, he saw a diverse and modern economy, the eighth largest in the Western world, with an estimated GDP of US$265 billion, as well as plenty of room for growth, with the world largest area of uncultivated arable land.[140]

Conclusion

The Bank of Montreal's international experience from the end of the Second World War to the end of the 1980s constituted a complex journey that put its operations, capabilities, strategy, and competitiveness to the test in ways that the domestic market could not. But there was a lot more going on than met the eye.

First, some understanding of the Bank's operational context is in order before rendering judgment on its performance. As a Canadian bank in a global financial market, the Bank of Montreal was immediately in the underdog position in the international field vis-à-vis other banks that originated from the great-banking-power countries. American, British, German, and French banks had several inherited competitive advantages. They had size. They could follow international champions and global brands across the world. Some leveraged political or imperial legacies in the post-war period.

Second, changing political, economic, and specific local environments in several key territories, particularly in the Caribbean and Central and South America, provided an additional set of challenges that would stretch the Bank's capabilities as options narrowed and events pressed Bank leaders of the era to make quick decisions about just how committed they were to certain foreign fields. Of course, it was not simply the external environment that drove decisions regarding international operations. If that were the case, other banks that remained in troubled territories would have followed the same route. By the mid-1970s, the Mulholland bank squarely focused on expansion beyond Canada, not only as a way to escape the constraints of a tight domestic market but also as a way to expand the horizons and the capacities and outlook of the Bank itself. If the Bank of Montreal was one of the oldest, most respected, and relevant financial institutions in the North Atlantic world, why would it simply sit on the sidelines when new worlds and new markets beckoned? Opening up to international horizons offered an opportunity to import substantial and remarkably able talent in international banking from the United States and the United Kingdom to expand the capabilities of the Bank. Remember the context: the Bank's leadership was trying to find the road of return – if not to its position of yore, then at least to a re-energized and revitalized bank that could once again find itself at the centre of the action.

Thus, for a number of reasons, Bill Mulholland was a convinced internationalist. He perceived that participating in the banking world beyond Canada represented an integral component of the Bank's modernization that included internal reforms and upgrades initiated by his predecessor. Mulholland embraced that internationalist vision out of recognition about "what was going on around the world."[141] He and his team knew that the Bank had to negotiate a transformation from a processing, lending-type business into a market-driven, market-competitive, market-making business. In the view of some of his contemporaries, that transformation motivated him to expand his relationships with international banking, selecting the Treasury function as a central component in the execution of that strategy.[142]

When BMO bankers actually took the field in the Caribbean, in Mexico and Central and South America, and in China, they consistently showed their strengths and abilities. They enabled the Bank to punch above its weight class in the international councils of global banking, a fact amply borne out by how much Bank of Montreal bankers were able not only to draw upon but also to maintain and enhance their reputation as first-class international bankers. Here, the presence of a Hart or a Mulholland in China, supported by a whole phalanx of men on the spot, made a significant difference. When it came time to make the hard decisions and depart the field, they typically did so while extracting favourable terms, especially when big circumstances seemed to force the Bank to retreat to continental fields or just outright return home.

In hindsight, the Bank's international strategy was generally hampered by a lack of the kind of constancy and commitment required to remain an international player in the local banking scene, as was the case in Mexico, in the Caribbean, and in Brazil. For many, the issue in the Mulholland era was consistency of vision – and the Bank's ability, despite everything else that was going, to stick with that vision. Consider the view of one senior international banker of the time:

> [What] has happened with our international operation or lack of success is "chopping and changing." We change horses all the time. One day we are a global bank. One day we are an international bank. Bill Mulholland spends all of this time and effort and money building an international bank. The next thing is, after he goes, we become a Canadian bank with international operations. Then we become a North American bank with a European support. And we don't even understand that. If we are a Canadian bank looking after our international clients, then do we need Bucklersbury House here in the City of London, with all the overhead that goes with it? If we are a North American bank, okay, what is it? We're a small Canadian bank with Chicago domestic business as a North American bank? We change all the time. The branch here [London] is now – it's a very small business. I don't know. Perhaps five or six people running the bank. There are, I don't know, a dozen or so clerical staff there. Is that a North American bank that is supporting its North American clientele's business in Europe? The equation doesn't work. I think we've changed too many times.[143]

An important part of understanding the Bank's international ventures in the post-war period has to do with the United States – in particular, the weight and impact of the Bank of Montreal's acquisition of the Harris Bank of Chicago in 1984. That generational strategic move into the American banking market (the subject of chapter 18) diverted executive energies and attention away from most of the Bank's foreign fields and toward the much closer, much better understood, and much more potentially lucrative markets of the American Midwest. Of course, there is no magic status conferred by international operations: sometimes it is right to leave or pull back as part of a sound strategy. In the case of the Bank of Montreal, unwillingness to invest or double down on questionable bets and getting out when and where they did arguably saved the organization from a worse fate. At the same time, the lack of a stable, long-term vision for international operations was undoubtedly a factor in the Bank's attenuated success in foreign fields.

The obvious exception in the entire period is China. There, the Bank took the measure of the possibilities of this massive market and took the long-range view. That vision was shared by successive chief executives who each built upon the achievements and successes of the last, down to contemporary times. This commitment involved risk-taking and long-term, careful cultivation. It also drew upon the ability of the Bank to count on a long experience and stable set of institutional relationships. While willing to take setbacks, the Bank of Montreal was in China for the long term. That put it in the top tier of global banks when it came time in China to modernize, expand, and reach out to the capitalist world.

Each departed jurisdiction had its own story, its own rationale. Frequently, it came with regrets at the missed opportunities, particularly from the men on the spot who had invested years of their lives in developing the Bank's business everywhere from South Korea to Japan to the seductive Caribbean islands that had beckoned an earlier generation of bank executives. Those departures also came with an equal, if not greater, sense of relief from head office executives anxious to rid themselves of foreign entanglements awash in risk and red ink. Their gaze was toward the American Midwest, and the opportunities that waited there. One senior executive of the era commented on the link between the Bank's "elegant culture" and its fate as a global presence – a culture that "has led us to be unable to handle global expansion well."

> We were screwed in Brazil by the Brazilians, we were screwed in Mexico by the Mexicans, we were screwed in Australia by the Australians, we were screwed in Europe by the Europeans. We have a terrible time with being outside of Canada because we are way too nice to the locals and they run over us like a Mack truck. Now, interestingly, China, where we have actually made 25, 30 years of progress – maybe

35, actually – their culture interestingly mirrors ours, which is it's very gracious, very respectful of seniors, very much done to the rules. And so there we are, blooming in a communist country because hopefully no one's screwing us.[144]

That colourful judgment, while opinion and not historical fact, is still a rather good example of the kind of frustration more than a few executives had with the international performance of the Bank. Again and again, we see the importance of a certain cultural set of assumptions and behaviours.

Beyond that, however, it was neither the objective nor within the realm of possibility to transform the Bank of Montreal into a major institutional player in global banking. This is true of all major Canadian chartered banks and, more broadly, true of Canada as a middle power in the Western world. The required scale and scope alone put any such idea beyond reach (though perhaps igniting the idea in the next decade of the need for a Canadian banking combination to level the playing field). Yet, the Bank's experience showed that it could translate its banking prowess to international fields – not always equally or everywhere, but enough to become a player. The experience of the 1970s and 1980s – in reality, the Bank of Montreal's first authentically foreign or international banking foray – demonstrated both the possibilities and the limits of projecting Canadian banking power in the world.

In spite of the reversals, the passage through international banking waters left a distinct legacy. It generated a broader capacity for international banking and a host of other capabilities. In multiple instances, it extended the Bank's relationship network significantly within and beyond the banking world, and within the countries it served. It also provided senior decision-makers with lessons and insights about what to pursue, and when and how to take BMO's considerable capabilities to the global market. In many instances, it underlined that timing the Bank's entry into the market was vital. Not least, the international experience brought home the importance of having a strong, unifying, and adaptable vision inside the Bank to ensure that when the time came, the Bank could fully leverage its competitive advantage at the times and places of its own choosing. In combination, these were part of the beneficial legacy from the Bank of Montreal's far journey in the world in the postwar period.

PART SEVEN

A Time to Every Purpose, 1990–2017

To every thing there is a season,
and a time to every purpose under the heaven
Ecclesiastes 3:1 (KJV)

Many things, having full reference
To one consent, may work contrariously
As many arrows, loosed several ways
Fly to one mark; as many ways meet in one town;
As many fresh streams meet in one salt sea
As many lines close in the dial's centre
So may a thousand actions, once afoot
End in one purpose, and be all well borne without defeat.
William Shakespeare, *Henry V*, Act I, Scene 2

The Beginning of the Long Dash

Part Seven of this book covers about three decades of the Bank of Montreal's most recent experience, beginning in 1990 and ending in 2017, the 200th year of its existence. It is comprised of two chapters: the first covers most of the 1990s, and the last brings the story up to the end of 2017. One of the astonishing observations about the last twenty-seven years is the density of events contained. Three chief executive officers led BMO in this period: Matthew W. Barrett (1990–98), F. Anthony Comper (1998–2006), and William A. Downe (2007–17). A fourth, W. Darryl White, began his term in November 2017. That quarter-century-plus bore witness to multiple long-run trends playing out in the wider world, where economic cycles produced recessions and recoveries; a dot-com tech bubble, as well as crash; a Great Recession; and a long but steady recovery. The long-term liberalization of the terms of trade and globalization continued to define the arc of economic history until relatively recently. For example, in Canadian banking, a comparison of the players in 1990 and in 2017 would find the usual suspects among the chartered banks in the league tables with little apparent change. The operative word is "apparent": banks in this period underwent far-reaching transformations, both seen and unseen.

The epigraphs that open Part Seven capture, in counterpoise, the two-sided nature of this period. The first suggests that elements are fleeting and time-bound for which there are seasons. Different times, different priorities: a time to every purpose. Change. The second suggests continuity, but also the connectedness of things. Many actions, many ways, many roads – but coalescing in a single purpose.

These overarching ideas represent a way of understanding the long-run experience: the time-limited purposes of the organization – that run for a season; and the long-term, inter-generational purposes with attendant challenges and goals – that over time converge. These considerations about purpose are also timely since recent years have seen a number of organizations undertake large cultural and organizational change projects under the banner of "purpose." These chapters strongly indicate that, in order to understand an authentic organizational purpose properly, the long run is a critical factor.

Before examining this important and eventful transformational period in the Bank, a note about sources. Access was allowed to corporate repositories up to the 1990 watershed. What to analyze today and what to leave to tomorrow is a bargain struck differently across organizations. In our case, legal, regulatory, and customer constraints and concerns precluded access to current and recent operational and board files. In time, when those may be unsealed, historians will have an opportunity to undertake a more detailed analysis of this period in the Bank's long-run experience.

Continuity and the Long Run

There is a fundamental continuity that brings the entire 1990–2017 era together – each BMO administration, across the generational divide. Some of the more persistent elements are obscured because of emergent events and circumstances. Nevertheless, several elements weave a thread that passes from administration to administration, beyond individuals and styles. The work on building the Bank's strengths in risk management – a process of constant adaption and refinement – never stopped. Technological transformation was another cross-generational dossier demanded by innovation and evolving customer expectations and by the changing nature of the industry. Marketing and brand were also constant priorities that followed a line of continuity, each era building on the previous. In particular, the faithful commitment to diversity and inclusion set BMO apart from its competitors in specific ways in each decade and each administration.

There is something else that unites these three decades and links them with the broader long-run experience of the Bank of Montreal: commitment to the nation. Throughout the period, the Bank's values were tried and tested multiple times. Here, it is not so much the philanthropy dollars or donations that are the subject – though those are also important. Rather, it is the spirit in which each administration viewed its obligations beyond statute or regulatory compliance to the financial stability of the Canadian system. It has a lot to do with the Bank's long-term place in the evolution of the country. Of course, its role has changed – from official bank to de facto reserve bank to a partner among other banks. In spite of its place in the league tables of Canadian banking, BMO has been able to retain a special role beyond its size. This manifested itself in times of urgency and emergency, and involved participation and engagement that cannot be explained simply by bottom-line considerations. It stemmed, moreover, from a living cultural memory of the Bank's continuing role in Canadian economic and financial life. That DNA of institutional continuity, encoded in the ways BMO executives responded to opportunities and challenges persisted in this period, and manifested itself in multiple ways.

Of course, long-run continuity did not easily translate into years of gentle transition. It certainly did not augur the perpetuation of sameness. The era can be divided into two broad periods that in some ways align with leadership, significant events, or circumstances. Those two elements – the impact of leaders and the weight of circumstance – often went hand in hand.

Beginning in 1990, the Bank's new leadership team under Matt Barrett and Tony Comper unleashed a sustained energy pulse of strategic and organizational change that transformed the Bank. It launched a bold North American strategy and embraced financial and communications technologies as a central strategic component. Internally, a quiet revolution of human capital was beginning through an unprecedented willingness to recast the relationship between the Bank and the people of BMO. The new administration ushered in a bold, innovative approach to employee training and development, and a sustained commitment to diversity and inclusion of historically overlooked groups – women, Indigenous peoples, and people with disabilities. The 1990s are remembered in the lore of the Bank as a remarkable period of renewal, especially in the wake of the Mulholland years, whose rigidified culture by the end of the 1980s had tested the patience of a younger generation of bankers. Post-Mulholland, the release of pent-up energy in the first year alone was in part an enthusiasm for the new and different.

The second period, 1999 to 2017, can itself be divided in two. Initially defined by the failure of a major strategy – the merger of the Bank of Montreal with the Royal Bank of Canada – it was followed shortly thereafter by the departure of Matt Barrett as CEO. Under his successor, Tony Comper, focus turned to organizational transformation through value-based management and to piloting the Bank through uncertain times. Here again, continuities asserted themselves as priorities – risk, technology, brand, and diversity – and in each category, measurable progress was made. The zeitgeist shifted to a more formal and defensive posture. The second half, between 2007 and 2017, proceeded under the helmsmanship of William A. Downe. Comper's successor possessed an intuitive grasp of the possibilities and limitations of the Bank he would lead. At pivot points in the history of both the Bank and the Canadian financial system during his term as CEO, Downe's breakout ability to conceptualize a strategy, build consensus, and appeal to a higher purpose characterized his achievements as a leader.

Each period in Part Seven is intense with stories, trends, currents, networks and relationships, hard workers, the seen and unseen, triumphs, and disappointments that come standard with any relevant institutional experience. More importantly, these years also contain important trend-lines in the relationships inside the Bank, the changing networks of power and influence, the shifts in the nature of work, the role of technology, the rise of capital markets, the perennial cultural and organizational challenge of bureaucratic rigidity every large organization contends with, and the changing place of the Bank in the wider world. These are important themes to understand for the future of BMO and Canadian banking, but their systematic study will be left to another time and another place. Here, we offer an overview of these fascinating and important years.

Chapters 20 and 21 reflect the periods described above, with the latter divided into two subsections. As these last chapters bring us closer to the present day, the book enters a temporal territory where long-run historical judgments hold less, and where the historian's jurisdiction gets progressively more circumscribed. Therefore, these accounts are of unequal size and scope.

CHAPTER TWENTY

The Great Regeneration,
1990–1997

On 15 January 1990, the Bill Mulholland era at the Bank of Montreal came to its official end at the Annual General meeting with his valedictory address that emphasized "challenges of change facing business in the '90s" and the "mixed blessings of technological advancements which make business more efficient, yet increase risk if not managed well."[1] It was a curiously downbeat exit for Mulholland and somewhat out of step with the technological optimists who were about to take the reins at the Bank. In fact, the focus of the incoming generation of leadership was just as distant from the reflections of a lion in winter. The new team, under the leadership of CEO Matthew Barrett, was young, impatient for change, and armed with a tremendous popular desire from the people of the Bank for a new style and approach.

The Regenerators

In retrospect, the early 1990s – the spirit of the age, the plans, the feeling, all of it – look like the Bank of Montreal was on the threshold of a great regeneration. If the era can be called the "Great Regeneration," then the senior executive team that provided the leadership deserve the title of "The Regenerators."[2] They were comparatively young, in the summer of their years. They were smart. They were articulate. They had come up through the chain of command under W.D. Mulholland, and had not only survived but also acquired the kind of [battle]field experience critical to understanding the kind of skill, strategy, and leadership required in the "post-war" period. They knew the

Bank inside and out. As individuals, they shone. More than that, they were ready, and as a team, they were greater than the sum of their talent: complementary, collaborative, focused, sometimes combative, but never divided. But the four who led, the four who ruled, were Matthew W. Barrett, chairman and CEO; F.A. Comper, president and chief operating officer; J.S. Chisholm, vice-chairman, corporate and institutional financial services; and A.G. McNally, vice-chairman, personal and commercial financial services. Their biographies merit a closer look.

Matt Barrett was born in 1944 in County Meath, Ireland, the son of a dance-band leader. He joined the Bank at age eighteen in London, England, as a "waste-book clerk" (of which Barrett said, "you had to be subhuman to have a position that was lower"[3]). He immigrated to Canada in 1967, cancelling his plans to return to the United Kingdom after he perceiving opportunities in Canada and at the Bank of Montreal.[4] Working his way up the ranks, Barrett was determined to take on the high-risk, high-reward tasks, earning a reputation as a "clean-up artist" and managing progressively larger problems as he went.[5] In 1978, he was rewarded for his Augean labours by being named to the executive team as a vice-president of management services. From the commanding heights, W.D. Mulholland began to look out for Barrett, the rising star, putting him in a variety of difficult assignments and positions from British Columbia to Ontario. Barrett became an executive vice-president of personal banking in 1985 and president of the Bank in November 1987.[6] One of his contemporaries rhapsodized him as a "banker extraordinaire" who was "action personified, an impact player," and, ultimately, in the "top quartile of the world's leading bankers."[7] Another journalistic admirer wrote that Matt was, "charming, affable and graced with matinee-idol looks ... a charismatic leader – a striking contrast to the frosty, autocratic figures who traditionally head up this country's big banks."[8] Another observer called him the "radical banker."[9] The normally staid financial press of the era fell over themselves reaching for superlatives under the glare of Barrett's megawatt charm.

Francis Anthony Comper, Barrett's second-in-command, was born in 1945, joining the Bank of Montreal in 1967 as part of the intake of Young Turks meant to revitalize an increasingly sclerotic institution. Comper's professional trajectory propelled him from domestic branches and the personnel department to operations and systems. His work in the latter group allowed him to play a major role in the evolution of the bank's nationwide, real-time computer system, a tour of duty that earned him an executive position as vice-president of system development. In 1982, he was promoted to senior vice-president and manager of the Bank's branch in London, after which he returned to a progressively more senior set of roles, culminating with the position of president in 1990. Comper's unparalleled operational knowledge of the Bank and his elegant, lower-key personality was a perfect counterpoint to Barrett's star personality. His deep involvement in community affairs, from university life to important causes such as Christian-Jewish understanding, was indicative of the character and mien of the Bank's number two.[10]

Jeffrey Scott Chisholm was born in Erie, Pennsylvania, in 1949. He was hired by Harris Trust and Savings Bank in Chicago in 1971, and rose to the rank of executive exactly a decade later. When BMO acquired Harris, Chisholm made the move to Toronto to work in treasury operations. In 1986, he became an executive vice-president and treasurer. Chisholm was a key member of the Barrett inner cabinet, assuming the role of vice-chairman and, in 1996, the presidency of mbanx. Chisholm's charisma and warmth made him a popular executive. His American pedigree brought a different perspective to a Canadian-centred bank, especially as continental destiny beckoned.[11]

Alan G. McNally was born in Quebec City in 1945. A trained engineer, McNally joined the Bank in 1975 after six years at the Aluminium Company of Canada (Alcan). Maybe as a sign of things to come, young McNally participated in the acquisition of the Harris Bank in 1984. He progressed quickly through the ranks, managing personal and commercial financial services from his post as vice-chairman. He joined Harris Bank as CEO and vice-chairman in 1993 and as chairman in 1995, at a time when BMO began to impose greater control over its Chicago bank.[12]

The leadership team of course included several others, some of whom we have already mentioned. But these four men were the ones who led. The leadership strength around the table was ideally suited to the challenges and the opportunities that awaited: the front man, the ops man, the tech man, and their man in Chicago. In time, if their plans were to bear fruit, there would be a lot more women joining those ranks, and in increasingly senior key positions.

Fiat Lux

The new administration moved swiftly and decisively to set a new tone and a new strategic vision. On 19 April 1990, at the Bristol Place Hotel, Barrett convoked a meeting of BMO executives from around the world to "affirm a new strategic plan" that was to set the tone for the decade.[13] With that began the great regeneration of the Bank of Montreal for the 1990s. The Bristol Place conference marked the "first time that every single executive of the Bank and the senior executives of [its] subsidiaries gathered to participate in one meeting."[14] In his summation at the conference, Barrett began by taking a frank account of the Bank's strengths and weaknesses. The latter included "earnings volatility from Less Developed Country (LDC) interest, subsidiaries struggling to achieve higher ROE [return on equity], undervalued shares, a decline in market share, a history of retention problems and a public image which, to put it charitably, could do with some polishing." He also identified an overall need to bolster confidence and spirit throughout the organization – likely an understatement.[15]

The executive team set to confront these challenges were, in Barrett's words, "old enough to know what doesn't work and young enough to try a few things that might." Barrett signalled a decisive break from the past: "not only will we dare to be different from the pack, we will strive to be."[16] The Bank's strengths – Harris, Nesbitt Thomson, the Brazilian subsidiary, an impressive spending discipline, a good loan book, a powerfully strong capital base – was prologue for what was to come. The Bank's international reputation was outstanding, Barrett declared, and, he added, he had tested that reputation firsthand around the world. The final strength was the Bank's employees, who "may not be madly in love with us, but they are fiercely loyal, tremendously hard-working and thirsting for leadership."[17] Barrett's generation-defining oration to the 240 executives of the Bank of Montreal was a communications tour de force. It was frank and fearless. The speech also cut to the heart of a number of issues that would have to be overcome in the 1990s. In particular, he cited the divisions between leadership as having to end: "I would like to suggest to you that railing against the forces of darkness on the 68th floor [the CEO command centre] these days is a little dated ... Anyway, there is no point in complaining about the past. We can't blame the past forever. There has to be a statute of limitations. There has to be a cutoff point, and I suggest April nineteenth 1990 is as good as any. What's past is prologue. Our task is to make history, not debate it."

The culture of complaint was Barrett's specific target. The regenerators – the generation of 1990 – were determined to change an entire culture with a new "open, give-and-take style of leadership," working more collaboratively, and critically, with the support of the Bank's employees. Barrett challenged the audience: "From time to time we have to ask ourselves: 'If there were an election for my job, would my subordinates vote for me?' Because, in fact, there is an election going on in your office all the time. It's not a popularity contest – you win it by earning respect and esteem ... If you think you might have trouble being re-elected, then it's time to change your campaign strategy."[18]

Barrett laid down the blueprint for his leadership that April evening in Toronto. He focused on new tools of motivation: pride ("to be able to say without hesitation or misgiving, 'I work at the Bank of Montreal'"); reputation ("a bureaucrat seeks anonymity; a professional builds a reputation"); promise ("providing people the opportunity to set their own agenda in the future as a reward for good work in the past."); broader career opportunities; and giving people a share of the value they help create. The conference was also the birthplace of the idea of what would become the Institute for Learning, or IFL. It was originally called the Centre for Management Development, and the Bank was "not going to scrimp. We're going to do it right. We will be funding the centre to the tune of $20 million, and it will be worth every penny." Barrett quipped, "I think old BMO U will do us proud."[19] At one point, Barrett answered a question often posed to him during his travels – one of those softball, open-ended town-hall questions he would come to routinely knock out of the park: "How do you want to be remembered?" "That question kept me up a few nights," he told the conference, but he was clear with the following answer: "I want to be remembered as part of the team that breathed new life and vitality into this grand old Canadian institution and set it on its new path."[20]

The Corporate Strategic Plan

The Corporate Strategic Plan, called "Excellence: Making the Commitment," was a forty-seven-page document that outlined plans to reform the entire gamut of the Bank's operations and relationships. It set out the vision and mission about business and customers, and asserted that North America was to be the "marketplace where we will pursue market share," with Canada as the first priority and the United States as a second priority, as well as other strategically important markets and regions.[21] The plan focused also on the leadership team's commitments to strategy, performance, marketing, training, and development. From the financial strategy perspective, shareholder value, profitability (a particular underperformance challenge, considering the dead weight of the LDC debt drag), maintaining a strong capital base, credit risk, productivity, customer service, and competitive advantage were the focus.[22] The US business was a particular area of emphasis, with pledges to increase its share of overall earnings to 50 per cent.

The Great Communicator

The plan was accompanied by a powerful and extremely detailed communications strategy intended to gain consensus among the employees during the spring and summer of 1990.[23] There followed a cross-country tour by Barrett, one of the great and most gifted communicators of his era in Canadian and international banking. Corporate communications, or at least executive communications, was entering a golden age at the Bank. As the Annual Report for 1990 recounted, Barrett "discussed the plan with some 10,000 employees and with customers from all market segments. From these sessions, it was clear that our own people and our customers have strongly endorsed the strategic plan, and by so doing, have underwritten its success."[24] Barrett's approach to the tour could be summarized in his approach to criticisms about the condition of some of the branches in the network: "We are prepared to make changes ... An assessment of the physical conditions in our branches made me keenly aware that some of them are – how shall I put it – not quite up to snuff? You know the ones I mean, the ones where the manager stands at the door handing out hard-hats to the customers as they walk in! Well, we have made a sizeable increase of the capital budget to tackle this problem and the higher spending will stay in place until every branch sparkles. This is a commitment you can bank on."[25]

Here, the communications genius of Richard O'Hagan did much to maximize Barrett's star power and, more importantly, the entire architecture of CEO communications. As a former key player in the Prime Minister's Office of Pierre Elliott Trudeau, O'Hagan understood the methods, the structures, and the art of shaping the public persona of the leader. O'Hagan had connections like few others, both in Ottawa and in the media, which allowed Barrett to pursue a powerful and impact-driven communications agenda, whose results were evident almost from the moment he took office. The Barrett-O'Hagan partnership stands as proof – if such proof is even needed in this communications-intensive world – that first-class communications advice, structure, and execution can make a material difference to the leadership of large organizations.

The Great Regeneration proceeded on multiple fronts. In terms of strategy, Bank leadership was moving toward the realization of a North American vision, exploiting BMO's unique competitive advantage in cross-border presence. As the 1991 Annual Report asserted, "in the longer term, we plan to generate 50 percent of our earnings from US operations, compared with about 31 percent in 1991. One way we will meet this objective is by expanding our business with major US corporations. Another way is for Harris to continue the expansion of its community bank network in the Chicago suburbs; adding branches and acquiring additional community banks." The report indicated that the Bank favoured the American Midwest because it was close, because of its size, and, more to the point, because the Bank was already there. "Further expansion within the Midwest," the Annual Report concluded, "will be eased by changes underway in US legislation that will remove restrictions on interstate banking."[26]

There was also to be a major refocus on decentralization, to promote "services that are more customer and market-driven, and bring our senior people closer to our customers, and we gave local staff more decision-making authority."[27] The infamous Domestic Development Progam (DDP) was buried. Decentralization also meant, across the Bank's territory, empowering a cadre of newly appointed vice-presidents armed with substantial credit-granting authority. In 1990 alone, the Bank committed \$111 million to investments in improved customer service and an additional \$38 million to technical and management training programs. Part of the regeneration package was to tackle corporate governance and a reform of the BMO board, reducing the number of directors from fifty-two in 1981 to twenty-nine in 1992.[28] This included recasting board committees to align more closely with the functions of the Bank in marketing and customer service, human resources management, technology and infrastructure management, community service management, financial management, risk management, and strategic management.[29]

Generating Human and Intellectual Capital

The Regenerators quickly translated Barrett's April 1990 declaration of a "business management college" into a set of architectural and organizational blueprints. Within the organization, two generation-defining initiatives were underway.

The Learning Curve

The first initiative, at a projected cost of \$40 million, was construction of a massive training centre in Scarborough that would become the Institute for Learning.[30] The Bank hired Raymond Moriyama, one of the greatest Canadian architects of his generation, to design the building and put his creative imprint on the project. The emphasis on employee development and in career progression was envisioned on a scale that precious few financial institutions of BMO's size had ever contemplated. "When completed in 1993," the Annual Report for 1990 declared, "this future banking 'college' will offer courses in English and French to some 15,000 employees each year."[31] The goal was to provide an average of five days of training per employee per year by 1997. The employee development centre attracted significant media attention when made public. "This represents a level of commitment to employee development matched by only a handful of corporations in North America," Barrett said. In typical style, he added that the \$40-million cost, as well as the commitment to spend about a further \$50 million by 1993, was "very self-serving of the Bank" because it would give it a leg up on its competitors. Ontario Premier Bob Rae called the Bank's commitment "a tremendous example to governments and other corporations" in the face of blistering global competition."[32]

The IFL would grow to become a central component of BMO's training, development, and leadership architecture. That stands as one of the more foresighted decisions of the Regeneration Generation. The institute's large and welcoming premises were the physical manifestation of an idea, a relationship, and a reminder of the importance of cultural, professional, and leadership experience in the future of the Bank itself. The IFL was to be the first purpose-built institution of its kind in Canada and one of the few in North America.[33] Prime Minister Jean Chrétien officially opened Bank of Montreal's Institute for Learning in May 1994.[34]

The Task Forces

The second shift envisioned and engineered was the establishment in October 1990 of the Task Force on the Advancement of Women in the Bank under the sponsorship of Tony Comper. Comper's experience in the Bank from virtually the beginning, and especially in technology and operations, sensitized him to the challenges that superbly qualified women faced in promotion through the ranks. His insights were transformed into a resolve to drive change. Comper deputized a young female executive, Marnie Kinsley, to work on the task force. Kinsley had joined BMO from KPMG in 1985 as an auditor and was appointed a vice-president in 1990, progressively earning more responsibility and more senior roles throughout the 1990s and into the 2000s. The task force's mandate was to "identify and dismantle barriers preventing women from moving ahead in the Bank and reaching the most senior ranks" and to "create an environment for women and men in which there will be true equality, with advancement based solely on merit."[35]

The position of women in the Bank was an increasingly inescapable challenge. In Barrett's first cross-country tour as CEO, he noticed that at branch meetings there would be "eight women and a male branch manager." So he said, "Right. Let's do something dramatic here. Let's actually establish something big and address it on behalf of all banks and do this advancement of women in the workplace."[36] As one senior BMO executive involved in the task force recalled, Harriet Stairs and Deanna Rosensweig, both in senior management, were asked to figure out what issues "were keeping women back. Why they're not up in the senior levels." One of the issues involved learning and training – and that women were not receiving the same access. All that was about to change.[37] There were also more deeply rooted reasons. As one executive later suggested, "the answer is something that has undeniably and demonstrably become part of the DNA." The message, especially from Comper, was that the Bank needed "to be representative of the communities in which we work and live and serve." This would be good for business, and also help establish a long-term competitive advantage.[38]

What about impact? In the words of one veteran participant, this and the other task forces were "*very* successful in terms of shifting that balance. It took a long time and it is still underway but of all the things that I felt could have a dramatic impact, because when you looked at our clients, the buying decisions for financial services are disproportionately made by women in families." From the human capital perspective, those key initiatives of the 1990s began to exert a fundamental influence on the values of the bank.[39] The task force published its findings in November 1991, providing a wide-ranging set of important data and analysis on the situation of gender and employment at the Bank, or as Tony Comper nicely put it in his introduction, "who we really are, and (even more revealing) who we really aren't."[40] The establishment of an Advisory Council on an Equitable Workplace and the creation of an executive position with responsibility for workplace equality followed, along with a detailed agenda for this generation of bankers to address this challenge. The task force report, its recommendations, and its action plan represented an important milestone in the regeneration of the Bank. As one long-term observer and participant within the Bank noted: "The task force had much more impact on Canadian society because ... the banks do copycat ... When the Bank of Montreal took a lead in this ... the other banks took notice and they started doing it in their own way, but all pushed the whole women's issue. They all did it. The CIBC did it very poorly. They just went and hired a whole lot of senior people and stuck them in and then three years later they quit."[41]

The report's impact on the Bank was substantial and long-lasting. As one executive recalled, "for all of us who were involved and for the people that participated in the surveys and so on, it was an eye opener of immense proportions, not necessarily just about the women but how the men felt about their work."[42] As a result, Bank of Montreal became the first non-US–based company, as well as the first bank, to win the coveted Catalyst Award, honouring innovative efforts for the advancement of women. In 1993, women's share of the executive promotions in the Bank rose from 29 per cent to 54 per cent.[43] The promotion of rising stars such as Karen Maidment to chief financial officer was seen by many female BMO bankers as a "transformational point" in the work environment. One young woman executive suggested that it was not only Maidment's position as CFO that was inspirational, but the way the Bank allowed her to work from home from time to time: "what a message that was. Being a mom and all that was acceptable."[44]

The initiatives expanded to other groups, including a similar Task Force on the Advancement of Aboriginal Employment, which reported its findings in September 1992.[45] The rather public suggestion of Assembly of First Nations Grand Chief Phil Fontaine, who suggested that the Indigenous peoples were invisible to Canadian financial institutions, added impetus to a subject that had its own momentum at BMO. Under the leadership of Ron Jamieson, the work began. As one executive involved in the program noted, the relationship between Canadian banking and Indigenous communities was virtually non-existent, but that BMO would find out that "they just want what you want. They want to be treated fairly. They want respect. They want to be able to trust you and that will take time." President Comper and his wife, Elizabeth, took a "sincere and active interest in the Aboriginal marketplace," going to branch openings and travelling far afield in Canada to open branches of the Bank of Montreal.[46] By 1994–95, the Bank added five full-service branches to its five already-existing ones in Aboriginal communities across Canada. As the Annual Report for that year recorded, "the new branches, which provide career opportunities as well as a wide range of financial services, are part of the Bank's continuing efforts to serve Canada's Aboriginal communities better."[47] A third study group, the Task Force on Employment of People with Disabilities, issued a report in 1993, which made recommendations supported by action plans to lead the Bank to further progressive change in the future.[48]

Vision 2002

By 1991–92, the Bank's new look, new leadership, and new media offensive began to attract major notice. The media reported that Barrett was "merrily pumping out new loans south of the border. In the past 12 months alone, his US corporate loan portfolio has grown by a hefty 28 percent, or $1 billion" in the midst of a US credit crunch. Another example: "The jaunty executive isn't exactly dallying on his home turf: In the face of a sharp Canadian recession that has idled almost 12 percent of the work force, Bank of Montreal has boosted its residential mortgages by 18 percent and its commercial loans by 15 percent in the past year." Barrett commented that the reason for all this was that his new team was "irreverent and full of energy."[49] Another "jaunty" example was the Bank's breaking of convention by announcing their interest rate cuts before the Bank of Canada. On multiple occasions between 1 August 1990 and 1993, the Bank led the industry in cutting the prime rate. This strategy and others were examples of what BMO could and did do in the market that its competitors either could not or did not do. The preparation required to execute that sort of action properly without loss indicated the strength of the Bank's capabilities at the time. These actions and others disrupted the status quo and, more importantly, sent a message that BMO was on the front foot. South of the border, just as American banks were distracted by credit problems and acquisitions, Barrett pushed the Bank to take advantage of the situation.[50]

Inside the organization, the Regenerators were making substantial progress. Interdisciplinary meetings of executives aimed to reintroduce executives to each other – treasurer Yvan Bourdeau recalls being aghast at just how estranged the officer corps was. The training and development, the task forces, and the new emphases on employees and on the wider world were meant to signal that the Bank of Montreal was an institution "transcending purely the bottom line ... trying for a fit between what we do for a living and something society is interested in."[51]

In June 1992, the Barrett team unveiled its official North American strategy for the 1990s: Vision 2002. "*Vision 2002* is much more than an organization chart of legal entities," the 1993 Annual Report reassured.

> We see, not a "parent bank" surrounded by a ring of subsidiaries, but for complementary line organizations, each with clear market, product, and geographic mandates ... and [a] strong regional bank in the American Midwest, operating through the prosperous eight-state region that is our target market for individual, small business, and middle-market corporate banking services, and with a national franchise for trust and cash management services. A continental corporate and institutional bank, offering a full range of credit, treasury, and operating services to major customers across North America and in their dealings with the world ... And a continental investment bank, offering creative government and corporate financing solutions, and value-added advice to institutional equity, fixed income, and individual clients.[52]

One of the most ambitious goals of the Bank's North American strategy was to triple the Bank's market share over the coming decade.[53] Under Alan McNally's leadership, acquisitions and additions to the Harris operation allowed Harris Bank to meet its branch expansion objectives "a full six years ahead of schedule by acquiring all 54 branches and 250,000 customers of the Household Bank in the greater Chicago area" with a mid-1990s expansion target of 1 million individual and small business customers by 2002.[54]

As part of Vision 2002 and for greater exposure in the United States, in 1994, the Bank listed its shares on the New York Stock Exchange as the "natural next step in our evolution."[55] Barrett personally bought 176 shares at $18.50 – one for every year the Bank of Montreal had been in business since 1817. The move was part of the overall expansion into the United States. By 1997, Harris had played a natural leading role in the "three-pronged American expansion strategy." Between 1993 and 1996–97, Harris tripled its number of retail and small-business customers to more than 800,000, with a book equity value reaching US$1.8 billion as it expanded in the Midwest and in other centres such as Florida and Arizona.[56] By the mid-1990s, the Bank would serve one out of every five households in the Chicagoland area.[57]

By the mid-2000s, the Bank had invested $2.4 billion in US retail acquisitions, "transforming a handful of private Chicago banks into a community banking network of nearly 200 branches in the Chicago area and Northwest

Table 20.1 | Bank of Montreal US acquisitions, 1984–2004

Date	Acquisition	Purchase Price CA$(000,000)
1984	Harris Bank	718
1985	First National Bank of Barrington	43
1987	Commercial State Bank (Phoenix)	3
1988	State Bank of St Charles and First National Bank of Batavia	31
1990	Libertyville Federal Savings and Loan	7
1990	Frankfort Bancshares	20
1994	Suburban Bancorp	300
1996	Household International	378
1999	Burke, Christensen & Lewis	59
2000	Village Banc of Naples	19
2000	Freeman Welwood	140
2000	Century Bank	24
2001	First National Bank of Joliet	337
2002	CSFB*direct*	854
2002	Northwestern Trust	19
2002	Self-directed online client accounts of Morgan Stanley Individual Investor Group	153
2002	myCFO	61
2003	Sullivan, Bruyette, Speros & Blayney	20
2003	Gerard Klauer Mattison	40
2004	Lakeland Community Bank	49
2004	New Lenox State Bank	314
Total		3,589
Total, excluding Harris Bank acquisition		2,871

Source: BMOA, Bank of Montreal Annual Report, 2004.

Indiana."[58] That work would largely unfold beyond the period of this chapter, piloted by Frank Techar, the Minnesota-born, Princeton-educated banker who served as president of BMO Harris Bank from 2002 to 2006.

South of the Rio Grande

The Barrett team's North American vision led south of the Rio Grande, to Mexico. In March 1996, the Bank acquired a 16 per cent stake in Grupo Financiero Bancomer S.A., Mexico's second largest bank, for US$456 million, a bet placed squarely on the North American Free Trade Agreement (NAFTA) and its transformative power. Caution was warranted, but the risk was worth it. The Bank paid for the purchase using $539 million worth of Mexican government Brady bonds that were denominated in US currency and backed by the US government, among other conditions.[59]

How did the move fare? One executive summed it up thus: "When you look at it from a pure investment perspective, it did very well for us because we got out of it many years later and made hundreds of millions of dollars in the process. They ran into another wall, and at that point we were faced with a strategic decision: 'Do we want to put a lot of our money behind this bank?' ... And we decided no, it was too much of a single bet for us. A Spanish bank was willing to do it, so we obviously sold out. But as I said, we made a good dollar on that particular investment relative to the country debt that we started with."[60]

China

Meantime, the Bank moved to increase its capabilities in international finance, particularly for its North American customers doing business abroad, adding $3 billion for trade, term, and project finance initiatives in key export markets. China was, of course, always in the executive sights, "another sign of management's continuing commitment to exploring international markets for future growth."[61] The Bank had opened a representative office in Beijing in 1983, followed by a representative office in Guangzhou a decade later. In 1995, the Guangzhou office was upgraded to a full-service branch, a first for the Bank of Montreal in China.[62] This was followed in 1997 by the opening of a branch in Beijing, making the Bank of Montreal the only Canadian bank with two branches in mainland China.[63] Robert Martin, the bank's managing director and regional executive for Asia, was bullish on the prospects: "We are confident that the bank's branches in Beijing and Guangzhou will provide our customers with an exclusive operating platform from which to invest in the fastest growing economy in Asia."[64] The Bank of Montreal was fortunate to have Roger Heng as its early navigator and relationship-maker in China. From Heng's appointment in 1987 until his retirement in 2017, Heng opened doors and pathways into the labyrinthine world of Chinese officialdom as governments sought to liberalize financial markets. Barrett continued and extended the BMO CEO traditions of his predecessor in attempting to gain a serious foothold in the Celestial Empire. As one executive recalled: "Matt Barrett, in one of his early activities as CEO, told the board that he wanted to expand into China. And we always had a little business in China, but Matt took it upon himself to get a bigger foothold ... And again, his great persuasion, he talked the Chinese government into giving us the first branch in Beijing;

the first Canadian branch in Beijing and one of the few foreign-owned banks in Beijing."[65]

In 1989, BMO executive Neil Tait was given an extraordinary mandate to strengthen the Bank's presence in Asia. Over the following decade, as Bill Downe later recalled, "through his efforts, we obtained banking licenses in Guangzhou, Beijing and Shanghai; we held a board of directors meeting in Beijing – a first for a Canadian company; and we secured a position on the prestigious International Business Leaders Advisory Council for the Mayor of Beijing." Tait later became special adviser to the Bank for Asia after his nominal retirement in 2001.[66]

The Bank's push for China also extended within Canada, as it increased its profile in the growing Chinese-Canadian community, particularly in Scarborough, Ontario, and Richmond, B.C. Accordingly, it purchased the personal banking business of Standard Chartered Bank of Canada in order to compete in that market. Many of the 35,000 people a year who were leaving Hong Kong in advance of its 1997 handover to China were entrepreneurs who brought both skills and money to Canada.[67] One Asia-Pacific executive, however, lamented the lack of serious long-term commitment to the region, expressing a "frustration about acknowledging how fast Asia was growing, where our opportunity could have been."[68]

Cruising Speed

By the mid-1990s, the story of the Bank was one of greater momentum, leadership, and strategic precision. "The last five years at the Bank of Montreal have been a major success story," noted John Switzer of Ernst & Young in 1995. Jean Monty at Northern Telecom (later a BMO director) agreed that Barrett had been "able to energize, to get everybody walking in the same direction."[69] In 1995 also, Matthew Barrett was named the Outstanding CEO of the Year, cited for innovative leadership and contribution to global competitiveness.[70] By 1997, the Bank could point to the fact that "since 1990, the year a strategic plan for the decade was unveiled by the new management team, market capitalization has grown from $3.8 billion to $15.9 billion. Dividends paid out for the same period totalled $2.5 billion for a total return to shareholders of $14.6 billion."[71] That momentum included a pronounced geographic diversification as a result of the North American strategy, and to an extent the efforts in Asia. That meant that over 50 per cent of the Bank's earnings came from outside Canada. "That was our goal for the year 2002," the Annual Report for that year wrote, "and reaching it has enabled us to advance more quickly to the next target – to achieve 60 percent of earnings from outside Canada."[72] The conclusion was clear to the Regenerator Generation: for many reasons, all told, "fiscal 1997 was a watershed for the Bank of Montreal." But it was not only that. The Bank of Montreal had built a sustained momentum. Things were going according to plan.

The Technological Turn and mbanx

A key element of the Bank's regeneration was the deployment and diffusion of technology as a competitive differentiator in the market. The 1990s were comparatively early days of the Internet, and that revolution was thought to have such deep transformative powers as to fundamentally change everything. Between 1990 and 1995, incremental but notable innovations were made in networking the branches, enhancing relationship banking with customers, and improving productivity.[73] In January 1995, the Bank established its presence on the Internet for the first time – the first of the Canadian domestic banks to do so, though the Royal attempted to claim the title by issuing the press release about their website first.[74] But for the Barrett team, a more ambitious grand strategy beckoned: a completely online-only banking presence.

Barret loved the idea. When the project team approached him in the summer of 1996, as one witness recalled: "Matt loved the idea so much he wanted a full, national launch by October!" instead of a test market planned for Calgary, then a possible national rollout. Barrett had his reasons beyond technology. He wanted to explore the whole "direct channel" idea of banking – through the Internet and call centres. Barrett also thought there was a technological solution, finally, to problems in the service culture. As one executive recalled, Barrett "was quite seized with the … lack of a customer-focused service culture in the retail bank, and wanted to set up some sort of internal competing force." Barrett understood the challenge and the opportunity. mbanx would also project modernity, and perhaps one day become the entire bank itself, one that captured the plenitude of the activities going on under the aegis of the Bank of Montreal. As one executive recalled, "the plurality of the mbanx name was favoured because we were absorbing investment banking, we were starting to branch out into different pillars … and so it was much more than just a technologically kind of buzzy name."[75] The idea was so seductive to decision-makers that the proposal to test the mbanx idea via a limited launch in Calgary was not only approved but also the team working on it was directed to launch nationally. One of those team members recalled the response: "We can't go national!" And Barrett saying, "Go national … go for it."[76] So the mbanx team, and the Bank itself, not only went for it but – in the parlance of the day – they went for it big time.

On 16 October 1996, the Bank of Montreal launched mbanx, "an entirely new virtual banking enterprise designed to meet the needs of financially

Under the leadership of W.D. Mulholland, pictured here with Chinese officials at Tiananmen Square, the Bank of Montreal opened its first representative office in mainland China in 1983, opting for the capital, Beijing. This was a big deal, as only forty-one other foreign banks had received approval to operate in China, with just four of them being Canadian. 1983.

(*above*) Expanding operations in China required putting in face-time and developing close and personal relationships. Beginning with G. Arnold Hart's visits to China in the 1970s, Bank of Montreal CEOs would travel to China with increasing frequency. 1983.

(*opposite*) The Domestic Development Program reorganized the Bank of Montreal into separate functions: retail ("Domestic Banking") and commercial ("Commercial Banking"). To help staff and customers alike get used to the change and new protocols, the Bank published a comic book about the superhero Domestic Development Man. Each page featured an episode with a customer who was unhappy with the service he or she received. Domestic Development Man then came to the rescue, explaining to staff how the new Domestic Development Program was designed to help them navigate and solve these problems. 1983.

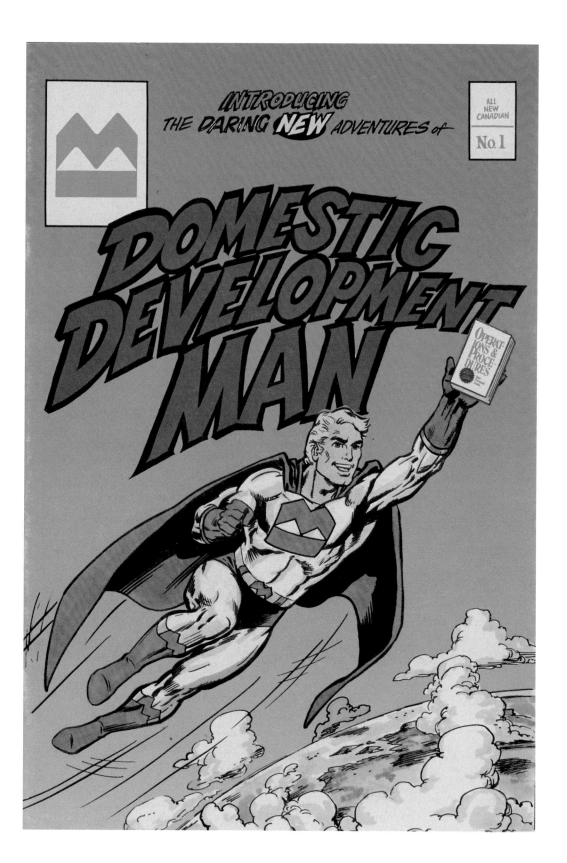

(*above*) The acquisition of Harris Bankcorp, Inc. of Chicago was one of the major milestones of the Mulholland era. This picture, taken that year, was part of a series of images taken for the merger. 1984.

(*opposite*) The acquisition of Harris Bankcorp, Inc. was a cause for celebration, both in Canada and in the United States. This picture was taken at a Harris branch in Chicago commemorating the event. 1984. Photo Ideas, Inc., Chicago, Illinois.

(*above*) In 1984, the Master Charge lineup was expanded with the introduction of MasterCard Gold, geared to "higher income, status-oriented professionals." Shown here, from left to right, are: Fredrick S. Eaton, T. Eaton Company Ltd president and CEO; William D. Mulholland, Bank of Montreal president and CEO; Russell E. Hogg, MasterCard International president and CEO; and Matthew Barrett, Bank of Montreal executive vice-president and group executive for domestic banking. 1985.

(*opposite*) In August 1987, the Bank of Montreal announced that it had acquired Nesbitt Thomson Corp. Inc., Canada's fifth-largest brokerage firm. The dealmakers, seen here strolling down St Jacques Street in Montreal, were, from left to right: Michael I. Sweatman, Matthew W. Barrett, W.D. Mulholland, and Brian J. Aune. 1987.

The acquisition of Nesbitt Thompson was historic. The Bank of Montreal was the first Canadian bank to purchase a Canadian brokerage firm, putting it ahead of its competitors and positioning it to deliver new services across the country. Pictured here are Nesbitt Thomson chairman J. Brian Aune (*left*) and Bank of Montreal CEO William D. Mulholland (*right*) at a press conference regarding the acquisition. 1987.

The 1990s saw the Bank of Montreal expand its presence to the Internet. In this picture, Terri McLennan (*left*) and Paul Gammal (*right*) are shown using the new BMO website, where consumers could apply for mortgages and get online approvals. 1990.

On 19 April 1990, BMO CEO Matthew Barrett convoked a meeting at the Bristol Place Hotel with BMO executives from around the world to "affirm a new strategic plan," which was to set the tone for the 1990s. Shown here, from left to right: (*top row*) Lloyd Darlington, Al McNally, and Tony Comper; (*middle row*) Michael Rayfield, Doug Gibson; (*bottom row*) L.R. O'Hagan, Dereck Jones, and Bernard Barth. 1990.

Following the adoption of the Bank of Montreal Corporate Strategic Plan, CEO Matthew Barrett embarked on a cross-country tour where he "discussed the plan with some 10,000 employees and with customers from all market segments." 1990.

In October 1996, the Bank of Montreal launched mbanx, "an entirely new virtual banking enterprise designed to meet the needs of financially active consumers across North America at the highest standards of speed, convenience and service quality." Shown here, from left to right, are Matthew Barret, Jeff Chisholm, and Andrew White announcing the launch of mbanx. 1996.

Under the leadership of Matthew Barrett and Tony Comper in the 1990s, the Bank of Montreal underwent tremendous changes. In April 1996, Barrett posed for the cover of *Report on Business Magazine* holding up a placard that read, "Can a Bank Change?" 1996.

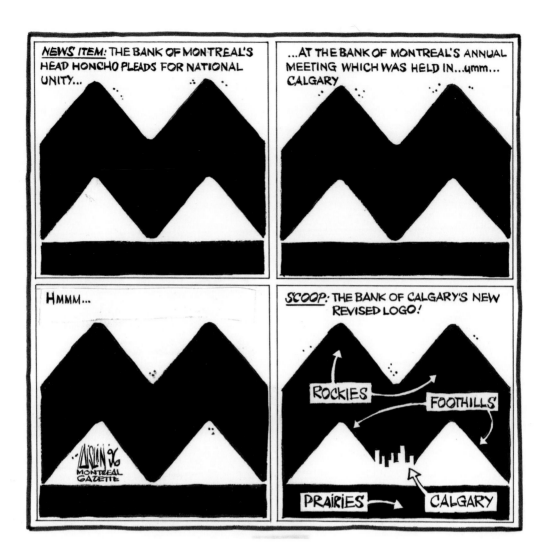

(*above*) In the wake of the 1995 Quebec Referendum and the possibility of another referendum in 1997, Matthew Barrett called for national unity and a "leaner, tauter federation." Artist Aislin (Terry Mosher) lampooned Barrett's sincere calls by highlighting the Bank of Montreal's strong presence in central Canada when compared to its presence in Canada's western provinces. 1996. Artist Aislin (alias Terry Mosher). Image courtesy of McCord Museum of Canadian History, M999.65.181.

(*opposite*) The front cover of *First Bank News*, the Bank of Montreal's internal staff magazine, hailed the progress made in the merger talks between the Bank of Montreal and the Royal Bank of Canada with the headline, "Merger Momentum. The BMO/Royal Bank Alliance: Getting Ready for Tomorrow." 1998.

INSIDE: ON THE ROAD • TAKING SURVEY STOCK

MAY/JUNE 1998

FirstBank News

THE PUBLICATION FOR EMPLOYEES OF THE BANK OF MONTREAL GROUP OF COMPANIES

MERGER

BMO/RBC   TD/CIBC   Citicorp/Travelers Group   NationsBank Corp./Bank America   First Chicago NBD/Banc One

MOMENTUM

The BMO/Royal Bank Alliance: Getting Ready for Tomorrow

In anticipation of the potential BMO-RBC merger in 1998, promotional pins were produced that highlighted the predicted growth potential of such a development. 1998.

Bank of Montreal executives visited China with increasing frequency in the 1990s. Pictured here are Tony Comper (*fourth from left*) and Bill Downe (*third from left*) with Canadian and Chinese officials. The 2000s would see tremendous expansion in China, culminating with establishment of the Bank of Montreal (China) Co. Ltd – or BMO ChinaCo – in October 2010. 2000.

In the aftermath of the failed merger of the Bank of Montreal with the Royal Bank of Canada and the departure of Matt Barrett as CEO, Tony Comper, pictured here, took the reins in challenging times. 2001.

The year 2004 marked the 10th anniversary of BMO's listing on the New York Stock Exchange. In the centre of the image, from left to right, is the Bank's senior leadership: Karen Maidment, senior executive vice-president and chief financial officer; Tony Comper, president and chief executive officer; and William Downe, deputy chair of BMO Financial Group and chief executive officer of BMO Nesbitt Burns. 2004. Image used courtesy of NYSE Group ©2004.

William Downe ascended to the position of chief executive officer in 2007. He steered the Bank through the Great Recession of 2008 and, in the words of governor of the Bank of Canada Mark Carney, "was instrumental in formulating Canada's response to the financial crisis." 2004. From BMO Corporate Communications.

Bank of Montreal CEO Darryl White took over in November 2017. He is pictured here speaking at the Leadership Council 2018 on 24 September. 2018. From BMO Corporate Communications.

Joanna Rotenberg (right), group head of BMO Wealth Management, in discussion with the historian Niall Ferguson at the Bank's annual Leadership Council 2018. 2018. From BMO Corporate Communications.

A generation of leadership, from left to right: Former CEOs Matt Barrett and Tony Comper, incoming CEO Darryl White, and, on his last day as CEO, Bill Downe unveil for posterity the bicentennial wall at the Montreal Main Branch on 29 October 2017. 2017.

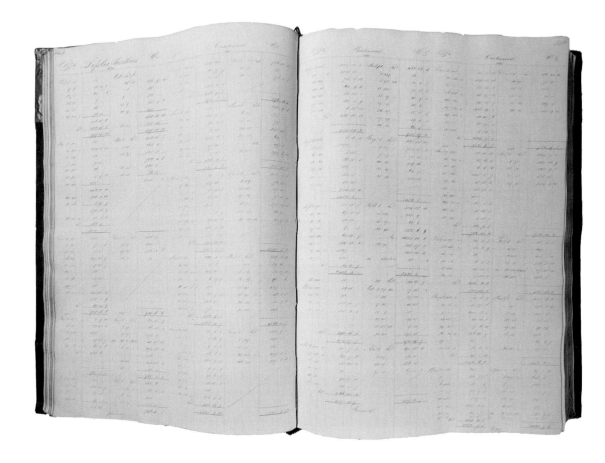

General ledger belonging to the Bank of the People, 1840–42. Owing to restrictions on banks operating branches outside their territory, the Bank of Montreal acquired this bank in 1840 in order to have access to Upper Canada.

active consumers across North America at the highest standards of speed, convenience and service quality."[77] The expectations placed on mbanx, which would be supported by the newly minted Electronic Financial Services Group, were truly remarkable. They also undoubtedly strained the creative talents of the Annual Report copywriters: "we have planted an acorn from which a truly mighty oak will grow"; mbanx is to be the "central thrust of our response to the steady growth of a world without boundaries."[78] The mbanx operations would deliver fully integrated electronic banking products in Canada, the United States, and eventually, it was planned, in Mexico. Here, the Bank's reputation as a technology pioneer in Canadian banking was reinforced. As one executive of the day suggested, "you know, we had a reputation of being innovative, even when it almost killed you."[79]

The mbanx operations attracted a lot of attention in 1996–97, as well as some of the best and brightest young minds in the Bank. Those who did a tour at mbanx during this time look back with great nostalgia. They were not only doing something new but also clearly doing something league-leading in an area (communications technology, the Internet) that had captured the public imagination as the millennium approached. The 1997 Annual Report suggested that "with more than 80,000 customers to date, mbanx has met or exceeded our customers' expectations, having placed in the top decile in customer loyalty rankings of financial services surveyed by an independent research firm. mbanx is definitive proof that Bank of Montreal can create and implement a dramatically new and different vision of banking in the Digital Age."[80] mbanx followed in the wake of a whole panoply of technological firsts – online auto leasing, online mortgage approvals, wireless banking, and Investorline.

And then there was the advertising, which created a remarkable splash. As Barrett colourfully explains, the campaign (which included buying the rights to Dylan's "The Times They Are A-Changin'" for $2 million) was in some ways a long-held dream that was realized:

I used to love the advertising side. I used to spend hours with the agencies. It's very creative and flaky and I loved it. But I remember as a kid in London these posters that were up in the subway. "H-U-D," they read. "Who is Hud?" All these goddamn posters going up everywhere. Turns out that it was a Paul Newman movie called Hud. I remember thinking how clever it was: everybody was talking about it. So we ran mbanx with no mbanx ... No explanation. No Bank of Montreal, nothing. Just a commercial with families walking through beautiful fields singing "The Times They Are A-Changin'." And there was an uproar from the public; everyone was talking about it. But I was catching flak everywhere because the boomers had this view that Dylan was the great anti-establishment man and that I had hijacked one of the great anthems of the '60s.[81]

mbanx was almost certainly a visionary and bold move, but the project also proved to be a serious overextension. As one manager recalled: "From the external [perspective], the launch looked very well done, but behind the scenes it was chaos. I mean, I remember in finance we were just throwing people at the business like crazy. Nothing was automated, nothing was documented, nothing was put in place. And it was just … chaos, literally. It was just basically being held together by plastic bands and tape and duct tape."[82]

The Bank would have to rely on old technology for the new platform, if they were to get it done quickly. "So the concept was, in some ways, brilliant. It was very much ahead of its time … So it got launched. The concept was great. The clients loved it. But it was one of those 'We lose two cents on every transaction. We'll make it up with volume.' In the end it just could not make sufficient revenues given the technology limitations, and not least because mbanx had to be end-to-end processing. As a result, its long-term fate was sealed."[83] The plug was quietly pulled in 1999.

A Mixed Verdict

mbanx was the technological vessel into which many of the Bank's fondest aspirations were poured. From the commanding heights of a Bank leadership already impatient for change and possessing a creditable track record for accomplishing that after 1990, taking the lead in Internet banking was the next step. How the Bank's leadership understood technological change was tied to several competing assumptions – the nature of the technology, the frustration of the pace of change across the branch network, and a certain search for a game-changing innovation that would answer the complex question of securing and maintaining competitive advantage. In the febrile atmosphere of the technological wave, executives viewed these technologies and saw the reflections of other fundamental technological shifts that would disrupt the status quo. Branch banking was thought to be in a death spiral – and that was the industry view. Nobody would go to branches anymore. As one participant recalls: "So a decision was made that we would take a bold step forward and really kind of move forward quickly and be the first bank to launch a totally virtual bank; you know, branded separately, everything."[84] This passage is a telling insight to the managerial mind of the mid-1990s. Chastened by the experience, the mbanx episode "hugely sensitized every senior executive to be careful." As one executive put it, "these grand strategies, if they aren't anchored in reality regarding consumer behavior, and [questions about] how long is it going to take and how much money is it going to take and what kind of people change is required and what kind of motivational systems are needed [aren't answered], these schemes in the sky can be hugely expensive and can hurt your image also." However, in 1997, the fate of mbanx was not yet sealed; that would come in 1999 and 2000.

The Spirit of the Age

It would be a mistake, however, to view the mbanx episode in the long-run experience of BMO as a failure, or at the least as something that did not take. In many ways, mbanx crystallized some of the enduring qualities of an evolving purpose for the Bank. One of the most persistent legacies of the mbanx era was the kind of cultural values that began to be articulated as a conscious program of organizational life. The five values were: (1) change is good; (2) we believe in better; (3) a promise is a promise; (4) make simple rules that work; and (5) everyone is important. Within the scope of those five declarations was the blueprint for the next two decades.

Value, vision, and purpose statements are often couched in soaring and aspirational rhetoric – what the organization imagines itself to be, and perhaps what it also aspires to be. If not handled properly, those statements can also resemble cut flowers – when fresh, they are stunning to look at: they motivate and inspire. But after a time, their beauty inevitably begins to fade. However, if those statements are deeply rooted in the DNA of the organization, meaningfully connected to its authentic experience and aspirations, they begin to take on a power and a life of their own. Carefully reflected-upon values and purpose make intuitive sense to those who receive them. It's something beyond mere marketing – something an organization is, and is in the process of becoming. Authentically reflected values are not something that can be bought and installed: they are first lived and shaped, and then recognized.

The values and mission – even the purpose, if you will – of the Bank of Montreal in the 1990s emerged out of the significant cultural shifts in the post-Mulholland era. Those shifts began to move the Bank measurably toward a greater engagement and dynamism on virtually all fronts. The authenticity of the values they articulated flowed from the renewed strength of the Bank – from its reinvigorated leadership and their plans. That special, kinetic spirit of the age manifested itself in multi-faceted ways – from the efforts to promote the advancement of women to a more forward posture on strategy, marketing, communications, and how to handle the competition. The new dynamism extended to such symbolically small things as scooping the Bank of Canada on prime interest rate reductions to such era-shaping events as entry into China or re-entry into Mexico. In the parlance of the era, Bank of Montreal had got its groove back.

Historians studying the transition from one great period to the next – from the waning of the Middle Ages to the Renaissance or, to choose a Canadian example, the advent of the Quiet Revolution in Quebec – will inevitably get round to telling you that change is a long-term process, that something started in a previous era could come to fruition in a subsequent time. So it is with the Bank's long-run experience. Many of the seeds – not to mention the people and the policies – of the Mulholland era were very much in evidence in the 1990s. So many of the habits, tendencies, and strengths of the past persisted in time as they inevitably do. It is equally true, however, that something important changed in that era in the Bank that could not be explained simply by recourse to what had come before. Dynamism, confidence, connection, engagement: that was the legacy of the BMO Regenerators, and the way in which that generation of leaders sought to master their own time.

Taken together, the seven years of the Great Regeneration represented seven good years, a clear but complex strategic triumph for the leadership and people of the Bank. Those years of regeneration would allow the Bank of Montreal to confront the trials and tests soon to come.

CHAPTER TWENTY-ONE

Trajectories, 1998–2017

Section 1: The Icarus Trap

When Daedalus had put the finishing touches to his invention, he raised himself into the air, balancing his body on his two wings, and there he hovered, moving his feathers up and down. Then he prepared his son to fly too. "I warn you, Icarus," he said, "you must follow a course midway between earth and heaven, in case the sun should scorch your feathers, if you go too high, or the water make them heavy if you are too low. Fly halfway between the two"... Drawn on by his eagerness for the open sky, he left his guide and soared upwards...
Ovid, *The Fall of Icarus*[1]

By 1997, or Year 7 of the Barrett administration, the strategy and performance of the Bank had yielded impressive results across all of its expanded activities, especially after 1994. The mbanx initiative had not yet demonstrated its fatal flaws. The 1994 purchase of Burns Fry added considerable capacity to the investment and capital markets dimension of the business. The North American strategy was moving apace, with growth in the United States and in Mexico. The long-run attention to China was also yielding major gains, culminating in a new branch in Beijing and expanded operations there. The deepening relationship was fully reflected in the 1997 decision to hold the first board meeting in the Bank's history outside of North America in Beijing, which saw former prime minister Pierre E. Trudeau, with his long-standing links to the PRC, in attendance. On the technology front, the decision to form mbanx was visionary, even if it was a much greater risk than other strategic moves because of the challenges. Internally, organizational transformation, a quiet revolution in training and development, and focus on a bank more open to women and minorities began a long wave of change in the workforce at the Bank. Board reforms streamlined corporate governance and ensured a more meaningful contribution of oversight. The Barrett administration's triumphs were substantial, yet somehow fell short of the ambitions the Regeneration Generation harboured for the Bank. In some quarters at least, and demonstrably at the top, the leadership yearned for something more, something bigger.

Meanwhile, the Bank's public pronouncements were increasingly focused around the idea of creating a serious, Canada-based, North American or global competitor to be reckoned with. "It's a mistake to be thinking of Canadian banks solely in the context of their size relative to Canada," Barrett said in 1997.[2] Here, having "scaled players" with an ability to compete was critical. The competition in "the emerging borderless era" would come from America, Europe, and Asia. The critical instrument to confront this emergent world was scale, a sentiment shared by other Canadian financial institutions in making representations to the federal government for regulatory reform in the period. For the Barrett bank, something had to give.

The need for consolidation in the financial services sector to compete continentally and globally was an accepted article of faith in global banking circles. Waves of deregulation in the North Atlantic world in the 1980s allowed banking and investment houses to come together. Globalization of the industry demanded a strong response from bankers to consider their scale and measure it against the challenges of the future. In the case of Canadian banking, there was local precedent: as we have seen in chapters 8 and 9, the Bank of Montreal and the Royal were especially active consolidators in the Canadian market between 1900 and 1920. Now, the markets were not only national but also continental; not only continental but also global. The success of Canadian banking in the financial history of the North Atlantic world could be transformed for export, but the battle would be lost before it began if Canadian players were not able to leverage scale. The near-universal view, particularly pushed by management consultants in the field, was that the path to international leadership and competitive advantage in banking required bigger players – much bigger players.

On 15 September 1998, the federal cabinet convened to discuss the Report of the Task Force on the Future of the Canadian Financial Services Sector, or the MacKay Report. The Privy Council Office note commended the report as providing "valuable and comprehensive input" for the evolution of a financial institution policy framework for the twenty-first century.[3]

The MacKay Task Force was heralded as the "most significant piece of work" in financial services since the Porter Commission in 1964. As a memorandum to the prime minister on the subject suggested, the report "corroborates the view that, to the extent possible, the government should have a clearly articulated policy framework for the financial sector as a backdrop to taking decisions on the bank mergers."[4] Though the memorandum suggested that "some may argue that the report was 'pro-bank'" because it was consistent with bank recommendations in a variety of areas, others would take note that the report was much more consumer focused than previous initiatives and, thus, was a "step in the right direction."[5] There were other potential land mines, such as the recommendation that the government acquire the legislative authority to approve "in exceptional cases" the takeover of a large Canadian financial institution by a widely held foreign financial institution."[6]

As early as 1991, BMO bankers began to form the conviction that the financial services industry in Canada was in progressively more urgent need of restructuring. As one central player recalled, restructuring meant more "bulk, more heft, more capital, more market capitalization." Fuelled by those assumptions about the future of financial services, throughout the 1990s, Canadian bankers discussed multiple scenarios and possible mergers. The key in the Canadian system, however, was to ensure that not only bankers but also, critically, the federal government was on board. In other words, the political economy of the situation would be pivotal to whether any such merger would happen. The bankers' market, so to speak, had reached some sort of consensus on the desirability of mergers. The political and public policy market was much harder to read.

In December 1997, the Bank of Montreal made its move. As one executive of the era recalled, on 19 December 1997, the day of the BMO Christmas party on the sixty-eighth floor of First Canadian Place, John Cleghorn, CEO of the Royal Bank, and Matthew Barrett of the Bank of Montreal agreed to "put something together" in terms of a merger.[7] The official announcement came on 23 January 1998, beginning eleven months of intense negotiation and collaboration between the two banks to amalgamate their operations. With some exhortation by corporate communications planners, Bank employees rallied to the colours and showed their support for the merger strategy "by writing letters to MPs, taking part in talk shows and organizing highly successful rallies in the streets of cities across Canada."[8] As Barrett wrote in the 1998 Annual Report, "I believe they did these things because they knew better than anyone that 1998 was a year when everything changed, a watershed year for Canadian banking."[9]

Reflecting on those years, one key member of the Regenerators viewed this major strategic move in the following terms: "for many years we had always taken a strategic view that consolidation in the industry would be a beneficial thing from a perspective of scale and scope of activities, shareholder value, expansion outside of Canada and things of that nature. I'm still of that view. And we've seen it because of the concentric circles ... we've been going through that. And so the proof positive of this has helped the banks but at that point in time, throughout the 90s, we were kind of sliding down the league tables and it was pretty apparent to Matt and me that if consolidation was going to occur at some point in time and, properly executed, it was probably going to be a beneficial thing." The Bank's inner cabinet had been preparing the board "for years and years and years before 1998": therefore, when the merger with the Royal Bank got past the initial courtship stages, the directors were familiar with the subject matter and the arguments for the action. Indeed, Barrett and his leadership team could count on the board being in complete strategic alignment.[10]

Meantime, the BMO senior leadership worked intensely to prepare the Bank for the transition. Its case was argued with shareholders, employees, and the public, and constant representations were made to government agencies, task forces (a more sober one headed by Harold McKay, and a more political one chaired by Toronto Liberal MP Tony Ianno), and regulators why the merger should proceed and why it would be good to create a "superbank out of Royal – the country's biggest – and the third-ranked Bank of Montreal."[11] Adding more complexity to the proceedings was the announcement in April 1998 of another major merger of Canadian banks, with the CIBC and the TD asserting what seemed to be a defensive counter-merger in light of the BMO–RBC plan.[12] Throughout the spring and summer of 1998, the machinery of the federal government ground on, and included reports, opinions, hearings, and political declarations. At the highest levels, however, it seemed as if bankers were losing the argument to ministers in the court of public opinion.

At a meeting of the federal cabinet on 3 November 1998, Finance Minister Martin noted that public opinion was "not in favour of the mergers" and that, in addition, the Caucus Task Force was expected to be heavily critical of mergers.[13] The cabinet briefing also noted that the cabinet would "need to manage this issue in caucus."[14] At that November meeting, the finance minister's presentation focused on the "negative public opinion with respect to the mergers" emanating from government polling on the subject.[15] Martin balanced this focus with discussions on "how globalization and technology were affecting traditional financial institutions (and how these institutions might respond, with or without mergers, and with or without major legislative changes)."[16]

Martin kept coming back to the theme of hostile public opinion in his prepared remarks to cabinet. He told his colleagues that polls conducted by the government had shown "that there is a phenomenally high level of public awareness of the two proposed mergers." The polls found that the awareness of the bank mergers was greater than any other major issue. Those same polls informed the government that the "majority of Canadians" did not believe that mergers were in the public interest, "irrespective of regional differences."[17] Martin concluded that there was "no mood in the public that the mergers should be approved," adding "this is not likely to change."[18] The Caucus Task Force, chaired by Toronto-area MP Tony Ianno, was also "very unsupportive" of any merger, citing negative implications for competition and consumer choice. Besides, Martin remarked, the bankers themselves were telling him that the probability of a merger approval went from a "slam dunk" in spring of 1998 to a probability of about "40 percent."[19]

Finance Minister Martin then laid out his proposed next steps, which included awaiting various reports from the Office of the Superintendent of Financial Institutions (OSFI) and the Competition Bureau before he could make a decision. But it was clear which way the wind was blowing that November in Room 323-S of the House of Commons where the cabinet was gathered. One of Martin's last points reinforced the feeling: "The banks have been trying to publicly put pressure on the government to move quickly," he suggested, "but the banks cannot be allowed to dictate our agenda. Instead, it will be dictated by the political environment and the government's own priorities."[20] No other issue related to financial institutions – for example, foreign bank entry into Canada or the weighty decision to allow demutualization of life insurance companies – came close in evoking such a strong reaction.

A few more twists and turns of the story continued throughout the autumn of 1998, with the coup de grâce coming with the Competition Bureau's 11 December letter to Barrett and Cleghorn, which concluded that the BMO–RBC merger was "likely to lead to a substantial lessening or prevention of competition that would cause higher prices and lower levels of service and choice for several key banking services in Canada."[21] On 14 December 1998, Finance Minister Paul Martin announced he would reject the two proposed bank mergers.

The broad outlines of what happened after the day Barrett and Cleghorn set the institutions they led on the bold trajectory of merging are captured, at least superficially, in available journalistic accounts and analyses. We know the contours of what happened, and some of why and how it happened. But the real history, the definitive story beyond those journalistic reports – the balance of the considerations – will have to wait at least until release of the government documents of the era. The main protagonists – Barrett, Cleghorn, and Martin – and the cast of hundreds driven into the public arena – bankers, communications flacks, politicians and parliamentarians, Canadian nationalists, economists, task force participants, and the wider public, most of whom came armed with vastly different motivations, understandings, and sophistication – made for an unusual chapter in the story of Canadian banking whose outcome bore the essential characteristics of Canadian political economy.

Skyfall?

The failure of the BMO–RBC merger had a strong yet differential impact on the leadership and people of the Bank of Montreal. If you were at the head office, "you thought the world had ended," in the words of one contemporary. At the same time, if you were in the field, in the branches, serving customers day after day, lending money, and helping people, you took a different view. "I think the branches were totally unaffected by this," one insider noted, suggesting that connection between what was happening at the centre and "what the real business of the business was" were affected differently.[22] There was no hiding the fact that the outcome caught the leadership of the Bank on the back foot. Some suggested that the dark mood in the post-merger-failure days was because there did not seem to be an alternative plan, and "so when it became obvious that we weren't going to be able to consummate that merger or whatever, we had to scramble. We had to scramble. We had to try to pump up the bank tire. That was very, very difficult to do."[23]

For the eight or nine central people who lived through that extraordinary year, the whole affair, in a paradoxical way perhaps, showed the Bank of Montreal leadership that, in the words of one of the central players, "we had a very strong executive group who could, at the minimum, compete [with the Royal], if not excel, in a number of key areas."[24] This statement captures rather well the spirit of the era at BMO – to surge ahead, to challenge the status quo, and to push in every direction in an attempt to assert its leadership in Canadian banking. There seemed to be no fear of investigating strategic options – even the ones requiring more than the usual risk. The Regeneration Generation's great play proved to be "quite rejuvenating for the company" – until, of course, it all came to a halt. Until then, it was, for those involved, "the most exciting of days."[25]

Let us leave the last word to Matt Barrett, reflecting on the events of 1998 sometime later: "I knew that, at best, we had a 50/50 chance. At best. The only thing I was certain of was that if I'd gone to Paul Martin he would have said no. I thought the only hope I had was to put news of the intended merger out there, which I'm permitted to do, and then see if I can fight it out in the court of public opinion." When asked about the presence or absence of a Plan B, Barrett suggested that while "I don't have the documents [to prove this] … there was a plan B strategy that in the event [the merger] didn't come off we would use the failure to address some of the deficiencies the merger was expected to take care of." The failure would, in his estimation, have given the Bank some leverage "to do things that might have been unpalatable otherwise." That meant eliminating cross-subsidy, sharpening the Bank's focus, deepening it on different areas, and getting "very, very aggressive on our productivity which was still lagging. So there was a whole plan of what we would do in the event that the merger didn't come off."[26]

Barrett's reflections also touch on 1998's titanic battle for public opinion. Even for the most charismatic bank chairman in modern times, he conceded that "you're out of your league taking on politicians. They're pretty good, you know." That realization had dawned on virtually every leader of the Bank since the days of Sir Vincent Meredith and Mackenzie King. Barrett suspected that Finance Minister Paul Martin's views about the merger might have been conditioned by his concerns about both "big doesn't buy big" and the importance of maintaining a broad consensus in the governing party. Others speculated about the impact of the finance minister's future plans on his calculations. Whatever the reality, the man who has been called one of the great finance ministers of his generation took the momentous decision to disallow the merger based on his prudential judgment. In so doing, he acted in the tradition of twentieth-century ministers of finance from W.S. Fielding to Jean Chrétien. Of course, he had to answer to cabinet and to the caucus of the governing party. Liberal backbenchers of the day were "anti-bank [and] anti-big bank," in the words of one observer.[27] Whatever the merits of their views on banking, these parliamentarians also represented an undeniable current of public opinion.

Moreover, sitting at the commanding height of government was one of the most canny politicians of the era, Prime Minister Jean Chrétien. He would ensure that any resolution of the merger question would not endanger either Liberal Party unity or the prospects of forming a third majority government (which came in 2000 after his victories in 1993 and 1997).

From a historical perspective, the Barrett administration's decision to take the bold strategic step in 1997 to merge the Bank of Montreal with the country's largest bank arguably represented the logical culmination of BMO's long-range strategic vision set into motion in 1990. Of course, in 1990, any contemplation of such a merger was a theoretical concept: the focus was squarely on renewal and regeneration from the inside, working within the established rules of the game in Canadian banking. As the 1990s unfolded, however, several patterns of thought clearly began to dominate the managerial mind as it contemplated the future, pointing to a larger conclusion.

The first discernible pattern (as expressed in the public actions and declarations of executives) was based on the success of the leadership's strategy grounded in the 1990 declarations. The Regenerators began to see their vision for the Bank being realized. A new and more self-confident institution began to emerge in the wake of sweeping internal renewal and transformation and a set of strategic initiatives that allowed the Bank to regain competitive advantage. The discussion in chapter 20 covers this in greater detail. By the mid-1990s, the leadership, and especially Matt Barrett, began to seek greater challenges and more ambitious objectives. The merger plans with RBC provided not only that grand challenge but also a mechanism by which the united banks could accelerate their plans to tackle global competition, as well as issues like productivity and capital ratios. As mentioned at the beginning of this chapter, the convictions of the Bank's leadership very much reflected the wider consensus in the banking world on the need to become big to compete globally. For Canadian bankers in particular, this was an even more urgent challenge, given the relatively small size of the country's financial players and financial sector in comparison with their competitors in the North Atlantic.

The second pattern is more deeply rooted in strategy. From the early 1990s, the elaboration of the Vision 2002 strategy emphasized a North American continentalist approach to growth. At the same time, the Bank's China aspirations were becoming more prominent in the calculations and considerations of where growth would come next. That continentalist/internationalist perspective led to a greater focus on whether the Bank of Montreal, at its current size and scope, would be able to take on the institutional banking behemoths of the United States and Europe. The Barrett administration was increasingly of the view that Canadian banking could only compete in the major leagues if it could, as it were, field a strong enough team. The advantages of scale seemed obvious, logical, and compelling.

The third pattern of thought involved how senior executives of the era regarded the future of banking. Their conceptualization was based on assumptions about the pace of technological change in the financial services sector and, in particular, the idea that the Bank and its industry were on the verge of a major technological transformation. This was clearly manifested in the Bank of Montreal's spectacular embrace of the technological turn in the mid-1990s with mbanx. Exploiting an exceptional technological moment required exceptional means and exceptional approaches and strengths that could confront the emergent future.

These three patterns of thinking in the managerial mind – a focus on greater challenges borne of internal renewal, the future of banking cast in strategic terms as continentalist and globalist, and the technological turn – coalesced around the necessity, perhaps the urgency, to project Canadian banking onto a much bigger stage. Furthermore, the forces at play convinced the Regeneration Generation that the logical next step had to be big and it had to be dramatic. A major merger was an idea demanded by the times, supported by the evidence, and worthy of the risk. The fact that other mergers were attempted after the BMO–RBC endeavour endorses this perspective.

Of course, in such momentous circumstances, executives have to contend with multiple worlds. There is the banking world and the broader market where bankers hold sway. There is also the political market and the political economy, an arena where bankers face much larger forces, interests and calculations, and public opinion in a game where they do not have home advantage. Typically, a high degree of agreement and consonance prevails. Yet, the long-run experience of the Bank's relationship with Canadian governments is remarkably instructive: partnership and collaboration usually reigned, though punctuated with disputes of varying complexity and intensity dealing with mergers, banking stability, political support, banking policy, central banking, and more. For at least a century, governments valued the contribution of Canadian banks, but would not hesitate to exercise public power against private interest, and to do so decisively on major issues. Those decisions were made, as ever, through a combination of public interest and political calculation. Here, public opinion mattered a great deal. The reputation of Canadian banks was sterling among elite circles but often as not was viewed with a mixture of fear, suspicion, and admiration. Taking a run against bank fees, dodgy technology, high loan rates, executive compensation, employment standards, or customer service was very much a populist pastime too tempting for some politicians to ignore. Recall, too, that the popular view of banks did not focus on their economic role or their success in maintaining stability, but rather on stereotypes related to pinstripes and power.

Once the issue was dragged into the political and regulatory arena, in the context of the day, the fate of the merger appeared sealed. The arguments for consolidation to allow Canada to compete on the world stage were swamped by counter-arguments ranging from its possible negative effects on competition and corporate concentration to branch closures and resulting unemployment. More adamant arguments were made by regulators fearful of violating the principle that "big cannot buy big" in this context, lest it create an institution so large as to be too powerful and at the same time too susceptible to severe contractions in the economic cycle.

Judging the events and the players of 1997–98 in hindsight runs the risk of falling into the "enormous condescension of posterity." If not applied properly, hindsight can trick the contemporary observer of these events into thinking that the outcomes were predetermined, or travelled along an inevitable track to their conclusion. They were not and did not. Much of history is contingent when it is being made. Outcomes depend on will, circumstance, and luck as well as strategy. In this case, a few questions arise. Were the strategists and planners of the merger in both banks operating in an intense but closed-circuit world where their assumptions about the merits of the proposal were so strong, the idea so compelling, that the political and regulatory risks were undervalued? If the risk of failure was, as one senior executive suggested, even odds, then what conclusions can we draw about the quality of the political and regulatory analysis applied to decision-making? What we do know is that the managerial minds at both the Bank of Montreal and the Royal were convinced that it was a *beau risque*. The historical question that arises over this important episode in Canadian financial history is whether it was lost on the merits of the case, or lost on a combination of bad timing, bad luck, and outclassed strategy and tactics. As virtually all the chapters in Part Four attest to, banking is not only a financial product but also a social, economic, and political product. From the very beginning in the early nineteenth century, banking has been an activity deeply shaped by public policy. As a result, major change – especially major structural change in size and ownership – is always going to involve bankers, regulators, politicians, and the public. Which realm decides on the right structures, rules, and limits is an uncertain one to predict.

Regarding the merits of the case, opinion is divided: politicians and senior public servants will stress this as the determining factor, and the unpopularity of the move among certain segments of the population as a subsidiary factor. It can be argued that one factor offered cover for the other. Bankers, by contrast, tend to question less the merits of the case and focus more on the perilous politics of the day as the motivating factor for the outcome. Yet, with the benefit of twenty years' distance, experience, and evolution of the banking sector, some of the most astute bankers view the quest for merger as a complicated way to be successful. Mergers and acquisitions, paradoxically, can function in the managerial mind as a panacea – a magic bullet – to solve problems of productivity, growth, and organizational or cultural change.

In the wider world, even years and decades later, the occasional editorial still appears, usually in the wake of a crisis or a financial reversal, citing the supposed wisdom of disallowing the merger on the counterfactual historical basis that BMORBCBank would have suffered more deeply than the individual banks. Perhaps. But such conjecture is just that: conjecture. It is equally possible that the combined institution would have given Canada opportunities and market power never before dreamt of except in the minds of Matt Barrett and John Cleghorn, and their teams.

In the event, the irresistible force of determined and convinced top Canadian bankers met the immovable object of the federal state. Something, as the song goes, had to give, and if twentieth-century Canadian political history is any guide, the "givers" on the big set pieces are typically the banks if there is no alignment. So it was with the events of 1998. The leadership at BMO and RBC forgot that long-run experience – or perhaps were well aware of it and took the risk they felt they must. Not unlike Icarus, who ignored Daedalus's admonition to fly midway between heaven and earth, they too fell into the trap of thinking their waxen wings could withstand the height of sky and heat of sun. With all his ancient Greek credentials, Daedalus would have made an ideal deputy minister of the Department of Finance in the 1990s, who, in true Canadian form, sought always to fly the middle course, come what may.

Numbers and Comparators: 1990–98

The following figures offer snapshots of the performance of the Bank of Montreal, both on its own and in comparison with the Big Five Canadian banks, across four categories: dividends per share, book value per common share, total assets, and market capitalization in the 1990–98 period. The pattern for BMO share dividends and book value (see figures 21.1 and 21.3) seems to follow a parallel pattern, with no change in the early 1990s, followed by increasingly strong performances posted in the 1994–98 period. For example, the dividend increases were raised 6 per cent in 1994, 7 per cent in 1995, 10 per cent in 1996, and 21 per cent in 1997. In 1998, the growth rate was scaled back to 10 per cent. The book value of shares tells a similar tale, with an average growth of 10 per cent per year. In each of these two categories, the performance of the Bank of Montreal was a strong second among the five Canadian banks (see figures 21.2 and 21.4).

The story of total assets in the period was also a positive one. Assets grew on average 12 per cent per year, with 1997 registering the highest gain at 22 per cent (see figure 21.5). The Regeneration Generation could also count this measure as a success, though by the end of the period, the battle for third-among-five ranking between the Bank of Nova Scotia and BMO was ceded to the former institution (see figure 21.6).

Market capitalization tells a story of strong growth, though some years were better than others. The high-water mark for growth was 1997, at 51 per cent growth. The average growth for the period, which included an 18 per cent loss in 1990, was 20 per cent (see figure 21.7). The strong results kept BMO very competitive in this measure, with a second-place finish at the end of the period (see figure 21.8).

With key financial measures registering strong performances, the 1990–98 period was an interesting and productive one for the Bank of Montreal.

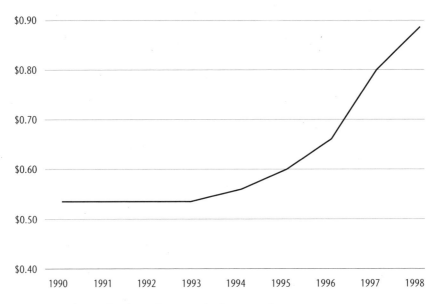

Figure 21.1 | Dividend per share, Bank of Montreal, 1990–98
Source: Data provided by Thomson Reuters.

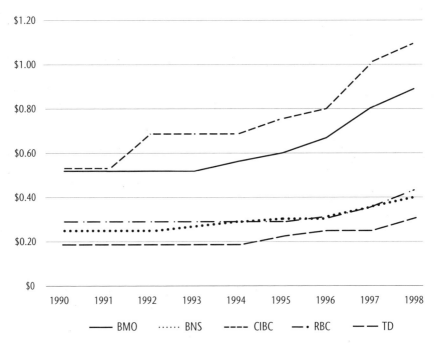

Figure 21.2 | Dividend per share, Big Five banks, 1990–98
Source: Data provided by Thomson Reuters.

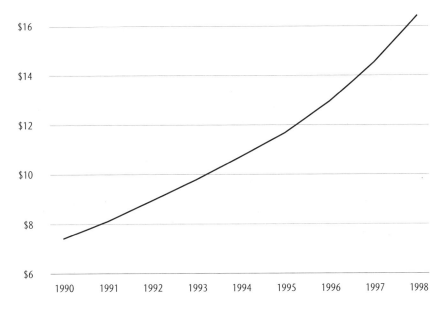

Figure 21.3 | Book value per common share, Bank of Montreal, 1990–98
Source: Data provided by Thomson Reuters.

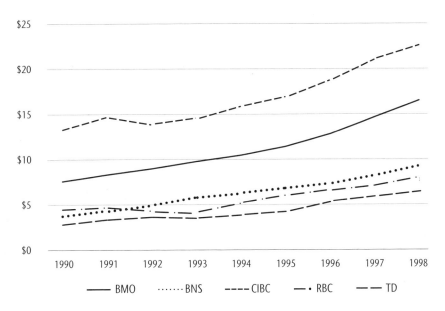

Figure 21.4 | Book value per common share, Big Five banks, 1990–98
Source: Data provided by Thomson Reuters.

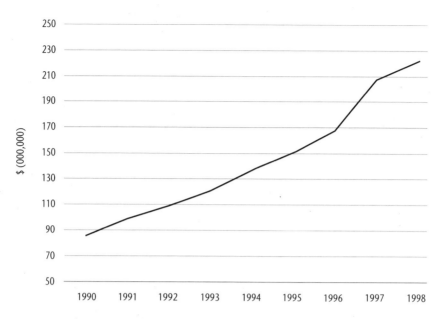

Figure 21.5 | Assets, Bank of Montreal, 1990–98

Source: Data provided by Thomson Reuters.

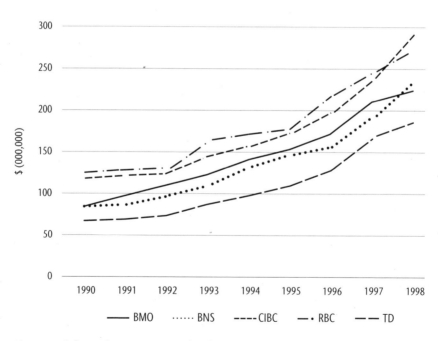

Figure 21.6 | Total assets, Big Five banks, 1990–98

Source: Data provided by Thomson Reuters.

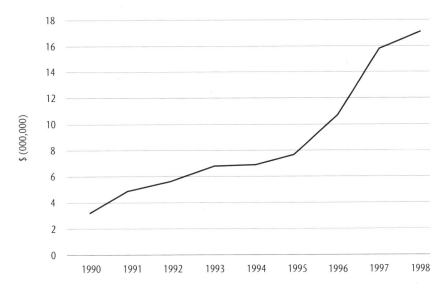

Figure 21.7 | Market capitalization, Bank of Montreal, 1990–98

Source: Data provided by Thomson Reuters.

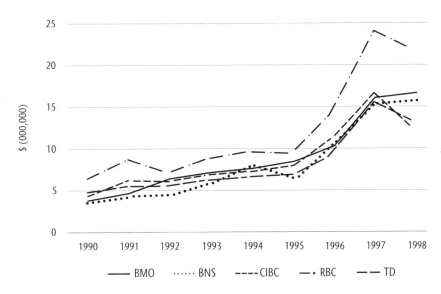

Figure 21.8 | Market capitalization, Big Five banks, 1990–98

Source: Data provided by Thomson Reuters.

Section 2: The Phoenix Protocol

The bird of wonder dies, the maiden phoenix,
Her ashes new create another heir
As great in admiration as herself; ·
So shall she leave her blessedness to one,
When heaven shall call her from this cloud of darkness,
Who from the sacred ashes of her honour
Shall star-like rise as great in fame as she was,
And so stand fix'd.
William Shakespeare,
King Henry VIII, Act V, Scene 5

On 24 September 2018, internationally renowned historian Niall Ferguson addressed BMO's Leadership Council – 320 top leaders of the current generation – on some of the vast changes taking place in the contemporary world as a result of the changing dynamics between the world of hierarchies and the world of networks. Ferguson's central thesis in his *The Square and the Tower* is that social networks have been much more important than we realize, and that we are living through one of the great networked eras of human history that portends some powerful opportunities as well as some great geopolitical, economic, and social challenges to the status quo. Insights about the febrile contemporary political environment, the age of populism, financial crisis, geopolitical competition, and powerful and profoundly inegalitarian social networks offered a bracing view of the world as it is. Novel networks, with "their impact magnified by new technology," would result in trouble for hierarchies and organizations that are not able to reform themselves.[28]

Yet, the underlying theme of Ferguson's talk was that this extraordinary present moment of change, when set in its proper historical context, is, as he once put it, "less unnervingly unprecedented and more familiar." The current generation of BMO leadership of the ten-generation, 200-year-old Bank has been tried and tested in the art of change and adaptation.[29] Indeed, the 2018 Leadership Council was an "extraordinary present moment" when set in the Bank's own proper historical context. The genial, strategically minded, and energetic chief executive officer, Darryl White, ten months into the job, paced the stage talking about momentum, about the Bank's strong position, and about the multiple competitive advantages the Bank had built over time. The Montreal-raised White joined BMO in 1994, coursing a path that took him through the investment and corporate banking side, and ultimately, capital markets. "Where we are right now in our journey," he suggested, "is the result of decades of focused investment and performance." The results – from net income (+14 per cent) to earnings per share (+16 per cent) and other key indicators – proved the point. The time had come to explore the Bank's growth ambition, to refocus strategic priorities, and to take on a renewed sense of purpose. Across the lines of business, the details were different but the story was the same – expansion, capabilities, earning production, mobilization for growth. There was a palpable sense that this, finally, in 2018, could be the inflection point, and that the team assembled around Darryl White could be the team to mobilize that hard-won set of earned advantages into quantum growth. That sense was tempered by the understanding that, in the words of the CEO, "we can't kid ourselves that we're at the end of the job" of challenging many of the existing practices that need to change across the organization.

The long run to that September morning moment in 2018 took the institution twenty years – eighty quarters – to reach. Those two decades between December 1998 and September 2018 began with a reversal and what seemed to many a retreat, followed by a regrouping, a renewal, and an impressive and sustained rally to return to form. In time, the Bank's leadership focused their discipline and strategy on the long fight ahead and were able to deliver that long-awaited future moment, in 2018, when the inflection point was within reach, if not within grasp. For the bankers of '98, that future must have seemed remote and impossibly distant. Yet, the story of September 2018 began there, on 15 December 1998, the day after Finance Minister Paul Martin declared the BMO–RBC merger dead on arrival.

The failure of the merger strategy was a significant setback, and the events of 1998 have entered into legend as a turning point in the long-run experience of Canada's first bank. A year of the Bank's vital energies – involving some of its most experienced and trusted bankers, and a surprising proportion of younger bankers and communications people, working late hours, flying to Ottawa, meeting in secure locations – all seemingly down the drain. Of course, there is plenty of evidence to show that 1998's big risk became 1999's big regret. But in the entire experience of banking, even the most careful management can come up against outcomes beyond its control. The Bank's own past evidenced how mercurial Fortune could be: In the 1910s and 1920s, as seen in Part Four, much depended on political decisions as well as market ones. In the 1930s, the establishment of the Bank of Canada is the example par excellence of the supremacy of political economy in national fiscal and monetary policy.

In spite of the result, the BMO–RBC merger proposal was put together on solid banking foundations. It was a shareholder winner; it addressed some long-standing issues about technology and productivity that were constant irritants to senior management; it seemed a logical extension of a carefully crafted and successful strategy that BMO's regeneration had put in place. The fact that it harboured a fatal flaw (unlikely acceptance by the government of the day) and did not proceed is obviously central to the story, but the rest is too often forgotten or dismissed. Throughout its late twentieth-century history, the Bank of Montreal has faced much more serious problems and events than the failure of a late-1990s merger. As we have seen in Part Six, the organization has a remarkable resilience. Its leadership and people seem to respond most strongly in the midst of adversity. The merger was a major issue to be overcome, not least because it came with a serious sense of disappointment and a temporary angst about the future, which could have been handled in time, though not without facing tough challenges. The deeper challenges began after the merger, with the announcement of Matt Barrett's departure two months after the failure of the merger; his acceptance of the position of CEO at Barclays PLC in London accelerated the departure timetable.[30] This meant the breakup and effective dissolution of the team that had guided the destiny of the Bank since 1990 – the team that restored its confidence, competitive spirit, and momentum at a critical time. Gone too was the special symbiosis, the creative tension, the complementary talents that made everything cohere. And it came at a time when the Bank's fortunes had suffered a public setback.

The board of directors of the Bank of Montreal faced what was likely the second momentous decision in two years (after the merger): the selection of a successor to Matthew W. Barrett. The person they chose would take the helm in a situation diametrically opposite in almost every way imaginable to that of his predecessor. In 1990, the Bank was ready for bold leadership and organizational change, and both the leadership and the people were primed to take on the grand challenges. The incoming executive team in 1990 had a world of opportunities before them and a plan to exploit them to the greater glory of the Bank of Montreal. Fast-forward nine years: the board would be putting a new leader in charge of an institution with something of a hangover, with its centrepiece strategy blown up and in pieces, and with all kinds of warning lights flashing on the dashboard – profitability, risk management, cash productivity ratio, shareholder value, and more. Moreover, the person they chose would follow one of the most popular and charismatic chief executives the country had produced. The person they chose would have to handle all that, and help chart a course for a complex, vital institution in need of direction. They chose fifty-three-year-old Tony Comper, Barrett's number two, the operations man, the Montreal banker par excellence. Appointed in February 1999 as CEO, he also became chairman a short time later.

The Bank's challenges in this era were large, complex, and well defined. However, Comper was assuming command with an unparalleled knowledge of the Bank's DNA, its operations, its strengths as well as its limitations, and with a sharp analytical mindset. He could also rely on a core of professional bankers who had proven both the Bank's ability to rally from reversals and its integrity. Inevitably, though, Comper would also govern under the long shadow of the failure of the merger and the departure of Barrett. Indeed, no CEO in the twentieth-century experience of the Bank had started his tenure under more challenging conditions – with the possible exception of Sir Charles Gordon in 1929. The Comper administration's game plan and its focus generally turned inward, toward solving the mounting internal challenges facing the Bank. The hard, unglamorous work of reorganization – of transforming thirty-three business lines under three divisions – was undertaken. Personal and commercial client services, private client services, and investment banking underwent an overhaul under the banner of value-based management theories. Streamlining of the management of the North American businesses was pursued, combined with a stated focus on cost control and the creation of greater shareholder value and a better return on equity. With mergers no longer a possible solution to these challenges, other means had to be found.

Comper's early focus on the thesis that traditional financial services such as banks were in a "death spiral," as he told the Canadian Club of Toronto in 1999, struck a darker, more urgent tone. "What I was doing was holding up a scenario that if we didn't address it, that would be the outcome," he said. "But I'm confident that we are addressing it and that it won't happen to us." The combination of technology and global deregulation had, indeed, created transformational conditions for global banking. The strategy internally focused on reorganization and on ensuring that the Bank's workforce – the "people part" – would be able to compete for the financial services customer in a world dominated by market-driven attention on financial products and services.[31]

The Comper administration drew inspiration from the deep experience of the Bank of Montreal in serving customers and "the emotionally charged and socially useful business of helping people manage their finances," as he stated in the 1999 Annual Report. In his view, Canada's banks, including BMO by the 1990s, had "used up all the instinctive goodwill most customers could manage. We have all talked a good story about improving customer relationships, and to a greater or lesser extent, we have all meant what we said – we certainly did here at Bank of Montreal. The problem has been in the execution." A back-to-the-fundamentals approach focusing on the customer was required "in building a bank for our time." That meant a large-scale reorganization.[32] On a parallel track, in 2002, the Bank officially changed its name to BMO Financial Group in an attempt to reinforce the Bank's visibility and unity.

The Bank that Tony Comper left to his successor in 2007 was marked by a reinforcement of BMO's position in credit risk and cash productivity ratios. Net income had also doubled, from $1.29 billion to $2.66 billion.[33] The American operations were primed for expansion, with 234 branches across the Midwest. The creation of BMO Capital Markets in 2006 was a major move, unifying corporate, government, and institutional businesses under one banner.[34] The focus on internal dynamics and on getting profitability back on track in the early twenty-first century were necessary and important correctives to maintain continuity in the Bank and, particularly, to navigate it away from more dangerous waters. That, too, came at a cost. The feeling was prevalent during this period of reassessment that the Bank was playing defence. In an important sense that is frequently missed in the casual accounts of this period, the unwritten mandate of the Comper years was to transform elements of the organization toward gathering its strength after the reversal of 1998 – to permit no harm to come to the organization and its people, and to execute the hard work required to bring the entire organization into a strategic and market position to once again assert itself. Comper also championed the values of diversity, equity, and renewed corporate governance – elements that are more valued a decade later than they were even at the time, and whose legacy has become a centrepiece of the contemporary Bank's approach to organization. In keeping with evolving best practices of corporate governance, Comper also relinquished his post as chairman of the board while CEO. This change was to have a remarkably strengthening effect on the Bank's governance structures at the top, and constitutes one of the under-reported achievements of the era. The emphasis on profitability and shareholder value, moreover, was a necessary antidote in dealing with the unfinished business of the 1990s. This was, by consensus of the leadership, the chosen path of those early years of the new millennium. This then was the challenge that Tony Comper accepted, the burden he took on, the call he answered.

By 2005–06, there was a growing sense of restlessness with the status quo and a feeling that the times demanded a new, more assertive approach. A consensus began to emerge that, while the fundamentals of banking were strictly observed and the bank was well run, the balance between dynamism and form had tipped decisively toward the latter. The focus on financial engineering had been necessary, but it was not sufficient. The future leadership rising through the ranks had seen the pendulum swings in the late 1990s and in the first few years of the twenty-first century, and were impatient to rally once again to a grand challenge. The banker favoured by Comper and anointed by the board to lead the Bank into the following decade was William A. Downe.

Downe was born in Montreal in 1952. He joined the Bank in 1983 as an assistant credit manager in Toronto. His BMO formative years were spent in Houston, in corporate and government banking, where he was admitted to the executive ranks in 1988 as vice-president, oil and gas division, corporate banking, US. His exposure to American business would be a determining factor in his formation as a banker. Downe was promoted through the ranks, eventually being appointed executive vice-president, North American corporate banking in 1996 and in 1998 piloting the integration of Global Fixed Income and Global Treasury. In 1999, he was appointed vice-chair, private client group as well as deputy chair of BMO Nesbitt Burns. In 2001, he directed BMO Harris Bank operations in Chicago, a city he's never really left. In 2006, he was appointed chief operating officer before assuming the top job.

Downe's star had risen consistently through the years as he gained a reputation for originality, collaboration, and a strong competitive instinct. Downe studied and mastered the "decision engine" within BMO, and possessed a commanding sense of how to get important things done with a minimum of disruption (and often by stealth). His perspective was very much that of a global banker at ease in China, Chicago, and Calgary. As Tony Comper suggested in his 2006 promotion announcement, "I have long considered Bill Downe a first-generation *North American* business leader, someone who is completely and utterly at home on both sides of the border."[35] Downe's appointment was the culmination of Comper's positioning of BMO as a North American institution.

The Will to Prevail

The decade that unfolded under the leadership of Bill Downe was underwritten with a solid confidence in the ability to prevail in spite of the situation BMO leadership found itself in at the beginning of the period in 2007 – weak earnings growth, overextended in capital markets, and an eye-popping scandal-ridden natural gas trading loss of $853 million, which set something of a record in the industry.[36] Once again, however, in a matter of days, BMO was upstaged by a far more spectacular trading loss at the Société Générale. Something in the order of US$7.2 billion had been lost at the hands of a young "rogue" trader, so one supposes BMO's situation could have been worse. The spotlight was immediately diverted to Paris and the offices of the SocGen.[37] It was reported that Downe began his first day by cutting 1,000 head-office jobs, then continued to manage $2 billion in writedowns in the wake of the financial crisis of 2008 (which nevertheless represented "less than a tenth of the $23 billion taken by Canadian banks").[38]

Bill Downe's reputation among friends, observers, and competitors alike points toward his lively competitive spirit – a man who relished the big challenges; a man driven by data, but with a superb instinct for timing and people; a commander who thrived in adversity and with the instinct for the counter-attack. By that standard, then, his first year or two at the helm of the Bank must have been, in a perverse way, a dream come true. Barely a year into Downe's mandate, outrageous fortune would place the Bank of Montreal's leadership before the greatest financial crisis since the Great Depression.

Facing the Financial Crisis of 2008

On 15 September 2008, Lehman Brothers, the fourth-largest investment bank in the United States, filed for bankruptcy protection.[39] A run on money-market mutual funds ensued, causing a domino effect that resulted in a severe contraction in the global economic cycle. The Lehman collapse was only the inflection point in a series of reversals across the financial landscape – BNP Paribas, in August 2007, moved to block withdrawals from its subprime mortgage funds.[40] In the United Kingdom, there was a run on Northern Rock – Britain's first bank run since the nineteenth century. Merrill Lynch was acquired by the Bank of America and Goldman Sachs and Morgan Stanley were the only two of the Big Five US investment banks still standing.[41] The insurer AIG was also headed for major trouble. The contagion spread to the broader economy: real GDP fell 8.2 per cent in the last quarter of 2008. As Alan Greenspan and Walter Woolridge note, global equities had lost $35 trillion in value, the American homeowner had lost $7 trillion in equity, and global equities globally had lost $50 trillion "or close to four-fifths of global GDP for 2008."[42]

The causes and roots of the crisis were multiple – a global bubble, a rapid rise in US housing prices, and securitization. Financial innovation and political pressure (in the subprime mortgage area) to water down stricter credit conditions created a much wider and deeper market for mortgages beyond conventional borrowers (that is, creditworthy customers). The complexity of financial products purporting to reduce or diffuse risk, but which bankers without doctorates in quantum mathematics had little hope of understanding, contributed to the collapse. Moreover, a complacency about leverage lulled regulators and investors into a similar complacency.[43] Alan Greenspan and others credit the "superior quality of the official response" as a major reason why the 2008 financial crisis did not develop into a Great Depression. That official response was deeply informed by those who understood the long-run experience of the North Atlantic economy: to "respond to emerging problems quickly and concoct practical but innovative solutions."[44]

The financial crisis that washed over the United States and Europe had a significantly lighter impact in Canada. In a famous paper on the subject, Michael D. Bordo, Angela Redish, and Hugh Rockoff suggest that the stability of Canadian banks was deeply rooted in the long-run experience and structure of Canadian banking. Canadian banking was concentrated and, in particular, had "absorbed the key sources of systemic risk – the mortgage market and investment banking – and was tightly regulated by one overarching regulator."[45] In other words, the Canadian financial system was able to ward off systemic risk because of its historic design.

The ivory-tower conclusions about the Canadian banking system are true and on point: Canada was spared the worst. Fortune favoured Canadian finance in this instance, and so did a robust regulatory system and industrial architecture. The conclusions do not quite capture the urgency with which Canadian banking leadership had apprehended those events south of the border. The dry run for the crisis in Canada was the issue of asset-backed commercial paper, or ABCP, a credit instrument that consisted of "30- and 60-day notes that paid interest earned from bundling assets like mortgages and loans together."[46] When the market for ABCPs seized in Canada, it took bankers and regulators alike by surprise. "None of us appreciated the size of it, or the level of risk that existed in [the] market," Downe told the *Globe and Mail* when reflecting on those events.[47] Then-governor of the Bank of Canada Mark Carney remembers that he "worked closely with Bill and the CEOs of Canada's major banks and pension funds to help devise an innovative re-structuring of the Canadian ABCP market. BMO constructively termed out its exposures to help stabilise the market and to ensure noteholders could mini-mise their losses." He adds that "it is widely underappreciated how important these steps were to stabilise the global financial system."[48]

Moreover, that was before the events of September 2008. When the un-folding events did confront Canada, the Bank of Canada and its governor Mark Carney, the Department of Finance and its minister James Flaherty, and the Canadian banks and investment houses came together in an unpreced-ented way to ensure that the Canadian financial system would not be subject to catastrophic reversals – losses yes, even significant losses, but not failures. As Gordon Nixon of the RBC recalled of those days: "It was the scariest period in my history by a huge margin. I lived through the crash of '87. Credit cycles. The technology crash. They all paled in comparison."[49]

Downe's national leadership in the events of 2008 – in his role as presi-dent of the Federal Advisory Council of the US Federal Reserve Board, and especially in his role as a key player in the discussions among Canadian bankers and policymakers on how to get through the crisis – earned him the respect and admiration of his colleagues. The urgent nature of the times compelled Downe to draw upon every assignment he had previously had to confront the crisis. He acted as a key point of reference in keeping the Can-adian banking system and its customers safe from the combustible materials catching fire in the United States. Downe's insider view of what was happen-ing in the United States provided a vital context for Canadian bankers. BMO's position and reputation in US banking made that possible; Downe's intui-tive command of the issue set him apart from other actors in that unfolding drama. If the Canadian system of banking and finance was able to emerge from that period of crisis – 2007 to 2009 – as one of the world's soundest and most admired, it was because of a unique Canadian combination of system architecture; close, collaborative relationships between public and private players; and the kind of leadership and strategic thinking that key protagonists such as Bill Downe brought to the situation. Confronting the crisis of 2008 without a Mark Carney, a Jim Flaherty, or a Bill Downe almost assuredly would have produced different results, universal banking model or not. As RBC's Nixon recalled, Downe was "very attuned to what was happening in the United States because of his role on the Fed board, and his history in the United States ... And so, during that period of time, I would say that Bill really showed some good leadership for the country, as well as for his institution."[50]

Downe's entry into the CEO position was in many ways a baptism by fire, with at least three major challenges – one internal and two external – posing varying levels of threat to the Bank and to the broader system. The strategic agility and ability to rally what were often disparate teams and interests in these cases prepared him well for the challenges that lay ahead. Mark Carney summarized Bill Downe's complex role in the crisis of 2008, in his service to both BMO customers and the nation: "Bill was instrumental in formulating Canada's response to the financial crisis. Cool under pressure, rigorous in analysis and decisive in action; Bill moved quickly to assess where BMO was most vulnerable. He then recognised losses were inevitable; and wanted to mitigate exposures and restructure portfolios wherever he could. At the same time, he remained resolutely outwardly focused, concentrating on his clients' needs and generally giving Canadians the justified confidence that their banking system would be there for them."[51]

The team Downe assembled faced some of the greatest and most sustained challenges faced by the institution, certainly in living memory. Yet one crisis – the commodity writedown – helped prepare the Bank for an even bigger systemic crisis. The Downe cabinet was able to return to first principles and to "slow down time," to deliberate and act without unnecessary anxiety. The balancing of the interests of BMO customers and the Bank's balance sheet as well as the continental system of banking was the result. The upgrading of the risk management systems, from people to processes to systems, the year before meant BMO was ahead of the game.[52]

Bill Downe and BMO's Strategic Thrust

The beginning of the Downe era at the Bank of Montreal coincided with a time when Canadian banks that were once considered a homogeneous group of institutions began to diverge in strategy. The TD pursued a retail focus, which extended to the Northeastern United States. Scotiabank pushed into a more global position, while the CIBC seemed intent on, in the words of one observer, "shrinking to greatness." The big cat, the RBC, pursued a global strategy as a high, wide, and handsome player among banking institutions. In this context, at this point in time, BMO required a clear plan and a leadership team that would go on the counteroffensive armed with a clear vision and a unified purpose.

Downe's core team included a group of seasoned professional bankers with an intuitive understanding of the Bank and a passionate conviction that it could prevail – and that there were yet untapped internal resources waiting to be harnessed. His comrade-in-arms, his number two, was Frank Techar: partner, colleague, and sounding board.

Techar's Bank career began in corporate banking in 1984. He made his way through increasingly important roles across BMO territory in the North Atlantic world, including the symbolically important and managerially essential London, England, posting. Those postings culminated in his appointment to head the BMO Harris operations in the United States in 2002. Out of his base in Chicago, he transformed Harris Bank into a consumer brand in the United States. His appointment to this strategically vital post in the Bank coincided with the need to overhaul retail banking operations and put them on a strong organizational footing. From 2006 to 2012, Techar served as head of Canadian personal and commercial banking and, in 2013, was made chief operating officer. "Brilliant at the Basics" was Techar's initiative to put retail banking on a sounder footing when BMO needed to move beyond smart talk to concrete achievements.

Downe's leadership core included a number of gifted individuals, each of whom had a specific role to play in pushing and pulling the Bank of Montreal back into a position primed for competitive advantage. The board directors in this period, led by chairs David A. Galloway (2004–12) and J. Robert S. Prichard (2012–current), acted as advisors, overseers, and guarantors of the overall destiny of the Bank. Their precise role represents one of the more interesting untold stories of this generation. The leadership also benefited immensely from the Bank's ability to attract major national figures onto its team to leverage its reputational and intellectual capital. L. Jacques Ménard, past president of BMO Quebec and one of the most celebrated and successful Quebec public figures and businessmen of his generation, was a great example of the calibre of people that the Bank gathered to itself. The contribution of three vice-chairs – Kevin G. Lynch, former Clerk of the Privy Council, perhaps the greatest public servant of his generation; Brian Tobin, former Newfoundland premier and long-serving federal MP and cabinet minister; and David Jacobson, a shrewd, strategically connected former United States ambassador to Canada – allowed the voices of "inside-outsiders" with remarkable depth, experience, and insight of the wider world to inform strategy and decision-making. Russ Robertson, who succeeded Karen Maidment as chief financial officer, brought deep experience and judgment, as well as an extraordinary commitment to his job, during those early days and in acquisitions to come. Tom Flynn, as the next chief financial officer, became Downe's most important partner in the greatest strategic move of the decade: the $4.1 billion acquisition of the $50 billion–asset Marshall & Ilsley Bank (M&I) of Wisconsin in 2011. Flynn's stints as treasurer and chief risk officer more than prepared him for this undertaking. That acquisition was the largest takeover in the history of the Bank of Montreal[53] and enshrined BMO's future as a North American bank by giving it critical mass (doubling US deposits and branches) in the key US Midwest market.[54] In July 2011, BMO then returned the $1.7 billion in US federal aid it had received in the wake of the 2008 financial crisis.[55]

The M&I acquisition was also a tribute to the agility, preparation, and right combination of urgency and timing of the Bank. In many ways, the landmark acquisition symbolized the Downe bank at its best. The organization had been actively reviewing at least five major acquisitions over a number of years. Fortune truly favoured the bold in this case: when the opportunity materialized, Downe and the team he led were prepared to act. Nothing, it seems, was left to chance. This was an opportunity to leverage the relative strength of Canadian banks while many American banks were on the back foot. Measured by capitalization levels alone, Canadian banks were miles ahead of their American counterparts. And among Canadian banks, BMO was the strongest.

With quarterly results posting routine records in terms of net income, revenue, and profit, the Bank by common consent was turning the corner, with the US market a key catalyst for that transformation. Another key acquisition among many of the era was the purchase of the UK-based Foreign and Colonial (F&C) Investment Trust, the world's oldest investment trust, established in 1868. The establishment in October 2010 of Bank of Montreal (China) Co. Ltd – or BMO ChinaCo. – and its deep involvement in that country represents another important chapter in the Downe decade. By 2013, BMO was the only Canadian bank and "one of only three North American banks with an established subsidiary bank in China."[56] The Bank's return to form was certified in its performance, its evolving strategic vision, and its ability to execute.

Discipline and Unity

The Bank of Montreal as an institution was able to sustain the discipline necessary for the comeback because of its collective ability to understand itself as a single, unified entity – its experience, its values, what it stood for in the market, and the broader economic and financial life of the territories it served. For large, multi-form firms in multiple lines of business, operating under a single, unified brand is a market challenge, a cultural challenge, and an organizational battle. BMO could be cited as a case study in this subject area. Multiple subcultures flourished in their lines of business – most notably the capital markets arm Nesbitt Burns and the Harris Bank operations. Bill Downe focused his considerable abilities on and fought relentlessly for the transformation of the Bank from a "house of brands" to a single, branded house. As one associate recalled, "the Brand was [his] near obsession," and, in effect, finished what Comper had started in his time.[57] The campaign was conducted on the terrain of both symbol and substance, sometimes overtly and sometimes by subtle or stealthy changes in nomenclature and even brand colours. Rallying to the colours under one brand and a single identity became possible for the first time – a remarkable achievement motivated by the conviction, in Downe's words, that "our customers were more important than our personal ambition."[58] The era of the brand fiefdom with the organization had seen its twilight. The unification of the brands portended a deeper organizational alignment – the outcome of a generation of work.

On a more existential plane, the Downe bank in these years began to articulate a more precise and purposeful statement of values and commitments, all tied to firmly entrenching its reputation as a leader in Canadian enterprise. Beyond a set of rhetorical commitments, to the BMO leadership of the day, this meant taking a meaningful position on the so-called ESG file – environment, social, governance. This included a commitment, made in 2008 and achieved in 2010, to become carbon neutral. It included the adoption of the Catalyst Protocol to promote board diversity. It also meant an overhaul to charitable giving, focusing on the intersection of poverty and education. Here, BMO's distinguished pedigree over two centuries of community development in Canada and elsewhere was revitalized and reinforced.[59] Employee participation in annual giving went from the low 30 per cent range to the truly remarkable mid-90 per cent range by 2017 – twice the level of its next highest peer in companies of similar size and position.

Downe and his contemporaries understood that banks had a unique institutional role to play – principally in the market – to sustain economic growth. They also had a broad social mandate to maintain capital strength, manage risk, act ethically, promote environmental sustainability, and maintain transparency and accountability in corporate governance practices.[60]

In addition, through the last two decades, the ability to understand and act upon BMO's performance, plans, and place as an organization in time was another competitive advantage. The key here was what one might term the Q-3-10 formula: delivering numbers on a quarter-by-quarter basis, investing against a three-year plan, and having a ten-year view of the future. The formula is reinforced by seeking a sophisticated understanding of a deeper context – the long-run experience of the Bank – to complete the picture. This is an organization with a well-defined sense of meaning and purpose over time and territory.

The simultaneous unified brand and managerial focus on the short, medium, and long term are two powerful reasons that the Bank, under Bill Downe's leadership, was able to offer a constellation of competitive advantages to the Darryl White generation of leadership that followed, enabling them to exploit and extend in an era of transformation. In an important sense, the successes and achievements of the Bank of Montreal under Bill Downe are only part of the evidence considered in the judgment of posterity. The managerial team in place today will also be the yardstick by which the previous team will be judged. If there is a palpable appetite for more risk in the contemporary bank, and a feeling that the Bank has the capability to reach major new heights of performance, the credit goes to those who built better than they knew at the beginning of this century.

The Bank's growing strength and momentum in the United States over the Bill Downe decade, its remarkably successful and top-rated capital markets arm, its personal and commercial banking successes, and a score of other lesser-known organizational achievements will constitute the raw material when the more recent experience of the Bank can be analyzed. But all of these stories are still in play, and part of a larger narrative yet to fully unfold. That said, some of the subjects that will occupy future historians are even now coming into view.

Next-Generation Leadership

Central among those subjects will be the dramatically changing composition of the senior leadership to include many more women. The Bank's specific long-term championship of and advocacy for throwing open the doors of leadership and opportunity for women, and the active promotion of diversity and inclusion in its ranks, will undoubtedly constitute an important chapter in the unfolding story of how Canada's first bank has adapted to the demands of the people and societies it serves in the last quarter-century. Those seeking to make sense of the long-run experience of this remarkable institution over that time will also focus on a wide variety of other themes; to start: strategy, performance, operations, corporate governance, and the capacity to adapt and change in the face of constant challenges. The changes in global capital markets and their formation, in investment strategy, wealth management, and accounting will be worthy of attention. As too the balance between hierarchies and networks within the organization, and the balance between centre and periphery. Future historians may also examine the fascinating trajectory of rhetoric and expression in official corporate communications, marketing, and promotion. Other focus may come to rest on the Bank's continuing role in influencing public policy both in financial services and in the broader economy as nations and regions struggle to adapt to transformations in trade, innovation, changing regulatory rules of the game, and heralded new industrial revolutions. The shifting nature of finance and money, the role of the customer and the customer experience, banking's evolution, organizational culture, the role of bureaucracy, the massive role of technology, artificial intelligence and machine learning, the transformation and future of work, the changing nature of leadership, and the role of training and development will all likely be on the radar.

Numbers and Comparators: 1999–2017

The following figures offer final snapshots of the performance of the Bank of Montreal, both on its own and in comparison with the Big Five Canadian Banks across four categories: dividends per share, book value per common share, total assets, and market capitalization. The Bank's share performance over the 1999–2017 period averaged 8 per cent growth year over year (see figure 21.9), with the average book value of BMO shares growing an average of 7 per cent year over year (see figure 21.11). The Bank's share performance in both measures was second among the Big Five Canadian banks (see figures 21.10 and 21.12). In terms of total assets, BMO's performance averaged 5 per cent between 1999 and 2006, and 8 per cent from 2007 to 2017 (see figure 21.13). In terms of comparative performance, the Bank ended the period with a strong fourth-place finish, with especially strong performances posted after 2013 (see figure 21.14). Finally, market capitalization: BMO's overall performance registered 9 per cent per year growth, with the 2009–17 period registering at 13 per cent per year growth (see figure 21.15). Its performance was, again, a fourth-place finish relative to the Big Five Canadian banks (see figure 21.16).

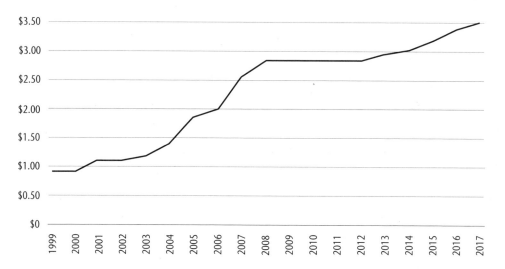

Figure 21.9 | Dividend per share, Bank of Montreal, 1999–2017
Source: Data provided by Thomson Reuters.

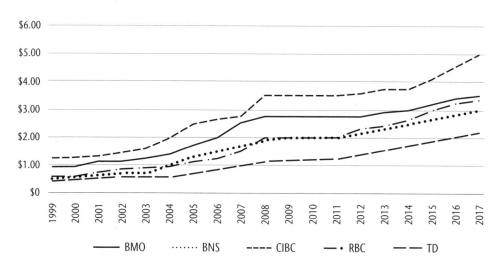

Figure 21.10 | Dividend per share, Big Five banks, 1999–2017
Source: Data provided by Thomson Reuters.

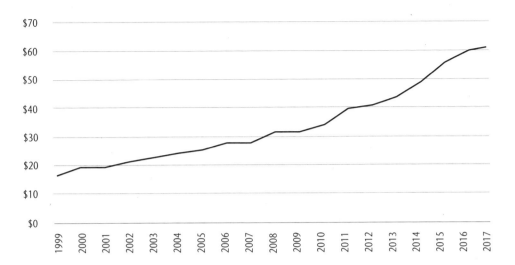

Figure 21.11 | Book value per common share, Bank of Montreal, 1999–2017

Source: Data provided by Thomson Reuters.

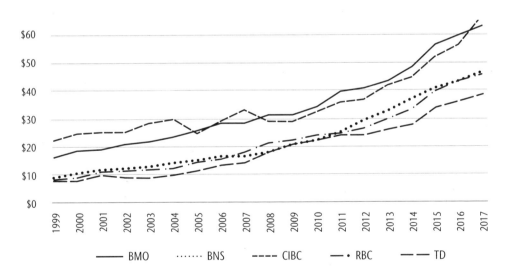

Figure 21.12 | Book value per common share, Big Five banks, 1999–2017

Source: Data provided by Thomson Reuters.

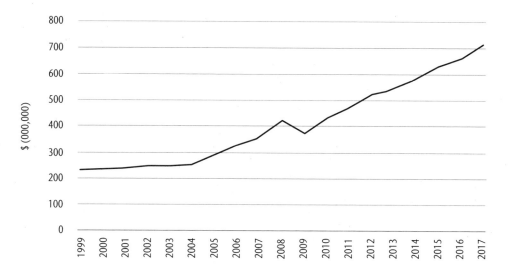

Figure 21.13 | Assets, Bank of Montreal, 1999–2017
Source: Data provided by Thomson Reuters.

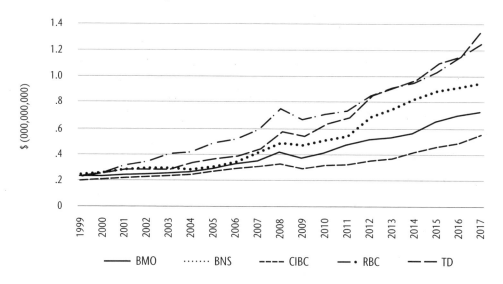

Figure 21.14 | Total assets, Big Five banks, 1999–2017
Source: Data provided by Thomson Reuters.

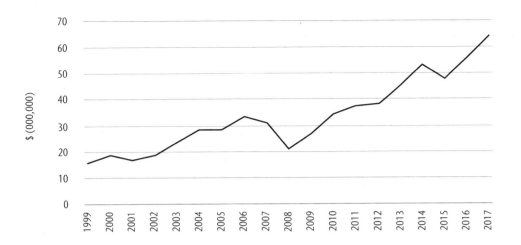

Figure 21.15 | Market capitalization, Bank of Montreal, 1999–2017
Source: Data provided by Thomson Reuters.

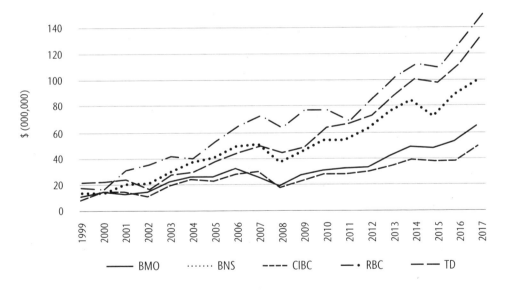

Figure 21.16 | Market capitalization, Big Five banks, 1999–2017
Source: Data provided by Thomson Reuters.

EPILOGUE

One Past, Many Possible Futures

*Every moment of our existence is linked by a peculiar triple thread
to our past – the most recent and the most distant – by memory.
Our present swarms with traces of our past. We are histories of
ourselves, narratives… It is memory that solders together the
processes, scattered across time, of which we are made. In this sense
we exist in time… To understand ourselves means to reflect on time.
But to understand time we need to reflect on ourselves.*
Carlo Rovelli, *The Order of Time*[1]

*It is the same! – For, be it joy or sorrow,
The path of its departure still is free,
Man's yesterday may ne'er be like his morrow;
Nought may endure but Mutability.*
Percy Bysshe Shelley, *Mutability*[2]

I chose the above quotations as a reflective way to end the journey in time we started over two centuries ago. The first, from *New York Times* best-selling author and theoretical physicist Carlo Rovelli, deals with the nature of time and memory, and the importance for us as individuals and organizations to see our experience as a whole in the context of time. The second, from English Romantic poet Percy Bysshe Shelley, reminds us that "mutability," or change, seems to be the only constant in the lives of humankind. Time, memory, reflection, change: appropriate themes with which to conclude.

The 200-year long-run experience of the Bank of Montreal represents an intimate part of the multiple historical flows that make up the economic and financial life of the North Atlantic world. In terms of geography, the Bank of Montreal's roots are Canadian, but its trajectory is, in the last three decades at least, increasingly North American and selectively global. In terms of historical turning points over two centuries, BMO leaders and people have been, according to time and place, everywhere: on the margins, in the centre of the action, and every point between. The long-run experience of the Bank of Montreal also constitutes one of the most compelling, continuous, long-term laboratories Canada has yet produced for the study of strategy, adaptation to change, and competitive performance over time. That laboratory, running multiple experiments in real time, has tested a remarkably impressive range of hypotheses in economic development, market change, political economy, regulation, international trade, global banking, wartime finance, central and reserve bank theory, leadership, mergers and acquisitions activity, capital markets, organizational behaviour, technology, and training and development. Also included were hundreds and hundreds more experiments that connected both to the big picture and to the individual shareholder, worker, depositor, saver, mortgage holder, entrepreneur, community project, enterprise, and mega project – relationships and networks that have extended from Montreal and the "empire of the St Lawrence" to a central place in the evolution of key regions of the North Atlantic world.

The Bank of Montreal experience has also provided a superb example of an institution that, from generation to generation, earned a sterling reputation in finance for a verifiable tradition of firsts, from 1817 down to the present day. It is an institution built to last. More than that, it is an institution that has deserved to last, through its strategy, discipline, and collaboration.[3] It is an institution that in its traditions, cohesion, and outlook went from strength to strength. The Bank also experienced its share of failures and reversals, and how to recover from them. From the retrospective gaze of posterity, that recovery process often seemed to take forever. But when the rally came, when the fight back started, as it did in recent years in the late 1970s and again in the mid-2000s, the leadership and people of the Bank of Montreal worked hard to create better futures for their institution and the wider world in which they operated. How? By finding the formula that would match their capabilities with their aspirations. That achievement is not just down to Bank of Montreal managers and executives over the years, but is also a collective accomplishment, co-signed by public policy and the structure of Canadian banking.

A few pages ago, I told you the story of CEO Darryl White and his remarks at the annual gathering of BMO's two-day Leadership Council in September 2018. As one can imagine, conferences in most large organizations are highly choreographed set pieces arranged by detail-oriented communications professionals and executed by a fast-moving group of headset-bearing assistants schooled in the art.[4] The universal risk in these affairs, of course, is that a tried-and-true choreography routine becomes an end in itself, where adherence to protocol and form become the false measures of success. It can be a parable, a symbol, for the challenge of change in organizations: the old choreography pitted against the new.[5] There was a different feel to the proceedings in that autumn of 2018 that relates directly to the question of forms. No doubt taking its cue in some part from the new chief executive, a more informal and direct style asserted itself among the leadership team – a style that was in counterpoint to, and at times transcended, the more restricted choreography. They wanted to get down to the content and de-emphasize the form. There seemed to be an earnest confidence in the leadership generation of 2018 in approaching its future. This was a team convinced that the institution it led was "built for more." Here again, that creative tension that has always existed between the structures that endure and the dynamism of new forms asserted itself – this time, between those familiar and comfortable with the tried-and-true structures of such public gatherings and the "main attractions" with their desire to signal a new approach. In a sense, the leadership's style, vision, and approach will shape the organization it will lead: this is how a generation matches its capabilities with its aspirations. This BMO generation also understands that while the current competitive environment is their great contemporary challenge, the Bank enterprise is the work of generations.

Darryl White will lead executives who have earned their positions at the table in various strategic areas and will together guide the destiny of the Bank into the 2020s. In this group we see the emerging face of leadership in North American finance for our own day – men and women who are transcending and redefining the role of bankers, as fits the times. In the coming months and years, it is for them to understand, in the given circumstances, what approaches Fortune will favour.

Both the author and the leaders who commissioned this work have aspirations for *Whom Fortune Favours*, markedly different from the first, popular volume *A Vision Greater Than Themselves*. One of the most fervent and straightforward aspirations is that distilling the Bank's long-run experience can translate into a deeper, more sophisticated context for contemporary decision-making. Normally, for the banker carrying out his and her daily duties, that context matters only theoretically or on the margins. The history seems as remote as an archival sepulchre. But, as almost every corporate and public leader I have ever met says, the higher you go, the more responsibility you have, the more important it is to understand the bigger picture and the patterns of the past in order to carry out your duties properly. When a journalist asked Bill Downe, a few months before his departure in 2017, what kind of conversations he was having with his successor Darryl White, the response was telling: "The conversation that we have been having now is that history matters, because there are analogs that you can look to."[6] Those "analogs" transmitted signals to Downe not just in reflective or retrospective moments but also in hours and days of crisis and heightened risk. As a leader, he understood how to decode those analog signals from the past and what to do with them, whether facing a financial crisis, a stock-market collapse, or the hundreds of smaller incidents inside and outside the organization that required depth of vision. That is how the Bank's unique institutional experience, set in context, can act as a powerful competitive and leadership advantage.

Elemental structures in the wiring of the Bank of Montreal leadership through time act as "live currents" between the past and the present. The job of leadership is to understand what has worked and what has not, and what needs adaptation. Armed with a clear sense of purpose and direction, the generation of 2018 has the best chance the Bank has had in decades of shaping a remarkable future.[7] Recently, one of the Bank's senior leaders posed a question to me that most historians usually dread:[8] the "what if?" question. This "what if" was not about Britain staying on the sidelines of the First World War or some other counterfactual world-historical topic. That would have been easier. This was along the lines of, "What if the Bank of Montreal had never existed: what difference would it have made?" So, one change in the timeline and what happens? This is the North American financial version of the butterfly effect, where the flutter of butterfly wings in one place creates weather events halfway around the world. So, if those nineteenth-century Montreal capitalists had not succeeded in creating Canada's first bank and making it, over the long run, a great financial force to be reckoned, would anyone really have noticed? Or perhaps we'd be celebrating the Bank of Hochelaga's two centuries of business?

Cynics might say that a world without the Bank of Montreal would largely be the same – we would still have banks, branches, head offices, bureaucracies, investments, capital markets, pinstriped suits, ATM fees, and the like – all of those categories seem eternal. They might *say* that, but I daresay they would not be looking at the larger picture. People and institutions exist in time. A small number of them have persisted over 200 years. The efforts of Montreal bankers over time has made the Bank a unique organism that responds to questions, challenges, opportunities, new markets, growing, adapting, and changing. If, in this scenario, we were given the consciousness of understanding what was missing, we would miss the original way in which Montreal bankers have approached their craft. Given the critical and continuing role that the Bank has played in the economic life of Canada and North America – from colonial times, to the great era of Confederation and the support for the Canadian Pacific Railway, to the early twentieth century, down to the financial crisis of 2008, and in countless examples between – Bank of Montreal leaders have taken their role as nation builders and system defenders deeply seriously. Bank of Montreal bankers have created an extraordinary record across time and space. We might miss the original style and thrust, and achievements, of the Montreal capitalists who pushed hard to make money and worked tirelessly to create a vision greater than themselves: to help build a nation and bind it together. We might miss the genius of individual leaders like Mount Stephen, Strathcona, Gordon, and Mulholland (because if the Bank is subtracted from history, it also take its leaders – that's the rule) and a thousand community leaders who led the Bank in a wild and untamed country. Can you imagine late-twentieth-century Canadian banking without Matthew W. Barrett? Even if you could, would you really want to? The point is that individual genius and institutional personality can matter far more than the study of impersonal historical forces might suggest.

The people who work in today's Bank, in everything from Capital Markets to Wealth Management to Personal and Commercial Banking, know that there is a BMO way, a BMO personality, a solidarity, an approach to people and projects, an earned reputation of standing by clients and getting through tough times together. Leaders of a large number of BMO clients in the small- and medium-sized enterprise sector, who survived the financial crisis of 2008 because their Bank stuck with them in the darker periods, would be the first to contradict the idea that a bank is a bank is a bank. At the very least, especially in the last quarter-century, the world of North American banking without the Bank of Montreal would have been a hell of a lot more boring. An analogy might help. In hockey, as with all team sports, every team that takes to the ice is a unique combination. No group of players has ever played the game in quite the same way – the mix of novelty, creativity, and innovation is unique. The best ones bring home the silverware from time to time (with the possible exception of certain Toronto teams). However, there are things that persist: the rules, the game, the referee, the league, the points system, the expensive parking, and the like. That balance, between the dynamics of a unique team and the structures of the game itself, produces something that cannot be easily replicated and, if eliminated, would be missed.[9]

As Darryl White's team at the Bank of Montreal takes the helm, I have three wishes for them. First, that they will approach the future armed with the knowledge and analytical insight borne of two centuries of experience. Second, that the leadership be energized by what ten generations have been able to build in one of the great financial institutions of the North Atlantic world. Finally, I hope that this generation, like the ones before it, will be inspired by the trust placed in them to make this institution work for the people, communities, nation, and world it serves, and will be mindful of their responsibility, when their time comes, to the next generation. Insight, energy, inspiration: three key pathways to how the leadership and people of the Bank of Montreal will continue to earn Fortune's favour and rise to the Bank's best and most illustrious traditions. By so doing, the current generation will step up to the mark that legacy, present opportunity, and future vision is creating for Canada's first bank.

AFTERWORD FOR ACADEMIC
READERS

A n explanation of the genesis and development of *Whom Fortune Favours* is in order for this book's academic readers. The entire project began in 2012, when Chief Executive Officer William A. Downe accepted my proposal to write not one, but two, works on the history of the Bank of Montreal. We believed that an initial, celebratory volume and a second scholarly or professional work would be an appropriate literary response to the 200th anniversary celebrations. As it turns out, we were right on the money. *A Vision Greater Than Themselves: The Making of the Bank of Montreal, 1817–2017*, published by McGill-Queen's University Press, delivered a unique and once-in-a-generation experience in word and image. The celebratory volume, as we called it, would have many benefits. One of the benefits for the historian in this two-publication strategy is that it gets to serve two sets of audiences. As a gorgeously illustrated work of history, *A Vision Greater* could effectively reach many popular audiences, from employees to customers.

As an independent work of scholarship, *Whom Fortune Favours* aimed to do the much heavier lifting of providing a scholarly history of one of Canada's and North America's founding financial institutions. It is the first scholarly history of the Bank of Montreal. Merrill Denison's two-volume chronicle *Canada's First Bank*, prepared for the Bank's 150th anniversary in 1967, represented a remarkable twelve-year effort, which among other things included carting station-wagon loads of documents from the National Archives of Canada to Port Dover, Merrill's summer home (with, of course, the permission of the dominion archivist, the remarkable W. Kaye Lamb). In some sense, the pursuit of those documents is an indication of how seriously Denison took his work. But his history was never conceived as a scholarly history: it was more of a romanticized account of the Bank of Montreal experience.

This project unfolded under the aegis of a book committee comprised of a small number of BMO employees, executives, and former executives. The committee provided an overall structure for the administration of the project and dealt with logistics and access issues. Committee members also reviewed earlier drafts of the manuscript and provided feedback as they were produced. The arrangements between BMO and the author were quite straightforward: I was to write a work of independent scholarship on the history of the institution. That arrangement meant, explicitly, that I was responsible for the conceptualization, research, and writing of this book, including its analysis and judgments. This key condition was not only respected, but respected to a fault by all concerned. That is not to say that everyone agreed fully at all times with the analysis offered: my early in-house readers were highly professional and knowledgeable skeptics, many of whom had lived through some of the period the book covers. Ultimately, however, I was free to reach my own conclusions. The arrangement also meant that the work would have to be submitted to the scholarly peer review process to ensure that it met the highest standards of scholarship, academic probity, and integrity. At the outset, therefore, it was agreed that this work would be published by a university press, where the mechanisms for review through anonymous experts in the field, and also through its own publications committee, would certify the academic rigor of the process. The natural choice for BMO, and for me, was the Montreal-based McGill-Queen's University Press.

Whom Fortune Favours was to cover the entire span of the Bank's existence to contemporary times. We jointly agreed that the end of W.D. Mulholland's era, in 1990, would constitute a watershed of sorts. The post-1990 experience would be covered and analyzed, of course, but would have to proceed with restricted access to documents for institutional and privacy reasons. Since 1990 coincided with a changing of the executive guard from Bill Mulholland to Matt Barrett, it provided enough distance for the historian to be able to carry out his office. Once again, from the outset, it was understood that responsibility for conceptualization, text, and length – including post-1990 – was mine alone, as an academic historian.

The main source for this work has been the Bank of Montreal Corporate Archives, which contains over 200 linear metres of documentary evidence on the evolution of Canada's first bank to contemporary times. It is an impressive archival repository; much has been saved down the years. In recent years, it has been served by dedicated, professional archivists. The formal organization of the archives seems to have begun with Merrill Denison's work on *Canada's First Bank* in 1955. But much has also been lost to time. The documentary evidence is, naturally, focused on the workings and strategy of the head office, senior executives, and the board of directors. The tens of thousands of documents that were examined in the preparation of this book provided a fascinating and, at times, forensically detailed picture of countless crises, booms, busts, and panics. At the same time, it should be stressed that the record often fell silent on a range of subjects. This challenge became more problematic as the study approached the contemporary era, when records were either not kept or were housed in different corners of the Bank. This project has encouraged contemporary management to begin the implementation of a systematic historical records management strategy.

Specific documents from the Bank of Montreal archives include board of director minutes (1817–1967) and related documents regarding decisions and discussions of the board, Annual Reports (1817–2017), correspondence, branch reports, memoranda, and employee and executive personnel biographical files (to approximately the 1960s). There were also personal diaries and recollections, ledger books, legal and regulatory filings, staff magazines, marketing material, business review summaries, business circulars, statements on public issues, corporate planning files, and corporate audit materials. Apart from the board minutes, I was given unrestricted access to archival documents to 1990.

I also consulted an array of regional, national, and international archives, in particular, a number of relevant record groups in Library and Archives Canada over multiple trips, specifically. These include Prime Ministerial Papers, records of various Royal Commissions, the Journal of the House of Assembly, records of the office of the Superintendent of Financial Institutions and the Department of Finance, as well as files dealing with federal external affairs, ranging from pre-1949 Newfoundland to London, and beyond. I also accessed Canadian regional archives, including the Nova Scotia Archives and the Provincial Archives of Newfoundland and Labrador, specific records of which can be found in the notes at the end of respective chapters. I visited the National Archives in the United Kingdom, looking at documents ranging from the Records of the Lord of the Treasury to the Office of the Committee of the Privy Council for Trade. I also visited the Bank of England Archive for their extensive "overseas department" holdings on Canada. Finally, financial data for Canada's Big Five banks – including the Bank of Montreal – in the late-twentieth century and early twenty-first century were obtained from Thomson Reuters.

Written sources included newspapers, magazines, and periodicals in Canada, United States, and the United Kingdom from 1818 to contemporary times, such as the *Calgary Herald, Financial Times, Globe, Globe and Mail, Monetary Times and Trade Review, Montreal Gazette, National Post, New York*

Times, *Ottawa Citizen*, *Toronto Globe*, and *Vancouver Sun* as well as a range of local national and international newspapers (a complete list can be found in the bibliography).

Finally, in 2008, the Bank asked me to interview a small number of its current and former executives in order to capture the rich institutional memory contained in individual experience. The success of that original project caused the Bank to expand the oral history project to approximately 150 confidential interviews of key personnel, which were conducted between 2009 and 2012. The typical interview lasted about two hours, with more senior personnel being interviewed several times. Those interviews formed an extraordinary foundation for understanding the experience of the Bank in the last half-century. Of course, they had to be handled with the usual due diligence of the historian and, for the most part, were anonymized if referred to in this work. The interviews very effectively supplemented the documentary archives, offering at various times nuance, greater depth, and diverse perspectives.

BMO's commitment to understanding its own long-run experience has resulted in a massive, multi-year research and writing effort. Its most senior executives submitted their cherished institution to an independent, honest accounting of its past. They were also ready to have the story published, understanding as they did the importance of the experience of the Bank of Montreal both to its own strategy and purpose and to Canadian and North American finance. The courage of such a commitment should never be underestimated: it is an all-too-rare quality among contemporary executives. More often than not, avoiding such beneficial scrutiny is the path of least resistance – to avoid imagined liability or reputational risk. It can be an undertaking that in some ways privatizes potential risk and, partly at least, socializes the potential benefit. Saying no is easy. BMO's decision-makers at the highest levels had both the courage and the commitment to do something that very few executives want to do: they voluntarily ceded "control of the narrative" in quite literal terms. But by loosing their grip, they allowed *Whom Fortune Favours* to take flight. This project was a public act, borne of confidence and a sophisticated sense of the institution's role in the wider world. The pay-off, I am certain, will benefit both BMO and the wider world that it serves. May this project be both a model and example to other similar firms. By saying yes to understanding the long-run experience, BMO joins a small group of global companies that understand how to generate insight from hindsight to confront contemporary challenges.

NOTES

Preface

1 "Treue Beobachter der Natur, wenn sie auch sonst noch so verschieden denken, werden doch darin miteinander übereinkommen, daß alles, was erscheinen, was uns als ein Phänomen begegnen solle, müsse entweder eine ursprüngliche Entzweiung, die hinter Vereinigung fähig ist oder eine ursprüngliche Einheit, die zur Entzweiung gelangen könnte, andeuten und sich auf eine solche Weise darstellen. Das Geeinte zu entzweien, das Entzweite zu einigen, ist das Leben der Natur; dies ist die ewige Systole und Diastole, die ewige Synkrisis und Diakrisis, das Ein- und Ausatmen der Welt, in der wir leben, weben, und sind." Johann Wolfgang von Goethe, *Zur Farbenlehre* (Herausgegeben von Karl-Maria Guth, Berlin: Hofenberg, 2016), 171.

Chapter Fourteen

The phrase contained in the title for chapter 14 was immortalized by Jean Fourastrié, *Les Trentes Glorieuses, ou, La revolution invisible de 1946 à 1975* (Paris: Fayard, 1979).

1 Stephen A. Marglin and Juliet B, Schor, eds., *The Golden Age of Capitalism: Reinterpreting the Postwar Experience* (Oxford: Clarendon Oxford University Press, 1990).

2 Magda Fahrni and Robert Rutherdale, "Introduction," in *Creating Postwar Canada: Community, Diversity, and Dissent 1945–1975*, eds. Magda Fahrni and Robert Rutherdale (Vancouver: University of British Columbia Press, 2008), 2.

3 Ibid.

4 Robert Bothwell, Ian Drummond, and John English, *Canada since 1945: Power, Politics, and Provincialism*, Revised Edition (Toronto: University of Toronto Press, 1989), 15.

5 Ibid., 21.

6 Ibid., 15.

7 Ibid., 21.

8 BMOA, Minutes of the Executive Committee of the Board, 3 September 1946.

9 BMOA, Minutes of the Executive Committee of the Board, 4 March 1948.

10 BMOA, Biography Files: Gardner, B.C.; "Man of the Week, B of M President Bertie C. Gardner," Standard, 17 April 1948.

11 Ibid.

12 BMOA, Biography Files: Gardner, B.C.; "BC Gardner Story 21/2/56," 12.

13 Ibid.

14 Laurence B. Mussio, *A Vision Greater Than Themselves: The Making of the Bank of Montreal, 1817–2017* (Montreal/Kingston: McGill/Queen's University Press, 2016), 23.

15 Ibid., 24.

16 BMOA, Biography Files: Fred H. McNeil; "McNeil of Bank of Montreal," in *Executive*, April 1973, 18.

17 BMOA, Biography Files: Fred H. McNeil, "Biography."

18 BMOA, Biography Files: Jensen, Arthur, J.L.

19 Ibid..

20 Ibid.; "Officials Names for Red Feather Advance Section," *Montreal Gazette*, 30 March 1955; "These Men Are Leaders of 1955's Red Feather Campaign," *Financial Post*, 30 July 1955.

21 BMOA, Biography Files: Mulholland, R.D.

22 BMOA, Biography Files: Walker, J.L. "John Leonard Walker, 1909–1973;" BMOA, Bank of Montreal Annual Report, 1973.

23 "The Bank in the Postwar Years," *Globe and Mail*, 7 December 1943.

24 BMOA, Bank of Montreal Annual Report, 1945.

25 BMOA, Bank of Montreal Business Summary, 21 December 1945.

26 BMOA, Bank of Montreal Business Summary, 22 November 1945.

27 Ibid.

28 BMOA, Bank of Montreal Business Summary, 22 December 1947.

29 Ibid.

30 BMOA, Bank of Montreal Business Summary, 22 December 1949.

31 Ibid.

32 Ibid.

33 For an excellent treatment of Canada's transition from wartime to a peacetime economy, see Joy Parr, *Domestic Goods: The Material, the Moral, and the Economic in the Postwar Years* (Toronto: University of Toronto Press, 1999). Parr argues that the Canadian government prioritized heavy industry and exports and focused on investments in the welfare state and income redistribution. All of this delayed the creation of a consumer society. This was in stark contrast to the United States, where the government actively encouraged consumption.

34 "Finance at Large: Production Hampered by Persistent Shortages and Dislocation of Cost-Price Relationships; Beware Grim Game of Leapfrog – Geo. Spinney," *Globe and Mail*, 6 December 1946.

35 BMOA, Bank of Montreal, Executive Committee of the Board, Minutes, 4 January 1945.

36 Mussio, *A Vision Greater Than Themselves*, 141.

37 Ibid.

38 BMOA, Bank of Montreal, Executive Committee of the Board, Minutes, 4 January 1945.

39 "Canada Economic Scene Reviewed by B of M Heads," *Globe and Mail*, 7 December 1948.

40 Bank of Montreal Annual Report, 1950.

41 "Tighter Monetary Policy Helpful but Inflation Battle Still to Be Decided, Warns B of M President," *Globe and Mail*, 4 December 1951.

42 BMOA, Bank of Montreal Business Summary, 21 December 1950.

43 BMOA, Bank of Montreal Business Summary, 18 December 1953.

44 Ibid.

45 BMOA, Bank of Montreal Business Summary, 16 December 1954.

46 BMOA, Bank of Montreal Business Review, 18 December 1957.

47 BMOA, "Confidential Memorandum for Mr Gardner – A Survey of the Bank's Earning Power," 16 March 1950.

48 Ibid.

49 Ibid.

50 Ibid.

51 Ibid.

52 Ibid.

53 Ibid.

54 BMOA, Executive Committee of the Board, Minutes, 1953: "Salient Features of 1952 Operating Results Based on Schedule Q and Related Data."

55 BMOA, Minutes of the Executive Committee of the Board, 24 October 1955.

56 BMOA, Minutes of the Executive Committee of the Board, 13 April 1956.

57 BMOA, Minutes of the Executive Committee of the Board, 13 February 1957.

58 Bank of Montreal, Executive Committee of the Board, Minutes, 15 July 1954.

59 BMOA, "Confidential Memorandum for Mr Gardner."

60 Ibid.

61 Ibid.

62 BMOA, Minutes of the Executive Committee of the Board, 11 March 1950.

63 BMOA, "Confidential Memorandum for Mr Gardner."

64 "Chicago Office Closed by B of M," *Globe and Mail*, 15 December 1952.

65 Bank of Montreal, Executive Committee of the Board, Minutes, 24 November 1952.

66 Ibid.

67 Bank of Montreal, Executive Committee of the Board, Minutes, 14 May 1959.

68 BMOA, Oral History Project, Testimony No. 64.

69 Ibid., Testimony No. 25.

70 Ibid., Testimony No. 69.

71 Ibid., Testimony No. 104.

72 BMOA, "The Girls of the Bank Are Doing Their Share," Bank of Montreal *Staff Magazine*, February 1945.

73 BMOA, "Gleanings from Letters of Members of the Staff Now Overseas," Bank of Montreal *Staff Magazine*, February 1945.

74 BMOA, "Personal and Sports Notes," Bank of Montreal *Staff Magazine*, February 1947.

75 See, for example, BMOA, Flt-Lt. L.R. Montgomery, Ottawa Branch, "Under the Hand of Nippon: Life Was Grim in Japanese Prisoner of War Camps," Bank of Montreal *Staff Magazine*, June 1946.

76 BMOA, Oral History Project, Testimony No. 105.

77 BMOA, "Personal and Sports Notes."

78 BMOA, "Bank's Loss Problems and Remedies," Bank of Montreal *Staff Magazine*, December 1945.

79 BMOA, "Black Gold: New Horizons for the Canadian West," Bank of Montreal *Staff Magazine*, December 1949.

80 BMOA, "Long May She Reign," Bank of Montreal *Staff Magazine*, June 1953.

81 BMOA, "Depression in Hamilton," Bank of Montreal *Staff Magazine*, June 1946.

82 BMOA, "Strictly Feminine," Bank of Montreal *Staff Magazine*, August 1948.

83 BMOA, "Operation Waterman: The Bank Goes Amphibious," Bank of Montreal *Staff Magazine*, October 1947.

84 BMOA, Minutes of the Executive Committee of the Board, 5 September 1947.

85 "Banker Estimates Bank Mortgage Loan Totals $100 Million," *Globe and Mail*, 14 December 1954.

86 Bank of Montreal, Executive Committee of the Board, Minutes, 31 July 1956.

87 LAC MG26 (n6), Vol. 1, Lester B. Pearson Papers, "Memorandum of a Conversation with Senator Salter Hayden," 6 October 1969.
    Note on date: This document is likely misdated. In the LAC collection the file comes after a related document dated 30 September 1959. Furthermore, Pearson refers to his status as "Leader of the Liberal Party." By October 1969, Pearson was no longer leader of the Liberal Party, further reinforcing the notion that the above document is from 6 October 1959, not 1969. Moreover, a 1959 date would put the merger talks firmly in the midst of other large mergers of the period: namely Toronto and Dominion (1955) and Commerce and Imperial (1961).

88 LAC MG26 (n6), Vol. 1, Lester B. Pearson Papers, "Memorandum of a Conversation with Senator Salter Hayden," October 6, 1969 [1959].

89 "Heavy Votes for Merging Commerce, Imperial Banks," *Globe and Mail*, 15 April 1961.

90 Bank of Montreal, Executive Committee of the Board, Minutes, 1 December 1958.

91 BMOA, Minutes of the Executive Committee of the Board, 15 September 1948, "Memorandum for the General Manager."

92 BMOA, Minutes of the Executive Committee of the Board, 30 November 1949.

93 BMOA, Minutes of the Executive Committee of the Board, 29 August 1950, "Memorandum for Mr Townsend – Staff – Salaries – Bonuses."

94 Ibid.

95 Bank of Montreal, Executive Committee of the Board, Minutes, 22 January 1960.

96 BMOA, Oral History Project, Testimony No. 105.

97 Ibid., Testimony No. 105.

98 BMOA, Bank of Montreal Business Review, 24 December 1958.

99 BMOA, Address of G. Arnold Hart to the 142nd Annual Meeting of the Bank of Montreal 7 December 1959.

100 BMOA, Bank of Montreal Business Review, 23 December 1958; Address of G. Arnold Hart to the 143rd Annual Meeting of the Bank of Montreal 5 December 1960.

101 Ibid.

102 BMOA, Bank of Montreal Business Review, 18 December 1964.

103 BMOA, Bank of Montreal Business Review, 17 December 1965.

104 BMOA, Bank of Montreal Business Review, 20 December 1967.

105 Canada. Privy Council Office. Royal Commission on Banking and Finance. Report of the Royal Commission on Banking and Finance/Dana Harris Porter, Chairman (Ottawa: Royal Commission on Banking and Finance, 1964).

106 Canada. Department of Finance. Budget Speech, 20 June 1961.

107 Canada. House of Commons Debates. 20 June 1961, 6648; LAC RG33-64, Vol. 37, Scrapbook No. 1, Newspaper Clippings.

108 LAC RG33-64, General Inventory.

109 Canada. Privy Council Office. Royal Commission on Banking and Finance. Report of the Royal Commission on Banking and Finance, Vol. I, 121.

110 Ibid., 122.

111 "Banks Startled by What They Told Probe, Now It's in Print," *Globe and Mail*, 28 April 1964.

112 "Have Times Changed Enough to Warrant Regional Banks?" *Globe and Mail*, 19 May 1964.

113 David W. Slater, "The 1967 Revision of the Canadian Banking Acts Part I: An Economist's View," in *Canadian Journal of Economics* 1 no. 1 (February 1968): 79.

114 Ibid.

115 James L. Darroch, *Canadian Banks and Global Competitiveness* (Montreal/Kingston: McGill-Queen's University Press, 1994), 278–9.

116 Ibid.

117 Ibid.

118 Slater, "The 1967 Revision of the Canadian Banking Acts Part I," 85.

119 Ibid., 84.

120 Darroch, *Canadian Banks and Global Competitiveness*, 278–9.

121 Canada. Privy Council Office, Royal Commission on Banking and Finance, Report of the Royal Commission on Banking and Finance.

122 LAC M-8935, Vol. 20, John G. Diefenbaker Series vii Reference Series, 1957–1967, "Memorandum Re: The Bank Act Bill C-102."

123 LAC M-8935, Vol. 20, John G. Diefenbaker Series vii Reference Series, 1957–1967, "New Bank Law: We've Fumbled It," *Toronto Star*, 31 May 1966.

124 LAC MG26 (n6), Vol. 1, Lester B. Pearson Papers, "Memorandum from the Cabinet Committee on Finance and Economic Policy to Minister of Finance, re: The General Approach to banking Legislation," 28 February 1966.

125 LAC MG26-M, Vol. 20, John G. Diefenbaker Series vii Reference Series, 1957–1967, "B of M Chief Calls Gordon View Timid," *Montreal Star*, 26 June 1966.

126 LAC MG26-M, Vol. 20, John G. Diefenbaker Series vii Reference Series, 1957–1967, "The Big Money Hassle: Is Sweeping Change Needed?" *Toronto Star*, 7 February 1966.

127 Michael Hart, *A Trading Nation: Canadian Trade Policy from Colonialism to Globalization* (Vancouver: University of British Columbia Press, 2002), 238.

128 LAC MG26 (n6), Vol. 1, Lester B. Pearson Papers, "Memorandum from the Cabinet Committee on Finance and Economic Policy to Minister of Finance."

129 Denis Smith, *Gentle Patriot: A Political Biography of Walter Gordon* (Edmonton: Hurtig Publishers, 1973), 311.

130 Darroch, *Canadian Banks and Global Competitiveness*, 278–9.

131 LAC M-8936, Vol. 20, John G. Diefenbaker Series vii Reference Series, 1957–1967, "US Envoy Denounces Our Curb on Citibank," *Toronto Star*, 10 December 1966.

132 LAC M-8936, Vol. 20, John G. Diefenbaker Series vii Reference Series, 1957–1967, "Personal & Confidential Memorandum for the Right Honourable Leader. Re – George McNamara and the Bank Act."

133 Ibid.

134 Ibid.

135 Ibid.

136 Ibid.

137 LAC M-8936, Vol. 18, John G. Diefenbaker Series vii Reference Series, 1957–1967, "Memo: General Views on the Bank Act, 26 June 1966."

138 "Mercantile Championed by Bank of Montreal," *Globe and Mail*, 8 June 1965.

139 BMOA, Bank of Montreal Annual Report, 1971.

140 Ibid.

141 Ibid.

142 Ibid.

143 BMOA, Lectures on Foreign Exchange and Foreign Trade (E.C. Winrow), March 1967, 1.

144 Ibid., 21.

145 Ibid., 22.

146 Ibid., App 5, 8.

147 BMOA, Oral History Project, Testimony No. 13.

148 "Women-only Bank Opens Doors," *Globe and Mail*, 9 December 1966.

149 Ibid.

150 BMOA, Bank of Montreal Annual Report, 1966.

151 "Women-only Bank Opens Doors."

152 BMOA, Minutes of the Executive Committee of the Board, 30 April 1957.

153 Mussio, *A Vision Greater Than Themselves*, 142.

154 Ibid.

155 Ibid.

156 Ibid.

157 E.P. Neufeld, *The Financial System of Canada. Its Growth and Development* (Toronto: MacMillan of Canada, 1972), 66–7.

158 Ibid., 67.

159 Ibid., 70.

160 Ibid., 94.

161 Ibid., 117.

162 Ibid., 121.

163 "F. Williams-Taylor Banker Knight Dies," *Toronto Daily Star*, 2 August 1945.

164 Victor Davis Hanson, *The Savior Generals: How Five Great Commanders Saved Wars that Were Lost – From Ancient Greece to Iraq* (New York: Bloomsbury Press, 2013), 2.

165 Ibid., 238.

166 Ibid., 240.

167 BMOA, Oral History Project, Testimony No. 105.

Chapter Fifteen

1 Christopher Wright and Matthias Kipping, "The Engineering Origins of the Consulting Industry and Its Long Shadow," in *The Oxford Handbook of Management Consulting*, eds. Matthias Kipping and Timothy Clark (Oxford: Oxford University Press, 2012), 29–50.

2 Ralph Cavanagh, "Making Friends with Mother Nature," Harvard Business School Alumni, www.alumni.hbs.edu/stories/Pages/story-bulletin.aspx?num=6334 (accessed 7 May 2017).

3 BMOA, Oral History Project, Testimony No. 85.

4 Ibid., Testimony No. 121.

5 Ibid.

6 BMOA, Bank of Montreal Annual Report, 1967, 1968.

7 BMOA, Oral History Project, Testimony No. 121.

8 Ibid.

9 Ibid., Testimony No. 63

10 Ibid., Testimony No. 121.

11 Canada. Privy Council Office. "Report of the Inquiry into the Collapse of the CCB and Northland/by the Honourable Willard Z. Estey, commissioner" (Ottawa: Privy Council Office, 1986), 354.

12 BMOA, Oral History Project, Testimony No. 121.

13 Ibid.

14 Ibid.

15 Ibid., Testimony No. 60.

16 Ibid., Testimony No. 95.

17 Ibid., Testimony No. 45.

18 Ibid., Testimony No. 60.

19 Ibid., Testimony No. 63.

20 Ibid.

21 Ibid.

22 Ibid., Testimony No. 20.

23 Ibid.

24 Ibid., Testimony No. 58.

25 Ibid., Testimony No. 69.

26 BMOA, Bank of Montreal Annual Report, 1946, 1954, 1961.

27 BMOA, Oral History Project, Testimony No. 108.

28 Ibid.

29 Ibid., Testimony No. 117.

30 Ibid., Testimony No. 64.

31 Ibid., Testimony No. 117.

32 Ibid.

33 BMOA, McKinsey: The Special Development Program, 3.

34 Ibid., 6.

35 Ibid.

36 Ibid., 7.

37 Ibid., 22.

38 Ibid., 11.

39 Ibid., 29.

40 BMOA, Oral History Project, Testimony No. 85.

41 Ibid., Testimony No. 74.

42 Ibid., Testimony No. 117.

43 "Financier Hartland Molson MacDougall Started Out as a Teller," *Globe and Mail*, 20 October 2014.

44 "Elsie Kuchta Stalls Off Another Hold-Up," Bank of Montreal *Staff Magazine*, April 1955; BMOA, Bank of Montreal Annual Report, 1973.

45 BMOA, Oral History Project, Testimony No. 117.

46 Ibid., Testimony No. 64.

47 Statistics Canada, Labour Force Survey CANSIM Table 282-0002. 89-503-X.

48 BMOA, Oral History Project, Testimony No. 66.

49 Ibid., Testimony No. 67.

50 Ibid..

51 BMOA, J.L. Walker's Archives, "Strengthening the Organization of the Montreal Branch, July 1967," 3.

52 Ibid.

53 Ibid.

54 Ibid., 5.

55 Ibid., 8.

56 Ibid., 3.

57 BMOA, Strategic Planning, "Memorandum from Donald K. Clifford Jr to J. Leonard Walker," 1 May 1969, 1.

58 Ibid.

59 Ibid.

60 BMOA, Strategic Planning, "Confidential: Strategic Planning Statement of Priorities," 20 March 1969, 2.

61 Ibid., 3.

62 Ibid., 4.

63 Ibid.

64 Ibid., 5.

65 BMOA, Strategic Planning, "International Banking – Detailed Plan," 2.

66 Ibid.

67 For more information, see Mussio, *A Vision Greater Than Themselves*, 142.

Chapter Sixteen

1 Patricia Meredith and James Darroch, *Stumbling Giants: Transforming Canada's Banks for the Information Age* (Toronto: University of Toronto Press, 2017), xiv.

2 Harry E. Mertz, quoted in James Cortada, *The Digital Hand: Volume II: How Computers Changed the Work of American Financial, Telecommunications, Media and Entertainment Industries* (Oxford: Oxford University Press, 2006), location 142 of 10474, Kindle.

3 See Andrew Tylecote, *The Long Wave in the World Economy: The Current Crisis in Historical Perspective* (London: Routledge, 1991): 36–70. As Cortada suggests, *The Digital Hand: Volume II*, location 8023. Tylecote describes a new style as "the most efficient and profitable, change in response to the appearance of new key *factors of production* which are: a) clearly very cheap by past standards, and tending to get cheaper; and b) potentially all pervasive."

4 Cortada, *The Digital Hand: Volume II*, location 465.

5 Quoted in Cortada, *The Digital Hand: Volume II*, location 12.

6 Cortada, *The Digital Hand: Volume II*, location 47.

7 Ibid., location 151.

8 Quoted in Cortada. Lauren Bielski, "Year of the Wallet?" *ABA Banking Journal* 99 (December 1999): 56, 58, 62–3.

9 Cortada, *The Digital Hand: Volume II*, location 163.

10 Ibid., location 171.

11 Ibid., location 234.

12 Ibid., location 280; Cf. David S. Evans and Richard Schmalensee, *Paying with Plastic: The Digital Revolution in Buying and Borrowing*, Second Edition (Cambridge: Massachusetts Institute of Technology, 2005).

13 James L. McKenney, with Duncan C. Copeland and Richard O. Mason, *Waves of Change: Business Evolution through Information Technology* (Boston: HBS Press, 1995): 41.

14 Paul Armer, *Computer Aspects of Technological Changes, Automation and Economic Progress* (Santa Monica, CA: The RAND Corporation, 1966), cited in Cortada, *The Digital Hand: Volume II*, location 769.

15 Cortada, *The Digital Hand: Volume II*, location 776.

16 Ibid., location 807f.

17 See James L. McKenney and Amy Weaver Fisher, "Manufacturing the ERMA Banking System: Lessons from History," *IEEE Annals of the History of Computing* 15, no. 4 (1993): 7. McKenney and Fisher suggest that this system's impact was felt not just by Bank of America but also by the entire banking industry – and they are surely correct. "The ERMA effort," they concluded, "clearly demonstrates that a knowledgeable user working with

competent technologists can design an implement a system that meets critical needs with state-of-the-art technology" (7).

18 BMOA, Bank of Montreal Annual Report, 1946, 1961.

19 See Laurence B. Mussio, *A Vision Greater Than Themselves: The Making of the Bank of Montreal, 1817–2017* (Montreal/Kingston: McGill-Queen's University Press, 2016), 87–8.

20 Cortada, *The Digital Hand: Volume II*, location 386.

21 Ibid., location 423.

22 See Joy Parr, *Domestic Goods: The Material, the Moral, and the Economic in the Postwar Years* (Toronto: University of Toronto Press, 1999).

23 BMOA, Bank of Montreal *Staff Magazine,* December 1962.

24 BMOA, Montreal GENIE Centre, "Press Release," 2 July 1963.

25 BMOA, Bank of Montreal Annual Report, 1969.

26 BMOA, Bank of Montreal Annual Report, 1973.

27 Ibid.

28 BMOA, Bank of Montreal Annual Report, 1958.

29 Ibid.

30 Ibid.

31 Ibid.

32 BMOA, Montreal GENIE Centre, "Press Release."

33 BMOA, Bank of Montreal Annual Report, 1958; "Electronics Come to Aid of Bank's Bookkeepers," *Albertan*, 3 January 1959; "Machine Speeds City Bank Work," *Calgary Herald*, 3 February 1959.

34 BMOA, "'New' Banking History Made ... Canada's First Bank Incorporates Many Firsts in New Head Office," Bank of Montreal Annual Report, 1960.

35 BMOA, "Setting the Pace in Progress ... in Automated Banking," Bank of Montreal Annual Report, 1963.

36 BMOA, Corporate Audit Files On-line (MECH) Pre-mechanization Studies and Reports, "Financial Management Report. Bank Mechanization Study," August 1969.

37 BMOA, "Setting the Pace in Progress ... in Automated Banking."

38 BMOA, Montreal GENIE Centre, "Bank of Montreal Introduce Fully Integrated Automatic Banking in Canada," *Toronto Stock Exchange Review*, September 1963.

39 BMOA, Montreal GENIE Centre, "Press Release."

40 BMOA, "Setting the Pace in Progress ... in Automated Banking."

41 Ibid.

42 BMOA, Bank of Montreal Annual Report, 1964.

43 Ibid.

44 Ibid.

45 BMOA, Bank of Montreal Annual Report, 1966.

46 BMOA, Corporate Audit Files On-line (MECH) Pre-mechanization Studies and Reports, "Final Management Report. Bank Mechanization Study," August 1969.

47 BMOA, Bank of Montreal *Staff Magazine*, December 1962.

48 James L. Darroch, *Canadian Banks and Global Competitiveness* (Montreal/Kingston: McGill-Queen's University Press, 1994), 49.

49 BMOA, Bank of Montreal *Staff Magazine*, April 1963.

50 BMOA, Bank of Montreal Annual Report, 1963.

51 Ibid.

52 BMOA, "These Are the Winners: GENIE Comes from Genius," Bank of Montreal *Staff Magazine*, August 1963.

53 BMOA, "More About the GENIE Prize Winners," Bank of Montreal *Staff Magazine*, October 1963.

54 BMOA, Audit Material, "Inspection and Controls for an E.D.P. System," 28 May 1963.

55 BMOA, Corporate Audit Files On-line (MECH) Pre-mechanization Studies and Reports, "Pre-survey Study Online Banking," June 1968.

56 Ibid.

57 Ibid.

58 Ibid.

59 Ibid.

60 Ibid.

61 Ibid.

62 Ibid.

63 BMOA, Corporate Audit Files On-line (MECH) Pre-mechanization Studies and Reports, "Survey – Phase I Bank Mechanization Study," February 1969."

64 BMOA, Corporate Audit Files On-line (MECH) Pre-mechanization Studies and Reports, "Financial Management Report. Bank Mechanization Study," August 1969.

65 BMOA, Corporate Audit Files On-line (MECH) Pre-mechanization Studies and Reports, "Pre-survey Study Online Banking."

66 BMOA, Corporate Audit Files On-line (MECH) Pre-mechanization Studies and Reports, "Letter from J. Britton to Mr O.C. Frood," 9 November 1970.

67 BMOA, "The Space Age of Banking," Bank of Montreal Annual Report, 1969.

68 Ibid.

69 BMOA, Bank of Montreal Annual Report, 1969

70 BMOA, J.L. Walker's Archives, "Some Domestic Banking Aspects of the Bank Mechanization System."

71 Ibid.

72 This is akin to an automated version of the character book. BMOA, Bank of Montreal Annual Report, 1969.

73 BMOA, "The Space Age of Banking."

74 BMOA, J.L. Walker's Archives, "Some Domestic Banking Aspects of the Bank Mechanization System."

75 BMOA, Corporate Audit Files On-line (MECH) Pre-mechanization Studies and Reports, "Bank of Montreal Mechanization System Sign-off by Shareholders' Auditors," 11 February 1976.

76 BMOA, Corporate Audit Files On-line (MECH) Pre-mechanization Studies and Reports, "Final Management Report. Bank Mechanization Study."

77 BMOA, J.L. Walker's Archives, "Some Domestic Banking Aspects of the Bank Mechanization System."

78 Ibid.

79 BMOA, Corporate Audit Files On-line (MECH) Pre-mechanization Studies and Reports, "Pre-survey Study Online Banking."

80 BMOA, J.L. Walker's Archives, "Some Domestic Banking Aspects of the Bank Mechanization System."

81 BMOA, Corporate Audit Files On-line (MECH) Pre-mechanization Studies and Reports, "Pre-survey Study Online Banking."

82 Ibid.

83 Ibid.

84 Darroch, *Canadian Banks and Global Competitiveness*, 55.

85 BMOA, Bank of Montreal Annual Report, 1973.
86 Ibid.
87 Ibid.
88 Ibid.
89 Ibid.
90 Ibid.
91 BMOA, Corporate Audit Files On-line (MECH) Pre-mechanization Studies and Reports, "Guidelines for a Bank Data Processing Services Concept., December 1968.
92 Ibid.
93 Ibid.
94 Ibid.
95 BMOA, Corporate Audit Files On-line (MECH) Pre-mechanization Studies and Reports, "Bank of Montreal Mechanization System Sign-off by Shareholders' Auditors."
96 BMOA, Corporate Audit Files On-line (MECH) Pre-mechanization Studies and Reports, "Pre-survey Study Online Banking."
97 BMOA, Bank of Montreal Annual Report, 1979.
98 BMOA, Corporate Audit Files On-line (MECH) Pre-mechanization Studies and Reports, "Pre-survey Study Online Banking."
99 Mussio, *A Vision Greater Than Themselves*, 136.
100 Ibid.
101 BMOA, Bank of Montreal Annual Report, 1974.
102 BMOA, Interac Launch press kit; CIRRUS press releases, "News Release – CIRRUS adds 2,900 ATMS, 8.7 mm cards, CIRRUS System Inc."
103 BMOA, Interac Launch press kit; CIRRUS press releases, "Fact Sheet: CIRRUS Systems Inc."
104 BMOA, CIRRUS Launch, 1985, "News Conference – 22 July 1985, Toronto, RE: CIRRUS."
105 BMOA, Gold Master Card Public Relations Program, "Gold Master Card Pays Interest and Provides Cheques," *Toronto Sun*, 23 November 1984.
106 BMOA, CIRRUS Launch, 1985, "Marketing/Communications Overview."
107 BMOA, Gold Master Card Public Relations Program, "Why the Banks Are Climbing into Bed," *Toronto Sun*, 25 November 1984.
108 BMOA, Interac Launch press kit; CIRRUS press releases, "Backgrounder – Interac Association."
109 Ibid.
110 BMOA, Interac Launch press kit; CIRRUS press releases, "News Release for Immediate Release – Interac Association."
111 BMOA, Interac Launch press kit; CIRRUS press releases, "Circular: ABM Sharing – New Developments."
112 Lizabeth Cohen, *A Consumer's Republic: The Politics of Mass Consumption in Postwar America* (New York: Vintage Books, 2004), 124.
113 "Here Comes Master Charge," *Concordia: Personnel Publication of the Bank of Montreal*, May 1973.
114 Ibid.
115 Ibid.
116 Ibid.
117 Ibid.
118 Ibid.
119 BMOA, Bank of Montreal Annual Report, 1973.

120 BMOA, Gold Master Card Public Relations Program, "Bank of Montreal Gold Mastercard Public Relations Program;" BMOA, Gold Master Card Public Relations Program, "Media-Reach, Business Report CFRB Toronto," 22 November 1984.

121 Lars Heide, "Retail Banking and the Dynamics of Information Technology in Business Organizations," in *Technological Innovation in Retail Finance: International Historical Perspectives*, eds. Bernardo Batiz-Lazo, J. Carles Maixé-Altés, and Paul Thomes (New York: Routledge, 2011), 275.

122 David Stearns, "Automating Payments: Origins of the Visa Electronic Payment System," in *Technological Innovation in Retail Finance: International Historical Perspectives*, eds. Bernardo Batiz-Lazo, J. Carles Maixé-Altés, and Paul Thomes, 270.

123 Ibid.

124 Heide, "Retail Banking and the Dynamics of Information Technology in Business Organizations," 280.

125 Stearns, "Automating Payments: Origins of the Visa Electronic Payment System," 246.

126 Ibid.

Part Six

1 *Lincoln* (2012), The Internet Movie Database. www.imdb.com/title/tt0443272/quotes (accessed 15 March 2016). Quoted in John Lewis Gaddis, *On Grand Strategy* (New York: Penguin Press, 2018), 17.

2 Canada would continue to post budget surpluses consistently between 1996 and 2008.

3 Richard S. Grossman, *Unsettled Account: The Evolution of Banking in the Industrialized World since 1800* (Princeton: Princeton University Press, 2010), 267; Joan Edelman Spero, *The Failure of the Franklin National Bank: Challenge to International Banking System* (Washington: Beard Books, 1999).

4 Philip Cross and Phillipe Bergevin, "Turning Points: Business Cycles in Canada since 1926," *C.D. Howe Commentary No. 366: Economic Growth and Innovation* (October 2012): 17.

5 Ibid.

6 Stacy L. Schreft, "Credit Controls: 1980," *Economic Review* 76, no. 6 (November/December 1990): 25–55.

7 Cross and Bergevin, "Turning Points," 18–19.

8 Clarence L. Barber and John C.P. McCallum, *Controlling Inflation: Learning from Experience in Canada, Europe, and Japan* (Toronto: James Lorimer & Company, 1982), 90–1.

9 Paul Boothe, and Douglas Purvis, "Macroeconomic Policy in Canada and the United States: Independence, Transmission, and Effectiveness," in *Degrees of Freedom: Canada and the United States in a Changing World*, eds. Keith Banting, George Hoberg, and Richard Simeon (Montreal/Kingston: McGill-Queen's University Press, 1997), 189–230, here 193.

10 Cross and Bergevin, "Turning Points," 20; the Government actually spent more on promoting the GST than on the Gulf War. Johnathan W. Rose, *Making "Pictures in Our Heads": Government Advertising in Canada* (Westport: Praeger, 2000), 157.

Chapter Seventeen

1 Victor Davis Hanson, *The Savior Generals: How Five Great Generals Saved Wars that were Lost – from Ancient Greece to Iraq* (New York: Bloomsbury Press, 2014), 2.

2 Ibid.

3 Ibid.

4 Ibid., 4. It seemed to me that Hanson's concept of the "Savior General" fit Mulholland and the Bank of Montreal almost perfectly, even though Dr Hanson is using it as a way of understanding the character, nature, and experience of his victorious generals.

5 Ibid., 2.

6 Ibid., 6.

7 See, for one of many such examples: BMOA, W.D. Mulholland, Patricia Chisholm, "Stepping Aside: A Combative Banker Hands Over the Reins," *Maclean's*, 30 January 1989. Also: BMOA, Oral History Project, Interview No. 8: "He reminded me of a marine general from the United States."

8 BMOA, Bio-File: W.D. Mulholland, Alexander Ross, "Bill Mulholland's Biggest Turnaround," *Canadian Business*, November 1978.

9 BMOA, W.D. Mulholland, "William Mulholland, Chairman and Chief Executive Officer, Bank of Montreal – Biography;" "Former BMO Chief, William Mulholland, Dies at 81," *Globe and Mail*, 10 September 2007; Waldo Heinrichs and Marc Gallicchio, *Implacable Foes: War in the Pacific, 1944–1945* (Oxford: Oxford University Press, 2017).

10 BMOA, Bio-File: W.D. Mulholland, "New York's Newest Banker," *Business Week*, 4 December 1978, 74.

11 BMOA, Bio-File: W.D. Mulholland, Ann Shortell, "The Lion in Winter," *Financial Times*, 13 February 1989.

12 Douglas M. Fouquet, "Business School's Prestige Grows as David Enters 10th Year As Dean," Harvard Crimson, 12 September 1951. www.thecrimson.com/article/1951/9/12/business-schools-prestige-grows-as-david/?utm_source=thecrimson&utm_medium=web_primary&utm_campaign=recommend_sidebar (accessed 18 February 2018).

13 "Ex-Dean of Business School Dies in Hyannis at Age 83," *The Harvard Crimson*, 17 April 1979.

14 Joseph Schull, *The Great Scot: A Biography of Donald Gordon* (Montreal/Kingston: McGill-Queen's University Press, 1979), 254–64.

15 "Former BMO Chief, William Mulholland, Dies at 81."

16 James L. Darroch, *Canadian Banks and Global Competitiveness* (Montreal/Kingston: McGill-Queen's University Press, 1994), 55–6.

17 BMOA, Bio-File: W.D. Mulholland, Ross, "Bill Mulholland's Biggest Turnaround."

18 See, for example, James P. Feehan and Melvin Baker, "The Churchill Falls Contract and Why Newfoundlanders Can't Get Over It," in *Policy Options/Options Politiques* (1 September 2010): 65–70. http://policyoptions.irpp.org/magazines/making-parliament-work/the-churchill-falls-contract-and-why-newfoundlanders-cant-get-over-it/ (accessed 31 January 2017). The authors conclude that "whatever the answers to these questions may be, the following conclusion is in order. It is inconceivable that any party to a commercial transaction would knowingly and willingly agree today to sell its services some 50 to 75 years in the future at a price fixed below the current price, except if either forced to do or given commensurate compensation; in this case, the latter did not happen. This and the ever-more lopsided outcome ensure that most Newfoundlanders will find it impossible to put the Churchill Falls contract behind them."

19 BMOA, Bio-File: W.D. Mulholland, Ross, "Bill Mulholland's Biggest Turnaround."

20 Ibid.

21 BMOA, Bio-File: W.D. Mulholland, "William Mulholland, Chairman and Chief Executive Officer, Bank of Montreal – Biography;" BMOA, Bank of Montreal Annual Report, 1989.

22 BMOA, Bank of Montreal Annual Report, 1989.

23 BMOA, Bio-File: William E. Bradford, "William E. Bradford – Biography."

24 BMOA, Bio-File: Grant L. Reuber, "Resolution of Appreciation to Grant L. Reuber"; BMOA, Bio-File: Grant L. Reuber, "Grant L. Reuber, President and Chief Operation Officer, Bank of Montreal"; BMOA, Bio-File: Grant L. Reuber, "CV: Grant Louis Reuber, O.C., B.A., A.M., PH.D., LL.D., F.R.S.C."

25 BMOA, Bank of Montreal Annual Report, 1985; BMOA, Bio-File: Keith O. Dorricott, "Keith O. Dorricott, Vice-Chair Office of Strategic Management, Bank of Montreal;" BMOA, Bio-File: Fred McNeil, "F.H. (Fred) McNeil, Chairman of the Board – Bank of Montreal, a Biography"; BMOA, Bio-File: W.D. Mulholland, Shortell, "The Lion in Winter"; BMOA, Bio-File: W.D. Mulholland, Ross, "Bill Mulholland's Biggest Turnaround."

26 BMOA, Bio-File: W.D. Mulholland, Ross, "Bill Mulholland's Biggest Turnaround."

27 "Sharp Drop in Bank of Montreal Revenue Balance Stuns Analysts," *Globe and Mail*, 31 August 1974.

28 Ibid.

29 BMOA, Bio-File: W.D. Mulholland, Shortell, "The Lion in Winter."

30 BMOA, Bio-File: W.D. Mulholland, "New York's Newest Banker."

31 BMOA, Bio-File: W.D. Mulholland, Ross, "Bill Mulholland's Biggest Turnaround."

32 BMOA, Oral History Project, Testimony No. 40.

33 Ibid.

34 Ibid., Testimony No. 41.

35 Ibid.

36 BMOA, Bio-File: W.D. Mulholland, Shortell, "The Lion in Winter."

37 Ibid.

38 Ibid.

39 BMOA, Oral History Project, Testimony No. 39.

40 Ibid., Testimony No. 51.

41 Ibid.

42 Ibid., Testimony No. 91.

43 Ibid.

44 Jim Armstrong, "The Changing Business Activities of Banks in Canada," *Bank of Canada Review* (Spring 1997): 11.

45 Ibid.

46 Sherrill Shaffer, "A Test of Competition in Canadian Banking," *Journal of Money, Credit and Banking* 25, no. 1 (February 1993): 58.

47 Parliament, 29th Parliament 2nd Session Vol. 2, House of Commons Debates, 27 February 1978, 3252, intervention of Mr David Orlikow (Winnipeg North).

48 Ibid.

49 See, for example, the Bank Act debates in February 1978 in the House of Commons. Canada. House of Commons Debates, 27 February 1978, 3250. See also: Canada. House of Commons Debates, 1 May 1980, 619, "Banks and Banking Law Revision Act, 1980."

50 Canada. House of Commons Debates, 1 May 1980, 626. This spirited and informed debate shows that people were engaged in attempting to shape the Bank Act. See also: Canada. House of Commons Debates, 14 November 1980; Canada. House of Commons Debates, 18 November 1980.

51 Armstrong, "The Changing Business Activities of Banks in Canada," 12.

52 Ibid.

53 Shaffer, "A Test of Competition in Canadian Banking."

54 Armstrong, "The Changing Business Activities of Banks in Canada," 16–22.

55 Stanley H. Hartt, "From a Bang to a Whimper: Twenty Years of Lost Momentum in Financial Institutions," *Policy Options Extra* (September 2005): 74–5.

56 BMOA, Bio-File: W.D. Mulholland, "Setting an Ambitious Course at Canada's No. 3 Bank," *Globe and Mail*, 24 August 1981.

57 BMOA, Oral History Project, Testimony No. 67.

58 Ibid.

59 Ibid.

60 BMOA, Bio-File: W.D. Mulholland, Ross, "Bill Mulholland's Biggest Turnaround"; BMOA, Bio-File: W.D. Mulholland, "New York's Newest Banker," 72.

61 BMOA, Oral History Project, Testimony No. 54.

62 Ibid., Testimony No. 81.

63 Ibid.

64 Ibid., Testimony No. 110.

65 Ibid., Testimony No. 91.

66 Ibid.

67 BMOA, Bio-File: W.D. Mulholland, "New York's Newest Banker," 74.

68 BMOA, Bank of Montreal Annual Report, 1975.

69 BMOA, Bank of Montreal Annual Report, 1981.

70 "Ad: Bank of Montreal World Corporate Banking," *Globe and Mail*, 18 November 1981.

71 BMOA, Bank of Montreal Annual Report, 1975.

72 Ibid.

73 BMOA, Oral History Project, Testimony No. 73.

74 Ibid.

75 Ibid., Testimony No. 80.

76 Ibid.

77 Canada. House of Commons Debates, 25 February 1977, 3457.

78 Lisa Fitterman, "Women's Rights Advocate Ruth Bell Refused to Be a 'Nice Girl.'" *Globe and Mail*, 17 January 2016.

79 Canada. House of Commons Debates. 25 February 1977, 3457.

80 BMOA, Elizabeth B. Wright, "Women Executives Realizing Ambitions, says Bank V.P." *First Bank News*, September 1986.

81 Ibid.

82 BMOA, Corporate Communications: Finance Committee Enquiry into Bank Profits – Q&A Briefing Book (Mulholland Era), "William Mulholland Testimony before the House of Commons Standing Committee on Finance, Trade, and Economic Affairs," 3 June 1982.

83 BMOA, Bank of Montreal Annual Report, 1980; BMOA, *First Bank News* March 1981.

84 BMOA, Bank of Montreal Annual Report, 1976.

85 "B of M Finally Cures Itself of Mechanization Hiccoughs," *Globe and Mail*, 4 September 1976.

86 BMOA, Bank of Montreal Annual Report, 1978.

87 BMOA, Oral History Project, Testimony No. 2.

88 BMOA, Bank of Montreal Annual Report, 1977.

89 "370 Banks in 15 Countries to Go SWIFT," *Globe and Mail*, 24 July 1976.

90 BMOA, Bank of Montreal Annual Report, 1979.

91 "Opinions Differ on Multi-branch Banking," *Globe and Mail*, 17 February 1979.

92 BMOA, Bank of Montreal Annual Report, 1985.

93 "B of M Joins Teller Network," *Globe and Mail*, 17 October 1985.

94 BMOA, Bank of Montreal Annual Report, 1985.

95 BMOA, Bank of Montreal Annual Report, 1986.

96 BMOA, Bio-File: W.D. Mulholland, Ross, "Bill Mulholland's Biggest Turnaround."

97 Ibid.

98 Ibid.

99 Ibid.

100 BMOA, Bio-File: W.D. Mulholland, "New York's Newest Banker," 74.

101 BMOA, Bio-File: W.D. Mulholland, Ross, "Bill Mulholland's Biggest Turnaround,"

102 Ibid.

103 "Bank of Montreal Plans to Stress West," *Globe and Mail*, 28 June 1979.

104 BMOA, DDP Case Study, "Bank of Montreal – Domestic Development Program (A)," 3–4.

105 Eventually, as a result of the new organization, the Bank of Montreal was able to offer new services as well: "Several new banking services and initiatives have been introduced across Canada by Bank of Montreal as the Domestic Development Program is implemented. They include: Business Advisory panels; Agricultural Advisory Panels; FirstBank Financial Agreement; Personal Line of Credit." (Lines of Credit were hitherto reserved for commercial clients, but new computer technology allowed the bank to extend this service to customers.) BMOA, Bank of Montreal, CBU Counselling, "Bank of Montreal Domestic Development Program Fact Sheet."

106 BMOA, DDP Case Study, "Bank of Montreal – Domestic Development Program (A)," 4.

107 Ibid., 5.

108 "Bank Is in Excellent Shape: My Appreciation to All of You" by Grant Reuber, *First Bank News*, 1984 special edition.

109 BMOA, DDP Case Study, "Bank of Montreal – Domestic Development Program (A)," 5.

110 This managerial oversight and control was something the Bank had desired from its early days: see Character Book.

111 BMOA, DDP Case Study, "Bank of Montreal – Domestic Development Program (A)," 5–6.

112 Ibid., 6

113 BMOA, DDP Case Study, "Bank of Montreal – Domestic Development Program (C)," 1.

114 BMOA, DDP Case Study, "Bank of Montreal – Domestic Development Program (B)," 1–2.

115 BMOA, DDP Case Study, "Bank of Montreal – Domestic Development Program (E)," 1.

116 BMOA, Bank of Montreal, CBU Counselling, "Bank of Montreal Domestic Development Program Fact Sheet."

117 Ibid.

118 Ibid.

119 Ibid.

120 BMOA, DDP Case Study, "Bank of Montreal – Domestic Development Program (D)," 2.

121 BMOA, Bank of Montreal, CBU Counselling, "Bank of Montreal Domestic Development Program Fact Sheet."

122 BMOA, DDP Case Study, "Bank of Montreal – Domestic Development Program (D)," 7.

123 BMOA, M.W. Barrett, AGM 1988 Binder, "A.J. Munsie – Domestic Development Program."

124 BMOA, DDP Case Study, "Bank of Montreal – Domestic Development Program (E)," 2.

125 Ibid.

126 BMOA, M.W. Barrett, AGM 1988 Binder, "A.J. Munsie – Domestic Development Program."

127 Ibid.

128 BMOA, DDP Case Study, "Bank of Montreal – Domestic Development Program (E)," 3–4.

129 BMOA, Oral History Project, Testimony No. 110.

130 Ibid., Testimony No. 117.

131 Ibid., Testimony No. 118.

132 Ibid., Testimony No. 125.

133 Ibid.

134 Ibid.

135 Ibid.

136 "Bank Shares Expected to Be Aided by New Act," *Globe and Mail*, 1 December 1980.

137 BMOA, House of Commons Standing Committee on Finance, Trade & Economic Affairs, 1982 – B/M Chairman: W.D. Mulholland, "Finance Committee Enquiry Into Bank Profits, Q&A Briefing Book," 2: Small Business Hardship Cases.

138 Ibid., n.p.: Mortgage Hardship Cases (2), Supplementary Point.

139 Ibid., 16: Mortgage Hardship Cases.

140 Ibid., 5: Are Bankers Knowledgeable of Farm Operations?

141 Ibid., 12: Small Business Versus Corporate Loan Profits.

142 Ibid., 2: Small Business Hardship Cases.

143 Ibid., 14: Undue Profits on Low Interest Funds.

144 Ibid., 36: Foreign Lending Policy.

145 BMOA, Bank Statement on Public Issues, Circa 1980, "A Reply by Mr McNeil to Questions at the 159th Annual General Meeting, 17 January 1977 (Reference: South Africa – 1977 Annual Meeting. Pages 3 to 8) Pages 10 to 13," 11.

146 BMOA, Bank Statement on Public Issues, Circa 1980, "Statement Release [*sic*] by President and Chief Executive Officer William Mulholland after the 20 May 1980 Reference Vote – 'NON'."

147 BMOA, Bank Statement on Public Issues, Circa 1980, "President William D. Mulholland, in an Address to Senior Management Conference Payment Systems, Inc., in New York, on 15 November 1979."

148 Ibid.

149 BMOA, Bank Statement on Public Issues, Circa 1980, "Mr Mulholland, in His Remarks to the Bank's 162nd annual general meeting, in Montreal, 14 January 1980;" BMOA, Bank of Montreal Annual Report, 1980.

150 Ibid.

151 BMOA, Oral History Project, Testimony No. 12.

152 Ibid., Testimony No. 86.

153 Ibid.

154 BMOA, Bank Statement on Public Issues, Circa 1980, "President William D. Mulholland, in an Address to the Canadian Club, in Montreal, 25 April 1980."

155 BMOA, Bank Statement on Public Issues, Circa 1980, "Chairman Fred H. McNeil, in His Address to the Bank's 162nd Annual General Meeting, 14 January 1980;" BMOA, Bank of Montreal Annual Report, 1980.

156 BMOA, Bank Statement on Public Issues, Circa 1980, "President William D. Mulholland, in an Address with the Title 'Toward a Mineral Industries Policy for Canada,' to the Annual Meeting of the Canadian Institute of Mining and Metallurgy, Toronto, 21 April 1980."

157 BMOA, Bank of Montreal Annual Report, 1986.

158 BMOA, Acquisition de Nesbitt Thomson 7aout au 1 oct 1987, "Nestbitt, Thomson Inc., Summary Statistical Sheet," 1.

159 BMOA, Acquisition de Nesbitt Thomson 7aout au 1 oct 1987, Philippe Dubuisson "Bank of Montreal: Great Expectations. Interview with Senior Management in Toronto," 31 August 1987.

160 BMOA, M.W. Barrett, AGM 1988 Binder, "Nesbitt Thomson Inc."

161 Ibid.

162 Ibid.

163 Charles Freedman, "The Canadian Banking System," Revised version of a paper delivered at the Conference on Developments in the Financial System: National and International Perspectives The Jerome Levy Economics Institute of Bard College Annandale-on-Hudson, New York, 10–11 April 1997, 10.

164 BMOA, Acquisition de Nesbitt Thomson 7 août au 1 oct 1987, "Briefing Note: BMO/Nesbitt Thomson Acquisition Ad"; Charles Calmès, "Regulatory Changes and Financial Structure: The Case of Canada," *Bank of Canada, Working Paper 2004–26*, 12–13; Freedman, "The Canadian Banking System," 11.

165 BMOA, Acquisition de Nesbitt Thomson 7aout au 1 oct 1987, "Briefing Note: BMO/Nesbitt Thomson Acquisition Ad."

166 Ibid.

167 Angela Redish, "It Is History but It's No Accident: Differences in Residential Mortgage Markets in Canada and the United States," in *Current Federal Reserve Policy Under the Lens of Economic History: Essays to Commemorate the Federal Reserve System Centennial*, ed. Owen F. Humpage (Cambridge: Cambridge University Press, 2015), 296–317 at 311; BMOA, Bene-fices economiques dus par l'acquisition, 26 nov 1987 au juin 1991, "Enclosure 1 to Circular #6922: Guidelines: Referral of Existing Bank Clients to Nesbitt Thomson."

168 Gordon F. Boreham, "Three Years after Canada's 'Little Bang,' *Canadian Banker* 87, no. 5 (September/October 1990): 6.

169 BMOA, Burns Fry Limited 18 juillet 1994 au 2 sept 1994, "Autonomy Unviable: Burns Can't Compete with Bank-owned and Foreign Brokerages," *Financial Post*, 19 July 1994.

170 Freedman, "The Canadian Banking System," 5.

171 BMOA, Acquisition de Nesbitt Thomson 7aout au 1 oct 1987, "Press Release, 12 August 1987."

172 Ibid.

173 Ibid.

174 BMOA, Acquisition de Nesbitt Thomson 7aout au 1 oct 1987, Philippe Dubuisson.

175 BMOA, Acquisition de Nesbitt Thomson 7aout au 1 oct 1987, "Nesbitt, Thomson Inc., Summary Statistical Sheet," 1.

176 BMOA, Acquisition de Nesbitt Thomson 7aout au 1 oct 1987, "Interview: Deregulation and the Acquisition of Nesbitt, Thomson, with W.E. Bradford, Phillippe Dubuisson, and Brian Smith," 24 August 1987.

177 BMOA, Acquisition de Nesbitt Thomson 7aout au 1 oct 1987, Philippe Dubuisson.

178 BMOA, Discrimination Linguistique 14 aout 1987 au 8 fev 1988, "Jean-Guy Dubuc, "Éditorial," *La Presse*, 17 August 1987.

179 BMOA, Acquisition de Nesbitt Thomson 7aout au 1 oct 1987, "Memorandum from L.R. O'Hagan to William E. Bradford, 'Media Coverage – Nesbitt, Thomson Acquisition'," 17 August 1987.

180 BMOA, Burns Fry Limited 18 juillet 1994 au 2 sept 1994, "B of M to Lift $100M from Merged Broker," *Financial Post*, 19 July 1994.

181 Ibid.

182 Ibid.

183 BMOA, Nesbitt Thomson/Burns Fry Merger, 1994, "Nesbitt Thomson and Burns Fry Announce Merger Plans."

184 BMOA, Burns Fry Limited 18 juillet 1994 au 2 sept 1994.

185 BMOA, Nesbitt Thomson/Burns Fry Merger, 1994.

186 BMOA, Burns Fry Limited 18 juillet 1994 au 2 sept 1994.

187 BMOA, Oral History Project, Testimony No. 3.

188 Ibid., Testimony No. 70.

189 Ibid., Testimony No. 107.

190 Ibid., Testimony No. 117.

191 Ibid., Testimony No. 118.

192 From 1950 to 1958, it was known as Dome Exploration (Western); "John Patrick Gallagher, Oil Pioneer," *Canadian News Facts*, 16 December 1998, 5798.

193 Jim Lyon, *Dome: The Rise and Fall of the House that Jack built* (Toronto: Avon Books of Canada, 1984).

194 "John Patrick Gallagher, Oil Pioneer."

195 Mike Byfield, "Empire Gallagher Built and Lost: Smiling Jack Passes on but the Arctic Oil Challenge Endures," *Alberta Report*, 11 January 1999, 13–15.

196 Kenneth M. Davidson, *Megamergers: Corporate America's Billion-Dollar Takeovers* (Washington: Beard Books, 2003), 65–6.

197 Byfield, "Empire Gallagher Built and Lost."

198 Ibid.

199 Ibid.

200 BMOA, Public Affairs "Dome Amoco" Media Coverage Binder, "MediaReach, CBC Radio: Sunday Morning," 5 July 1987; BMOA, Various Public Affairs documents, regarding the "Dome Petroleum-Amoco" litigation, "Fact Sheet: Dome Petroleum Limited," June 1987, 2.

201 BMOA, Public Affairs "Dome Amoco" Media Coverage Binder, "Banking Wire: Dome Waivers," 10 July 1987; BMOA, Public Affairs "Dome Amoco" Media Coverage Binder, "Banking Wire: Dome Talks Continue," 26 May 1987.

202 BMOA, Public Affairs "Dome Amoco" Media Coverage Binder, "Banking Wire: Dome Waivers."

203 BMOA, Public Affairs "Dome Amoco" Media Coverage Binder, "Lenders Milking Dome for Billions," *Calgary Herald*, 9 July 1987.

204 BMOA, Public Affairs "Dome Amoco" Media Coverage Binder, "Creditors Push Dome into Financial Limbo," *The Citizen*, 10 July 1987; BMOA, Various Public Affairs documents regarding the "Dome Petroleum-Amoco" litigation, "Fact Sheet: Dome Petroleum Limited," 2.

205 BMOA, Public Affairs "Dome Amoco" Media Coverage Binder, "Media Tapes and Transcripts, Special Report: Senate Hearings into Sale of Dome Petroleum," 8 July 1987.

206 BMOA, Public Affairs "Dome Amoco" Media Coverage Binder, "Banking Wire: Dome Fight Not Over," 16 June 1987.

207 BMOA, Public Affairs "Dome Amoco" Media Coverage Binder, "Media Tapes and Transcripts, Special Report: Senate Hearings into sale of Dome Petroleum."

208 BMOA, Public Affairs "Dome Amoco" Media Coverage Binder, "Media Tapes and Transcripts, State Governments Ask for Investigation of Dome/Amoco deal," 8 July 1987.

209 BMOA, Public Affairs "Dome Amoco" Media Coverage Binder, "Banking Wire," 4 June 1987.

210 BMOA, Public Affairs "Dome Amoco" Media Coverage Binder, "Banking Wire: Dome Fight Not Over."

211 BMOA, Various Public Affairs documents regarding the "Dome Petroleum-Amoco" litigation, "J.H. Macdonald Press Conference," 22 April 1987.

212 BMOA, Public Affairs "Dome Amoco" Media Coverage Binder, "Banking Wire: Cool Reception to Amoco Offer," 19 May 1987.

213 BMOA, Public Affairs "Dome Amoco" Media Coverage Binder, "Media Tapes and Transcripts, Amoco Won't Offer More Cash for Dome," 20 May 1987.

214 BMOA, Various Public Affairs documents regarding the "Dome Petroleum-Amoco" litigation, "Memorandum from Harry W. Macdonell to L. Richard O'Hagan," 19 June 1987.

215 BMOA, Public Affairs "Dome Amoco" Media Coverage Binder, "Banking Wire," 4 June 1987.

216 BMOA, Bank of Montreal Annual Report, 1987.

217 BMOA, Various Public Affairs documents regarding the "Dome Petroleum-Amoco" litigation, "Chronology of Recent Events Related to Dome-Amoco proposal," 1987.

218 BMOA, Public Affairs "Dome Amoco" Media Coverage Binder, "Media Tapes and Transcripts, Bank of Montreal Continues Effort to Block Sale of Dome," 3 July 1987; BMOA, Public Affairs "Dome Amoco" Media Coverage Binder, "Media Tapes and Transcripts, Bank of Montreal Loses Bid to Block Dome Sale," 2 May 1987.

219 BMOA, Public Affairs Affairs "Dome Amoco" Media Coverage Binder, "Media Tapes and Transcripts, Bank of Montreal Loses Bid to Block Dome Sale"; BMOA, Various Public Affairs documents regarding the "Dome Petroleum-Amoco" litigation, "Chronology of Recent Events Related to Dome-Amoco Proposal."

220 BMOA, Public Affairs "Dome Amoco" Media Coverage Binder, "Media Tapes and Transcripts, Bank May Be Held Responsible for Losses to Dome's Creditors," 9 July 1987.

221 BMOA, Public Affairs "Dome Amoco" Media Coverage Binder, "Bank Used Same Tactic, Dome says," *Calgary Herald*, 9 July 1987.

222 BMOA, Public Affairs "Dome Amoco" Media Coverage Binder, "Amoco, CIBC Threaten Bank of Montreal," *Globe and Mail*, 9 July 1987; BMOA, Public Affairs "Dome Amoco" Media Coverage Binder, "Bank Lawyers Clash at Hearing to Reopen Dome Bidding," *Toronto Star*, 9 July 1987.

223 BMOA, Public Affairs "Dome Amoco" Media Coverage Binder, "Media Tapes and Transcripts, Legal Action Threatened Against the Bank of Montreal," 13 July 1987.

224 BMOA, Public Affairs "Dome Amoco" Media Coverage Binder, "MediaReach, CBC Radio: Sunday Morning," 5 July 1987.

225 BMOA, Various Public Affairs documents regarding the "Dome Petroleum-Amoco" litigation, "Memorandum from Harry W. Macdonell to L. Richard O'Hagan."

226 BMOA, Public Affairs "Dome Amoco" Media Coverage Binder, "MediaReach, CBC Radio: Sunday Morning."

227 BMOA, Public Affairs "Dome Amoco" Media Coverage Binder, "Banking Wire: Ways to Save Dome Pete," 14 May 1987.

228 BMOA, Public Affairs "Dome Amoco" Media Coverage Binder, "MediaReach, CTV TV: Canada AM," 15 May 1987.

229 "Bank Misses Deadline for Early Dome Appeal," *Toronto Star*, 9 September 1987.

230 "Amoco Said Exploring an Improved Offer for Dome Pete," *Toronto Star*, 17 September 1987.

231 "Amoco Offers Dome's Banks $100 million More," *Toronto Star*, 27 August 1987.

232 "Amoco Raises Offer for Dome Petroleum," *Toronto Star*, 8 October 1987.

233 "Study Finds Dome Worth More than Amoco's Offer," *Toronto Star*, 19 October 1987.

234 BMOA, Various Public Affairs documents regarding the "Dome Petroleum-Amoco" litigation, "Chronology of Recent Events Related to Dome-Amoco Proposal."

235 "Amoco Offer for Dome Climbs $400 million," *Toronto Star*, 18 November 1987.

236 "Company News: Amoco Completes Takeover of Dome," *The New York Times*, 2 September 1988.

237 BMOA, Bank of Montreal Annual Report, 1988.

238 BMOA, Bio-File: W.D. Mulholland, "Tough Bosses: William Mulholland," Unknown publication, December 1987.

239 Ibid.

240 BMOA, File: W.D. Mulholland, "The Toughest Guy at the Top," *Canadian Business*, July 1987.

241 BMOA, Bio-File: W.D. Mulholland, "New York's Newest Banker," 74.

242 BMOA, Oral History Project, Testimony No. 123.

243 BMOA, Bio-File: W.D. Mulholland, Daniel Stoffman, "Management by Mayhem," *Report on Business Magazine*, May 1989, 42.

244 Ibid., 43.

245 Ibid., 44.

246 BMOA, Oral History Project, Testimony No. 6.

247 Ibid., Testimony No. 40.

248 Ibid., Testimony No. 12.

249 Ibid.

250 Ibid., Testimony No. 109.

251 BMOA, Bio-File: W.D. Mulholland, Chisholm, "Stepping Aside: A Combative Banker Hands Over the Reins,"

252 BMOA, Bio-File: W.D. Mulholland, Shortell, "The Lion in Winter."

253 BMOA, Bio-File: W.D. Mulholland, Terence Corcoran, "Mulholland's Heir Needs to Build Team," *Financial Post*, 18 January 1989.

254 Brünnhilde in Richard Wagner's Götterdämmerung (Trans: "My heritage yields now the hero."). Excerpted from DM's Opera Site: www.murashev.com/opera/G%C3%B6tterd%C3%A4mmerung_libretto_English_German (accessed 8 September 2018)

255 BMOA, Bio-File: W.D. Mulholland, Shortell, "The Lion in Winter."

256 BMOA, Bio-File: W.D. Mulholland, Larry Welsh, "Bad Boy Bill Mulholland to Quit Bank of Montreal," *Toronto Star*, 17 January 1989.

257 Ibid.

258 BMOA, Bio-File: W.D. Mulholland, Corcoran, "Mulholland's Heir Needs to Build Team."

259 BMOA, Bio-File: W.D. Mulholland, Welsh, "Bad Boy Bill Mulholland to Quit Bank of Montreal."

260 BMOA, Bio-File: W.D. Mulholland, Corcoran, "Mulholland's Heir Needs to Build Team."

261 BMOA, Oral History Project, Matthew Barrett.

262 Ibid., Testimony No. 9.

263 Ibid., Testimony No. 21.

264 Ibid., Testimony No. 40.

265 Inspired by the insight of John Lewis Gaddis, *On Grand Strategy* (New York: Penguin Press, 2018), 56.

266 For a discussion of this leadership phenomenon, see Gaddis, *On Grand Strategy*, 47.

267 Shakespeare's Ulysses in *Troilus and Cressida*, Act 1, Scene 3, lines 112–27, paraphrased in Gaddis, *On Grand Strategy*, 47. "Then every thing includes itself in power, Power into will, will into appetite, And appetite, an universal world, So doubly seconded with will and power, Must make perforce an universal prey, And last east up himself. Great Agamemnon, This chaos, when degree is suffocate, Follows the choking. And this neglection of degree it is That by a pace goes backward, with a purpose, It hath to climb."

268 BMOA, Oral History Project, Testimony No. 4.

269 Ibid., Testimony No. 6.

270 Ibid., Testimony No. 40.

Chapter Eighteen

1 BMOA, Bank of Montreal Annual Report, 2017.

2 Jay Pridmore, *Harris: A History of the Bank* (Chicago: History Works, 2009), 190.

3 BMOA, Harris Bank, Pre-purchase "Blue Book" + Information on Harris + BMO fit, "Status Report as at 21 April 1983: Description of Park," 1.

4 Ibid.

5 Ibid., 1–4.

6 Ibid., 6.

7 Ibid.

8 Ibid., 8.

9 Ibid., 11–12.

10 An Edge Act Bank is a subsidiary that carries out international banking and financing operations under the Edge Act of 1919. See "Edge Act and Agreement Corporations in International Banking and Finance," *Federal Reserve Monthly Review*, May 1964, 88.

11 BMOA, Harris Bank, Pre-purchase "Blue Book" + Information on Harris + BMO fit. "Status Report," 13.

12 Ibid., 21.

13 For a detailed, informative, and entertaining examination of the history of the Harris Bank, see Pridmore, *Harris*. The book was commissioned by the bank a quarter century after its acquisition by the Bank of Montreal. See also Laurence B. Mussio, *A Vision Greater Than Themselves: The Making of the Bank of Montreal, 1817–2017* (Montreal/Kingston: McGill-Queen's University Press, 2016), 61, 147.

14 Pridmore, *Harris*, 167–8.

15 Ibid., 172.

16 BMOA, Harris Bank, Pre-purchase "Blue Book" + Information on Harris + BMO fit, "Status Report," 20–1.

17 Ibid.

18 Pridmore, *Harris*, 173.

19 BMOA, Oral History Project, Testimony No. 31.

20 Ibid.

21 The 1982 Competitive Situation Report, prepared by Greenwich Research Associates, quoted in BMOA, Harris Bank, Pre-purchase "Blue Book" + Information on Harris + BMO fit, "Status Report," 28.

22 Ibid., 20–1.

23 BMOA, Harris Bank, Pre-purchase "Blue Book" + Information on Harris + BMO fit, "Project Park: Peer Group Comparison," 1.

24 Ibid., 1.

25 BMOA, Harris Bank, Pre-purchase "Blue Book" + Information on Harris + BMO fit, "Legal Matters: Restructuring of BMO Necessary to Permit Acquisition," 1.

26 Ibid., 1.

27 Ibid., 1–4.

28 Ibid.

29 BMOA, Harris Bank, Pre purchase "Blue Book" + Information on Harris + BMO fit, "Fit between Park and BMO – Potential Synergies," 3.

30 Ibid., 3.

31 Ibid.

32 Ibid., 4.

33 Ibid.

34 Timothy H. Hannan and Stephen A. Rhoades, "Acquisition Targets and Motives: The Case of the Banking Industry," *The Review of Economics and Statistics* 69, no. 1 (1987): 67–74, here 67.

35 "B of M Talks in US Get Mixed Reactions," *Globe and Mail*, 11 November 1978.

36 Ibid.

37 Ibid.

38 BMOA, Oral History Project, Testimony No. 12.

39 Ibid., Testimony No. 9.

40 BMOA, Preliminary Application for Federal Reserve, Board Approval – Harris Merger, "Statement of Reasons Supporting Bank of Montreal's Application to Acquire Harris Bankcorp, Inc.," 3.

41 Pridmore, *Harris*, 192; Mussio, *A Vision Great Than Themselves*, 61; BMOA Chicago, Harris Bankcorp, Inc. Annual Report, 1983; BMOA, Bank of Montreal Annual Report, 1983; BMOA, Corporate Communications/Harris Acquisition Public Affairs File, "Summary: Agreement and Plan of Merger," 2 October 1983; "No Hurdle Seen in Bank Merger," *Globe and Mail*, 28 July 1984; "B of M Sees Completion of Merger," *Globe and Mail*, 22 August 1984; "Bank of Montreal Completes Purchase of Harris Bankcorp.," *Wall Street Journal*, 5 September 1984.

42 Pridmore, *Harris*, 191.

43 "Bank of Montreal Completes Purchase of Harris Bankcorp."; BMOA, Corporate Communications/Harris Acquisition Public Affairs File, "Summary: Agreement and Plan of Merger"; BMOA, Harris Acquisition Closing, Public Affairs File, "Possible Questions and Suggested Answers Relating to the Acquisition of the Harris Bank," 2, 3.

44 BMOA Chicago, "Two Years After the Merger: A Special Look," *Harris Herald*, September 1986, 3.

45 BMOA, Preliminary Application for Federal Reserve, Board Approval – Harris Merger, "Statement of Reasons Supporting Bank of Montreal's Application to Acquire Harris Bankcorp, Inc.," 4; BMOA, Harris Acquisition Closing, Public Affairs File, "Possible Questions and Suggested Answers Relating to the Acquisition of the Harris Bank," 1, 2, 3.

46 BMOA Chicago, Harris Bankcorp, Inc. Annual Report, 1983.

47 BMOA, Preliminary Application for Federal Reserve, Board Approval – Harris Merger, "Statement of Reasons," 21, 23–9.

48 BMOA, Preliminary Application for Federal Reserve, Board Approval – Harris Merger, "Statement of Reasons Supporting Bank of Montreal's Application to Acquire Harris Bankcorp, Inc.," Bank of Montreal Capital Adequacy Discussion Paper (DRAFT), 24 September 1983.

49 Ibid.

50 Ibid.

51 BMOA Chicago, BMO Acquisition Various Documents, "Federal Reserve Press Release, 25 July 1984." See also the State of Illinois Office of Commissioner of Banks and Trust Companies, 29 August 1984. Change of Control acknowledgement of the deal, notarized by William C. Harris.

52 BMOA Chicago, Harris Bankcorp, Inc. Annual Report, 1983.

53 Ibid.

54 Ibid.

55 Ibid.

56 Ibid.

57 BMOA Chicago, Harris Acquisition Closing, Public Affairs File, "A New Chapter in Our History."

58 BMOA Chicago, Harris Acquisition Closing, Public Affairs File, "Merger Salute," *Belleville News Democrat*, 5 September 1984; "We Bought a US Bank," *Edmonton Sun*, 5 September 1984.

59 BMOA Chicago, Harris Acquisition Closing, Public Affairs File, "Harris Bank Takeover Is Official," *Globe and Mail*, 5 September 1984. See also "Merger," *Dallas Times-Herald*, 5 September 1984; "Bank Merger Official," *Chesterton Tribune*, 5 September 1984; "Two Flags, One Venture," *Detroit News*, 9 September 1984.

60 BMOA Chicago, "Opportunities Look Better for All," *Harris Herald*, November 1983, 1.

61 BMOA Chicago, BMO Acquisition Various Documents, "The Harris Connection: Remarks by W.E. Bradford Deputy Chairman Bank of Montreal to Canadian Association for Corporate Growth, 26 March 1985."

62 Ibid., 3.

63 Ibid., 6.

64 Ibid.

65 Ibid., 7.

66 For a more detailed account of this era from the Harris perspective, see Pridmore, *Harris*, chapter 8.

67 BMOA Chicago, "Two Years After the Merger: A Special Look," 2.

68 Ibid.

69 Ibid., 3.

70 BMOA Chicago, Harris Bankcorp, Inc. Annual Report, 1986.

71 BMOA, Bank of Montreal Annual Report, 1997.

72 BMOA Chicago, "Two Years After the Merger: A Special Look," 3.

73 Ibid.

74 Ibid., 5.

75 BMOA, Oral History Project, Testimony No. 92.

76 Ibid., Testimony No. 44.

77 Ibid., Testimony No. 74.

78 Ibid., Testimony No. 92.

79 Ibid., Testimony No. 29.

80 Quoted in Pridmore, *Harris*, 202.

81 BMOA, Oral History Project, Testimony No. 74.

82 Ibid., Testimony No. 99.

83 Ibid.

84 Ibid., Testimony No. 51.

85 Ibid.

86 Ibid., Testimony No. 29.

87 Ibid., Testimony No. 114.

88 Ibid., Testimony No. 23.

89 Ibid., Testimony No. 73.

90 Ibid., Testimony No. 81.

91 Ibid., Testimony No. 23.

92 Ibid., Testimony No. 124.

93 Ibid., Testimony No. 32.

94 Maurizio Zollo and H. Singh, "Deliberate Learning in Corporate Acquisitions: Post-acquisition Strategies and Integration Capability in US Bank Mergers," *Strategic Management Journal* 25 (2004): 1233–56 at 1251.

95 Maurizio Zollo, "Superstitious Learning with Rare Strategic Decisions Theory and Evidence from Corporate Acquisitions," *Organization Science* 20, no. 5 (2009): 894–908 at 894.

96 Ibid.; Barbara Levitt and James G. March, "Organizational Learning," *Annual Review of Sociology* 14: 319–40 at 325.

97 Zollo, "Superstitious Learning," 894–908 at 904.

98 Harry G. Barkema and Mario Schijven, "Toward Unlocking the Full Potential of Acquisitions: The Role of Organizational Restructuring," *The Academy of Management Journal* 51, no. 4 (2008): 696–722 at 696; Wouter Dessein, Luis Garicano, and Robert Gertner, "Organizing for Synergies," *American Economic Journal: Microeconomics* 2 (2010): 77–114; Günter K. Stahl and Andreas Vogt, "Do Cultural Differences Matter in Mergers and Acquisitions? A Tentative Model and Examination," *Organization Science* 19, no. 1 (2008): 160–76.

99 *Lincoln* (2012), The Internet Movie Database. www.imdb.com/title/tt0443272/quotes (accessed 15 March 2016). Quoted in John Lewis Gaddis, *On Grand Strategy* (New York: Penguin Press, 2018), 17.

100 To extend the metaphor a bit far, scientists have suggested four ways that the universe could meet its end: the Big Freeze, the Big Crunch, the Big Change, and the Big Rip, which, with the exception of the last one, would not be a bad way to describe the phases of integration between the Bank of Montreal and the Harris Bank. See Adam Becker, "How Will the Universe End, and Could Anything Survive?" 2 June 2015, www.bbc.com/earth/story/20150602-how-will-the-universe-end (accessed 5 September 2016).

Chapter Nineteen

1 What's Behind the Rorschach Inkblot Test? *BBC News*, 25 July 2012. www.bbc.com/news/magazine-18952667 (accessed 24 July 2018).

2 For this idea, see G.K. Chesterton, "Orthodoxy," in G.K. Chesterton, *Three Apologies of G.K. Chesterton: Heretics, Orthodoxy & the Everlasting Man* (Bristol: Mockingbird Press, 2018).

3 G.K. Chesterton, *Three Apologies*.

4 P. Nagy, *The International Business of Canadian Banks* (Montreal: Centre for International Business Studies, École des Hautes Études Commerciales, Montreal, April 1983), 389.

5 Ibid., 41.

6 BMOA, Oral History Project, Testimony No. 13.

7 James Darroch, "Global Competitiveness and Public Policy: The Case of Canadian Multinational Banks," *Business History* 34, no. 3 (1992): 153–75, here 157.

8 Stefano Battilossi, "Financial Innovation and the Golden Ages of International Banking: 1890–1931 and 1958–81," *Financial History Review* 7, no. 2 (2000): 141–75, here 145.

9 Ibid., 146; R. Cameron, "Introduction," in *International Banking 1870–1914*, eds. R. Cameron and V.I. Bovyking (Oxford: Oxford University Press, 1991), 12–14.

10 Battilossi, "Financial Innovation," 157.

11 Ibid., 158.

12 Ibid., 169.

13 Darroch, "Global Competitiveness and Public Policy," 162.

14 Ibid., 163.

15 Ibid.

16 Ibid., 164.

17 BMOA, Executive Committee of the Board, Minutes, 10 March 1970.

18 Wallace Clement, *Continental Corporate Power: Economic Elite Linkages between Canada and the United States* (Toronto: McClelland and Stewart, 1977), 119, 312.

19 Ibid., 119.

20 BOLSA was founded in 1923.

21 BMOA, "BOLSA Investigation, January 1958," 62.

22 Ibid.

23 Ibid.

24 Ibid.

25 Ibid.

26 Ibid., 11.

27 Ibid., 49.

28 Ibid., 15.

29 Ibid., 13.

30 BMOA, BOLAM, 1959–1961, "For the Information of the Board – 16 December, 1958: Bank of London & Montreal Limited."

31 Ibid.

32 BMOA, Executive Committee of the Board, Minutes, date illegible – 4 or 8 November 1963.

33 Ibid.

34 Carlo Edoardo Altamura, *European Banks and the Rise of International Finance: The Post-Bretton Woods Era* (New York: Routledge, 2017), 42.

35 BMOA, BOLAM, 1959–1961, "Strictly Confidential Letter from George Bolton to Julian S. Crossley," 20 February 1959.

36 BMOA, BOLAM, 1959–1961, "Strictly Confidential Letter from Julian S. Crossley to George Bolton," 16 February 1959.

37 Ibid.

38 BMOA, Executive Committee of the Board, Minutes, 15 October 1964.

39 BMOA, Bank of Bahamas, "Letter from P.R. Shaddick, Executive Vice-President International Banking, to Carleton E. Francis, Minister of Finance, Commonwealth of the Bahama Islands," 16 February 1970.

40 BMOA, Executive Committee of the Board, Minutes, 27 January 1970.

41 Ibid. The Bahamas branches excluded BOLAM's International Department and the Trust Department, which operated in Nassau.

42 BMOA, Executive Committee of the Board, Minutes, 27 January 1970.

43 Ibid.

44 "Trinidad Moves to Take Over Canadian Bank," *Globe and Mail*, 24 March 1970.

45 Ibid.

46 BMOA, Bank of Montreal Annual Report, 1970.

47 "Bank of Montreal Plans for Acquisitions," *Globe and Mail*, 25 March 1970.

48 Ibid.

49 "New Jamaican Company Planned by Royal Bank," *Globe and Mail*, 8 December 1970.

50 "Jamaica Plans to Control 3 Banks," *Globe and Mail*, 21 January 1977.

51 "Important Notice from the Bank of Surrey, Ltd," *Kingston Gleaner*, 6 July 1978.
    Note: One of the possible reasons why the Bank of Montreal was able to operate in Jamaica for much longer than in Trinidad might be because of resentment toward the British. While both Jamaica and The Bahamas remained part of the Commonwealth after independence (in 1962 and 1973, respectively), Trinidad did not.

52 BMOA, Bank of Montreal Annual Report, 1970.

53 BMOA, Bank of Bahamas, "Presentation to The Government of The Bahamas By Bank of Montreal Re: Canadian Caribbean Banking Corporation," 16 February 1970.

54 Ibid.

55 BMOA, Executive Committee of the Board, Minutes, 24 March 1970.

56 BMOA, Bank of Bahamas, "Presentation to The Government of The Bahamas."

57 BMOA, Bank of Bahamas, "Bank of Montreal Bahamas Ltd Selling Paper, Bank of Montreal Bahamas Corporate Planning, September 1985."

58 BMOA, Bank of Bahamas, "Review – Bank of Montreal Bahamas Ltd."

59 BMOA, Bank of Bahamas, "Review Bank of Montreal Bahamas Ltd, Bank of Montreal Bahamas Corporate Planning," 1985.

60 Ibid.

61 BMOA, Bank of Bahamas, "Review Bank of Montreal Bahamas Ltd, Bank of Montreal Bahamas Corporate Planning, Appendix A: Detailed Overview of Trends," 1985.

62 Ibid.

63 Ibid.

64 Ibid.

65 Ibid.

66 BMOA, Oral History Project, Testimony No. 4.

67 Ibid., Testimony No. 73.

68 BMOA, Bank of Bahamas, "Review Bank of Montreal Bahamas Ltd, Bank of Montreal Bahamas Corporate Planning."

69 BMOA, Bank of Bahamas, "Bank of Montreal Bahamas Ltd Selling Paper."

70 BMOA, Bank of Bahamas, "Potential Sale of Bank of Montreal Bahamas Limited," 21 June 1985.

71 BMOA, Closing of the Bahamas Branch, "Memorandum from the Deputy Chairman, G.L. Reuber, to the Chairman and CEO, William D. Mulholland," 23 August 1988.

72 BMOA, "Bank Agreement," *The Nassau Guardian*, 1 September 1988.

73 Ibid.

74 BMOA, Mexico, Memos & Precis, 1926–1927; Mexico – Report on Accounts, "Mexico Branch Business," 20 October 1923.

75 BMOA, Executive Committee of the Board, Minutes, 4 January 1945.

76 BMOA, Correspondence – Closure of Mexican branches, "Memorandum for Mr Spinney," 17 January 1945.

77 "Canadian Bank Back in Mexico," *Financial Post*, 12 September 1964.

78 BMOA, Mexico – General File, 1930–1990s, "Up Mexico Way," *Canadian Business*, January 1997.

79 Ibid.

80 BMOA, Mexico – General File, 1930–1990s, "B of M Closes Deal to Buy 16% of Mexican Bank," *Globe and Mail*, 30 March 1996.

81 BMOA, Bank of Montreal Annual Report, 1928.

82 BMOA, "Bank of Montreal & Trade with China: A Historical Perspective."

83 Ibid.

84 Ibid.

85 Ibid.

86 Ibid.

87 BMOA, Chairman's Visit to the People's Republic of China, "Confidential: Chairman's Visit to the People's Republic of China," 23 June 1971, 1.

88 BMOA, Bank of Montreal Annual Report, 1954, "Nothing Ever Happens to a Banker ..."

89 BMOA, Chairman's Visit to the People's Republic of China, "Confidential," 2.

90 Ibid., 5.

91 Ibid., 7–8.

92 Ibid., 16.

93 Ibid., 24.

94 Ibid., 27.

95 Ibid., Appendix 2.

96 BMOA, Chairman's Visit to the People's Republic of China, "Call Report 14 June 1971, Call made by G. Arnold Hart and H.C. Hartmann."

97 Ibid.

98 Ibid.

99 Ibid.

100 Ibid.

101 BMOA, Chairman's Second Visit to the People's Republic of China, "Chairman's Second Visit to the People's Republic of China, May 1975."

102 On the subject of entertainment, for example, Hart reported that "the hotel seemed filled with people of every nationality, including about twelve thug-like individuals who turned out to be members of the PLO [Palestinian Liberation Organization]. They invariably arrived at breakfast and departed in a group. On our subsequent trip to the Great Wall of China, we encountered them on the Wall as they were having a group photograph taken. I promptly filmed them with my movie camera to the displeasure of at least one member who was dressed in a camouflage outfit. I think my wife and the van Dongens [of the Hong Kong Office] envisaged me, camera and all, being hurled over the Wall on the Mongolian side!" BMOA, Chairman's Second Visit to the People's Republic of China, "Chairman's Second Visit." A later correspondent admonished Hart for not taking the threat seriously enough.

103 BMOA, Chairman's Second Visit to the People's Republic of China, 1975, "TM Burns Senior Asst. Deputy Minister International Trade from Acting General Director, Pacific, Asia and Africa Bureau, RE: China – Meeting with Mr Arnold Hart, Chairman of the Board, Bank of Montreal, 10 April 1975.

104 Ibid.

105 BMOA, Chairman's Second Visit to the People's Republic of China, 1975, "Peking 13 May 1975 – Bank of China People's Republic of China, Peking, G. Arnold Hart, C. van Dongen).

106 Ibid., 3.

107 Ibid., 12.

108 Ibid., 12–13.

109 Ibid., 13.

110 BMOA, Chairman's Second Visit to the People's Republic of China, 1975, "P. Papadopoulos and Y. Sûsé, 'The People's Republic of China: A Survey of Current Trends in Politics, Economics and Foreign Trade,'" 11 April 1975 (update of study of 30 April 1972).

111 BMOA, Trips – South-Asia, "Memorandum of Call, Bank of China Hong Kong Branch, 31 October 1978: Senior Executive Visit to Foster B/M Bank of China Relationship and to Explore Business Opportunities Given PRC Attitude Change re: Economic Growth and Borrowing."

112 BMOA, Press Releases – English, 1983, "China's Involvement in International Affairs a Key Development of Our Time, Says Bank of Montreal's Chairman," 16 March 1983.

113 BMOA, "China Welcomes Bank Team," *First Bank News*, March 1983.

114 BMOA, "... and Bank Team Visits China Site," *First Bank News*, July 1985.

115 BMOA, "Bank of Montreal in Asia," *First Bank News*, August 1987.

116 Ibid.

117 Ibid.

118 Ibid.

119 Ibid.

120 BMOA, Oral History Project, Testimony No. 98.

121 Ibid.

122 BMOA, "Bank of Montreal & Trade with China: A Historical Perspective."

123 Ibid.

124 Ibid.

125 BMOA, "Hong Kong/China: How Private Banking Centre Funnels Business Back to Canada," *First Bank News*, 1991. For more on this, see Margaret Cannon, *China Tide: The Revealing Story of the Hong Kong Exodus to Canada* (Don Mills: Harper & Collins, 1989).

126 BMOA, Oral History Project, Testimony No. 15.

127 Ibid.

128 "Brazil to Suspend Interest Payments to Foreign Banks," *New York Times*, 21 February 1987.

129 BMOA, Oral History Project, Testimony No. 71.

130 Ibid., Testimony No. 124.

131 "Brazil to Suspend Interest Payments to Foreign Banks."

132 BMOA, Oral History Project, Testimony No. 12.

133 Ibid.

134 BMOA, Brazilian Debt to Equity Conversions, 1987, "Bank of Scotland Converts Brasil Debts to Investments in Sao Paulo [*sic*]."

135 BMOA, Oral History Project, Testimony No. 9.

136 BMOA, Brazilian Debt to Equity Conversions, 1987, "Investor Relations Issues, Question 9."

137 BMOA, Brazilian Debt to Equity Conversions, 1987, "New Approach to Debt-Equity Swaps to Be Applied to Brazil."

138 Ibid.

139 BMOA, Brazilian Debt to Equity Conversions, 1987, "Strictly Private and Confidential: Report on Establishment of Brazilian Investment Vehicles through Debt-To-Equity Conversions," 30 March 1970 – Appendix 12: Communications Plan.

140 BMOA, Brazilian Debt to Equity Conversions, 1987, "Brazil: Economic Prospects and Outlook."

141 BMOA, Oral History Project, Testimony No. 67.

142 Ibid.

143 Ibid., Testimony No. 120.

144 Ibid., Testimony No. 39.

Chapter Twenty

1 BMOA, "Retiring Chairman Exits in Style," *First Bank News*, 14, no. 1: 1990.

2 Apologies to Ramsay Cook, the late Canadian historian, who wrote an award-winning book by that name.

3 BMOA, Quoted in Matthew Barrett Biofile F1-S5120, John Greenwood, "Matthew Barrett," *Financial Post Magazine*, November 1995.

4 Ibid.

5 Ibid.

6 BMOA, Matthew Barrett Biofile F1-S5120, Ann Shortell, "Can Matthew Barrett Revive the Ailing Bank of Montreal?" *Financial Times of Canada*, 23 January 1989.

7 BMOA, Matthew Barrett Biofile F1-S5120, Dick O'Hagan, "A Fond Farewell to M. Barrett," *Globe and Mail*, 6 March 1999.

8   BMOA, Matthew Barrett Biofile F1-S5120, Greenwood, "Matthew Barrett."

9   BMOA, Quoted in Matthew Barrett Biofile F1-S5120, Judy Steed, "The Radical Banker," *Toronto Star*, 19 November 1995.

10 BMOA, F. Anthony Comper Biofile F1-S5120.

11 BMOA, Jeffrey S. Chisholm, F1-S5120, "Jeffrey S. Chisholm Biography, January 1997."

12 BMOA, Alan G. McNally Biofile, F1_S5120, March 2001.

13 BMOA, Bank of Montreal Annual Report, 1990.

14 BMOA, "Matthew W. Barrett, Bristol Place Conference Evening Address, 19 April 1990," 1.

15 Ibid., 2.

16 Ibid., 3.

17 Ibid., 4.

18 Ibid., 8, 10, 12.

19 Ibid., 18, 20.

20 BMOA, "Change and Teamwork Highlight New Strategic Plan," *First Bank News* 14, no. 3 (1990), 3.

21 BMOA, Corporate Strategic Plan, Excellence: Making the Commitment.

22 BMOA, "Executive Officer Meeting Bristol Place Hotel, Financial Strategy," by K.O. Dorricott, Executive Vice-President and Chief Financial Officer, 19 April 1990.

23 BMOA, Communication Guide: Excellence: Making the Commitment.

24 BMOA, Bank of Montreal Annual Report, 1990.

25 BMOA, Bristol Place Conference, 19 April 1990.

26 BMOA, Bank of Montreal Annual Report, 1991.

27 Ibid.

28 See BMOA, Matthew W. Barrett, "Shaping a Board of Directors for the Future," James Gillies Alumni Lecture, May 1992.

29 Ibid.

30 BMOA, Bank of Montreal Annual Report, 1991.

31 BMOA, Bank of Montreal Annual Report, 1990.

32 "Bank of Montreal Unveils Plan for Employee Training Centre," *Toronto Star*, 2 October 1991.

33 BMOA, Bank of Montreal Annual Report, 1993.

34 BMOA, Bank of Montreal Annual Report, 1994.

35 BMOA, Bank of Montreal Annual Report, 1990.

36 BMOA, Oral History Project, Testimony No. 39.

37 Ibid., Testimony No. 92.

38 Ibid., Testimony No. 125.

39 Ibid., Testimony No. 26.

40 BMOA, "Report of the Task Force on the Advancement of Women in the Bank," November 1991, 3.

41 BMOA, Oral History Project, Testimony No. 92.

42 Ibid., Testimony No. 19.

43 BMOA, Bank of Montreal Annual Report, 1994.

44 BMOA, Oral History Project, Testimony No. 11.

45 BMOA, "Report of the Task Force on the Advancement of Aboriginal Employment," September 1992.

46 BMOA, Oral History Project, Testimony No. 119.

47 BMOA, Bank of Montreal Annual Report, 1995.

48 BMOA, Bank of Montreal Annual Report, 1992.

49 Steve Klinkerman, "Bank of Montreal's Barrett Maps Aggressive Expansion," *The American Banker*, 5 October 1992.

50 Ibid.

51 Ibid.

52 BMOA, Bank of Montreal Annual Report, 1993.

53 Ibid.

54 BMOA, Bank of Montreal Annual Report, 1996.

55 "Bank of Montreal Now Listed on NYSE," *Hamilton Spectator*, 28 October 1994.

56 BMOA, Bank of Montreal Annual Report, 1997.

57 BMOA, Bank of Montreal Annual Report, 1999.

58 BMOA, Bank of Montreal Annual Report, 2005.

59 Paul Waldie, "B of M Closes Deal to Buy 16 Percent of Mexican Bank," *Globe and Mail*, 30 March 1996.

60 BMOA, Oral History Project, Testimony No. 124.

61 BMOA, Bank of Montreal Annual Report, 1995.

62 "BMO Set to Open Branch in Beijing," *Gazette* (Montreal), 29 August 1997.

63 BMOA, Bank of Montreal Annual Report, 1997.

64 "BMO Set to Open Branch in Beijing."

65 BMOA, Oral History Project, Testimony No. 6.

66 Bill Downe, "Congratulatory Message to Neil Tait, Special Advisor to China, BMO Financial Group," 22 December 2014, from in-house collection, "Messages from Bill Downe, Chief Executive Officer BMO Financial Group, 2007–2017," 395.

67 Rick Haliechuk, "Bank Buys Two Asian Branches," *Toronto Star*, 1 September 1994.

68 BMOA, Oral History Project, Testimony No. 27.

69 BMOA, Matthew Barrett Biofile F1-S5120, Greenwood, "Matthew Barrett."

70 BMOA, Bank of Montreal Annual Report, 1995.

71 BMOA, Bank of Montreal Annual Report, 1997.

72 Ibid.

73 BMOA, Bank of Montreal Annual Report, 1995.

74 Rick Haliechuk, "2 Banks Gear Up for Information Highway," *Toronto Star*, 12 January 1995.

75 BMOA, Oral History Project, Testimony No. 96.

76 Ibid., Testimony Nos. 8, 96.

77 BMOA, Bank of Montreal Annual Report, 1996.

78 Ibid.

79 BMOA, Oral History Project, Testimony No. 101.

80 BMOA, Bank of Montreal Annual Report, 1997.

81 BMOA, Oral History Project, Matthew Barrett.

82 Ibid., Testimony No. 49.

83 Ibid., Testimony No. 90.

84 Ibid., Testimony No. 49.

Chapter Twenty-One

1 Ovid, *The Fall of Icarus*, trans. Mary Innes (London: Penguin Classics First Edition, 2015), location 123, Kindle.

2 Bertrand Marotte, "Banks Need Mergers to Compete Globally, Barrett Says," *Ottawa Citizen*, 12 September 1997.

3 The documents referred to in this and subsequent notes under "Privy Council Office" are never-before-released documents were obtained under the Access to Information Act, Request A-2018-00410. Government of Canada, Privy Council Office (hereafter GOC/PCO) Secret. Cabinet Meeting, Tuesday, 15 September 1998, 10:00 a.m.–12:00 noon, File 28620-98/09/15, 222, 231, 239; see also, GOC/PCO, Jocelyne Bourgon, Memorandum for the Prime Minister. "Summary of the Report of the Task Force on the Future of the Canadian Financial Services Sector," 282.

4 GOC/PCO, Jocelyne Bourgon, Memorandum for the Prime Minister. "Summary of the Report of the Task Force on the Future of the Canadian Financial Services Sector," 283.

5 Ibid., 284.

6 Ibid., 286.

7 BMOA, Oral History Project, Testimony No. 117.

8 BMOA, Bank of Montreal Annual Report, 1998.

9 Ibid.

10 BMOA, Oral History Project, Testimony No. 104.

11 Bertrand Marotte, "Merger Is Music to Barrett's Ears: Bank of Montreal Shareholders Meet Today to Hear the Merits of Proposed 'Superbank' Talks with Royal," *Southham Newspapers*, 24 February 1998.

12 "CIBC, Toronto Dominion Announce Plans to Merge," *Wall Street Journal*, 20 April 1998.

13 GOC/PCO, Cabinet Meeting Annotated Agenda, Tuesday, 3 November 1997, 10:00 a.m.–12:00 noon [note that the year has a typographical error – it should be 1998, not 1997]. Financial Institution Reform, 503.

14 Ibid., 505.

15 GOC/PCO, Cabinet Meeting Annotated Agenda. Secret. Tuesday, 3 November 1997, 10:00 a.m.–12:00 noon [note that the year has a typographical error – it should be 1998, not 1997]. Financial Institutions, 525.

16 Ibid.

17 GOC/PCO, C. Scott Clark to Minister of Finance. Secret. "Speaking Points on Proposed Bank Mergers for Cabinet, 3 November 1998," 30 October 1998, 531.

18 Ibid., 531, 532.

19 Ibid.

20 Ibid., 531, 535.

21 Konrad von Finckenstein to John E. Cleghorn and Matthew W. Barrett, 11 December 1998. See www.competitionbureau.gc.ca/eic/site/cb-bc.nsf/eng/01612.html (accessed 12 August 2018).

22 BMOA, Oral History Project, Testimony No. 42.

23 Ibid., Testimony No. 42.

24 Ibid., Testimony No. 71.

25 Ibid., Testimony No. 76.

26 Ibid., Matthew Barrett.

27 Ibid., Testimony No. 104.

28 Niall Ferguson, *The Square and the Tower: Networks and Power, from the Freemasons to Facebook*, (New York: Penguin Press, 2018), 48.

29 Ibid.

30 For an entertaining account of Barrett's tenure at Barclay's, see Philip Augar, *The Bank that Lived a Little: Barclays in the Age of the Very Free Market* (London: Allen Lane, 2018), especially Part II, chapter 10.

31 See Katherine Maklem, "B of M Chief Has Plan to Ward Off 'Death Spiral': New Business Strategy: Warns that Demise of Traditional Banks not Exaggerated," *Financial Post*, 9 November 1999.

32 BMOA, Bank of Montreal Annual Report, 1999.

33 BMOA, Bank of Montreal Annual Report, 2006.

34 Ibid.

35 BMOA, Tony Comper, "Message to Colleagues on Appointment of Chief Operating Officer," 19 January 2006.

36 Doug Alexander and Sean B. Pasternak, "Downe Transforms Bank of Montreal from Laggard to Top Bank Stock," *Vancouver Sun*, 4 June 2010; see also "Trader Pleads Guilty in $853M BMO fraud; Optionable's ex-CEO Admits Role in Inflating Natural Gas Stock Value," *Toronto Star*, 16 August 2011.

37 Nicola Clark and David Jolly, "French Bank Says Rogue Trader Lost $7 Billion," *New York Times*, 25 January 2008; Doug Sanders, "Europe's Enron Moment Has Arrived," *Globe and Mail*, 30 January 2008; Daniel Bouton, "A chaque crise, la Société Générale en est ressortie plus forte," *Le Monde*, 12 février 2008.

38 Alexander and Pasternak, "Downe Transforms Bank of Montreal."

39 Alan Greenspan and Adrian Wooldridge, *Capitalism in America: A History* (New York: Penguin Press, 2018), location 5305, Kindle.

40 Ibid.

41 Laurence M. Ball, *The Fed and Lehman Brothers: Setting the Record Straight on a Financial Disaster* (Cambridge: Cambridge University Press, 2018), location 1377, Kindle.

42 Greenspan and Wooldridge, *Capitalism in America*, location 5328.

43 Ibid., location 5427.

44 Ibid., location 5476.

45 Michael D. Bordo, Angela Redish, and Hugh Rockoff, "Why Didn't Canada Have a Banking Crisis in 2008 (Or in 1930, Or 1907, Or ...)?" *National Bureau of Economic Research Working Paper Series*, Working Paper 17312 (2011): 1–40.

46 Tim Kiladze, Tara Perkins, Grant Robertson, Jacqueline Nelson, Boyd Erman, Joanna Slater, Jeffrey Jones, and Paul Waldie, "The 2008 Financial Crisis: Through the Eyes of Some Major Players," *Globe and Mail*, 14 September 2013.

47 Ibid.

48 Private correspondence between the author and Gov. Mark Carney, 14 January 2019.

49 Kiladze, Perkins, Robertson, Nelson, Erman, Slater, Jones, and Waldie, "The 2008 Financial Crisis."

50 Armina Ligaya, "How Bill Downe Turned 200-year-old BMO from Laggard to Leader," *National Post*, 20 July 2017.

51 Private correspondence between the author and Gov. Carney, January 2019.

52 BMOA, Oral History Project, Testimony No. 1.

53 Doug Alexander, "BMO Agrees to Buy Marhsall & Ilsley; Deal Worth $4.1 Billion Will Increase Canadian Bank's Branches in US," *Ottawa Citizen*, 18 December 2010.

54 Ibid.

55 Matthew Monks, "Bank of Montreal Chief Aims to Buy More in US," *American Banker* 176, no. 104 (July 2011), 1, 7.

56 BMOA, Bank of Montreal Annual Report, 2013.

57 Author interview with BMO executive (Ref: Viz), 24 October 2018.

58 Ibid.

59 Here, the work of the director of corporate donations, Nada Ristich, has been one of the many unsung yet remarkable success stories of the past generation. Ristich's long-run experience and unsurpassed network of relationships in Canada's philanthropic world developed since her arrival at BMO in May 1994 has allowed successive administrations to maximize the impact of corporate giving and philanthropy.

60 BMOA, Bill Downe, "Address to Annual General Meeting of Shareholders," 22 March 2011, from in-house collection, "Messages from Bill Downe, Chief Executive Officer BMO Financial Group, 2007–2017."

Epilogue

1 Carlo Rovelli, *The Order of Time* (New York: Riverhead Books, 2018), 178.

2 Percy Byssche Shelley, "Mutability ['We are as clouds that veil the midnight moon']." *Poetry Foundation.* www.poetryfoundation.org/poems/54563/mutability-we-are-as-clouds-that-veil-the-midnight-moon (accessed 17 January 2018).

3 The points that John Lewis Gaddis makes in *On Grand Strategy* (New York: Penguin Press, 2018), 25.

4 For the last approximately two decades, the person who has been responsible for executing that perfect choreography for the Bank's most senior executives has been Kelley Millage, nicknamed "Field Marshal von Millage" for her unsurpassed attention to detail in executing flawless events. I mention Ms Millage here as a tribute to the dozens of people who, down the years, have laboured behind the scenes to ensure the executives they support have every chance of getting their message across to the Bank and to the world. If one pulls back the veil in many organizations of the calibre and size of the Bank of Montreal, one will find that what appears the work of a few is really the labour of many.

5 Here, the medium can send mixed messages. Imagine, for example, if the Regeneration Generation in April 1990 had chosen to deliver its clarion call for the renewal of the Bank using the same lexicon, forms, and venue that Bill Mulholland had used. They emphatically did not – and that major change represented an entirely new choreography, if you will, that along with the venue, the Bristol Place Hotel, is forever associated in the annals of the Bank of Montreal with the start of an extraordinary transformation. This is how the Barrett bank, to extend the dance metaphor, announced to the world that the Bank of Montreal was "busting a move."

6 Armina Ligaya, "How Bill Downe Turned 200-year-old BMO from Laggard to Leader," *National Post*, 20 July 2017.

7 Gaddis, *On Grand Strategy*, 21.

8 Except Niall Ferguson, of course.

9 I am indebted to Bishop Robert Barron for this general observation, and his reading of Paul Tillich.

BIBLIOGRAPHY

Archives

BEA   Bank of England Archives

BMOA   Bank of Montreal Archives, Montreal, Quebec, Canada, and Chicago, Illinois, United States

LAC   Library and Archives Canada, Ottawa, Ontario, Canada

NAUK   National Archives, London, United Kingdom

NSA   Nova Scotia Archives, Halifax, Nova Scotia, Canada

PANL   Provincial Archives of Newfoundland and Labrador, St John's, Newfoundland and Labrador, Canada

PAS   Provincial Archives of Saskatchewan, Regina, Saskatchewan, Canada Thomas Reuters Corporation, Toronto, Ontario, Canada

Newspapers

Alberta Report
American Banker
Calgary Herald
Financial Times
Globe
Globe and Mail
Hamilton Spectator
Hamilton Times
Kingston Gleaner
Lethbridge Herald
Milwaukee Sentinel
Monetary Times & Trade Review
Montreal Gazette
Montreal Herald
National Intelligencer
National Post
New York Times

Ottawa Citizen
Southam newspapers
Toronto Globe
Toronto Star
Vancouver Sun

Secondary Sources

Ackert, Lucy F., Bryan K. Church, and Richard Deaves. "Emotion and Financial Markets." *Federal Reserve Bank of Atlanta: Economic Review* (2003): 33–41.

Ackrill, M., and L. Hannah. *Barclays: The Business of Banking, 1690–1996*. Cambridge: Cambridge University Press, 2001.

Adams, Donald R. Jr. "The Beginning of Investment Banking in the United States." *Pennsylvania History* 45, no. 2 (1978): 99–116.

Ahamed, Liaquat. *Lords of Finance: 1929, the Great Depression, and the Bankers Who Broke the World*. London: Windmill Books, 2010.

Alef, Daniel. *Henry Goldman: Goldman Sachs and the Beginning of Investment Banking*. United States: Titans of Fortune Publishing, 2010.

Allaire, Gratien. "Thomas Thain." *Dictionary of Canadian Biography*. www.biographi.ca/009004-119.01-e.php?&id_nbr=3165 accessed 1 October 2016. (accessed 7 November 2013).

Allen, Jason. *Are Canadian Banks Efficient?: A Canada-US Comparison*. Ottawa: Bank of Canada, 2006.

– *Efficiency and Economies of Scale of Large Canadian Banks*. Ottawa: Bank of Canada, 2005.

Allen, Jason, and Ying Liu. "Efficiency and Economies of Scale of Large Canadian Banks." *The Canadian Journal of Economics/Revue canadienne d'Economique* 40, no. 1 (2007): 225–44.

Alston, Lee J., Wayne A. Grove, and David C. Wheelock. "Why Do Banks Fail? Evidence from the 1920s." *Explorations in Economic History* 31 (1994): 409–31.

Altamura, Carlo E. *European Banks and the Rise of International Finance: The Post-Bretton Woods Era*. New York: Routledge, 2017.

Amatori, Franco, and Geoffrey Jones. *Business History Around the World*. Cambridge: Cambridge University Press, 2003.

Andreades, Andreas Michael. *History of the Bank of England, 1640–1903*. New York: A.M. Kelley, 1966.

Andreas, Peter. *Smuggler National How Illicit Trade Made America*. New York: Oxford University Press, 2013.

Andrews, Michael. *Size, Competition and Concentration in Canadian Financial Services*. Ottawa: Conference Board of Canada, 1993.

Archer, Keith. *Political Choices and Electoral Consequences: A Study of Organized Labour in the New Democratic Party*. Montreal/Kingston: McGill-Queen's University Press, 1990.

Armer, Paul. *Computer Aspects of Technological Changes, Automation and Economic Progress*. Santa Monica: The RAND Corporation, 1966.

Armstrong, Christopher. *Blue Skies and Boiler Rooms: Buying and Selling Securities in Canada, 1870–1940*. Toronto: University of Toronto Press, 1997.

Armstrong, Christopher, and H.V. Nelles. "A Curious Capital Flow: Canadian Investment in Mexico, 1902–1910." *The Business History Review* 58, no. 2 (1984): 178–203.

– *Southern Exposure: Canadian Promoters in Latin America and the Caribbean, 1896–1930*. Toronto: University of Toronto Press, 1988.

Armstrong, Frederick H. "David Torrance." *Dictionary of Canadian Biography*. www.biographi.ca/009004-119.01-e.php?&id_nbr=5298 (accessed 5 September 2014).

Armstrong, Jim. "The Changing Business Activities of Banks in Canada." *Bank of Canada Review* (Spring 1997): 11–38.

Ashenfelter, Orley, and Timothy Hannan. "Sex Discrimination and Product Market Competition: The Case of the Banking Industry." *The Quarterly Journal of Economics* 101, no. 1 (1986): 149–74.

Atindéhou, Roger B., and Jean-Pierre Gueyle. "Canadian Chartered Banks' Stock Returns and Exchange Rate Risk." *Management Decision* 39, no. 4 (2001): 285–95.

Augar, Philip. *The Bank that Lived a Little: Barclays in the Age of the Very Free Market*. London: Allen Lane, 2018.

Babad, M., and C. Mulroney. *Pillars: The Coming Crisis in Canada's Financial Industry*. Toronto: Stoddart, 1993.

Baker, Andrew. *The Group of Seven: Finance Ministries, Central Banks and Global Financial Governance*. New York: Routledge, 2006.

Baker, Mae, and Michael Collins. "Methodological Approaches to the Study of British Banking History." *Revue Économique* 58, no. 1 (2007): 59–78.

Bal, Simarjit, S. "Banking on Identity: Constructing a Canadian Banking Identity One Branch at a Time." *Journal of Historical Sociology* 31, no. 2 (2018): 196–212.

Ball, Laurence M. *The Fed and Lehman Brothers: Setting the Record Straight on a Financial Disaster*. Cambridge: Cambridge University Press, 2018.

Balleisen, Edward J., Sally Clarke, Johnathan M. Karpoff, and Jonathan Macey, "Corporate Reputation Roundtable." *Business History Review* 87, no. 4 (2013): 627–42.

Baltazar, Ramon, and Michael Santos. "The Benefits of Banking Mega-Mergers: Event Study Evidence from the 1998 Failed Mega-Merger Attempts in Canada." *Canadian Journal of Administrative Sciences/Revue Canadienne des Sciences de l'Administration* 20, no. 3 (2003): 196–208.

Bank of America. *The Bank of America*. New York: The De Vinne Press, 1887.

Bank of Canada. *About the Bank*. Ottawa: Bank of Canada, 2010.

Bank of Montreal. *The Centenary of the Bank of Montreal, 1817–1917*. Montreal: The Bank of Montreal, 1917.

Bank of Nova Scotia. *The Bank of Nova Scotia, 1832–1932*. Canada: The Bank of Nova Scotia, 1932.

– *History of the Bank of Nova Scotia, 1832–1900. Together with Copies of Annual Statements*. Halifax: The Bank of Nova Scotia, 1901.

Barber, Clarence L., and John C.P. McCallum. *Controlling Inflation: Learning from Experience in Canada, Europe, and Japan*. Toronto: Lirmer & Company, 1982.

Barkema, Harry G., and Mario Schijven. "Toward Unlocking the Full Potential of Acquisitions: The Role of Organizational Restructuring." *The Academy of Management Journal* 51, no. 4 (2008): 696–722.

Barnes, Andrew Wallace. *History of the Philadelphia Stock Exchange, Banks and Banking Interests*. United States: Cornelius Baker, 1911.

Baskerville, Peter. "Robert Cassels." *Dictionary of Canadian Biography*. www.biographi.ca/009004-119.01-e.php?&id_nbr=5424 (accessed 22 July 2015).

Baskerville, Peter A. *The Bank of Upper Canada: A Collection of Documents*. Toronto: Champlain Society and the Ontario Heritage Foundation, 1987.

– "Entrepreneurship and the Family Compact: York-Toronto, 1822–55." *Urban History Review/Revue d'Histoire Urbaine* 9, no. 3 (1981): 15–34.

Baskin, Jonathan Barron. "The Development of Corporate Financial Markets in Britain and the United States, 1600–1914: Overcoming Asymmetric Information." *The Business History Review* 62, no. 2 (1988): 199–237.

Bátiz-Lazo, Bernardo, and D. Wood. "An Historical Appraisal of Information Technology in Commercial Banking." *Electronic Markets – The International Journal of Electronic Commerce & Business Media* 12, no. 3 (2002): 192–205.

Bátiz-Lazo, Bernardo, and Trevor Boyns. "The Business and Financial History of Mechanisation and Technological Change in Twentieth-Century Banking." *Accounting, Business & Financial History* 14, no. 3 (November 2004): 225–32.

Battilossi, Stefano. "Financial Innovation and the Golden Ages of International Banking: 1890–1931 and 1958–1981." *Financial History Review* 7, no. 2 (2000): 141–75.

Baum, Daniel Jay. *The Banks of Canada in the Commonwealth Caribbean: Economic Nationalism and Multinational Enterprises of a Medium Power*. New York: Praeger, 1974.

Beales, H.L. "Revisions in Economic History: The Great Depression in Industry and Trade." *The Economic History Review* 5, no. 1 (1934): 65–75.

Beaverstock, Jonathan V. "Re-thinking Skilled International Labour Migration: World Cities and Banking Organizations." *Geoforum* 25, no. 3 (1994): 323–38.

Becker, Adam. "How Will the Universe End, and Could Anything Survive?" *BBC*. www.bbc.com/earth/story/20150602-how-will-the-universe-end (accessed 12 January 2017).

Beckhart, B.H. *The Banking System of Canada*. New York: Holt, 1929.

Bercuson, David J. *Confrontation at Winnipeg: Labour, Industrial Relations, and the General Strike*. Montreal/Kingston: McGill-Queen's University Press, 1990.

Berger, Allan N., and David B. Humphrey. "Efficiency of Financial Institutions: International Survey and Directions for Future Research." *European Journal of Operational Research* 98 (1997): 175–212.

Berger, Allan N., Anil K. Kashyap, Joseph M. Scalise, Mark Gertler, and Benjamin M. Friedman. "The Transformation of the US Banking Industry: What a Long, Strange Trip It's Been." *Brookings Papers on Economic Activity* 1995, no. 2 (1995): 55–218.

Bergeron, L.D. "Pretended Banking?: The Struggle for Banking Facilities in Kingston, Upper Canada, 1830–1837." MA thesis, University of Ottawa, 2007.

Bergerson, David. "Funding the War of 1812," *Bank of Canada Museum Research Papers* (2012): 1–15.

Berton, Pierre. *The National Dream: The Great Railway, 1871–1881*. Canada: Anchor Canada, 1970.

Bielski, Lauren. "Year of the Wallet." *ABA Banking Journal* 99 (1999).

Bisson, Pierre. "Le Club Mont Royal." In *Les Chemins de le Mémoire: Monuments et Sites Historiques du Quebec*. Quebec: Commission des biens culturels, 2001.

Blaug, Mark. "On the Historiography of Economics." *Journal of the History of Economic Thought* 12, no. 1 (1990): 27–37.

Bodenhorn, Howard. "Free Banking and Bank Entry in Nineteenth-Century New York." *Financial History Review* 15, no. 2 (2008): 175–201.

– *A History of Banking in Antebellum America: Financial Markets and Economic Development in an Era of Nation-Building*. Cambridge: Cambridge University Press, 2000.

– *State Banking in Early America: A New Economic History*. New York: Oxford University Press, 2003.

Bodnar, Gordon M., and William M. Gentry. "Exchange Rate Exposure and Industry Characteristics: Evidence from Canada, Japan, and the USA." *Journal of International Money and Finance* 12, no. 1 (1993): 29–45.

Booth, Laurence, and Wendy Rotenberg. "Assessing Foreign Exchange Exposure: Theory and Application Using Canadian Firms." *Journal of International Financial Management & Accounting* 2, no. 1 (1990): 1–22.

Boothe, Paul, and Douglas Purvis. "Macroeconomic Policy in Canada and the United States: Independence, Transmission, and Effectiveness." In *Degrees of Freedom: Canada and the United States in a Changing World*, edited by Keith Banting, George Hoberg, and Richard Simeon, 189–230. Montreal/Kingston: McGill-Queen's University Press, 1997.

Boothe, Paul, and Heather Edwards. *Eric J. Hanson's Financial History of Alberta, 1905–1950*. Calgary: University of Calgary Press, 2003.

Bordo, Michael D., and Angela Redish. "Credible Commitment and Exchange Rate Stability: Canada's Interwar Experience." Working Paper No. 2431 for the *National Bureau of Economic Research* (1987): 1–37.

– "Seventy Years of Central Banking: The Bank of Canada in International Context, 1935–2005." Working Paper No. 11586 for the *National Bureau of Economic Research* (2005): 1–16.

– "Why Did the Bank of Canada Emerge in 1935?" *The Journal of Economic History* 47, no. 2 (1987): 405–17.

Bordo, Michael D., Hugh Rockoff, and Angela Redish. "A Comparison of the United States and Canadian Banking Systems in the Twentieth Century: Stability vs. Efficiency?" Working Paper No. 4546 for the *National Bureau of Economic Research* (1993): 1–34.

– "The US Banking System from a Northern Exposure: Stability versus Efficiency." *The Journal of Economic History* 54, no. 2 (1994): 325–41.

– "Why Didn't Canada Have a Banking Crisis in 2008 (Or in 1930, Or 1907, Or...?)." Working Paper No. 17312 for the *National Bureau of Economic Research* (2011): 1–40.

Bordo, Michael D., and Richard Eugene Sylla. *Anglo-American Financial Systems: Institutions and Markets in the Twentieth Century*. New York: Irwin Professional Pub., 1995.

Boreham, Gordon F. "Three Years after Canada's 'Little Bang'." *Canadian Banker* 97, no. 5 (1990): 6–16.

Boreham, Gordon Francis, and William Howard Steiner. *Money & Banking: Analysis & Policy in a Canadian Context*. Canada: Holt, Rinehart and Winston of Canada, 1979.

Born, Karl Erich. *International Banking in the 19th and 20th Centuries*. United States: Palgrave Macmillan, 1983.

Bothwell, Robert, Ian Drummond, and John English. *Canada, 1900–1945*. Toronto: University of Toronto Press, 1990.

Boyer, Kate. "'Miss Remington' Goes to Work: Gender, Space, and Technology at the Dawn of the Information Age." *The Professional Geographer* 56, no. 2 (2004): 201–12.

– "'Neither Forget nor Remember Your Sex': Sexual Politics in the Early Twentieth-Century Canadian Office." *Journal of Historical Geography* 29, no. 2 (2003): 212–29.

Brassard, Michèle, and Jean Hamelin. "Sir George Alexander Drummond." *Dictionary of Canadian Biography*. www.biographi.ca/009004-119.01-e.php?&id_nbr=6683 (accessed 1 March 2015).

Brean, Donald J.S., Lawrence Kryzanowski, and Gordon S. Roberts. "Canada and the United States: Different Roots, Different Routes to Financial Sector Regulation." *Business History* 53, no. 2 (2011): 249–69.

Brecher, Irving. "Canadian Monetary Thought and Policy in the 1920's." *Canadian Journal of Economics and Political Science/Revue canadienne d'Economique et de Science politique* 21, no. 2 (1955): 154–73.

Breckenridge, Roeliff Morton. *The Canadian Banking System, 1817–1890.* New York: Macmillan & Company, 1893.

Breslaw, Jon A., and James McIntosh. "Scale Efficiency in Canadian Trust Companies." *Journal of Productivity Analysis* 8 (1997): 281–92.

Breton, Albert. "The Behaviour of the Aggregate Reserve Ratio of Canadian Chartered Banks." *The Canadian Journal of Economics/Revue canadienne d'Economique* 2, no. 3 (1969): 435–42.

Breton, Gaétan, and Louise Côté. "Profit and the Legitimacy of the Canadian Banking Industry." *Accounting, Auditing & Accountability Journal* 19, no. 4 (2006): 512–39.

Brooks, Leonard J. "Business Ethics in Canada: Distinctiveness and Directions." *Journal of Business Ethics* 16, no. 6 (1997): 591–604.

Browde, Anatole. "Settling the Canadian Colonies: A Comparison of Two Nineteenth-Century Land Companies." *Business History Review* 76, no. 2 (2002): 299–335.

Brown, M.A. *The Second Bank of the United States and Ohio (1803–1860).* New York: Edwin Mellen Press, 1998.

Bryan, Lowell. *Breaking Up the Bank: Rethinking an Industry under Siege.* Homewood: Dow Jones Irwin, 1988.

Bryan, Lowell, and Diana Farrell. *Market Unbound: Unleashing Global Capitalism.* New York: John Wiley & Sons, 1996.

Buckle, Mike, and John Thompson. *The UK Financial System: Theory and Practice.* Manchester: Manchester University Press, 1992.

Buckley, K. *Capital Formation in Canada, 1896–1930.* Toronto: University of Toronto Press, 1955.

Burbidge, John, and Alan Harrison. "(Innovation) Accounting for the Impact of Fluctuations in US Variables on the Canadian Economy." *The Canadian Journal of Economics/Revue Canadienne d'Economique* 18, no. 4 (1985): 784–98.

Burley, David G. "Hugh Cossart Baker." *Dictionary of Canadian Biography.* www.biographi.ca/009004-119.01-e.php?&id_nbr=3761 (accessed 2 March 2015).

Cain, P.J. "Gentlemanly Imperialism at Work: The Bank of England, Canada, and the Sterling Area, 1932–1936." *Economic History Review* 49, no. 2 (1996): 336–57.

Cain, P.J., and A.G. Hopkins. *British Imperialism: 1688–2000.* London: Longman, 2002.

– "The Political Economy of British Expansion Overseas, 1750–1914." *The Economic History Review* 33, no. 4 (1980): 463–90.

Calmès, Christian. "Regulatory Changes and Financial Structure: The Case of Canada." Working Paper 2004-26 for the *Bank of Canada* (July 2004): 1–43.

Calmès, Christian, and Ying Liu. "Financial Structure Change and Banking Income: A Canada-US Comparison." *Journal of International Financial Markets, Institutions and Money* 19, no. 1 (2009): 128–39.

Calomiris, Charles W. "Bank Failures in Theory and History: The Great Depression and Other 'Contagious' Events." Working Paper No. 13597 for the *National Bureau of Economic Research* (November 2007): 1–30.

Calomiris, Charles, and Stephen H. Haber. *Fragile by Design: The Political Origins of Banking Crises and Scarce Credit.* Princeton: Princeton University Press, 2014.

Calomiris, Charles, and Jason Karceski. "Is the Bank Merger Wave of the 1990s Efficient? Lessons from Nine Case Studies." In *Mergers and Productivity*, edited by Steven N. Kaplan, 93–178. Chicago: University of Chicago Press, 2000.

Cameron, Rondo. "Introduction." In *International Banking 1870–1914*, edited by R. Cameron and V.I. Bovyking, 3–22. Oxford: Oxford University Press, 1991.

Campbell, Bryan, and Steve Murphy. "The Recent Performance of the Canadian Forecasting Industry." *Canadian Public Policy/Analyse de Politiques* 32, no. 1 (2006): 23–40.

Campbell, Karen. "The Embargo Act of 1808." In *The Vermont Encyclopedia*, edited by John J. Duffy, Samuel B. Hand, and Ralph H. Orth, 114. Biddeford: University of New England, 2013.

Canadian Bankers' Association. *A Canadian Banking Perspective on Trade in Financial Services under a North American Free Trade Agreement*. California: The Association, 1991.

Capie, Forrest, and Mark Billings. "Evidence on Competition in English Commercial Banking." *Financial History Review* 11 (2009): 69–103.

Capie, Forrest, and T.C. Mills. "British Bank Conservatism in the Late Nineteenth Century." *Explorations in Economic History* 32 (1995): 409–20.

Capie, Forrest, and Geoffrey E. Wood, eds. *The Lender of Last Resort*. New York: Routledge, 2007.

Carlson, Avery Luvere. *A Banking History of Texas 1835–1929*. United States: Copano Bay Press, 2007.

Carlson, Mark, and Kris James Mitchener. "Branch Banking, Bank Competition, and Financial Stability." *Journal of Money, Credit and Banking* 38, no. 5 (2006): 1293–1328.

Carr, Jack, Frank Mathewson, and Neil Quigley. "Stability in the Absence of Deposit Insurance: The Canadian Banking System, 1890–1966." *Journal of Money, Credit and Banking* 27, no. 4 (1995): 1137–58.

Cassis, Youssef. *Capitals of Capital: The Rise and Fall of International Financial Centres, 1780–2009*. New York: Cambridge University Press, 2010.

Cavanagh, Ralph. "Making Friends with Mother Nature." *Harvard Business School Alumni*. www.alumni.hbs.edu/stories/Pages/story-bulletin.aspx?num=6334 accessed (accessed 23 February 2016).

Chandler, Robert J. *Wells Fargo*. Chicago: Arcadia Publishing, 2006.

Chant, John F. *Bank Lending and Entrepreneurial Finance: The Performance of Canadian Banks*. Vancouver: The Fraser Institute, 2008.

Chapman, Stanley D. *The Rise of Merchant Banking*. London: Allen & Unwin, 1984.

Checkland, S.G. "Banking History and Economic Development: Seven Systems." *Scottish Journal of Political Economy* 16, no. 1 (1969): 144–66.

Chernow, Ron. *The House of Morgan: An American Banking Dynasty and the Rise of Modern Finance*. New York: Atlantic Monthly Press, 1990.

Chesterton, G.K. *Three Apologies of G.K. Chesterton: Heretics, Orthodoxy & the Everlasting Man*. Bristol: Mockingbird Press, 2018.

Chou, David C., and Amy Y. Chou. "A Guide to the Internet Revolution in Banking." *Information Systems Management* 17, no. 2 (2000): 1–7.

Chown, John. *A History of Monetary Unions*. New York: Routledge, 2003.

Chu, Kam Hon. "Bank Mergers, Branch Networks and Economic Growth: Theory and Evidence from Canada, 1889–1926." *Journal of Macroeconomics* 32 (2010): 265–83.

Clarke, Matthew St Claire, and David A. Hall. *Legislative and Documentary History of the Bank of the United States*. Washington: Gales and Seaton, 1832.

Cleaveland, John, and G.S. Hutchinson. *The Banking System of the State of New York*. United States: Ayer Publishing, 1864.

Clement, Wallace. *Continental Corporate Power: Economic Elite Linkages between Canada and the United States*. Toronto: McClelland and Stewart, 1977.

Coffey, W.J., and M. Polèse. "Le déclin de l'empire montréalais: Regards sur l'économie d'une métropole en mutation." *Recherches Sociographique* 34 (1993): 417–37.

– "The Impact of Cultural Barriers on the Location of Producer Services: Some Reflections on the Montreal-Toronto Rivalry and the Limits of Urban Polarization." *Canadian Journal of Regional Science* 14 (1991): 433–46.

Cohen, Lizabeth. *A Consumer's Republic: The Politics of Mass Consumption in Postwar America*. New York: Vintage Books, 2004.

Coleman, W., and T. Porter. "Playin' Along: Canada and Global Finance." In *Changing Canada: Political Economy as Transformation*, edited by Wallace Clement and Leah F. Vosko, 241–64. Montreal/Kingston: McGill-Queen's University Press, 2003.

Coleman, William D. "Financial Service Reform in Canada: The Evolution of Policy Dissension." *Canadian Public Policy/Analyse de Politiques* 18, no. 2 (1992): 139–52.

– *Financial Services, Globalization and Domestic Policy Change: A Comparison of North America and the European Union*. United States: Macmillan Press, 1996.

Collard, E.A. *Chalk to Computers: The Story of the Montreal Stock Exchange*. Montreal: Bibliothèque Nationale du Québec, 1974.

Collins, Michael. "The Banking Crisis of 1878." *The Economic History Review* 42, no. 4 (1989): 504–27.

– *Banks and Industrial Finance in Britain 1800–1939*. Cambridge: Cambridge University Press, 1995.

Conference Board of Canada. *Big Bank, Little Bank? Canadian Concentration: An International Comparison*. Ottawa: The Conference Board of Canada, 2000.

Co-operative Commonwealth Federation. "Security for All." In *Canadian Party Platforms 1867–1968*, edited by D. Owen Carrigan, 168–78. Toronto: The Copp Clark Publishing Company, 1968.

Cortada, James. *The Digital Hand: Volume II: How Computers Changed the Work of American Financial, Telecommunications, Media and Entertainment Industries*. Oxford: Oxford University Press, 2006.

Courchene, Thomas J. "An Analysis of the Canadian Money Supply: 1925–1934." *Journal of Political Economy* 77, no. 3 (1969): 363–91.

Cowen, David J. "The First Bank of the United States and the Securities Market Crash of 1792." *The Journal of Economic History* 60, no. 4 (2000): 1041–60.

– *The Origins and Economic Impact of the First Bank of the United States, 1791–1797*. New York: Garland Press, 2006.

Cowton, C.J. "Integrity, Responsibility and Affinity: Three Aspects of Ethics in Banking." *Business Ethics: A European Review* 11, no 4 (2002): 393–400.

Crafts, Nicholas F.R. "British Industrialization in and International Context." *Journal of Interdisciplinary History* 19, no. 3 (1989): 415–28.

Creighton, Phillip. "Robert Henry Bethune." *Dictionary of Canadian Biography*. www.biographi.ca/009004-119.01-e.php?&id_nbr=5975 (accessed 12 January 2015).

Crompton, Rosemary. "Women in Banking: Continuity and Change since the Second World War." *Work, Employment & Society* 3, no. 2 (1989): 141–56.

Cross, Philip, and Phillipe Bergevin. "Turning Points: Business Cycles in Canada since 1926." *C.D. Howe Commentary No 366: Economic Growth and Innovation* (2012).

Cuneo, Carl J. "Surplus Labour in Staple Commodities Merchant and Early Industrial Capitalism." *Studies in Political Economy* 7 (1982): 61–87.

Cyril, James F. *The Growth of Chicago Banks*. New York: Harper & Row, 1969.

Daniels, Belden L. *Pennsylvania, Birthplace of Banking in America*. Pennsylvania: Pennsylvania Bankers Association, 1976.

Darroch, James, and Gerry Kerr. "From Partners in Nation Building to the Two Solitudes: The Canadian Chartered Bank-Federal Government Relations." In *Canada and the New World Economic Order: Strategic Briefings for Canadian Enterprise, Third Edition*, edited by Tom Wesson, 288–308. Ontario: Captus Press Inc., 2007.

Darroch, James L. "Canadian Banking Strategy in North America." In *Banking in North America: NAFTA and Beyond*, edited by Jerry Haar and Krishnan Dandapani, 81–101. New York: Pergamon, 1999.

– *Canadian Banks and Global Competitiveness*. Montreal/Kingston: McGill-Queen's University Press, 1994.

Darroch, James L., and Charles J. McMillan. "Entry Barriers and Evolution of Banking Systems: Lessons from the 1980s Canadian Western Bank Failures." *Canadian Public Administration* 50, no. 2 (2007): 141–65.

Das, Sanjiv R., and Ashish Nanda. "A Theory of Banking Structure." *Journal of Banking & Finance* 26, no. 6 (1999): 863–95.

Davidson, Kenneth M. *Megamergers: Corporate America's Billion-Dollar Takeovers*. Washington: Beard Books, 2003.

Davis, Lance E. *Institutional Change and American Economic Growth*. New York: Cambridge University Press, 1971.

Davis, Lance E., and Robert E. Gallman. *Evolving Financial Markets and International Capital Flows: Britain, the Americas, and Australia, 1870–1914*. Cambridge: Cambridge University Press, 2001.

Deaves, Richard. "Forecasting Canadian Short-Term Interest Rates." *The Canadian Journal of Economics/Revue canadienne d'Economique* 29, no. 3 (1996): 615–34.

Debelle, Guy. "The Ends of Three Small Inflations: Australia, New Zealand and Canada." *Canadian Public Policy/Analyse de Politiques* 22, no. 1 (1996): 56–78.

Delong, J. Bradford. *Did J.P. Morgan's Men Add Value? An Economist's Perspective on Financial Capitalism*. Cambridge: Harvard Institute for Economic Research, 1991.

Denison, Merrill. *Canada's First Bank: A History of the Bank of Montreal*, 2 vols. Toronto: McClelland and Stewart, 1966, 1967.

Désilets, Andrée. "Marc-Damase Masson." *Dictionary of Canadian Biography*. www.biographi.ca/009004-119.01-e.php?&id_nbr=5132 (accessed 11 October 2015).

Deslauriers, Peter. "James Millar." *Dictionary of Canadian Biography*. www.biographi.ca/009004-119.01-e.php?&id_nbr=3564 (accessed 13 October 2015).

– "John Fleming." *Dictionary of Canadian Biography*. www.biographi.ca/en/bio/fleming_john_6E.html (accessed 1 November 2015).

– "Samuel Gerrard." *Dictionary of Canadian Biography*. www.biographi.ca/009004-119.01-e.php?&id_nbr=3931 (accessed 23 August 2014).

Desmond, Bruce Lincoln. *Canadian Banks and US Financial Groups*. Hamilton: McMaster University, 1979.

Dessein, Wouter, Luis Garicano, and Robert Gertner. "Organizing for Synergies." *American Economic Journal: Microeconomics* 2 (2010): 77–114.

Dimand, Robert W. "David Hume on Canadian Paper Money: An Overlooked Contribution." *Journal of Money, Credit and Banking* 37, no. 4 (2005): 783–7.

Dombrowski, Peter. *Policy Responses to the Globalization of American Banking*. Pittsburgh: University of Pittsburgh Press, 1996.

Drummond, Ian. "Canadian Life Insurance Companies and the Capital Market, 1890–1914." *Canadian Journal of Economics and Political Science* 28 (1962): 204–24.

– *Progress without Planning: The Economic History of Ontario from Confederation to the Second World War*. Toronto: University of Toronto Press, 1987.

– "Why Did Canadian Banks not Collapse in the 1930s?" In *The Role of Banks in the Interwar Economy*, edited by Harold James, Hakan Lindgren, and Alice Teichova, 232–50. Cambridge: Cambridge University Press, 1991.

Drummond, Ian M. "Capital Markets in Australia and Canada." PhD dissertation, Yale University, 1974.

Dubuc, Alfred. "John Molson." *Dictionary of Canadian Biography*. www.biographi.ca/009004-119.01-e.php?&id_nbr=3567 (accessed 14 July 2014).

Eagle, John A. "Monopoly or Competition: the Nationalization of the Grand Trunk Railway." *Canadian Historical Review* 62, no. 1 (1981): 3–30.

Easterbook, W.T., and Hugh G.J. Aitken. "Money and Banking in Canadian Development." In *Canadian Economic History*, edited by W.T. Easterbrook and Hugh G.J. Aitken, 445–75. Toronto: University of Toronto Press, 2002.

Easterbrook, W.T., and M.H. Watkins. *Approaches to Canadian Economic History*. Toronto: McClelland and Stewart Inc., 1967.

Eckhardt, H.M.P. "Modes of Carrying Cash Reserves." *Journal of the Canadian Bankers' Association* 16 (1909): 98–105.

Eggertsson, Gauti B., and Benjamin Pugsley. "The Mistake of 1937: A General Equilibrium Analysis." *Monetary and Economic Studies* 24 (2006): 151–208.

Eichengreen, Barry. *Elusive Stability: Essays in the History of International Finance, 1919–1939*. New York: Press Syndicate of the University of Cambridge, 1990.

Eliason, Adolph Oscar. *The Rise of Commercial Banking Institutions in the United States*. New York: B. Franklin, 1970.

Elster, Jon. "Emotions and Economic Theory." *Journal of Economic Literature* 36, no. 1 (March 1998): 47–74.

England, Kim, and Kate Boyer. "Women's Work: The Feminization and Shifting Meanings of Clerical Work." *Journal of Social History* 43, no. 2 (2010): 307–40.

Esbitt, Milton. "Bank Portfolios and Bank Failures during the Great Depression: Chicago." *The Journal of Economic History* 46, no. 2 (1986): 455–62.

Estey, Willard Z. *Report of the Inquiry into the Collapse of the CCB and Northland Bank*. Canada: Minister of Supply and Services Canada, 1986.

Evans, David S., and Richard Schmalensee. *Paying with Plastic: The Digital Revolution in Buying and Borrowing*. Cambridge: Massachusetts Institute of Technology, 2005.

Evans, L.T., and N.C. Quigley. "Discrimination in Bank Lending Policies: A Test Using Data from the Bank of Nova Scotia, 1900–37." *The Canadian Journal of Economics/Revue canadienne d'Economique* 23, no. 1 (1990): 210–25.

Fahrni, Magda, and Robert Rutherdale. "Introduction." In *Creating Postwar Canada: Community, Diversity, and Dissent, 1945–1975*, edited by Madga Fahrni and Robert Rutherdale, 1–20. Vancouver, University of British Columbia Press, 2008.

Farr, David M.L. "Sir John Rose." *Dictionary of Canadian Biography*. www.biographi.ca/009004-119.01-e.php?&id_nbr=5808 (accessed 1 September 2015).

Fay, Terence J. "Winnipeg and Minneapolis Bank Resources Compared, 1876–1926." *Urban History Review/Revue d'histoire urbaine* 14, no. 1 (1985): 23–36.

Fayerweather, John. *The Mercantile Bank Affair: A Case Study of Canadian Nationalism and a Multinational Firm*. New York: New York University Press, 1974.

Feehan, James P., and Melvin Baker. "The Churchill Falls Contract and Why Newfoundlanders Can't Get Over It." *Policy Options/Options Politiques* (1 September 2010): 65–70.

Ferguson, Niall. *The Ascent of Money: A Financial History of the World*. New York: Penguin Press, 2008.

– "An Evolutionary Approach to Financial History." *Cold Spring Harbor Symposia on Quantitative Biology* 74 (2010): 449–54.

– *The House of Rothschild: Volume 1: Money's Prophets, 1798–1848*. London: Penguin Books, 2000.

– *The Square and the Tower: Networks and Power, from the Freemasons to Facebook*. New York: Penguin Press, 2018.

– *The World's Banker: The History of the House of Rothschild*. London: Weidenfeld & Nicolson, 1998.

Field, Alexander J. *A Great Leap Forward: 1930s Depression and US Economic Growth*. United States: Yale University Press, 2011.

Fine, L. *Souls of the Skyscraper: Female Clerical Workers in Chicago, 1870–1930*. Philadelphia: Temple University Press, 1991.

Finkel, Alvin. *The Social Credit Phenomenon in Alberta*. Toronto: University of Toronto Press, 1989.

First National Bank (Scranton, Pennsylvania). *History: The First National Bank of Scranton, PA*. Princeton: Princeton University Press, 1906.

First National Bank of Boston. *The First National Bank of Boston, 1784–1934: A Brief History of its 150 Years of Continual Existence with Emphasis on the Early Days of Its First Forebear, the Massachusetts Bank*. Michigan: The University of Michigan, 1934.

Flandreau, Marc, and Frédéric Zumer. *Development Centre Studies: The Making of Global Finance 1880–1913*. Paris: OECD Publishing, 2009.

Flick, Donald H. "Early Money in Nova Scotia: A Short History of Currency, Exchange and Finance." *Nova Scotia Historical Review* 1, no. 2 (1981): 4–15.

Foerster, Stephen R., and Stephen G. Sapp. "The Changing Role of Dividends: A Firm Level Study from the Nineteenth to the Twenty-First Century." *The Canadian Journal of Economics/Revue Canadienne d'Economique* 39, no. 4 (2006): 1316–44.

Fombrun, Charles. "The Building Blocks of Corporate Reputation: Definitions, Antecedents, Consequences." In *The Oxford Handbook of Corporate Reputation*, edited by Michael L. Barnett and Timothy G. Pollock, 94–113. Oxford: Oxford University Press, 2014.

Fouquet, Douglas M. "Business School's Prestige Grows as David Enters 10th Year as Dean." *Harvard Crimson* (1951).

Fourastrié, Jean. *Les Trentes Glorieuses, ou, La revolution invisible de 1946 à 1975*. Paris: Fayard, 1979.

Frankel, Jeffrey A. "The 1807–1809 Embargo against Great Britain." *The Journal of Economic History* 42, no. 2 (1982): 291–308.

Freedman, Charles. "The Canadian Banking System (Technical Paper no. 81)." Ottawa: *The Bank of Canada*, 1998. Paper presented to the conference on Development in the Financial System: National and International Perspectives, The Jerome Levy Economics Institute of Bard College, New York (1997).

– "Financial Innovation in Canada: Causes and Consequences." *The American Economic Review* 73, no. 2 (1983): 101–6.

– "Financial Structure in Canada: The Movement towards Universal Banking." In *Universal Banking: Financial System Design Reconsidered*, edited by A. Saunders and I. Walter, 724–36. Chicago: Irwin Professional Publishing, 1996.

– "Universal Banking: The Canadian View." In *Financial Regulation: Changing the Rules of the Game*, edited by D. Vittas, 369–90. Washington: The World Bank, 1992.

Freeman, Mark, Robin Pearson, and James Taylor. "'A Doe in the City': Women Shareholders in Eighteenth- and Early Nineteenth-Century Britain." *Accounting, Business & Financial History* 16, no. 2 (2006): 265–91.

Friedman, Milton, and Anna J. Schwartz. *A Monetary History of the United States, 1867–1960*. Princeton: Princeton University Press, 1971.

Gaddis, John Lewis. *On Grand Strategy*. New York: Penguin Press, 2018.

Galles, D.L.C. "The Bank of Nova Scotia in Minneapolis, 1885–1892." *Minnesota History* 42, no. 7 (1971): 268–76.

Garon, André. "James Leslie." *Dictionary of Canadian Biography*. www.biographi.ca/009004-119.01-e.php?&id_nbr=5099 (accessed 1 June 2014).

Geithner, Timothy, F. *Stress Test: Reflections on Financial Crises*. New York: Crown Publishing Group, 2014.

George, Peter, and Philip Sworden. "The Courts and the Development of Trade in Upper Canada, 1830–1860." *The Business History Review* 60, no. 2 (1986): 258–80.

Germain, A., and D. Rose. *Montréal: The Quest for a Metropolis*. New York: Wiley, 2000.

Germain, Richard. *Dollars through the Doors: A Pre-1930 History of Bank Marketing in America*. Westport: Greenwood Publishing Group, Inc., 1996.

Gertler, Mark. "Financial Structure and Aggregate Economic Activity: An Overview." Working Paper No. 2559 for the *National Bureau of Economic Research* (1988): 1–51.

Ghossoub, Edgar A., Thanarak Laosuthi, and Robert R. Reed. "The Role of Financial Sector Competition for Monetary Policy." *Canadian Journal of Economics/Revue canadienne d'Economique* 45, no. 1 (2012): 270–87.

Giammarino, Ronald, Eduardo Schwartz, and Josef Zechner. "Market Valuation of Bank Assets and Deposit Insurance in Canada." *The Canadian Journal of Economics/Revue Canadienne d'Economique* 22, no. 1 (1989): 109–27.

Gibbons, Alan O. "Foreign Exchange Control in Canada, 1939–1951." *The Canadian Journal of Economics and Political Science/Revue Canadienne d'Economique et de Science Politique* 19, no. 1 (1953): 35–54.

Gibbons, J.S. *The Banks of New-York, Their Dealers, the Clearing House, and the Panic of 1857*. New York: D. Appleton & Co., 1859.

Gilbert, R. Alton. "Bank Market Structure and Competition: A Survey." *Journal of Money, Credit and Banking* 16, no. 4 (1984): 617–45.

Gillett, Margaret. "William Lunn." *Dictionary of Canadian Biography*. www.biographi.ca/009004-119.01-e.php?&id_nbr=5665 (accessed 10 September 2015).

Gillis, Robert Peter. "John Hamilton." *Dictionary of Canadian Biography*. www.biographi.ca/009004-119.01-e.php?&id_nbr=5562 (accessed 10 September 2016).

Glassford, Larry A. "Meighen, Arthur." *Dictionary of Canadian Biography*. www.biographi.ca/en/bio/meighen_authur_18E.html (accessed 23 March 2016).

Goddard, Thomas H. *A General History of the Most Prominent Banks in Europe: Particularly the Banks of England and France; The Rise and Progress of the Bank of North*

America; A Full History of the Late and Present Bank of the United States. New York: H.C. Sleight, 1831.

Goethe, Johann Wolfgang von. *Zur Farbenlehre.* Herausgegeben von Karl-Maria Guth. Berlin: Hofenberg, 2016.

Greenspan, Alan, and Adrian Woolridge. *Capitalism in America: A History.* New York: Penguin Press, 2018.

Greenwood, F. Murray. "John Richardson." *Dictionary of Canadian Biography.* www.biographi.ca/009004-119.01-e.php?&id_nbr=3096 (accessed 30 September 2014).

Grodzinski, John R. "Commissariat." In *The Encyclopedia of the War of 1812: A Political, Social, and Military History,* Vol. 1., edited by Spencer C. Tucker, 148–9. Santa Barbara: ABC-Clio, 2012.

Grossman, Richard S. "The Shoe That Didn't Drop: Explaining Banking Stability during the Great Depression." *The Journal of Economic History* 54, no. 3 (1994): 654–82.

– *Unsettled Account: The Evolution of Banking in the Industrialized World since 1800.* Princeton: Princeton University Press, 2010.

Gup, Benton E. *The Financial and Economic Crises: An International Perspective.* Cheltenham: Edward Elgar Publishing Limited, 2012.

Hague, George. "The Late Mr E.H. King, Formerly President of the Bank of Montreal." *Journal of Canadian Bankers Association* 9 (1896–97): 20–9.

Hale, Geoffrey. *Uneasy Partnership: The Politics of Business and Government in Canada.* Ontario: Broadview Press, 2006.

Hammond, Bray. "Banking in Canada before Confederation, 1792–1867." In *Approaches to Canadian Economic History: A Selection of Essays,* edited by W.T. Easterbrook and M.H. Watkins, 127–68. Toronto: McClelland and Stewart, 1967.

– *Banks and Politics in America from the Revolution to the Civil War.* Princeton: Princeton University Press, 1967.

Hannan, Timothy H., and Stephen A. Rhoades. "Acquisition Targets and Motives: The Case of the Banking Industry." *The Review of Economics and Statistics* 69, no. 1 (1987): 67–74.

Hanson, Victor Davis. *The Savoir Generals: How Five Great Commanders Saved Wars that Were Lost – From Ancient Greece to Iraq.* New York: Bloomsbury Press, 2013.

Harold, James, Håkan Lindgren, and Alice Teichova. *The Role of Banks in the Interwar Economy.* New York: Cambridge University Press, 1991.

Harris, Stephen. "Financial Sector Reform in Canada: Interests and the Policy Process." *The Canadian Journal of Political Science/Revue canadienne de science politique* 37, no. 1 (2004): 161–84.

– "The Globalisation of Finance and the Regulation of the Canadian Financial Services Industry." In *Changing the Rules: Canadian Regulatory Regimes and Institutions,* edited by G. Bruce Doern, 361–81. Toronto: University of Toronto Press, 1999.

Hart, Michael. *A Trading Nation: Canadian Trade Policy from Colonialism to Globalization.* Vancouver: University of British Columbia Press, 2002.

Hartt, Stanley H. "From a Bang to a Whimper: Twenty Years of Lost Momentum in Financial Institutions." *Policy Opinions* (2005): 73–6.

Haubrich, Joseph G. "Nonmonetary Effects of Financial Crises: Lessons from the Great Depression in Canada." *Journal of Monetary Economics* 25 (1990): 223–52.

Heffernan, Shelagh. *Modern Banking.* New Jersey: John Wiley & Sons Inc., 2005.

Heide, Lars. "Retail Banking and the Dynamics of Information Technology in Business Organizations." In *Technological Innovation in Retail Finance: International Historical Perspectives*, edited by Bernardo Batiz-Lazo, J. Carles Maixé-Altés, and Paul Thomes, 275–86. New York: Routledge, 2011.

Heinrichs, Waldo, and Marc Gallicchio. *Implacable Foes: War in the Pacific, 1944–1945*. Oxford: Oxford University Press, 2017.

Hendrickson, Jill M., and Mark W. Nichols. "How Does Regulation Affect the Risk Taking of Banks? A US and Canadian Perspective." *Journal of Comparative Policy Analysis: Research and Practice* 3, no. 1 (2001): 59–83.

Hidy, Ralph W., and Muriel E. Hidy. "Anglo-American Merchant Bankers and the Railroads of the Old Northwest, 1848–1860." *The Business History Review* 34, no. 2 (1960): 150–69.

Higgins, B.H. *The War and Postwar Cycle in Canada, 1914–1923*. Ottawa: Advisory Committee on Reconstruction, 1943.

Hilt, Eric. "The Panic of 1825: Financial Innovation, Crisis and Regulatory Reform." *Financial History* 96 (2010): 26–38.

Hinchley, Christine. *Foreign Banks in the Canadian Market*. Ottawa: Statistics Canada, 2006.

Hoberg, George. "Canada and North American Integration." *Canadian Public Policy/ Analyse de Politiques* 26 (2000): 35–50.

Hobsbawm, Eric J. *The Age of Capital, 1848–1875*. New York: World Publishing, 1975.

– *The Age of Empire, 1875–1914*. New York: World Publishing, 1987.

– *The Age of Revolution, 1789–1848*. New York: World Publishing, 1962.

Hubbard, J.T.W. *For Each, the Strength of All: A History of Banking in the State of New York*. New York: New York University Press, 1995.

Hunter, Larry W., Annette Bernhardt, Katherine L. Hughes, and Eva Skuratowicz. "It's Not Just the ATMs: Technology, Firm Strategies, Jobs, and Earnings in Retail Banking." Working Paper Prepared for the *Wharton Financial Institutions Center* (2000): 1–44.

Innis, Harold A. *A History of the Canadian Pacific Railway*. Toronto: McClelland and Stewart, 1923.

Inwood, K., and T. Stengos. "Discontinuities in Canadian Economic Growth, 1870–1985." *Explorations in Economic History* 28 (1991): 274–86.

James, Marquis, and Bessie R. James. *The Story of Bank of America: Biography of a Bank*. Washington: Beard Books, 1954.

Jamieson, A.B. *Chartered Banking in Canada*. Toronto: The Ryerson Press, 1953.

Jaremski, Matthew. "National Banking's Role in US Industrialization, 1850–1900." *Journal of Economic History* 74, no. 1 (2014): 109–40.

Jaremski, Matthew, and Peter L. Rousseau. "Banks, Free Banks and US Economic Growth." *Economic Inquiry* 51, no. 2 (2013): 1603–21.

Jedwab, Jack. "Jacob Henry Joseph." *Dictionary of Canadian Biography*. www.biographi.ca/009004-119.01-e.php?&id_nbr=6815 (accessed 12 October 2015).

Jenks, Leland H. "Railroads as an Economic Force in American Development." *The Journal of Economic History* 4, no. 1 (1944): 1–20.

Johnson, J.F. "The Canadian Banking System and Its Operation under Stress." *Annals of the American Academy of Political and Social Science* 36, no. 3 (1910): 60–84.

Johnson, Leo A. "John Simpson." *Dictionary of Canadian Biography*. www.biographi.ca/009004-119.01-e.php?&id_nbr=5832 (accessed 12 October 2015).

Johnston, Charles M., and Wendy Cameron. "William McMaster." *Dictionary of Canadian Biography*. www.biographi.ca/009004-119.01-e.php?&id_nbr=5699 (accessed 29 October 2016).

Jollie, Rose Marie. *On the Grow with Cleveland: A Brief History of Cleveland and the Central National Bank of Cleveland on the Occasion of the Bank's Seventy-Fifth Anniversary, 1890–1965*. Cleveland: Central National Bank of Cleveland, 1965.

Jones, Geoffrey. *British Multinational Banking 1830–1990*. United States: Oxford University Press, 1995.

Jones, Geoffrey, and Tarun Khanna. "Bring History (back) into International Business." *Journal of International Business Studies* 37, no. 4 (2006): 453–68.

Kaplan, Edward S. *The Bank of the United States and the American Economy*. United States: Greenwood Press, 1999.

Kerr, Donald. "Some Aspects of the Geography of Finance in Canada." *The Canadian Geographer* 9 (1965): 175–92.

Kerridge, Eric. *Trade and Banking in Early Modern England*. New York: Manchester University Press, 1988.

Kim, Jongchul. "How Modern Banking Originated: The London Goldsmith-Bankers' Institutionalisation of Trust." *Business History* 53, no. 6 (2011): 939–59.

Kimmel, David. "Sir Byron Edmund Walker." *Dictionary of Canadian Biography*. www.biographi.ca/009004-119.01-e.php?&id_nbr=7878 (accessed 12 March 2016).

Kindleberger, Charles P. *Manias, Panics, and Crashes: A History of Financial Crises*. New York: Basic Books, 1978.

King, Brett. *Bank 3.0: Why Banking Is No Longer Somewhere You Go, but Something You Do*. Singapore: John Wiley & Sons, 2013.

Klebaner, B.J. *American Commercial Banking: A History*. Boston: Twayne Publishers, 1990.

Knox, F.A. "Canadian War Finance and the Balance of Payments, 1914–18." *Canadian Journal of Economics and Political Science/Revue canadienne d'Economique et de Science politique* 6, no. 2 (1940): 226–57.

Koslowski, Peter. *The Ethics of Banking: Conclusions from the Financial Crisis*. Germany: Springer, 2009.

Kryzanowski, Lawrence, and Gordon S. Roberts. "Bank Structure in Canada." In *Banking Structures in Major Countries*, edited by G.G. Kaufman, 1–58. Boston: Kluwer Academic Publishers, 1991.

– "Canadian Banking Solvency, 1922–1940." *Journal of Money, Credit and Banking* 25, no. 3 (1993): 361–76.

– "Perspectives on Canadian Bank Insolvency during the 1930s." *Journal of Money, Credit and Banking* 31, no. 1 (1999): 130–6.

Kryzanowski, Lawrence, and Nancy Ursel. "Market Reaction to Announcements of Legislative Changes and Canadian Bank Takeovers of Canadian Investment Dealers." *Journal of Financial Services Research* 7 (1993): 171–85.

Kyte, Elinor Sr, and James H. Lambert. "David, David." *Dictionary of Canadian Biography*. www.biographi.ca/009004-119.01-e.php?&id_nbr=2824 (accessed 12 November 2014).

Laird, Pamela W. *Pull: Networking and Success since Benjamin Franklin*. Cambridge: Harvard University Press, 2007.

Lamalice, André L.J. "François-Antoine Larocque." *Dictionary of Canadian Biography*. www.biographi.ca/009004-119.01-e.php?&id_nbr=4538 (accessed 12 November 2014).

Lamoreaux, Naomi R. *Insider Lending: Banks, Personal Connections, and Economic Development in Industrial New England.* Cambridge: Cambridge University Press, 1996.

Lanier, Henry Wysham. *A Century of Banking in New York.* United States: George H. Doran, 1922.

Lazonick, W., and M. O'Sullivan. "Finance and Industrial Development, Part I: The United States and the United Kingdom." *Financial History Review* 4 (1997): 7–29.

Lebowitz, Michael A. "Review of 'Canada's First Bank: A History of the Bank of Montreal.' by Merrill Denison." *Journal of Economic History* 28, no. 4 (1968): 660–1.

Lee, Thomas A. "American Accountants in 1880." *Accounting, Business & Financial History* 17, no. 3 (2007): 333–54.

Lepler, Jessica M. "A Crisis of Interpretation: Precursor to the Panic of 1837." *Financial History* 109 (2014): 30–3.

– *The Many Panics of 1837: People, Politics and the Creation of a Transatlantic Financial Crisis.* Cambridge: Cambridge University Press, 2013.

Levine, Allan. "Hugh McLennan." *Dictionary of Canadian Biography.* www.biographi.ca/009004-119.01-e.php?&id_nbr=6287 (accessed 23 November 2015).

Levitt, Barbara, and James G. March. "Organizational Learning." *Annual Review of Sociology* 1 (1988): 319–40.

Little, John. *Loyalties in Conflict: Canadian Borderland in War and Rebellion, 1812–1840.* Toronto: University of Toronto Press, 2008.

Lo, Andrew W. *Adaptive Markets: Financial Evolution at the Speed of Thought.* Princeton: Princeton University Press, 2017.

Longley, Ronald Stewart. *Sir Francis Hincks, A Study of Canadian Politics, Railways, and Finance in the Nineteenth Century.* London: Oxford University Press, 1943.

Lott, Susan M. *Bank Mergers and the Public Interest.* Ottawa: Public Interest Advocacy Centre, 2005.

Lowe, Graham. "Class, Job and Gender in the Canadian Office." *Labour/La Travail* 10 (1982): 11–37.

– *Women in the Administrative Revolution: The Feminization of Clerical Work.* Toronto: University of Toronto Press, 1987.

Lower, Arthur R. *Colony to Nation: A History of Canada.* Toronto: McClelland and Stewart, 1981.

Luna, Sergio A. *Banking in North America.* Montreal: Institute for Research on Public Policy, 2004.

Lynch, James J. *Banking and Finance: Managing the Moral Dimension.* Cambridge: Gresham Books, 1994.

Lyon, Jim. *Dome: The Rise and Fall of the House that Jack Built.* Toronto: Avon Books of Canada, 1984.

Machiavelli, Nicolò. *The Prince.* Translated by W.K. Marriott. Ballingslöv: Wisehouse Classics, 2015.

MacIntosh, Robert. *Different Drummers: Banking and Politics in Canada.* Toronto: Macmillan Canada, 1991.

MacIntosh, Robert M. "The Buck Starts Here." *The Beaver* (August–September 2006): 43–8.

Makhoul, Anne. *RBC Financial Group from Accommodation to Inclusion.* Ottawa: Caledon Institute of Social Policy, 2005.

Marchildon, Gregory P. "British Investment Banking and Industrial Decline before the Great War: A Case Study of Capital Outflow to Canadian Industry." *Business History* 33, no. 3 (1991): 72–92.

– "'Hands across the Water': Canadian Industrial Financiers in the City of London, 1905–20." *Business History* 34, no. 3 (1992): 69–96.

– *Profits and Politics: Beaverbrook and the Gilded Age of Canadian Finance.* Toronto: University of Toronto Press, 1996.

Marchildon, Gregory P., and Duncan McDowall. *Canadian Multinationals and International Finance.* London: Frank Cass and Company Limited, 1992.

Marglin, Stephen A., and Juliet B. Schor, eds. *The Golden Age of Capitalism: Reinterpreting the Postwar Experience.* Oxford: Clarendon Oxford University Press, 1990.

Markham, Jerry W. *A Financial History of the United States: Volume I: From Christopher Columbus to the Robber Barons (1492–1900).* New York: M.E. Sharpe, Inc., 2002.

– *A Financial History of the United States: Volume II: From J.P. Morgan to the Institutional Investor (1900–1970).* New York: M.E. Sharpe, Inc., 2002.

Masters, D.C. "Toronto vs. Montreal: The Struggle for Financial Hegemony, 1860–1875." *Canadian Historical Review* 22, no. 2 (1941): 133–46.

Matthews, Philip W., and Anthony William Tuke. *History of Barclays Bank Limited.* London: Blades, East & Blades Ltd, 1926.

McCallum, John. *Unequal Beginnings: Agriculture and Economic Development in Quebec and Ontario until 1870.* Toronto: University of Toronto Press, 1980.

McCullough, Alan Bruce. *Money and Exchange in Canada to 1900.* Toronto: Dundurn Press, 1984.

McDowall, Duncan. "Edson Loy Pease." *Dictionary of Canadian Biography.* www.biographi.ca/009004-119.01-e.php?&id_nbr=7956 (accessed 22 November 2016)

– *Quick to the Frontier: Canada's Royal Bank.* Toronto: McClelland & Stewart, 1993.

– "Sir Henry Vincent Meredith." *Dictionary of Canadian Biography.* www.biographi.ca/009004-119.01-e.php?&id_nbr=8294 (accessed 23 November 2016).

McDowell, Linda, and Gillian Court. "Missing Subjects: Gender, Power, and Sexuality in Merchant Banking." *Economic Geography* 70, no. 3 (1994): 229–51.

McIntosh, James. "Scale Efficiency in a Dynamic Model of Canadian Insurance Companies." *The Journal of Risk and Insurance* 65, no. 2 (1998): 303–17.

– "A Welfare Analysis of Canadian Chartered Bank Mergers." *The Canadian Journal of Economics/Revue Canadienne d'Economique* 35, no. 3 (2002): 457–75.

McKeagan, David. "Development of a Mature Securities Market in Montreal from 1817 to 1874." *Business History* 51, no. 1 (2009): 59–76.

McKenna, Christopher, and Rowena Olegario. "Corporate Reputation and Regulation in Historical Perspective." In *The Oxford Handbook of Corporate Reputation*, edited by Michael L. Barnett and Timothy G. Pollock, 260–77. Oxford: Oxford University Press, 2014.

McKenney, James L., Duncan C. Copeland, and Richard O. Mason. *Waves of Change: Business Evolution through Information Technology.* Boston: Harvard Business School Press, 1995.

McKenney, James L., and Amy Weaver Fisher. "Manufacturing the ERMA Banking System: Lessons from History." *IEEE Annals of the History of Computing* 15, no. 4 (1993): 7–26.

McKinsey and Company. "L'évolution du secteur des services financiers au Canada: De nouvelles forces, de nouveaux compétiteurs, de nouveaux choix." Document de recherché préparé pour *le group de travail sur l'avenir du secteur des services financiers canadien* (1998).

McMurry, R.N. "Efficiency, Work-Satisfaction and Neurotic Tendency: A Study of Bank Employees." *Personnel Journal* 11 (1932): 201–10.

Meredith, Patricia. "Why the Frog Does Not Jump Out of the Boiling Water: A Multi-level Exploration of the Limited Responses of the Canadian Banks to Disruptive Changes in the Canadian Residential Mortgage Industry from 1975 to 2008." PhD. dissertation, York University, 2009.

Meredith, Patricia, and James Darroch. *Stumbling Giants: Transforming Canada's Banks for the Information Age.* Toronto: University of Toronto Press, 2017.

Michie, Ranald C. "The Canadian Securities Market, 1850–1914." *The Business History Review* 62, no. 1 (1988): 35–73.

Miles, Barbara L. *The Canadian Financial System.* New York: Novinka Science Publishers, Inc., 2003.

Miller, Carman. "John Gray." *Dictionary of Canadian Biography.* www.biographi.ca/009004-119.01-e.php?&id_nbr=2897 (accessed 2 July 2014).

– "Sir Edward Seaborne Clouston." *Dictionary of Canadian Biography.* www.biographi.ca/009004-119.01-e.php?&id_nbr=7286 (accessed 23 August 2015).

– "Thomas Brown Anderson." *Dictionary of Canadian Biography.* www.biographi.ca/009004-119.01-e.php?&id_nbr=4794 (accessed 24 August 2015).

"Thomas Porteous." *Dictionary of Canadian Biography.* www.biographi.ca/009004-119.01-e.php?&id_nbr=3078 (accessed 12 September 2015).

Mitchener, Kris James. "Bank Supervision, Regulation, and Instability during the Great Depression." *The Journal of Economic History* 65, no. 1 (2005): 152–85.

Moessner, Richhild, and William A. Allen. "Banking Crises and the International Monetary System in the Great Depression and Now." *Financial History Review* 18, no. 1 (2011): 1–20.

Mollan, Simon, and R.C. Michie. "The City of London as an International Commercial and Financial Center since 1900." *Enterprise & Society* 13, no. 3 (2012): 538–87.

Momryk, Myron. "Daniel Sutherland." *Dictionary of Canadian Biography.* www.biographi.ca/009004-119.01-e.php?&id_nbr=3151 (accessed 22 November 2015).

– "Frederick William Ermatinger." *Dictionary of Canadian Biography.* www.biographi.ca/009004-119.01-e.php?&id_nbr=2860 (accessed 1 October 2014).

Monet, Jacques, and Gerald J.J. Tulchinsky. "Austin Cuvillier." *Dictionary of Canadian Biography.* www.biographi.ca/009004-119.01-e.php?&id_nbr=3340 (accessed 2 October 2014).

Monteith, Kathleen E.A. "Competition between Barclays Bank (DCO) and the Canadian banks in the West Indies, 1926–45." *Financial History Review* 7 (2000): 67–87.

Moore, B.J. "Capitalization and Profitability in Canadian Banking." *The Canadian Journal of Economics an Political Science/Revue canadienne d'Economique et de Science politique* 27, no. 2 (1961): 192–204.

Morris, Henry Crittenden. *The History of the First National Bank of Chicago.* United States: R.R. Donnelley & Sons Co., 1902.

Muller, Nicholas H. "Smuggling into Canada: How the Champlain Valley Defied Jefferson's Embargo." *Vermont History* 38, no. 1 (1970): 5–21.

Murphy, Sharon Ann. "Banks and Banking in the Early American Republic." *History Compass* 10, no. 5 (2012): 409–22.

Mussio, Laurence B. *A Vision Greater Than Themselves: The Making of the Bank of Montreal, 1817–2017.* Montreal/Kingston: McGill-Queen's University Press, 2016.

Musson, A.E. "The Great Depression in Britain, 1873–1896: A Reappraisal." *The Journal for European Economic History* 19, no. 2 (1959): 199–228.

Nagy, Pancras J. *The International Business of Canadian Banks.* Montreal: The Centre for International Business Studies, 1983.

Nathan, Alli, and Edwin H. Neave. "Competition and Contestability in Canada's Financial System: Empirical Results." *The Canadian Journal of Economics/Revue canadienne d'Economique* 22, no. 3 (1989): 576–94.

– "Operating Efficiency of Canadian Banks." *Journal of Financial Services Research* 6, no. 3 (1992): 265–76.

Naylor, R.T. *The History of Canadian Business, 1867–1914: Volume One: The Banks and Finance Capital.* Michigan: J. Lorimer, 1975.

– "The Rise and Decline of the Trustee Savings Bank in British North America." *Canadian Historical Review* 65, no. 4 (1984): 511–41.

Neary, Peter. *Newfoundland in the North Atlantic World, 1929–1949.* Montreal/Kingston: McGill-Queen's University Press, 1996.

– "'That Thin Red Cord of Sentiment and Blood:' Newfoundland in the Great Depression, 1929–1934." Draft. Centre for Newfoundland Studies copy. Courtesy of the author.

– "With Great Regret and after Most Anxious Consideration: Newfoundland's 1932 Plan to Reschedule Interest Payments." *Newfoundland Studies* 10, no. 2 (1994): 165–297.

Neave, Edwin H. *Financial Systems: Principles and Organisation.* New York: Routledge, 1998.

Neldner, Manfred. "Marktversagen oder falsche gesetzliche Restriktionen? Erfahrungen mit Vielnotenbanken-Systemen ohne Zentralbank in der Schweiz, Schweden und Kanada." *Vierteljahrschrift für Sozial- und Wirtschaftsgeschichte* 88, no. 4 (2001): 454–68.

Nelles, H.V. *The Art of Nation Building: Pageantry and Spectacle at Québec's Tercentary.* Toronto: University of Toronto Press, 2000.

Neufeld, Edward Peter. *Bank of Canada Operations and Policy.* Toronto: University of Toronto Press, 1958.

– *The Financial System of Canada: Its Growth and Development.* Toronto: Macmillan of Canada, 1972.

– *Money and Banking in Canada.* Toronto: McClelland and Stewart Limited, 1964.

– "Reshaping Canada's Financial System: Who Wins, Who Loses?" In *Financial Growth in Canada,* edited by P.J.N. Halpern, 419–29. Calgary: University of Calgary Press for Industry Canada Research Series, 1997.

Nevins, Allan. *History of the Bank of New York and Trust Company, 1784–1934.* New York: Bank of New Work and Trust Company, 1934.

Newton, Lucy, and Philip L. Cottrell. "Female Investors in the First English and Welsh Commercial Joint-Stock Banks." *Accounting, Business & Financial History* 16, no. 2 (2006): 315–40.

Nichols, Mark W., and Jill M. Hendrickson. "Profit Differentials between Canadian and US Commercial Banks: The Role of Regulation." *The Journal of Economic History* 57, no. 3 (1997): 674–96.

Noiseux, Marie Hélène. *Canadian Bank Mergers, Rescues and Failures.* Montreal: Concordia University, 2002.

Northcott, Carol Ann. "Competition in Banking: A Review of the Literature." Working Paper 2004-24 for the *Bank of Canada* (2004): 1–36.

O'Huallachain, Breandán. "Foreign Banking in the American Urban System of Financial Organization." *Economic Geography* 70, no. 3 (1994): 206–28.

Olegario, Rowena, and Christopher McKenna. "Introduction: Corporate Reputation in Historical Perspective." *Business History Review* 87, no. 4 (2003): 643–54.

Ontario Legislative Assembly. *Role of the Bank of Canada*. 1991.

Orr, Dale. "The Economic Determinants of Entry into Canadian Banking, 1963–7." *The Canadian Journal of Economics/Revue canadienne d'Economique* 7, no. 1 (1974), 82–99.

Osborn, Alan. *Banking and Financial Institutions in the UK* London: Foreign & Commonwealth Office, 2001.

Ovid. *The Fall of Icarus*. Translated by Mary M. Innis. London: Penguin Books, 2015.

Owram, Doug. "Economic Thought in the 1930s: The Prelude to Keynesianism." *Canadian Historical Review* 66, no. 3 (1985): 344–77.

Pak, Susie. *Gentlemen Bankers: The World of J.P. Morgan*. Cambridge: Harvard University Press, 2014.

– "Reputation and Social Ties: J.P. Morgan & Co. and Private Investment Banking." *Business History Review* 87, no. 4 (2013): 703–28.

Park, Y. Goo. "Depression and Capital Formation in the United Kingdom and Germany, 1873–1896." *The Journal for European Economic History* 26, no. 1 (1997): 511–34.

Parker, George L. "Robert Armour." *Dictionary of Canadian Biography*. www.biographi.ca/009004-119.01-e.php?&id_nbr=3748 (accessed 29 November 2016).

Parr, Joy. *Domestic Goods: The Material, the Moral, and the Economic in the Postwar Years*. Toronto: University of Toronto Press, 1999.

Peria, Maria Soledad Martinez, Andrew Powell, and Ivanna Vladkova-Hollar. "Banking on Foreigners: The Behavior of International Bank Claims on Latin America, 1985 2000." *IMF Staff Papers* 52, no. 3 (2005): 430–61.

Perkins, Edwin J. *Financing Anglo-American Trade: The House of Brown, 1800–1880*. Cambridge: Harvard University Press, 1975.

Piédalue, Gilles. "Les Groupes Financiers et la Guerre du Papier au Canada, 1920–1930." *Revue d'histoire de l'Amérique française* 30, no. 2 (1976): 223–58.

Piercy, Day, and Anne Ladky. *Women Employed vs. Harris Bank: A Case Study*. Chicago: Women Employed Institute, 1982.

Piva, Michael J. *The Borrowing Process: Public Finance in the Province of Canada, 1840–1867*. Ottawa: University of Ottawa Press, 1992.

Polèse, Mario, and Richard Shearmur. "Culture, Language, and the Location of High Order Service Functions: The Case of Montreal and Toronto." *Economic Geography* 80, no. 4 (2004): 329–50.

Pomfret, Richard. *The Economic Development of Canada*. New York: Taylor & Francis, 2006.

Poole, Phebe-Jane. *Women in Banking: The First Year of Employment Equity*. Ottawa: Canadian Centre for Policy Alternatives, 1989.

Pratt, John Tidd. *The History of Saving Banks in England, Wales, Ireland, and Scotland*. London: Shaw and Sons, 1842.

Pridmore, Jay. *Harris: A History of the Bank*. Chicago: History Works, 2009.

Quigley, Neil. "The Chartered Banks and Foreign Direct Investment in Canada." *Studies in Political Economy* 19 (1986): 31–57.

Quigley, Neil C. "The Bank of Nova Scotia in the Caribbean, 1889–1940." *The Business History Review* 63, no. 4 (1989): 797–838.

Ramírez, Carlos D. "Bank Fragility, 'Money under the Mattress,' and Long-Run Growth: US Evidence from the 'Perfect' Panic of 1893." *The Journal of Banking and Finance* 33, no. 12 (2009): 2185–98.

Ratnovski, Lev, and Rocco Huang. *Why Are Canadian Banks More Resilient?* IMF Working Paper, 2009.

Redford, Alexander. "Donald Alexander Smith, 1st Baron Strathcona and Mount Royal." *Dictionary of Canadian Biography*. www.biographi.ca/009004-119.01e.php?&id_nbr=7710 (accessed 1 December 2016).

– "Richard Angus Bladworth." *Dictionary of Canadian Biography*. www.biographi.ca/009004-119.01-e.php?&id_nbr=8008 (accessed 30 November 2016).

Redish, Angela. "It Is History but It's No Accident: Differences in Residential Mortgage Markets in Canada and the United States." In *Current Federal Reserve Policy under the Lens of Economic History: Essays to Commemorate the Federal Reserve System Centennial*, edited by Owen F. Humpage, 296–317. Cambridge: Cambridge University Press, 2015.

– "Why Was Specie Scare in Colonial Economies? An Analysis of the Canadian Currency, 1796–1830." *The Journal of Economic History* 44, no. 3 (1984): 713–28.

Reeves, M.A., and W.A. Kerr. "Implications of the Increasing Emphasis on Monetary Policy for the Federal State: The Case of Canada." *Journal of Commonwealth & Comparative Politics* 24, no. 3 (1986): 254–68.

Regehr, T.D. "Banks and Farmers in Western Canada." In *The Developing West: Essays in Canadian History*, edited by J.E. Foster, 303–36. Edmonton: University of Alberta Press, 1983.

Regini, Marino, Jim Kitay, and Martin Baethge. *From Tellers to Sellers: Changing Employment Relations in Banks*. United States: MIT Press, 1999.

Rich, Georg. "Canadian Banks, Gold, and the Crisis of 1907." *Explorations in Economic History* 26 (1989): 135–60.

– *The Cross of Gold: Money and the Canadian Business Cycle, 1867–1913*. Ontario: Carleton University Press, 1988.

Richards, David L., and Ronald D. Gelleny. "Banking Crises, Collective Protest and Rebellion." *Canadian Journal of Political Science/Revue canadienne de science politique* 39, no. 4 (2006): 777–801.

Richards, R.D. *The Early History of Banking in England*. New York: Routledge, 1929.

Richardson, A.J.H. "William Finlay." *Dictionary of Canadian Biography*. www.biographi.ca/009004-119.01-e.php?&id_nbr=2870 (accessed 23 February 2016).

Richardson, Alan J. "The Canadian Audit Market in the First Half of the Twentieth Century." *The Accounting Historians Journal* 28, no. 2 (2001): 109–39.

– "Institutional Responses to Bank Failures: A Comparative Case Study of the Home Bank (1923) and Canadian Commercial Bank (1985) Failures." *Critical Perspectives on Accounting* 3, no. 2 (1992): 163–83.

Rindova, Violina P., and Charles J. Fombrun. "Constructing Competitive Advantage: The Role of Firm-Constituent Interactions." *Strategic Management Journal* 20, no. 8 (1999): 691–710.

Roberge, Ian. "Autonome malgré tout! L'internationalisation et la réforme des marches financiers au Canada." *Canadian Public Policy* 31, no. 3 (2005): 259–72.

– "For Better or Worse: The Politicization of Canadian Finance." Paper presented at the Canadian Political Science Association Annual Convention (2006): 1–18.

Robert, Jean-Claude. "Horatio Gates." *Dictionary of Canadian Biography.* www.biographi.ca/009004-119.01-e.php?&id_nbr=2885 (accessed 15 September 2014).

Roberts, Alasdair. *America's First Depression: Economic Crisis and Political Disorder after the Panic of 1837.* Ithaca: Cornell University Press, 2012.

Roberts, Richard, and David Kynaston. *The Bank of England: Money, Power, and Influence, 1694–1994.* Oxford: Oxford University Press, 1995.

Rockoff, Hugh. "The Free Banking Era: A Reexamination." *Journal of Money, Credit and Banking* 6, no. 2 (1974): 141–67.

Romer, Christina D. "What Ended the Great Depression?" Working Paper No. 3829 for the *National Bureau of Economic Research* (1991): 1–51.

Rose, Johnathan W. *Making Pictures in Our Heads: Government Advertising in Canada.* Westport: Praeger, 2000.

Ross, Victor. *A History of the Canadian Bank of Commerce*, 2 volumes. Toronto: Oxford University Press, 1922.

Rota, Mauro, and Francesco Schettino. "The Long-Run Determinants of British Capital Exports, 1870–1913." *Financial History Review* 18, no. 1 (2011): 47–69.

Rousseau, Peter L. "The Market for Bank Stocks and the Rise of Deposit Banking in New York City, 1866, 1867." *The Journal of Economic History* 71 (2011): 976–1005.

Rovelli, Carlo. *The Order of Time.* New York: Riverhead Books, 2018.

Royal Bank of Canada. *Fiftieth Anniversary of the Royal Bank of Canada, Established October Eighteenth, 1869; A Record of its Progress during the Past Half Century, 1869–1919.* Montreal: The Royal Bank of Canada, 1920.

Rubery, Jill. "Internal Labour Markets and Equal Opportunities: Women's Position in Banks in European Countries." *European Journal of Industrial Relations* 1, no. 2 (1995): 203–27.

Rudin, R.E. "Edward Henry King." *Dictionary of Canadian Biography.* www.biographi.ca/009004-119.01-e.php?&id_nbr=6197 (accessed 22 May 2016).

– "George Baillie Houliston." *Dictionary of Canadian Biography.* www.biographi.ca/009004-119.01-e.php?&id_nbr=6170 (accessed 30 May 2015).

– "George Stephen, 1st Baron Mount Stephen." *Dictionary of Canadian Biography.* www.biographi.ca/009004-119.01-e.php?&id_nbr=8375 (accessed 22 May 2016).

– "Henry Starnes." *Dictionary of Canadian Biography.* www.biographi.ca/009004-119.01-e.php?&id_nbr=6441 (accessed 22 July 2016).

– "William Weir." *Dictionary of Canadian Biography.* www.biographi.ca/009004-119.01-e.php?&id_nbr=7135 (accessed 31 July 2016).

Rudin, Ronald. "A Bank Merger Unlike the Others: The Establishment of the Banque Canadienne Nationale." *Canadian Historical Review* 61, no. 2 (1980): 191–212.

– "Banker's Hours: Life behind the Wicket at the Banque d'Hochelaga, 1901–1921." *Labour/Le Travail* 18 (1986): 63–76.

– *Banking en Français: The French Banks of Quebec, 1835–1925.* Toronto: University of Toronto Press, 1985.

– "Montreal Banks and the Urban Development of Quebec, 1840–1914." In *Shaping the Urban Landscape: Aspects of the Canadian City-Building Process*, edited by Gilbert A. Stelter and Alan F.J. Artibise, 65–83. Ottawa: Carleton University Press, 1982.

Safarian, A.E. *The Canadian Economy in the Great Depression.* Toronto: University of Toronto Press, 1959.

Saul, S.B. *The Myth of the Great Depression, 1873–1896*. London: Macmillan, 1969.

Saunders, Anthony, and Berry Wilson. "The Impact of Consolidation and Safety-Net Support on Canadian, US, and UK Banks: 1893–1992." *Journal of Banking and Finance* 23 (1999): 537–71.

Sawyer, Deborah C. "Bank of Montreal." *The Canadian Encyclopedia Online.* www.thecanadianencyclopedia.com/articles/bank-of-montreal (accessed 1 March 2014).

Schembri, Lawrence L., and Jennifer A. Hawkins. "The Role of Canadian Chartered Banks in US Banking Crises: 1870–1914." *Business History* 34, no. 3 (1992): 122–52.

Schreft, Stacy L. "Credit Controls: 1980." *Economic Review* 76, no. 6 (1990): 25–55.

Schull, Joseph. *The Great Scot: A Biography of Donald Gordon*. Montreal/Kingston: McGill-Queen's University Press, 1994.

– *100 Years of Banking in Canada: A History of the Toronto-Dominion Bank*. Vancouver: Copp Clark, 1958.

– *The Scotiabank Story: A History of the Bank of Nova Scotia, 1832–1982*. Toronto: Macmillan of Canada, 1982.

Schweikart, Larry. "US Commercial Banking: A Historiographical Survey." *The Business History Review* 65, no. 3 (1991): 606–61.

Scott, James C. *Seeing like a State: How Certain Schemes to Improve the Human Condition Have Failed*. New Haven: Yale University Press, 1998.

Sears, Louis M. *Jefferson and the Embargo*. Durham: Duke University Press, 1927.

Sexton, Jay. "Transatlantic Financiers and the Civil War." *American Nineteenth Century History* 2, no. 3 (2001): 29–46.

Shaffer, Sherrill. "A Test of Competition in Canadian Banking." *Journal of Money, Credit and Banking* 25, no. 1 (1993): 49–61.

Sharp, Paul F. *The Agrarian Revolt in Western Canada: A Survey Showing American Parallels*. Regina: Canadian Plains Research Centre, University of Regina, 1997.

Shearer, Ronald A. "The Canadian Financial System." In *New Palgrave Dictionary of Money and Finance*, edited by John Eatwell, Murray Millgate, and Peter Newman, 274–6. London: Palgrave Macmillan, 1992.

– "The Foreign Currency Business of Canadian Chartered Banks." *The Canadian Journal of Economics and Political Science/Revue canadienne d'Economique et de Science politique* 31, no. 3 (1965): 328–57.

– "The Porter Commission Report in the Context of Earlier Canadian Monetary Documents." *The Canadian Journal of Economics/Revue canadienne d'Economique* 10, no. 1 (1977): 34–49.

Shearer, Ronald A., and Carolyn Clark. "Canada and the Interwar Gold Standard, 1920–1935: Monetary Policy without a Central Bank." In *A Retrospective on the Classical Gold Standard 1821–1931*, edited by Michael D. Bordo and Anna J. Schwartz, 277–310. Chicago: University of Chicago Press, 1984:

Sheppard, G. *Plunders, Profit and Paroles: A Social History of the War of 1912 in Upper Canada*. Montreal/Kingston: McGill-Queen's University Press, 1994.

Shortt, Adam. *Adam Shortt's History of Canadian Currency and Banking, 1600–1880*. Pennsylvania: The Association, 1986.

– "The Early History of Canadian Banking: Canadian Currency and Exchange under French Rule." *Journal of the Canadian Bankers' Association* 5 (1898).

– "History of Canadian Currency, Banking and Exchange." *Journal of the Canadian Bankers' Association* 10 (1903): 35–9.

Siklos, Pierre L. "Understanding the Great Depression in the United States versus Canada." In *World Economy and National Economies in the Interwar Slump*, edited by Theo Balderston, 27–57. Basingstoke: The MacMillan Press, 2000.

Siles, William H. "Quiet Desperation: A Personal View of the Panic of 1837. *New York History* (1986): 89–92.

Skogstad, Grace. "Globalization and Public Policy: Situating Canadian Analyses." *Canadian Journal of Political Science/Revue canadienne de science politique* 33, no. 4 (2000): 805–28.

Skully, Michael T. "Financial Institutions and Markets in Australia." In *Financial Institutions and Markets in the Southwest Pacific: A Study of Australia, Fiji, New Zealand, and Papua New Guinea*, edited by Michael T. Skully, 1–93. London: Macmillan Press, 1985.

Slater, David W. "The 1967 Revision of the Canadian Banking Acts, Part I: An Economist's View." *Canadian Journal of Economics* 1, no. 1 (1968): 79–91.

Smith, Andrew. "Continental Divide: The Canadian Banking and Currency Laws of 1871 in the Mirror of the United States." *Enterprise & Society* 13, no. 3 (2012): 455–503.

Smith, Denis. *Gentle Patriot: A Political Biography of Walter Gordon*. Edmonton: Hurtig Publishers, 1973.

Smith, Norman Walker. *A History of Commercial Banking in New Hampshire, 1793–1843*. Wisconsin: University of Wisconsin-Madison, 1967.

Spero, Joan Edelman. *The Failure of the Franklin National Bank: Challenge to the International System*. Washington: Beard Books, 1999.

Spraakman, Gary. "Internal Audit at the Historical Hudson's Bay Company: A Challenge to Accepted History." *The Accounting Historians Journal* 28, no. 1 (2001): 19–41.

Spraakman, Gary, and Julie Margret. "The Transfer of Management Accounting Practices from London Counting Houses to the British North American Fur Trade." *Accounting, Business & Financial History* 15, no. 2 (2005): 101–19.

Stahl, Günter K., and Andreas Vogt. "Do Cultural Differences Matter in Mergers and Acquisitions? A Tentative Model and Examination." *Organization Science* 19, no. 1 (2008): 160–76.

Stairs, Denis, and Gilbert R. Winham. *The Politics of Canada's Economic Relationship with the United States*. Toronto: University of Toronto Press, 1985.

Ste Croix, Lorne. "Benjamin Holmes." *Dictionary of Canadian Biography*. www.biographi.ca/009004-119.01-e.php?&id_nbr=4499 (accessed 15 December 2014).

Stearns, David. "Automating Payments: Origins of the Visa Electronic Payment System." In *Technological Innovation in Retail Finance: International Historical Perspectives,* edited by Bernardo Batiz-Lazo, J. Carles Maixé-Altés, and Paul Thomes, 246–73. New York: Routledge, 2011.

Storey, John, Peter Cressey, Tim Morris, and Adrian Wilkinson. "Changing Employment Practices in UK Banking: Case Studies." *Personnel Review* 26, no. ½ (1997): 24–42.

Street, Kori. "Bankers and Bomb Makers: Gender Ideology and Women's Paid Work in Banking and Munitions during the First World War in Canada." *Dissertation Abstracts International* 62, no. 4 (2001): 1544.

Sutton, Brent. *Out from Behind the Great Wall: Emerging Opportunities for Canadian Financial Institutions in China*. Ottawa: Conference Board of Canada, 1995.

Sweeny, Robert. "Peter McGill." *Dictionary of Canadian Biography*. www.biographi.ca/009004-119.01-e.php?id_nbr=4069 (accessed 17 July 2016).

Sylla, R. "Federal Policy, Banking Market Structure and Capital Mobilization in the United States, 1863–1913." *Journal of Economic History* 29, no. 4 (1969): 657–86.

Sylla, R., J.B. Legler, and J.J. Wallis. "Banks and State Public Finance in the New Republic: The United States, 1790–1860." *The Journal of Economic History* 47 (1987): 391–403.

Talman, James J. "Review of 'Canada's First Bank: A History of the Bank of Montreal' by Merrill Denison." *The American Historical Review* 74, no. 1 (1968): 334–5.

Taylor, Norman W. "The Effects of Industrialization – Its Opportunities and Consequences – upon French-Canadian Society." *The Journal of Economic History* 20, no. 4 (1960): 638–47.

Teeple, Gary. *Capitalism and the National Question in Canada*. Toronto: University of Toronto Press, 1972.

Tilly, Richard. "Universal Banking in Historical Perspective." *The Journal of Institutional and Theoretical Economics* 154, no. 1 (1998): 7–32.

Tilly, Richard H. "Banking Institutions in Historical and Comparative Perspective: Germany, Great Britain and the United States in the Nineteenth and Early Twentieth Century." *Journal of Institutional and Theoretical Economics* 145, no. 1 (1989): 189–209.

Tooze, Adam. *Crashed: How a Decade of Financial Crises Changed the World*. New York: Viking Press, 2018.

Toronto-Dominion Bank, and Oscar D. Skelton. *Fifty Years of Banking Service, 1871–1921*. Toronto: Toronto Dominion Bank, 1922.

Totta, Johanne M., and Ronald J. Burke. "Integrating Diversity and Equality into the Fabric of the Organization." *Women in Management Review* 10, no. 7 (1995): 32–9.

Trenton Banking Company. *Trenton Banking Company: A History of the First Century of Its Existence*. New Jersey: Trenton Banking Company, 1907.

Tschoegl, Adrian E. "FDI and Internationalization: Evidence from US Subsidiaries of Foreign Banks." *Journal of International Business* 33, no. 4 (2002): 805–15.

Tulchinsky, Gerald J. *The River Barons: Montreal Businessmen and the Growth of Industry and Transportation, 1837–53*. Toronto: University of Toronto Press, 1977.

Tulchinsky, Gerald J.J. "Adam Ferrie." *Dictionary of Canadian Biography*. www.biographi.ca/009004-119.01-e.php?&id_nbr=4422 (accessed 25 May 2014).

– "George Auldjo." *Dictionary of Canadian Biography*. www.biographi.ca/009004-119.01-e.php?&id_nbr=3222 (accessed 25 May 2014).

– "George Garden." *Dictionary of Canadian Biography*. www.biographi.ca/009004-119.01-e.php?&id_nbr=2882 (accessed 25 May 2014).

– "George Moffatt." *Dictionary of Canadian Biography*. www.biographi.ca/009004-119.01-e.php?&id_nbr=4602 (accessed 25 May 2014).

– "John Forsyth." *Dictionary of Canadian Biography*. www.biographi.ca/009004-119.01-e.php?&id_nbr=3389 (accessed 25 May 2014).

– "John Frothingham." *Dictionary of Canadian Biography*. www.biographi.ca/009004-119.01-e.php?&id_nbr=4439 (accessed 26 May 2014).

– "Robert Gillespie." *Dictionary of Canadian Biography*. www.biographi.ca/009004-119.01-e.php?&id_nbr=4451 (accessed 26 May 2014).

Tulchinsky, Gerald J.J., and Alan R. Dever. "Thomas Ryan." *Dictionary of Canadian Biography*. www.biographi.ca/009004-119.01-e.php?&id_nbr=5815 (accessed 25 September 2015).

Turley-Ewart, John. "The Bank that Went Bust." *The Beaver* 84, no. 4 (2004): 36–41.

Turley-Ewart, John A. "Henry Collingwood McLeod." *Dictionary of Canadian Biography*. www.biographi.ca/009004-119.01-e.php?&id_nbr=8290 (accessed 25 September 2016).

Tylecote, Andrew. *The Long Wave in the World Economy: The Current Crisis in Historical Perspective*. London: Routledge, 1991.

Unterman, Katherine. "Boodle over the Border: Embezzlement and the Crisis of International Mobility, 1880–1890." *The Journal of the Gilded Age and Progressive Era* 11, no. 2 (2012): 151–89.

Urban, Scott, and Tobias Straumann. "Still Tied by Gold Fetters: The Global Response to the US Recession of 1937–1938." *Financial History Review* 19, no. 1 (2012): 22–48.

Vallières, Marc. "John Smythe Hall." *Dictionary of Canadian Biography*. www.biographi.ca/009004-119.01-e.php?&id_nbr=6759 (accessed 25 January 2016).

Vardy, Jill. *The Bank of Canada: An Illustrated History*. Ottawa: Bank of Canada, 2005.

Verdier, Daniel. "The Rise and Fall of State Banking in OECD Countries." *Comparative Political Studies* 33, no. 3 (2000): 283–318.

Wagster, John D. "Bank Capital and Implicit Government Support: Sources of Stability for Canadian Banks during the Great Depression." Presented at FMA European Conference at Turin (2008).

– "Canadian-Bank Stability during the Great Depression: The Role of Banking Consolidation and Safety-Net Support." Southern Finance Association at Key West, FL (20–22 November 2008).

– "Impact of the 1988 Basle Accord on International Banks." *Journal of Finance* 51, no. 4 (1996): 1321–46.

– "Wealth and Risk Effects of Adopting Deposit Insurance in Canada: Evidence of Risk Shifting by Banks and Trust Companies." *Journal of Money, Credit and Banking* 39, no. 7 (2007): 1649–79.

Wainwright, Nicholas B. *History of the Philadelphia National Bank: A Century and a Half of Philadelphia Banking, 1803–1953*. Philadelphia: Historical Society of Pennsylvania, 1953.

Wardley, P. "The Commercial Banking Industry and Its Part in the Emergence and Consolidation of the Corporate Economy in Britain before 1940." *Journal of Industrial History* 3, no. 2 (2000): 71–97.

Watts, George S. *The Bank of Canada: Origins and Early History*. Ontario: Carleton University Press, 1993.

Weber, Robert F. "Structural Regulation as Antidote to Complexity Capture." *American Business Law Journal* 49, no. 3 (2012): 643–738.

Weiman, David F., and John A. James. "The Political Economy of the US Monetary Union: The Civil War Era as a Watershed. *American Economic Review* 97, no. 2 (2007): 271–5.

Weissbourd, Robert. "Banking on Technology: Expanding Financial Markets and Economic Opportunity." A report prepared for the Brookings Institution Centre on Urban and Metropolitan Policy, the Financial Services Roundtable, and Ford Foundation (2002): 1–42.

Wessells, John H. *The Bank of Virginia: A History*. Virginia: University Press of Virginia, 1973.

White, Eugene Nelson. "A Reinterpretation of the Banking Crisis of 1930." *The Journal of Economic History* 44, no. 1 (1984): 119–38.

Whittington, Les. *The Banks: The Ongoing Battle for Control of Canada's Richest Business*. Toronto: Stoddart Publishing Co. Limited, 1999.

Wilkins, Mira. *The History of Foreign Investment in the United States, 1914–1945*. United States: President and Fellows of Harvard College, 2004.

Williams, Ben Ames. *Bank of Boston 200: A History of New England's Leading Bank, 1784–1984*. United States: Houghton Mifflin, 1984.

Williams, R.A. "Mergers if Necessary, but not Necessarily Mergers: Competition and Consolidation at Canada's 'Big Banks'." In *The Real Worlds of Canadian Politics, Cases in Process and Public Policy, Fourth Edition*, edited by R. Campbell, L. Pal, and M. Howlett, 155–214. Toronto: Broadview Press, 2004.

Williams, Russell Alan. "Exogenous Shocks in Subsystem Adjustment and Policy Change: The Credit Crunch and Canadian Banking Regulation." *The Journal of Public Policy* 29, no. 1 (2009): 29–53.

Willis, Henry Parker. *American Banking*. Chicago: Ayer Publishing, 1916.

Witham, John. "Andrew White." *Dictionary of Canadian Biography*. www.biographi.ca/009004-119.01-e.php?&id_nbr=3196 (accessed 25 June 2015).

Wood, John H. *A History of Central Banking in Great Britain and the United States*. New York: Cambridge University Press, 2005.

World Trade Press. *Canada Money and Banking: The Basics on Currency and Money in Canada*. Petaluma: World Trace Press, 2010.

Wright, Christopher, and Matthias Kipping. "The Engineering Origins of the Consulting Industry and Its Long Shadow." In *Oxford Handbook of Management Consulting*, edited by Matthias Kipping and Timothy Clark, 29–50. Oxford: Oxford University Press, 2012.

Wright, Richard W. *International Dimensions of Canadian Banking*. Montreal: The Institute of Canadian Bankers, 1983.

Wright, Richard W., and Susan Huggett. *A Yen for Profit: Canadian Financial Institutions in Japan*. Halifax: The Institute for Research on Public Policy, 1987.

Wright, Robert E. *Origins of Commercial Banking in America, 1750–1800*. Lanham: Rowman & Littlefield Publishers, Inc., 2001.

Xu, Jixin. "An Empirical Estimation of the Portfolio Diversification Hypothesis: The Case of Canadian International Banking." *The Canadian Journal of Economics/Revue canadienne d'Economique* 29, no. 1 (1996): 192–7.

Young, Brian J. "George Burns Symes." *Dictionary of Canadian Biography*. www.biographi.ca/009004-119.01-e.php?&id_nbr=4735 (accessed 25 June 2016).

Young, Brian J., and Gerald J.J. Tulchinsky. "Sir Hugh Allan." *Dictionary of Canadian Biography*. www.biographi.ca/009004-119.01-e.php?&id_nbr=5336.

Young, George R. *Upon the History, Principles, and Prospects of the Bank of British North America, and of the Colonial Bank*. London: W.S. Orr, P. Richardson, and J. Ridgway, 1838.

Zollo, Maurizio. "Superstitious Learning with Rare Strategic Decisions Theory and Evidence from Corporate Acquisitions." *Organization Science* 20, no. 5 (2009): 894–908.

Zollo, Maurizio, and H. Singh. "Deliberate Learning in Corporate Acquisitions: Post-Acquisition Strategies and Integration Capability in US Bank Mergers." *Strategic Management Journal* 25 (2004): 1233–56.

INDEX

Roman page numbers indicate Volume One
Italicized page numbers indicate Volume Two
f = figure; t = table

Assembly of First Nations, *220*
asset-backed commercial paper (ABCP), *253*
Atlantic Acceptance Corporation, *32*
Atlantic provinces. *See* Maritimes
Auldjo, George, and Alexander, *12*
Aune, J. Brian, *130, 133*
automated teller machines (ATMs), xvi, *69, 87, 88, 90, 117*

Bahamas, *43, 176–7, 180, 183–90*
Ball, Gordon R., *8–10, 18, 24–5, 39, 180*
Banco La Guaria, *182*
Banco de Montreal Investimento S.A., *201–2*
Bancomer (Mexico), *192, 223*
Bank Act, xxxiii, 72, 97–100, 175, 242, 255, *30*; Bank Act of 1871 (Canada), 84, 99, 120, 136, 145, 146, 175; revisions: (1901), 138, 149, 171; (1910), 147, 156; (1913), 206; (1923), 209; (1934), *30*; (1944), 299; (1954), *17, 24*; (1967), *29–34, 51, 108, 115*; (1980), *108, 112, 122, 123*; (1987), *108, 128–9*; (1991), *201–2*. *See also* Bank of Canada Act
Bank of America (BOA), *71, 89, 252*
BankAmerica Corp., *132*
BankAmericard. *See* Chargex
Bank of British Columbia, *196*
Bank of British North America (BBNA), 26, 38, 49, 62, 75, 79, 88, 115, 122, 139, 160, 172t, 173–4, 192, 195, 205, *9, 176*
Bank of Canada (1818), *12, 26, 31*
Bank of Canada (1858). *See* Canadian Bank of Commerce
Bank of Canada (1934) (Central Bank), xvii, xviii, xxix, 213, 228, 229, 234, 236, 240, 253–86, 292, 299, *28, 30, 33, 124, 221, 229, 247, 253*
Bank of Canada Act, *271–7, 30*
Bank of China, *193–6, 199*
Bank of Commerce (New York), 101
Bank of England, xviii, 35, 70, 78, 95, 98, 101, 110, 166, 228–9, 254, 256, 259, 262,

264, 265–9, 271, 272, 274, 275, 278, 280, 282–4, 292, 294, *179, 273*
Bankers Trust New York Corp., *160*
Bank of International Settlements, 259
bank of issue, 62–3, 76, 97, 98, 261
Bank of Liverpool, 92
Bank of London and Montreal (BOLAM), *10, 36, 176, 177–81, 192*. *See also* Bank of London and South America (BOLSA)
Bank of London and South America (BOLSA), *11, 176–85*
Bank of Lower Canada, 5, 6, 14
Bank of Montreal (BMO)
  amalgamations. *See* amalgamation of banks; mergers
  annual meeting, 59, 122, 123, 124, 130, 130f, 131, 141f, 149, 152, 157, 158, 166, 168, 277, 279, 295, *11, 14, 17, 29, 112, 126, 127, 193, 198*
  Big Five banks comparison, *147–9f, 242–5f, 260–3f*
  branch banking. *See* Bank of Montreal, branches
  branches, xvi–xviii, 25, 26, 35, 36, 41, 43–5, 50–1, 53, 55, 58, 64, 67, 68, 81, 86–9, 95, 97, 99, 107, 116, 118, 120, 130, 133–40, 145, 150, 153, 154, 170, 177, 180, 185–7, 192, 195, 196, 200t, 205–10, 222, 223, 226, 239, 242, 244–5, 249, 254–7, 260, 277–8, 281, 292, 296, *2, 3, 5, 9, 11, 19–23, 27, 28, 31, 32, 33, 37, 44, 49, 51–6, 58–63, 69, 71, 73, 75–6, 87–8, 90, 102, 109–11, 116, 117, 119–21, 130, 161, 176–7, 180–8, 190–2, 195, 198, 200, 213, 217, 219, 226, 228, 231, 236, 239, 268, 273*; in China, *224–5*; closures of, 62–3, 227, 233, 289; in France, *204–5*; and Harris Bank, *155, 158–9, 165, 221–2*; and mechanization, *78–9, 81–4*; in Mexico, *167–8, 201–4*; and online banking, *113–14*; in United Kingdom, *160–2, 166, 184–5, 296–9, 204*; in United States,

Clifford, Donald K. Jr, *49, 60, 61t*

Clouston, Sir Edward, 114, 116–18, 122–4, 139, 146, 149, 154, 155, 156, 167–9, 201, 249

Colonial Bank, 205

commercial banking. *See* Bank of Montreal, commercial banking

Commercial Banking Units (CBUs), *119*

Commercial Bank of Kingston, 94

Commercial Bank of the Midland District, 49, 74

Commercial Bank of Newfoundland, 242

Commercial Bank of Scotland, xvi, 55

Commission of Government (Nfld), 251–2

Comper, F. Anthony (Tony), xxiii, *145, 151, 208, 210, 213, 219–21, 248–51, 257*

Competition Act, 35

Confederation, xvii, 24, 49, 65, 79, 89, 106, 108, 118, 120, 121, 132, 136, 137, 143, 146, 163, 171, 181, 215, 224, 251, 254, 275, *43, 269*

conscription, 191, 192, 289–90

Conservative Party, *95*

Co-operative Commonwealth Federation (CCF), 239

Corporate Banking Group (BMO), *111, 117*

Corporate Strategic Plan (BMO), *216, 304*

Corporation Agencies, 249

Costello, Ellen, *171*

Court of Queen's Bench of Alberta, *137*

Coyne, James E., *30*

Crédit Lyonnais, 298

Crossley, Julian, *182–3, 300*

Cunliffe Committee, 259

Currency Act, 246

Currie, Sir Arthur W., 194, 290–1

Cuvillier, Augustin, xvi, 9–11, 17

Davison, Stan, *50, 104, 116*

Demerara Electric Company, 168

deposits, 199t, 208–9, 211, 240, 255–6, 261, 272, 279, *12, 31, 71, 195*. *See also* Bank of Montreal, deposits

depressions and financial crises, xviii, xxxix, 51–2, 63, 70, 81, 83, 104, 109, 115, 121–4, 131, 190, 214, 222, 227, 234, 236, 241, 242, 252–3, 255, 257, 259, 261–2, 272–3, 278, 280–1, 287, *xiii, 2, 6, 7*. *See also* Great Depression (1929–39)

Detroit and Milwaukee Railroad, 94

Diefenbaker, John, *25, 29, 30, 32*

Distillers-Seagram, 231

Dodds, Jackson, 224, 230, 231, 233, 242–6, 249–50, 255, 264–6, 278–9, 282, 290–1

Dome Petroleum Ltd, *135–9, 144*

Domestic Development Man (cartoon), *119–20*

Domestic Development Program (DDP), *102, 118–22, 150, 217*

Dominion Bank, 200t, *16t*, 25, *42t*

Dominion Government Account, 146

Dominion of Newfoundland. *See* Newfoundland

Dominion-Provincial Conference on Reconstruction, 300

Dominion Securities, *129*

Dominion Textile Company, 194, 231

Dorricott, Keith O., *104*

Downe, William (Bill) A., xx, xxi, xxii, *208, 210, 225, 250–8, 268, 271*

Drummond Colliery, 116

Drummond, Sir George Alexander, xvi, 114t, 116t, 118–19, 156, 161, 167–8

Drummond, Huntly R., 195, 224, 288–9, *293, 8*

Dunning, Charles A., *8*

East India Company, 66, 68

Economic Reform Association, 260–1

Edge Act banks, *155, 159*

Edmonton, *10, 30, 125*

Electronic Financial Services Group, 227

Electronic Recording Machine-Accounting (ERMA), *71*

England. *See* United Kingdom

Erie Canal, 47

Estey, Willard Z., *108*

London (Ontario), 50, 111, 194

London (United Kingdom), xvii, xviii, xxxi, xxxiii, xxxix, 3, 5, 7, 9, 22, 24, 25, 30, 31, 33, 37–8, 40–1, 43, 44, 46, 48, 51, 55, 56, 58, 59–60, 62, 64–6, 68–9, 71, 74–5, 84, 85, 88, 90, 92, 93, 98, 104, 107, 110, 112, 115, 116, 118, 120, 121, 123, 131, 132, 139, 140, 143, 144, 146–9, 158–62, 165–7, 169–70, 174, 179, 184, 200, 204–5, 215, 224, 227, 229, 241, 250–2, 256, 262, 265, 271, 282, 283, 289, 290, 296, 297, 298, *10, 11, 21, 28, 36, 41, 125, 128, 155, 173, 174, 176–7, 179t, 180, 183, 184, 204, 213, 227, 248, 255, 273*

London and Colonial Bank, 115

London committee (or board; of Bank), xvii, 86, 144, 169–70, 204, 227

London money market, 148, 158

Lord Strathcona's Horse (Royal Canadians), 144

Lower Canada, 5, 8, 11, 12, 14, 22, 25, 30, 31, 34, 36–9, 48, 59, 60, 62, 65–7, 74, 117. *See also* Quebec (province)

lumber, 4, 24, 83, 131, 154, 166, 168, 202, 227, 232t

Lynch, Kevin G., xxii, *255*

MacArthur, Douglas, *103*

Macdonald, J. Howard, *136–7*

Macdonald, Sir John A., 117

MacDougall, Hartland M., *57–8*

MacKay Report. *See* Task Force on the Future of the Canadian Financial Services Sector

Macmillan, Lord Hugh, 258, 271, 282–3

MacMillan Bloedel, *10*

Macmillan Commission, 259, 271

MacNamara, George, *34*

Magnetic Ink Character Recognition (MICR), 71, 74

Magnetic Telegraph Company, xvii, 50

Maidment, Karen, *220, 256*

Manitoba, 118, 137, 151, 154, 200t, *10, 135*

Manley, Michael, *185*

Maple Leaf Club, 160–1, 298

Maritimes, 138, 160, 174

Marshall & Ilsley Bank (M&I), *154, 256*

Marshall Plan, 6

Martin, Paul, *234–7, 247*

Mastercard 73, *86, 88–90, 91, 105*

Master Charge. *See* Mastercard

mbanx, xix, *214, 226–9, 231, 232, 238*

M-Bar, *38, 64*

McGill, Peter, xvi, 25, 30, 31, 33, 34, 37, 39, 41, 51, 71, 81–2, 86, 119

McGill University, 119, 275, 278, *58*

McKinsey & Company, *1, 49, 52–7, 59–61, 63, 65, 116*

McLaughlin, W. Earle, *112*

McMaster, Ross H., *8*

McMaster, William, 98, 100

McNally, Alan G., *171, 213–14, 222*

McNeil, Fred H., *8, 10, 27, 41, 45, 47, 49, 50, 64, 73, 74, 85, 89, 95, 104, 105, 113, 116, 125, 127, 192, 197*

Ménard, Jacques L., *255*

Mercaldo, Ed, *143*

mercantile, xxix, 5, 6, 10, 14, 15, 22, 25, 31, 32, 41, 43, 46, 68, 87, 99, 131, 145, 166

Mercantile Bank of Canada, *32, 33–4*

Merchants Bank of Canada, 95, 96, 139, 172t, 201, 205, 206–7, 217, *10*

Merchants Bank of Halifax, 249

Meredith, Sir H. Vincent, 114t, 119, 124, 150, 157–60, 173–4, 182, 185, 187, 188, 192–6, 198, 204, 210 213, 214, 216, 219, *27, 237*

mergers, xix, xxxiii, 105, 137–9, 164, 165, 167, 171–5, 188, 205–10, 225, 226, 249, 299, *10, 25–6, 99, 130–3, 139, 159–60, 163, 164–5, 169, 170, 210, 232–40, 247–9, 266. See also* amalgamation of banks

Merrill Lynch, *252*

Mesa Petroleum, *135*

Mexican Light and Power Company, 118, 167–8